AGAMEMNON

OF

AESCHYLUS

CAMBRIDGE
UNIVERSITY PRESS
LONDON : Fetter Lane
C. F. CLAY, Manager

NEW YORK
The Macmillan Co.
BOMBAY, CALCUTTA and
MADRAS
Macmillan and Co., Ltd.
TORONTO
The Macmillan Co. of
Canada, Ltd.
TOKYO
Maruzen-Kabushiki-Kaisha

AGAMEMNON
OF
AESCHYLUS

WITH VERSE TRANSLATION, INTRODUCTION AND NOTES

BY

WALTER HEADLAM, Litt.D.

LATE FELLOW AND LECTURER OF KING'S COLLEGE, CAMBRIDGE

EDITED BY

A. C. PEARSON, M.A.

CAMBRIDGE
AT THE UNIVERSITY PRESS
1925

First Edition 1910
Reprinted by photographic process 1925

PRINTED IN GREAT BRITAIN

"I am honoured and gratified by your proposal to dedicate to me your version of the *Agamemnon.* I regard the *Oresteia* as probably on the whole the greatest spiritual work of man."

Extract from a letter to
Walter Headlam from A. C. Swinburne.
October 2nd, 1900.

NOTE

Shortly after the publication of the first edition it was discovered that, owing to a confusion in Dr Headlam's papers, the *Introduction* and a few of the Notes were the work of Mr A. E. A. W. Smyth, late Fellow of Trinity College, Cambridge, now Librarian of the House of Commons.

A full explanation of the mistake was given in a letter written by Dr M. R. James to the *Athenaeum*, 15 July, 1911.

EDITOR'S PREFACE

AT the time of his death in 1908 Dr Walter Headlam had been for some years under engagement to prepare an edition of the *Agamemnon* for the Syndics of the Cambridge University Press. Unfortunately he was not able to complete it; but the Syndics were nevertheless desirous that a book the preparation of which had engrossed long periods of enthusiastic labour, should if possible be published.

With this end in view the existing material was entrusted to me to be sifted and arranged for the Press. The various parts of the work proved on investigation to be in different stages of progress; for, whereas the Introduction and Verse Translation were nearly complete, and had undergone considerable revision at the hands of their author, the recension of the text had not been carried through, there were no critical notes, and the commentary only existed in fragments. The deficiencies were however less serious than might appear from this statement. Dr Headlam had devoted himself for twenty years to the study of Aeschylus; he had ransacked the whole of the extant Greek literature in order to equip himself for the task of emending, explaining, and illustrating his favourite author; he had published from time to time in the philological periodicals critical studies on most of the difficulties which the text of the *Agamemnon* presents; and, when repeatedly working through the play, he had collected in note-books and in the margins of his printed copies abundant stores of evidence, which though not in their final shape were available in support of the conclusions he had reached.

I must now endeavour briefly to explain how I have dealt with this material.

So far as it went, the Introduction was finished, with the exception of the opening pages; but there can be no doubt that at least a section bearing on the textual criticism of the play would have been added. In order to make the critical notes intelligible, I have added a short account of the most important MSS., taken principally from Wecklein. The Verse Translation had undergone constant revision, as will be apparent from a comparison of such extracts as have appeared in the occasional contributions with the complete text as now printed. The author was a severe critic of his own productions, and finality was not easily reached. The manuscript bears many indications that the text had not been definitely settled; and I have sometimes been compelled to choose between alternatives, neither of which was considered entirely satisfactory. The number of cases where the addition of a word or words was necessary is fortunately so small as to be negligible.

In constituting the text I have been guided mainly by the evidence contained in an interleaved copy of Wecklein's *Aeschylus* (1885). This book was intended by Dr Headlam to be the basis of his own recension, and here he was accustomed to enter such textual corrections as he considered final. Further assistance has been derived from the notes to the prose translation written for Messrs Bell's Classical Translations (London, 1904), in which he professed to record such of the readings adopted as were likely to be unfamiliar. In the few cases where these notes conflicted with the 'final' Wecklein, the testimony of the latter was taken as conclusive. There remained a number of passages where the editor had not made up his mind on the reading to be printed; but in most of these either the translation, verse or prose, or the notes show what he considered to be probable, and the actually doubtful points are both few and unimportant.

For the convenience of readers I have added below the page a brief record of the MS. evidence, wherever the text departs from it. For the most part this is taken from Wecklein's apparatus, whose authority I have generally followed in attributing to their authors such conjectures as it was necessary or desirable to mention.

The material available for the commentary was as follows: (1) note-books and loose sheets containing notes in course of preparation; (2) notes and references written in the margin of printed copies of the play, the most important of which were in the interleaved copy of Wecklein already mentioned; (3) printed contributions to the *Classical Review* and *Journal of Philology*, and the notes to the prose translation. Dr Headlam had planned his commentary on an elaborate scale, seeking by illustrations drawn from every age of Greek literature to rest his criticism and interpretation upon the secure foundation of established usage. The complete design was never realised: the written notes which remain are intermittent and generally incomplete, and so far as they exist cover only a small portion of the text. On the other hand, many of the notes previously published required modification before they could be suitably incorporated in a commentary; and many others being superseded by later views had ceased to be of importance. In spite of these difficulties, it was thought better not to miss the opportunity of collecting the permanent results of Dr Headlam's criticism on the *Agamemnon*; and it is hoped that the new matter will be welcomed by those who are already familiar with his published work. It must be understood that, though in many instances I am responsible for the outward form which the note has ultimately assumed, the substance is in every case taken from one or more of the sources indicated above. No attempt has been made to work up rough material unless the design of the author in collecting it was established beyond reasonable doubt. Those who have endeavoured to sift numbers of references not always easy to find with the object of discovering the clue which holds the secret of their connexion will realise that the task I have undertaken is not without difficulty. I can only say that I have acted according to the best of my judgment, and if the result is to preserve for students some valuable fruits of the labours of one who has illuminated so many dark places in Greek poetry, I shall be more than satisfied. In the few cases where I have made additions to the notes I have distinguished them by square brackets.

For the principles by which the translator was guided in composing his version readers must be referred to the Preface to the *Book of Greek Verse* (Cambridge University Press, 1907); but I am permitted to quote the following extract from a letter written to Miss J. E. Harrison on Feb. 3rd, 1903, which has a peculiar interest as referring to the translation of the *Agamemnon*:

"The blank verse seemed to me to require the large language of the dramatists and Milton (without the slang of the dramatists)...The trouble comes with the Lyrics. They had to be in the same language to harmonise with the rest. That limits you very much in metre; you must forgo in the first place anapaestic rhythm. And whatever metre you use, there is one condition that prevents them ever being done to satisfaction. In the Greek they were the words written for music, to be sung; and in English there is nothing corresponds. English unhappily is not a singing language, as Italian is, or German; and the moment you try to write in English what is singable—which is hard in itself—you get for our ears too much tune. English 'lyrics' such as Shelley wrote are capable of the loveliest and subtlest effects, but they are effects for reading; and the lovelier and subtler they are, the less they can be sung."

I desire to thank the proprietors of the *Classical Review* and of the *Journal of Philology* for permission to make use of the various articles which have appeared in those periodicals; Messrs George Bell and Sons for a similar liberty in respect of the notes to the prose translation; Mr J. T. Sheppard, who not only lent me a series of notes taken in 1904, when he was reading the play with Dr Headlam, but also looked over some of the proof-sheets; Mr H. H. Sills for sending me several Lecture-Room papers containing passages from the *Agamemnon*; and Mr L. W. Haward for information on sundry points of detail.

A. C. P.

23rd July 1910.

CONTENTS

INTRODUCTION.

THE STORY.

ATREUS son of Pelops son of Tantalus, reigning in Argos, banished his brother Thyestes, who had corrupted his wife Aerope and disputed his rule. When Thyestes returned in the guise of a suppliant, his life was spared by Atreus but only that he might suffer a more horrible injury. Pretending to celebrate his home-coming by a special feast, Atreus slew and served up to him his two young children. The father, misled for the moment, with a cry of agony kicked over the table and uttered a curse 'that so might perish all the race of Pleisthenes.' He was afterwards banished a second time together with his third son Aegisthus, then a mere infant[1].

Of Atreus we hear no more, but he was succeeded on the throne by Agamemnon and Menelaus, who ruled conjointly in Argos. The two brothers married two sisters, Clytaemnestra and Helen the daughters of Tyndareus and Leda. In the course of their reign they were visited by Paris or Alexander, son of King Priam, of the famous and opulent town of Troy, whom they hospitably entertained. He repaid their kindness by seducing Helen, the wife of Menelaus, and carrying her off with a quantity of treasure on board his ship to Troy, leaving the husband disconsolate and speechless[2].

Agamemnon, against the wish of his oldest advisers, espoused his brother's quarrel, and assembled a vast fleet of a thousand vessels to avenge the rape and recover Helen. The male population of Argos, except those too old for military service and those too young, embarked on the enterprise. The government was left in the hands of Clytaemnestra assisted by a body of elders who remained behind[3]. At the moment of setting out

[1] vv. 1583—1606. [2] vv. 42—44, 409—28, 537—9, etc.
[3] vv. 72—82, 270—2, 790—5, etc.

the attitude of Heaven was declared by a significant omen. Two eagles differently marked were observed preying together on a pregnant hare. From this omen the prophet Calchas drew a twofold conclusion partly favourable, partly the reverse. Recognising in the two birds the two kings different in nature but now unanimous for war, he foretold from their action that Troy should one day fall and her gathered riches be despoiled. But as the fate of the hare and her unborn young must of necessity be displeasing to Artemis, the protectress of such creatures, he saw reason to dread the displeasure of the goddess against the army when assembled at her own port of Aulis[1], which had been assigned as the point of departure for the fleet. Then, taking leave of the sign, in language vague but ominous, he deprecated the occurrence of a storm which must lead to a monstrous sacrifice, breeding enmity between a husband and a wife, and entailing vengeance for a child[2].

As the prophet had feared, so it fell out. The fleet was detained by foul weather at Aulis; the ships began to go to pieces; provisions were running short; and every resource suggested by the diviners proved vain. Agamemnon himself was impatient under these trials and would perhaps have seized the excuse for abandoning his design, leaving it to Heaven to punish the seducer of his brother's wife. Before taking this step, however, he was informed of a remedy which would prove efficacious. This was nothing less than the sacrifice of his own daughter Iphigeneia to Artemis. The cruel alternative now lay before him, either of killing his child, or of refusing a personal sacrifice on behalf of the allies whom he had summoned to take part in a personal quarrel. After weighing the motives on either side, his calculating head got the better of his heart. In a moment of moral obliquity he consented to the sacrifice, and the fleet sailed. Ten years of labour and privation awaited him at Troy. The allies, for whose sake he had resigned so much, proved half-hearted in the end. By the loss of life abroad, he forfeited the sympathy of all but a scanty remnant of those who had been left behind. He made of his wife a concealed but implacable enemy; and he gave his bitterest foe the chance

[1] See Pausan. IX. 19, 6—8.

[2] vv. 113—63.

to cut him off in the very hour of his triumph over his great rival of the East[1].

For there was one person who had not sailed with the sailing of the fleet. Aegisthus[2], son of Thyestes, had grown up in exile, nursing projects of revenge, and not forgetful of his unhappy father's claim to the crown. In the absence of the kings and their force, he found means of access to Clytaemnestra, herself burning to revenge the death of her daughter Iphigeneia. He obtained her love, and (more fortunate than his father) might enjoy it in peace, together with the reality, if not the semblance, of power in Argos. The adultery was not openly avowed; but enough was known for those who remained faithful to the absent king to shake their heads and hold their peace. Orestes, the lawful heir to the throne, was sent away to be brought up by Strophius of Phocis, a friend of the family[3].

This state of things could only last so long as Agamemnon was abroad; and accordingly the guilty pair took measures to provide against the day of his return. It had been arranged between the king and his consort that the fall of Troy should be communicated by a series of beacons extending from mount Ida in the Troad to mount Arachnaeus in the neighbourhood of Argos; and a watchman had been stationed to look out for the signal for a year before the city fell. This appointment, no doubt innocently devised to communicate the important event as soon as possible, resulted in giving the conspirators ample warning of the king's approach. Aegisthus had got together a body of troops, either companions of his exile or drawn from the disaffected generation which had by this time grown up at Argos. He now arranged that, on the king's arrival, the cunning and capable queen should receive her husband with all appearance of affection, should conduct him to the bath previous to the usual sacrifice, should there drop the valance or canopy over him, and

[1] vv. 194—233, 452—64, 560—71, 829—33, etc.

[2] The importance of the part played by Aegisthus, in the version of the story which Aeschylus followed, was first emphasised by Dr Verrall, to whom here, as elsewhere, I am much indebted. While I cannot agree with Dr Verrall (as will be seen later) about the precise nature of Aegisthus' plot, I think it clear from v. 1609 that a plot of some considerable kind is presupposed.

[3] vv. 553—5, 871—2, 1585, 1608, 1625—7, etc.

despatch him thus entangled; while he himself, being precluded from appearing in public, should lurk in the vicinity, and, upon a signal of Clytaemnestra's action in the palace[1], should overpower with his partisans the following of the king, and join hands with his accomplice before the royal castle. From this stronghold he meant to govern Argos with absolute power, bribing some and coercing others. In the event the plan was much simplified by the fact that Agamemnon's fleet was utterly dispersed by a storm on the way home, so that the conqueror of Troy landed with the crew of a single ship, and fell an easy victim[2]. The return of the king, his murder by Clytaemnestra, and the usurpation of Aegisthus, form the subject of the *Agamemnon*.

THE DRAMA.

This action, of which the preliminaries (so far as they are stated or seen to be implied in the play itself) have been narrated above, is disposed by the poet into four broad chapters. The first is taken up with the announcement of the fall of Troy; the second with the return of the king; the third with his murder; the fourth with the immediate sequel of the murder. Each of the first three divisions is subdivided, on a rough principle of symmetry, into two parts. The reception of the news from Troy precedes by a considerable interval its public declaration at Argos; the entrance of Agamemnon's herald precedes the entrance of the king himself; and the prediction of his murder by the prophetess Cassandra (whom he brings in his train) precedes, by a very short interval, its actual execution. The last division likewise falls into two parts, the first of which consists of Clytaemnestra's open justification of her act, and the second of Aegisthus' exposition of his conspiracy; the whole accompanied by recriminations between each of these persons and the body of faithful elders who compose the Chorus of the play. We will now trace the course of the action down to the entrance of the herald, at which point a question of some importance arises.

[1] This detail is doubtful, but see v. 1354.

[2] vv. 327—8, 666—8, 1636—40, 1650, etc.

The scene, which is laid before the royal palace, opens at night. A watchman is discerned on the roof. He explains that his business is to look out for the beacon, complains of his hardships, utters a few dark hints about the state of affairs within, and expresses a forlorn wish for the conclusion of his watch. While the word is yet in his mouth, the fire appears. He greets it with a cry of joy, raises a shout to apprise Clytaemnestra, executes a dance, adds a few more hints of a dubious nature, and disappears (1—39).

By the queen's orders offerings are despatched to all the neighbouring shrines, and flames arise through the darkness. A group of elders, ignorant of the news, assembles to inquire the reason. In despondent tones they observe that the kings and their army have been absent at Troy for close on ten years, yet the war still continues. They comment on their own feebleness, which caused them to be left behind. The queen enters to kindle the altars near the palace, and they question her in the hope of some comforting news. For the present she does not answer, but goes off, apparently to complete the ceremony by leading the sacrificial chant to which she alludes later (40—103).

The Chorus, left alone, relate the omen which attended the departure of the kings, its exposition by Calchas, his prophecy of good and evil, and yet of further evil. Then, after a preface justifying the ways of Zeus to men, they proceed to the sacrifice of Iphigeneia. The father's tears, hesitation and eventual submission are depicted. The sacrifice itself is partly described; but they stop short of the fatal stroke, and pray that the good foretold by Calchas may now come about, as then the evil, dismissing his prediction of further evil as so much premature sorrow. On this note of uncertainty the ode concludes (104—269).

The night is far spent, when the queen reappears and announces the fall of Troy. The elders, with tears in their eyes, question her as to the proof and period of the capture. Pointing to the dawn, which ushers in her glad news, she informs them that it occurred in the night just past. They ask how she could learn so quickly, and in reply she narrates the transmission of the fiery signal from hill to hill, over sea and plain, by means of successive beacons. At the end of her rapid narrative the elders invite her to repeat it for their fuller comprehension. She contents herself with restating the chief fact, and goes on to draw a picture of the captured city, with its medley of victors and vanquished; deprecates any wanton sacrilege on the part of the former, who have still to get home with the blood of the dead upon their hands; and concludes by excusing her fears as natural to a woman, and praying that all may be well in no doubtful sense. The elders, having had leisure to reflect during this speech, accept her evidence as certain, and turn to praise Heaven for its mercy (270—366).

They begin by celebrating the power of Zeus, and his unerring chastisement of guilt, as seen in the case of Paris. This judgment refutes the saying that Heaven is indifferent to human sin, a doctrine traceable to the temper engendered by a sudden plethora of riches. Wealth without righteousness insures a man's ruin, his children's ruin, his nation's irreparable harm. It brings him to a bloody end, unregarded of God or man. The crime of Paris, the flight of Helen, the desolation of the Argive home, are then described in verses famous for their tender beauty. But instead of reverting to the theme of divine justice, the Chorus passes, by an easy but remarkable transition, to the general grief at Argos, caused by the death of kinsmen at Troy. The private quarrel of the Atridae has made them hateful at home. They may have conquered, but they have slain many; the gods take note of that. They may have won great glory; let not their hearts be lifted up, or Zeus will blast them. A middle station between conquest and captivity is the best. The tone of triumph with which the ode began has relapsed into one of dark foreboding. At the very close they call in question the truth of the fiery message which prompted them to sing. With a short lyric colloquy to this effect the music dies away. In the next scene Agamemnon's herald is observed approaching (367—507).

Here, then, we must pause to touch on a matter which has caused some discussion in recent times. An ancient commentator remarks: 'Some find fault with the poet that he represents the

Greeks as returning from Troy on the same day[1].' A modern commentator, Mr Sidgwick, remarks[2]: 'Observe that the herald arrives from Troy, announcing the return of Agamemnon, immediately after the beacon fires, on the morning after the capture. Such violations of possibility were held quite allowable by the licence of dramatic poetry.' Dr Verrall, justly objecting that neither the theory nor the practice of the Athenian drama bears out the last assertion, founds on this apparent discrepancy of times a new interpretation of the play. On a certain night a fiery signal announces the capture of Troy. In the course of the next morning the victorious king arrives, after having demolished Troy and traversed the whole length of the Aegaean Sea. One or other of these statements must be false. But, as it is certain that the king does arrive in the latter part of the play, while it is equally certain that a fiery signal is received in the first part, it would seem to follow that this signal cannot announce the capture of Troy. From the entrance of Agamemnon to the close of the play it is never mentioned. The story told by Clytaemnestra, of the chain of beacons extending from Ida to Arachnaeus, is improbable in itself; still more so if, as we learn later, a violent storm was raging in the Aegaean at the time of transmission. What, then, was the meaning of the signal? According to Dr Verrall, there was but one beacon altogether, and it was kindled on Arachnaeus by the conspirator Aegisthus, who there kept watch for the return of the king; and it was intended to warn Clytaemnestra in the city, and his adherents elsewhere, of Agamemnon's approach, that all their plans might be ready for the murder of the king and the seizure of the citadel which commanded the country. A watchman had been set on the palace roof to look out for its appearance. To avoid suspicion, he was chosen from among the loyal servants of the house; to account for his task, he was told that a beacon was expected, announcing his master's success at Troy; and 'his vigilance and silence were secured by threats and bribes.' On the night of Agamemnon's return, when the signal was fired, the queen,

[1] Schol. v. 509 τινὲς μέμφονται τῶι ποιητῆι ὅτι αὐθημερὸν ἐκ Τροίας ποιεῖ τοὺς Ελληνας ἥκοντας.

[2] Note to v. 504 (509).

desirous to secure the persons of her principal opponents, sent for the elders to the palace, and informed them that Troy had fallen that very night. In reply to their inevitable question as to the receipt of the news, she swept them off their legs with a graphic but fictitious narrative of the transmission of the light from Troy to Argos. Left to themselves, the elders naturally began to entertain doubts as to the truth of the story, when Agamemnon's herald appeared, confirming indeed the fall of Troy, but, by the very fact of his arrival, showing the queen's relation to be false. By a train of accidents, however, the elders allowed the herald to depart without advising him of their suspicions. Meanwhile the plot grew ripe for execution, and was subsequently carried out.

Such, in brief outline, is Dr Verrall's account of the story, presumed as familiar at Athens, which Aeschylus undertook to illustrate. By reducing the circuit of the action it does at least avoid the absurdity of supposing that events which must necessarily take several days happen within the course of a few hours. Although it is itself open to several objections of detail, chief among which is the astounding falsehood in which the queen involves herself, without apparent necessity, by choosing to impart to the elders her secret information of the capture of Troy, I do not propose to follow these out. A graver objection is that, by making the business of the watchman a blind and the plurality of the beacons imaginary, the first part of the play is reduced from a substantial to a factitious transaction, and the massive structure of the drama, with its three broad chapters of the announcement, the return, and the murder, seriously undermined. I will therefore state the reasons which, in my opinion, make it needless to resort to this new interpretation.

It is buttressed by various arguments, but it rests on the assumption that the time of the action is continuous from start to finish; or rather, that it is contained 'within the early hours of one morning.' Now, if, in the first part of the play, a fiery signal purports to announce the capture of Troy; and if, in the second part, the destroyer of Ilion himself appears, the first and most natural supposition is that the events of the play are not closely consecutive in time, but are divided by an interval sufficient to permit of this happening. Is there anything in the play which absolutely forbids such a supposition? I venture to assert that there is nothing at all; that there is not a single circumstance which compels us to suppose that the events which follow v. 493 occur on the same day, or within the same week, as those which precede; that the criticism mentioned by the old commentator is unfounded; that Mr Sidgwick's observation falls to the ground; and that Dr Verrall has taken hold of the wrong limb of the difficulty. Instead of inferring that the beacon cannot announce the capture of Troy, we ought to infer that the king does not arrive in the course of the next morning. How this interval was conveyed to the audience, we can only guess; but Blomfield's suggestion is probable, that the Chorus leaves the theatre for a short space after v. 493.

On what arguments does the supposed circumscription of the time depend? Dr Verrall says, 'Language could not be clearer than that in which we are told that the herald arrives while the queen's announcement of the beacon-message is passing from lip to lip.' This is quite true; but it would be a nine days' wonder, if not more. While the report of the great event was still unconfirmed, nothing else would be talked about at Argos. Is it surprising, then, that the topic of discourse on either side of v. 493 is the same? And is it anything but the mere sequence of verses in the page, which prevents our imagining the requisite interval of time between that verse and the next? The break is not so directly patent as at *Eum.* 235 and again at *Eum.* 566, because at both these places the scene is changed as well; but if the language is closely scanned, the fact betrays itself sufficiently. The elders have been discussing with one another the probability of the fiery message being true. Suppose the time perfectly continuous. One of them catches sight of a herald, and expresses himself thus:

> *τάχ' εἰσόμεθα λαμπάδων φαεσφόρων*
> *φρυκτωριῶν τε καὶ πυρὸς παραλλαγάς,*
> *εἴτ' οὖν ἀληθεῖς εἴτ' ὀνειράτων δίκην*
> *τερπνὸν τόδ' ἐλθὸν φῶς ἐφήλωσεν φρένας.*

Would anyone, who had just the moment before been keenly

discussing the fire, and who now saw his chance of settling the truth at once, stop to talk about 'successions of light-bearing torches, of beacon-watches, and of fire'? He would simply say 'the fire.' It is fairly clear that an interval has elapsed, probably marked by the departure of the Chorus from the scene, and that this recapitulation is designed to fix the attention of the audience on the resumption of the subject. The poetical excuse for it is no doubt, as Dr Verrall remarks, that a certain tone of contempt is here in place; but this contempt is even more appropriate after the lapse of an interval than when the fiery message is still recent.

But the herald upon entering salutes the risen sun, addresses the gods whose statues face it, observes that the king has returned 'bringing a light in darkness,' and narrates the fierce gale which befell the Greek fleet one night upon the sea[1]. The expressions are suitable to a morning hour. However, there are more mornings in the year than one, and the language would be equally pointed on any morning that the king's vessel happened to arrive. Indeed, for the expression 'a light in darkness' to receive its full force, the herald should be conceived as arriving shortly after dawn. But if the action all takes place on one day, the dawn is long since past[2]. The greater part of one episode, and a complete choric ode of a hundred lines, have intervened, which means much in a Greek play. If the action is continued on a different day, we can imagine the herald's entrance at whatever hour we like.

On receiving the news of the capture, the queen institutes a sacrifice. On the return of the king a sacrifice is also got ready. Dr Verrall identifies these two, or supposes the one to be the completion of the other, both alike occurring on the same day. I see no reason for this view. So far as can be determined, the first appears to be an offering of oil and incense, or other combustible substances, hastily made to celebrate the glad news[3]. The other is a grand and elaborate affair, in which sheep are to be slaughtered, prepared to express thanksgiving for the king's safe and unexpected arrival, and to provide the household with a

[1] vv. 513, 524, 527, 658. [2] v. 291.
[3] vv. 83—96, 599—602.

feast for the occasion[1]. When the herald arrives, and is interviewed by the queen, she remarks that she made the first celebration 'long ago[2]', on receipt of the fiery message; whereupon she excuses the herald from reciting the complete story, and goes off to make preparation for a second.

These, so far as I can discover, are the sole grounds for asserting that the time of the drama is limited to a single day, and for ascribing to the poet either a plain absurdity or a design which does not appear on the face of the text. The *Agamemnon*, like the *Eumenides*, does not conform to the 'unity of time'; nor is there any objection to this, which is founded on reason. Aristotle tells us that Tragedy at first obeyed the circumscription of time no more than Epic poetry. Manifestly not; for the passages of action and declamation were brought into it to give relief to a choir between its separate songs; and there was no reason why the subjects of the choral songs should be more restricted in their range than the incidents of Homer's epic. But with the progress of the art, when the dancing and singing element united with the speaking and acting element to embody one connected and consistent action, Tragedy 'endeavoured, as far as possible, to confine itself to a single revolution of the sun[3].' The reason of this was clearly stated by Lessing. It was designed to preserve the identity of the Chorus. It was improbable, if the action extended over a long time, or was removed to a great distance, that the same group of persons would throughout be present as interested spectators; and since the Chorus was still regarded as the foundation of the drama, a different Chorus meant a different play. But when this restriction could be eluded, a Greek dramatist had few further scruples either about identity of place or continuity of time. In the *Eumenides* the Chorus consists of supernatural beings, who can be present in any place at any time; therefore the time is severed and the scene is changed. In the *Agamemnon* the Chorus is conceived as a corporate body, or council of state, who would naturally assemble all together, from time to time, in a definite place. Therefore the time is broken, but the scene remains unchanged.

As regards the further difficulty, that the story of the beacons,

[1] vv. 1040—2. [2] v. 592. [3] *Poet.* 1449 b 12.

if presented as a substantial occurrence, violates probability, the gravest (because the most gratuitous) part of it vanishes with the separation of the events in time. We are relieved from supposing that the message was transmitted in the midst of a howling storm. For what remains, that the distances are too great, the poet himself has frankly acknowledged as much in the first word of the description[1]. If the reader feels, or thinks an Athenian audience would feel, that Aeschylus has taken an inexcusable liberty, it must be set down as a fault in his economy. The greater number, I am sure, will consider that he was justified in calling in a god to defend the minor probabilities, and delighting his hearers with a splendid poetic narrative.

Lastly, in reply to the objection, that the beacons are never once mentioned after the entrance of the king, three things may be urged. First, a dramatist cannot always advert to matters which have gone before, especially when they have taken place 'long ago,' and when there are more pressing matters to be considered. Secondly, the beacons are mentioned as a matter of course in the presence of the herald[2], which is sufficient evidence of good faith. Thirdly, it is equally remarkable that, if the events are all supposed to happen on the same day, not a syllable should escape one of the characters after v. 493, which makes it absolutely certain that this is the case.

We may now resume the thread of the action from v. 493 to the end of the play, after which some remarks will be offered on the whole.

The herald enters, and after saluting the gods in a rapture of joy, announces the return of the king and the utter destruction of Troy. The Chorus, with veiled meaning, inform him that their desire for the army's return was as great as the army's desire to get home. The herald betrays some surprise at their words, but instead of pressing his inquiries, embarks on a description of the hardships of the campaign, the sufferings of the army on land and sea, by night and day, and ends by asserting that all is compensated by the happy issue. Clytaemnestra now appears. She remarks that the event has

[1] v. 293. [2] v. 593.

justified her belief in the beacon message, but declines to hear the complete account from any but her husband, to whom she sends back the herald with a message to come quickly and an assurance of her unshaken fidelity. Before the herald departs, the Chorus affectionately inquire after Menelaus. The herald, who prides himself on telling the truth, confesses that Menelaus is lost; at the same time, being a scrupulous observer of form, he shows some reluctance to mix bad news with good, but at length avows that the Greek fleet was partly destroyed, and partly dispersed, by a terrible storm on the way home, from which the king's vessel escaped by miraculous aid. After consoling his auditors with the hope that Menelaus may yet return, he goes on his way (494—685).

In the lovely ode which follows, the theme of divine justice left incomplete in the last, while the report of the capture was still unconfirmed, is once more resumed. As the former ode dealt with the mischief wrought by Paris at Argos, the latter treats of the ruin brought by Helen on Troy. Her name and her action alike marked her out as the instrument of divine vengeance against the city. She reached the foreign shore in safety, but a host of enemies followed in her train. She was received with hymns of joy; but even before the foemen came, those hymns were turned to lamentation. Peace, luxury, and love were suggested by her advent; in the end she proved a curse. Was it the prosperity of Priam which provoked this judgment from Heaven? No, but an old taint of wickedness in the race, which in the fulness of time brought forth fresh wickedness, and with it the punishment of the whole. The upright house is prosperous for ever; but Justice loves the smoky cottage better than the guilty palace. Hardly have the solemn words been uttered, when Agamemnon enters in a chariot, followed (it is said[1]) by another chariot containing Cassandra and the spoils of Troy (686—773).

The Chorus accost him with honest warmth, not omitting to observe the prevalence and success of more interested friendship. They had never approved of the war for Helen's sake, but they

[1] In the Greek *argument*.

heartily rejoice at its conclusion, and look to the king to decide between true loyalty and false (774—800).

The king begins by acknowledging his debt of gratitude to Heaven for its aid in the punishment and destruction of Troy. He proceeds to corroborate the sentiment of the Chorus from his own experience of simulated zeal. He ends by announcing his intention of taking salutary measures for the better government of Argos. The queen enters, and in a long address, remarkable alike for its poetic expression and its dramatic irony, describes her afflictions caused by the king's absence, by the frequent rumours of his death, by the fears of a popular rising. She hails his return in a series of beautiful but extravagant images, and invites him to enter. At a given word, her women spread the king's path with purple tapestries. The king, taken aback by this display, severely reproves her extravagant laudation and her extravagant action, as more suited to an eastern despot than to one who entertains a proper fear of God and man. After a brief altercation, however, he is prevailed upon to tread the purple carpets, but not before he has evinced his humility by removing his shoes and commending the captive Cassandra to merciful treatment. The queen defends her prodigal action by reminding him of the wealth of the house, and the propriety of expense on such an auspicious occasion as the return of its lord. After expressing a prayer for the accomplishment of her vows, she follows her husband into the palace (801—965).

During the foregoing scene, what with the king's scruples and the queen's ambiguous language, an indefinable feeling of alarm has been created, which receives explicit utterance in the following choric ode. Despite the visible evidence of the army's return, the elders cannot enter into the full joy of the occasion, cannot banish the obstinate forebodings which have taken possession of their breasts, and yet cannot explain them at all. They reflect on the near neighbourhood of great prosperity to imminent decay. Loss of wealth may be repaired; a plentiful harvest may obliterate a famine; but when blood has been shed, nothing can remedy that. They suppose it to be the will of Heaven that joy shall not run to excess, but always be limited by some admixture of sorrow (966—1018).

Clytaemnestra returns, and hastily orders Cassandra within. As she remains obstinately silent, the elders gently urge her to comply. The queen impatiently repeats her command, observing that the business of the sacrifice will not suffer her to wait. Still receiving no response, she contemptuously remarks that Cassandra is mad, and leaves her and the compassionate elders alone (1019—1055).

Cassandra now breaks silence. Wildly calling on Apollo, who had begun her ruin before and has completed it now, in a series of rapt prophetic cries she touches on the previous crimes of the house, the new crime—the murder of a husband by his wife—which is about to follow, the horrible manner of its execution, and her own miserable end, following on the destruction of her city. The elders, here and there perceiving her drift, but for the most part utterly bewildered, answer her cries with expressions of reproof, amazement, perplexity, alarm, incredulity, and pity. The vision then becomes distinct, and she commands the credit of the Chorus by dwelling in a more coherent fashion on the ancient misdeeds of the house of Atreus. The elders are surprised at her knowledge, and she informs them that she received the gift of prophecy from Apollo, but that she was doomed to disbelief because she foiled his love. In a second burst of inspiration she mentions the feast of Thyestes, and all but reveals the plot of Aegisthus and Clytaemnestra against the newly returned king. The Chorus, convinced by the first fact, are puzzled and terrified by her intimation of the second. She then explicitly foretells the death of Agamemnon; but before she can calmly make all clear, a third access of frenzy seizes her, in which she forecasts her own death, reproaches Apollo for his cruelty, but predicts the vengeance of Orestes, and resigns herself to die. The Chorus, falling in with her humour, seek to console her. She waves aside their consolation, and approaches the doors, but recoils (as she says) at the smell of blood. She then invites the elders to witness the truth of her prediction in the day of vengeance; prays to the sun for its fulfilment; utters a general lament over the state of man, and enters the house (1056—1329).

Reflecting on her words, the Chorus observe that, if they

come true, if Agamemnon must atone for former bloodshed, prosperity is a fickle thing indeed. In the midst of their reflections the cry of the king is heard twice within. The elders hastily take counsel as to the best way of proceeding, and each in turn delivers his opinion. They are about to enter the palace, when the bodies of Agamemnon and Cassandra are exposed, with Clytaemnestra standing over them (1330—1370).

The queen now makes a clean breast of her duplicity and of her long cherished purpose of revenge. She dwells on the details of the murder, and openly glories in her action as a just retribution. To the elders, who reprove her effrontery, she expresses her indifference. They predict her cutting-off as a public pollution; but she retorts the former impurity of Agamemnon, who sacrificed his own daughter. They ascribe her defiant language to the maddening effect of bloodshed, and threaten her with retaliation. She rejoins that she has no fears; the love of Aegisthus and the infidelities of Agamemnon are her defence. She remarks that Cassandra keeps the latter's company even in death, adding a relish to her own passion for the former (1371—1448).

The Chorus, unequal to this audacity, pray for death to take them after their beloved master. They exclaim against Helen, who began the mortal work which her sister has completed. The queen reproves their desire for death and their denunciation of Helen. They allege the evil genius of the race, who, incarnate in the two sisters, has wrought by each an equal havoc; a change of statement which the queen approves. After deploring the fierceness of the demon and appealing to Zeus, by whose will all must have happened, they turn to bewail the king slain by a violent end. Clytaemnestra protests that the deed is none of hers, but of the avenging spirit in her semblance, atoning for the crime of Atreus. The Chorus will not exculpate her, but admit that an avenger raised by Atreus may have cooperated to the destruction of his son. Once more they bewail the end of the king slain by craft. Clytaemnestra retorts the crafty death of Iphigeneia. The elders, in utter perplexity, know not what to think or do. They forecast the swamping of the house in blood; for justice now demands fresh bloodshed. They would fain have died before seeing their king ignobly killed, with none to bury, none to weep, none to praise. The queen bids them dismiss these cares; she will bury him, and Iphigeneia will welcome him below. To this scoff the elders have no reply. They can only assert the eternal law, that the guilty must suffer. When a house is accurst, there is no remedy until it perish. The queen assents, but professes herself satisfied, for her part, if the evil spirit will now remove to some other family; she will be content to resign much of the house's wealth, if only bloodshed may now cease (1449—1576).

Hereupon Aegisthus enters with his soldiers. Pointing to the dead Agamemnon, he congratulates himself on the justice of his punishment for the crime of his father Atreus. He then narrates the story of the Thyestean feast, and the curse uttered upon the race; remarks on the propriety of his being the instrument of its fulfilment, as being the author of the whole conspiracy; and professes himself ready to die. The elders assure him that his death is certain. He turns savagely upon them, and threatens them with imprisonment or worse. They taunt him with his cowardice in laying this treacherous plot for a brave and heroic king. He replies that only thus could he compass his revenge, and intimates his resolve to make Argos submit to his power. The Chorus reproach him with polluting the land by joining the wife in the murder, and invoke Orestes to slay them both. Aegisthus, furious at this, directs his soldiers to take action. The elders on their side prepare for defence; but before the parties come to blows, the queen interposes, dissuades any further bloodshed, and advises both antagonists to depart to their several homes. Aegisthus continues to protest against the language of the Chorus, and threatens them with ultimate vengeance. The elders reply with spirit, threatening him with the return of Orestes. A few contemptuous words from the queen close the altercation; and so the first part of the trilogy of the *Oresteia* concludes (1577—1673).

REMARKS ON THE STORY.

That this account of the return and death of Agamemnon differs in several important respects from the story as it appears in Homer, has often been observed. There are four chief passages of the *Odyssey* which allude to the matter. From the first two of these[1], which are quite consistent with each other, we learn that Aegisthus, for some reason, did not join the muster of the Greek fleet, but remained behind 'in the nook of horse-feeding Argos'; that he was divinely warned against the temptation of conspiracy against the absent king and of making overtures to his wife; that he nevertheless prevailed upon the latter, after much entreaty and contrary to his own expectation, to leave the house of Agamemnon for his own; that he slew Agamemnon on his return, reigned seven years in Mycenae, and in the eighth was slain by Orestes. We further learn that his enterprise was aided by the dispersion of Menelaus' fleet by a storm, as he was rounding Cape Malea on his way to Sparta, so that he could not come to his brother's assistance. Of the sixty ships which Menelaus led to Troy, all but five were wrecked off Crete. With these five he was carried away to Egypt, and only returned seven years later, just in time for the funeral feast which Orestes made after the slaying of Aegisthus and his mother. From this account we should infer that Agamemnon, returning to Mycenae with a remnant of his host, found himself involved in a conflict with a rebellious subject, who had taken means to strengthen himself in his absence; and that, deprived of the succours which he might have expected from his brother, he was overwhelmed and slain.

But this version of the matter was evidently not the only one current; for in the third passage of the *Odyssey*[2] we find a more minute account of the death of Agamemnon, which is inconsistent with the foregoing. From this we learn that Agamemnon, thanks to the aid of Hera, escaped the storm which befell Menelaus; but that, as he was doubling Cape Malea, he himself encountered a gale which drove him on to a part of the coast which bounded

[1] *Od.* 1. 35—43 and 3. 262—312. [2] *Od.* 4. 512—47.

a certain territory, where Aegisthus had his residence in succession to his father Thyestes. Luckily the wind changed, and Agamemnon reached his native land in safety. Upon disembarking, however, he was espied by a watchman, whom Aegisthus had set to look out for his return, fearing that he might get past unobserved and subsequently engage in hostilities. Upon receiving the intelligence, Aegisthus placed a hundred men in ambush, and went with chariots and horses to fetch the king and his followers to a banquet at his house. In the midst of the feast he fell upon his guests, and slew them all, though all his own men perished in the conflict. In this account nothing is said of Clytaemnestra, but there is an allusion to the vengeance of Orestes and the arrival of Menelaus in time for the funeral of Aegisthus. The fourth passage of the *Odyssey*[1] agrees with the third in representing Agamemnon as slain at a banquet in the house of Aegisthus, but assigns a prominent share in the plot to Clytaemnestra. It is alone in making mention of Cassandra, who is declared to have been slain at the same time by Clytaemnestra herself. Indeed there is a verse in this passage, and another in a later book, to which we may perhaps trace the germ of the story that Clytaemnestra despatched her husband with her own hands[2].

Now, taking these two versions together as the sum of Homer's contribution to the legend, we may notice that nothing is said in either of the enmity of Atreus and Thyestes, of the banishment of Aegisthus, or of the sacrifice of Iphigeneia, which form the chief springs of the dramatic action. On the other hand, we collect the hostility of Aegisthus and Agamemnon; the infidelity of Clytaemnestra and her share in the enterprise of Agamemnon's death; the death of Cassandra by her hand; and the dispersion of Menelaus' ships by a storm, from which Agamemnon himself escapes by divine aid, only to fall a victim to treachery on land. So much a later poet could consistently put together from the separate accounts. But in one particular the two versions are inconsistent. The statement in the second

[1] *Od.* 11. 405—53.

[2] *Od.* 11. 453 *πάρος δέ με πέφνε καὶ αὐτόν*, and 24. 200 *κουρίδιον κτείνασα πόσιν* (the subject in both places is Clyt.).

that Agamemnon, on his return voyage, had got safely as far as Cape Malea, assumes that his home is not at Mycenae, as in the *Iliad*, but at Sparta; therein agreeing with the view of the lyric poets, Stesichorus, Simonides, and Pindar. To suit this version we must apparently conceive of Aegisthus as a prince whose hereditary domain lies in the peninsula which terminates in Cape Malea. Agamemnon is first carried to the east coast of this territory. He escapes thence, doubles the cape, and disembarks on his own territory of Sparta. But in order to reach his inland fortress, he is still obliged to pass along the western border of Aegisthus' land, where a watchman had been stationed for a year to give notice of his progress up the valley of the Eurotas. He is directed to the castle of Aegisthus, whither Clytaemnestra had previously removed, and is treacherously murdered at a banquet.

This conception of the matter differs considerably from that of the first version, in which the centre of interest is Mycenae. The difference is not without interest, for it marks the first stage in the passage of the legend to the form in which we find it in Aeschylus. It can hardly be doubted that the second version, which places the seat of Agamemnon's rule at Sparta, is the older of the two. First, it is conformable to what we know of the earliest kingships that Agamemnon should be represented as reigning, not at Mycenae, like his father Atreus, nor at Pisa, like his grandfather Pelops, but on the other hand, like his grandfather, his father, and his brother, at the home of his wife, that is, at Sparta[1]. Secondly, this version presupposes an archaic state of society, in which two chieftains dwelling on adjacent territories are at feud with each other, and one may get the better of his rival by the simple device of inviting him to a banquet at his castle. The whole relation smacks of something primitive, as indeed do those portions of the *Odyssey* from which it is extracted. But even before the Trojan war, as Thucydides tells us[2], this state of society had become antiquated by the growth of commerce and maritime intercourse, and the congre-

[1] Frazer, *Early History of the Kingship*, p. 240, where the reason of this is explained.

[2] Thuc. I. 7, 8.

gation of men into walled cities. Now that expedition itself was by all accounts due to the concentration of naval power in the hands of Agamemnon. Hence it was a plausible conception, doubtless resting on some basis of fact, to shift the seat of Agamemnon's power from the poor and backward country of Laconia to the fortified town of Mycenae, with its dependencies of Argos and Tiryns, right in the trading area of Corinth, Cleonae, Sicyon, Troezen, and Epidaurus. Therefore Mycenae appears as his capital throughout the *Iliad.* To these altered conditions the poet of the *Odyssey* had to adapt the story of Aegisthus' feat, which is nothing else than a variation on the immemorial theme of the *Odyssey* itself. Clytaemnestra is a more pliable Penelope, who is left at home in the charge of a minstrel[1], while her husband is absent on a distant war. Aegisthus is a successful Antinous, who persuades the queen to remove to his own residence. Agamemnon is a less fortunate Odysseus, who, upon returning home with the remnant of his followers, is promptly murdered by his rival. Orestes is a retributive Telemachus. But by the time that Mycenae has become prominent, the conception of two rival chieftains living each on his several estate has sunk into the background; and how, in the new circumstances, Aegisthus might execute his project, the poet of the *Odyssey* did not know. Therefore, when he places the scene of the exploit at Mycenae, he is obliged to leave the details of Agamemnon's murder vague, covering up his ignorance by saying that Menelaus was not at hand to help his brother. But when, in a later book, he wishes to give the details of the plot, he simply has recourse to the primitive version, and is thus compelled to leave the scene in the open and uncentralised country of Laconia.

Perhaps it was a perception of this inconsistency which led Stesichorus and Simonides to adopt the older account, which placed Agamemnon's residence near Lacedaemon[2]; and the same thing is implied in Pindar. According to the eleventh *Pythian*, the murder of Agamemnon took place at Amyclae, that is, about two and a half miles below Sparta in the vale of Eurotas. It is natural to suppose that Pindar, who calls Orestes a Laconian,

[1] *Od.* 3. 267. [2] Schol. Eur. *Or.* 46.

regards Lacedaemon as the seat of Agamemnon's power; that Amyclae, a town long independent of Sparta, represents to a later age, familiar with cities, what the primitive version broadly calls the territory of Thyestes and Aegisthus; and that here the stratagem took place by which Agamemnon was slain. In other respects Pindar agrees with Homer in leaving the actual slayer of Agamemnon vague, while affirming that Cassandra was slain at the same time by Clytaemnestra. Two alternative motives are assigned for her act. The one on which the poet lays most stress is her passion for Aegisthus, which could not be kept dark; but he mentions another, traceable in part to the *Cypria* of Stasinus, her anger at the sacrifice of Iphigeneia.

For Pindar, a lyric poet, whose chief purpose it was to adorn a naked theme with a romantic incident, such a conception was still admissible. He was not obliged to give the details of Agamemnon's death, and his auditors might suppose it to have happened in much the same way as Homer describes. But for Aeschylus, a dramatic poet, whose business it was to present this same transaction to the eyes of a fifth-century audience, and to interest them in it for its own sake, the details of the epic narrative were unsuitable. The primitive Homeric version was out of relation to life as actually lived at the moment; and without an effort of historical imagination, which is rather a modern gift, those circumstances could not be reproduced at once faithfully and probably. He was faced by the same difficulty as the poet of the *Odyssey*, when, to suit the story to changed historical conditions, he shifted the scene from the neighbourhood of Lacedaemon to the great capital of Mycenae. Ten years before the date of our play Mycenae had been destroyed by Argos; and Argos is the name which Aeschylus, apparently for the sake of some political allusions in the last act of the trilogy, chooses to give to Agamemnon's realm. But the problem, though slightly intensified by this greater air of historical reality, was in its essence the same for both poets. That problem was to substitute for the ancient version, in which one border chieftain with his retainers cuts off by stratagem another border chieftain with his retainers, an account of the enterprise of Aegisthus conformable to a more settled and political state of society. As we have seen, the poet of the *Odyssey*, who evidently felt the difficulty[1], did not take the pains to construct, perhaps could not even imagine a train of incidents by which the king of men, the lineal sovereign of a strong and wealthy town, the suzerain of a number of petty states, might himself be murdered, and his throne usurped, by a rebellious subject of no great personal courage. He takes refuge in the statement, that the revolution occurred when Menelaus was away.

But Aeschylus, or some predecessor whom Aeschylus followed, had a better idea of how such an attempt as that of Aegisthus might come about. With the growth of wealth and commerce in Greece, and the collection of its inhabitants into fortified cities, it became evident to political experience that freedom from external aggression was more than compensated by the danger of dissension within. The enterprise of Aegisthus is conceived as an incident of *stasis* or party faction, a feature of Greek politics whose beginning was traced by Attic thought to the influx of wealth which occurred a little before the Trojan War[2]. That this mature political conception of the matter has governed the shaping of the story between Homer and Aeschylus, is tolerably plain. In the drama, of course, it does not assume any great prominence; but enough details are given to show that it underlies the presentation, and is used to make it intelligible to a fifth-century audience. The scene is removed from an outlying tract of country to the heart of a city state. The origin of the dissension is ascribed to a personal quarrel between two members of the reigning family. Thyestes disputes the power of his brother Atreus, and is banished from the city. Even such uncouth incidents as the seduction of Aerope and the feast of Thyestes find some historical warrant in what was related of Gyges in Sardis and of Harpagus in Persia[3]. The feud continues into the next generation, and the hopes of the inferior faction centre on Aegisthus. He is to be conceived as hanging about in exile, intriguing with his adherents in the city, and waiting for a favourable moment for taking vengeance on his

[1] See *Od.* 3. 248—52. [2] Thuc. 1. 2, 3.
[3] Her. 1. 11; 1. 119.

enemies[1]. His opportunity came with the Trojan War. Thucydides informs us that the protracted nature of that expedition gave a great chance to the malcontents in the Greek cities to overthrow the government, in the midst of which commotions most of the old hereditary monarchies went down, and were replaced by tyrannies[2]. The temporary eclipse of one such monarchy is depicted in the *Agamemnon*[3]. The disaffection against the royal house of Argos is ascribed by the poet to the prolonged, costly, and selfish enterprise against Troy[4], which may be regarded as swelling the number of Aegisthus' partisans, and thus making the success of his attempt conceivable. A principal element in his plan, as in that of most Greek seditions, was to occupy the citadel which commanded the township. This might easily have been done in the absence of the kings, but it would have been a more difficult matter to retain it on their return. Besides, so long as the regent Clytaemnestra was his friend, there was nothing to be gained by premature action. His policy was to lie low until the day of Agamemnon's return, exciting as little suspicion as possible, and to overpower his enemies by a surprise; a thing manifestly impossible if he had already seized the fortress. But it was necessary for himself to be prepared against the surprise of their return, and to be ready for instant action. To such necessity we may perhaps attribute the introduction into the story of the beacon signal, which, while plausibly designed to announce the fall of Troy, has the secondary effect of giving the conspirators timely notice of their enemy's approach. On the day of the king's arrival, the conspirator who could draw nearest to his person, with the least suspicion, would be his wife; and to this circumstance we may naturally ascribe the bold invention which represents Agamemnon as overtaken in his privacy and murdered by his queen. In the interval between the murder and the appearance of Aegisthus on the stage, we may suppose the latter to have executed his part of the plan, originally a difficult part, but vastly simplified by the storm, that of overpowering the followers of the king.

[1] v. 1668. [2] Thuc. I. 12, 13.
[3] The character of this sovereignty is defined by *Cho.* 54—60 and *Cho.* 863—5.
[4] vv. 452—64.

This is the basis on which the drama rests. But as that part of it which is assigned to Clytaemnestra—the public intercourse with the elders, the reception of the king at his own home, and above all his actual murder—is obviously the part best fitted for dramatic treatment on the Greek stage, almost the whole interest of the presentation centres upon her; while Aegisthus, who cannot even openly appear, is relegated to the background. It is only from the last scene that we gather that he is at the bottom of the whole conspiracy. There remains one minor circumstance, for which the reason is not at once evident. Why does Aeschylus represent Agamemnon and Menelaus as reigning jointly at Argos?

It may be said that the concentration of interest which results—the desolation of the house at Argos by the wicked act of Paris, set off against the destruction of the house of Priam by the act of Helen—greatly increases the force and symmetry of the picture; and that the interest imparted to Menelaus provides several effective passages in the drama, such as the description of the storm. All this is true; but it may be doubted whether Aeschylus would have taken this liberty with history, simply for these reasons, if he had not found some warrant for it in the works of his predecessors. In the earliest version, as we have seen, both Agamemnon and Menelaus live in Laconia. There Agamemnon is murdered by Aegisthus, who in his turn is slain by Orestes, the latter exploit being regarded as just as simple an affair as the former[1]. But when the murder was transferred to Mycenae, the execution of Orestes' feat became an equally difficult matter with that of Aegisthus. How could he escape the consequence of his attack on the master of a fortified town? Again the poet of the *Odyssey* passes over the details, but he is careful to retain, and to emphasise, the fact that Menelaus arrived from Egypt on the very day of the funeral feast of Aegisthus[2]. The purpose of this retention is plain; the arrival of Menelaus accounts for the immunity of Orestes. But it involves the startling novelty that the home of Menelaus,

[1] *Od.* 4. 546—7.

[2] *Od.* 3. 311. It will be remembered what use Euripides makes of this synchronism in the *Orestes*.

no less than that of Agamemnon, is at Mycenae. Why else should Menelaus, sailing from Egypt, go there at all? Of course the poet does not intend this inference; everywhere else he assumes that Menelaus lives at Sparta. But, having transferred the scene of Agamemnon's death to Mycenae, he is obliged by the sequel of this particular story to bring Menelaus thither also. Now later writers, such perhaps as Agias of Troezen (author of the *Nosti*), having to explain in detail the achievement of Orestes, could by no means give up the opportune advent of Menelaus from Egypt; and having to account for his landing at Mycenae, they would incline to assert that Mycenae was his home. Hence the two brothers would be represented, in post-Homeric versions, as reigning together at Mycenae, just as in the earliest version they had reigned together at Lacedaemon. The seat of their joint government is merely transferred by Aeschylus, in conformity with his whole design, from the locality of Mycenae to the neighbouring locality of Argos.

MORAL AND RELIGIOUS IDEAS.

The riper political experience, which had befallen the Greek world since the time of Homer, is one of the chief causes which impart to the poet's treatment of the legend a seriousness and weight that are not felt to belong to it in the epic. Throughout the drama we are conscious that his eye is not really fixed on a remote antiquity, but that his sentiments and reflexions are drawn from that impressive age of Greek politics, which lies between the date of Peisistratus and the date of Pausanias; a period of wealth, commerce, and maritime adventure, in which parties fought in the several states, in which a combination of the states miraculously repulsed the national foe, in which individuals rose to power, yielded to their passions, and fell. Troy is the typical city of Asia Minor, a seat of wealth and luxury, where the decay of moral principle leads directly to political ruin. Argos is the scene of civic disunion terminating in tyranny. Another source of profound difference is the application to the story of certain theological ideas, some of which seem in their origin to lie behind Homer, others to be the fruit of more refined speculation working on the simple and careless religion of Olympus. The first class of ideas, those which are concerned with the ritual of the tomb, the powers of the underworld, the peculiar effects of bloodshed, and the like, are less prominent in the *Agamemnon* than in the *Choephori*, where the religion of the grave is presented in all its sombre and mystic power, or in the *Eumenides*, where part of the poet's object is to fuse the system of Olympus with the conflicting system of the Earth and of the dead. After Aeschylus these ideas appear to have become antiquated, so far as literature was concerned, and to have died a natural death. Interesting as they are in themselves, they do not directly concern us here.

The second class of ideas, which, though modified by the transition of the Greek mind from theology to philosophy, continued to provide the staple of later thought, figures more largely in our play. The questions which exercise the poet are the old pair. What is the nature of the Power which governs the order of events? Does this Power interfere to punish the successful sinner? First of all, that there is such a Power, the poet does not doubt. He calls it by the traditional name of Zeus; but what sort of a Being corresponds to this name, he does not profess to know[1]. To Zeus he ascribes the universal succession of causes and effects[2]; his contact with the temporal order is one of spiritual direction; the principle of his operation is justice[3]; the smoothness and ease of it is a sign of his power. In these matters the poet is the pupil of Xenophanes. When Xenophanes says[4], 'Among gods and men there is one greatest God, neither in body nor mind resembling mortal man....He is all eye, all ear, all thought....He sways all things without exertion by the notion of his mind....He remains always in the selfsame place, not moved at all, nor does it become him to travel hither and thither....There never was, nor ever will be, any man that knew the certain truth about the Gods, and what I affirm about all things; for although he might chance to state the fact as

[1] v. 170. [2] v. 1487. [3] v. 773.

[4] See frags. 23—6 and 34 (Diels).

nearly as possible, yet he knows it not himself; but opinion is formed upon all things'—the substance of his language is reproduced by Aeschylus: 'Zeus, whosoever he is, if so it please himself to be called, by this name I address him. When I ponder all things, I can make no guess to fill the gap, except Zeus, if I must cast off, to the very name, the vain obsession of the mind[1]....Zeus employs no violence; (every act of Deity is without exertion); throned aloft, his thought somehow effects its end, even from where it is, on its holy seat[2]....What merit has a Deity who should use violence on his awful throne[3].... The Father disposes all things, turning them upside down, panting not at all in his might[4].' In his dealings with men, the justice of Zeus is embodied in two laws, which distinguish his reign from that of those who might claim to have preceded him. The first law is, that moral wisdom is reward of painful experience[5]. The second is, that the guilty must suffer[6].

As regards the first, the point of interest is to observe how the religious soul of Aeschylus converts to its own use a circumstance which had discouraged less elevated minds. Other writers, such as Solon, had contrasted the complacent hopes of man, his ardent pursuit of various ends, with his utter ignorance of the future and his liability to complete and unexpected disaster: 'Hazard is annexed to every work, nor does any man know, when a business is beginning, where it will end[7].' The purpose of Aeschylus is not to lament this inferiority of human constitution, but to justify and even applaud it. This he does by considering it in the light of a nobler object, not that of a man's practical success, but that of his moral perfection. He regards the suffering in which the 'blind hopes' of men so often terminate as a necessary discipline of human character. Even if a man had complete foreknowledge, nothing would ensure his acting right. Laius was thrice divinely warned of the consequences of committing a certain action, but he committed it none the less[8]. Agamemnon was divinely warned of the consequences of sacrificing his daughter, but he did not repent

[1] vv. 170—7. [2] *Suppl.* 97—102. [3] vv. 192—3.
[4] *Eum.* 650—1. [5] vv. 183—8, 261—2. [6] vv. 1562—3.
[7] See Solon, frag. 4. 33—70 (Bergk). [8] *Theb.* 745.

till it was too late[1]. But if men will sin with their eyes open, instead of deploring the fact that a man's aims miscarry through his ignorance of the future, we ought rather to be thankful that, when suffering comes, it operates to man's amendment. Hence it is not as a matter of complaint, but as part of a solemn hymn of praise, that he enunciates the maxim *πάθει μάθος*. In some remarkable lines he touches on the stealthy and unconscious transformation of character by pain[2]. It is an instance of the gentle but thorough process by which the Deity effects all change.

But it is the devout assertion of the second law which is the test of a truly religious mind, inasmuch as it appears to conflict with the evident facts of life. Long before Aeschylus there had been misgivings about the continued impunity of the wicked, and various attempts had been made to account for it. The view of Homer, if it can be called a view, was that Zeus suffered men to trade on their wickedness, that he might take it out in fuller measure later on: 'Although the Olympian punishes not at once, yet he does so at the last, and they pay with heavy interest, with their persons, and with their wives, and with their children[3].' The wise Solon, having an eye on these words, gave a somewhat different explanation. Zeus surveys the end of all things; therefore he does not flare up, like an irascible man, at each particular sin. He waits till all has mounted up, and then he makes a clean sweep, as a vernal wind scatters the clouds, and restores the naked purity of sky[4]. But how if the sinner dies in prosperity, before the clearance comes? The answer of Solon is unsatisfactory but interesting: 'None that has a guilty mind escapes His notice for ever and ever, but in all case is shown up at the last. Only, while one pays forthwith, another pays later on; or if they themselves get off, before the visitation of Heaven catches them, it comes afterwards in any case: their deeds are paid for by the innocent, either by their children or by their posterity after them[5].' We see here that the ends of justice are equally supposed to be satisfied, whether the punishment falls upon the sinner himself, or upon

[1] vv. 228—31. [2] vv. 189—91. [3] *Il.* 4. 160—2.
[4] frag. 4. 17—26. [5] frag. 4. 27—32.

his innocent children or descendants. Theories of divine justice have usually been modelled on the scheme of human justice prevailing at the time; and it is well known that in early times the unit of which the law took cognisance was not the individual, but the family. If one member of a family did wrong, he was not himself directly punished, but indirectly, as a limb of the system of blood-relationship, on which as a whole the forfeit fell. But this community of interest embraced not only the members of the family living at the time; it extended also to the dead, between whom and the living the mere fact of dissolution made no essential rupture. The ancestor who committed a crime might at any time be penalised in the person of his descendant, on whom he depended for vital nourishment and his degree of honour among the dead. If the descendants were extinguished altogether, the fate of the ancestors would be miserable indeed. It was important to perpetuate the race and to keep it clear of guilt; but once the fatal act had been committed, once the curse had been entailed, it was not felt to be unfair that the living should be involved in the punishment of the dead. The divine retribution, like the human retribution, was assessed upon the whole; and the life which was subjected to justice was that which began with the earliest forefather and terminated with the last descendant.

The advantage of this collective view of responsibility was that, by giving the Deity an indefinite space of time in which to operate, it might at least be maintained that guilt was certain sooner or later to meet with its reward. But when the importance of the individual eclipsed that of the family, the dilatory character of divine justice assumed a new and perplexing aspect. What had hitherto been regarded as a deferred payment on the part of the family, now took the offensive shape of a vicarious punishment inflicted on the innocent. And yet to surrender this latitude of action on the part of Heaven was to give up the most plausible ground of experience on which it could be asserted that sin was always punished. Impressed with the conviction that compensation must somehow be made, but faced with the fact that the original sinner often ended his days in peace, it is perhaps not surprising that the moral sense of men acquiesced in the belief, rooted in an earlier notion of responsibility, that if the fathers had eaten sour grapes, the children's teeth should be set on edge. Such is the opinion of Solon in the passage quoted above. We perceive a slight trace of dissatisfaction with it in his use of the word 'innocent'; though this is perhaps designed to excite indignation against the sinner rather than to impugn the fairness of the divine execution.

In the *Oresteia* there is a general inclination to reconcile beliefs surviving from a rude past with the conscience of a more humane and enlightened age. Thus, while in the *Choephori* the old law of reviling for reviling, blood for blood, is asserted in all its stern rigour, because it seems just that Clytaemnestra and Aegisthus should suffer for their crime, in the *Eumenides*, where the conscience instinctively takes sides with Orestes, the severity of the law is relaxed in obedience to a higher claim. The court of Areopagus is instituted to inquire into cases of justifiable homicide. In the *Agamemnon* there is a like attempt, on the one hand to uphold the just principle that guilt must be paid for, and on the other, to mitigate the conclusion by which alone this principle could be shown to have a sure basis in fact. The poet does not deny that the sins of the fathers are visited on the children. He admits that the crime of Atreus may have contributed to the destruction of his son[1]. Nay, he points out how this might happen, through the physical link of blood connecting the two, which, in the control of a supernatural minister, fatally constrained Agamemnon to his doom[2]. The same blood which had sinned higher up in Atreus was punished lower down in Agamemnon. But the physical connexion which enabled the retribution to be made, even after the original sinner had escaped, might also be used to palliate its injustice. The continuity in blood might import a transmission of moral qualities also. Hence the poet asserts that, if an ancestor sins, he bequeaths to his descendant a tendency to sin himself[3]. The ancient crime of Laomedon came to birth again in the wicked act of Paris; then followed the punishment. The guilt of Atreus propagated itself afresh in the guilt of Agamemnon. It is the poet's cue, so to speak, to exhibit the personal culpability

[1] vv. 1508—9. [2] vv. 1510—3. [3] vv. 755—66.

of the latter. This is why, in the forefront of his drama, he lays so much emphasis on the sacrifice of Iphigeneia It is important to observe that this act does not take in Aeschylus, as it does in Sophocles, the form of restitution to Heaven, wiping out a previous offence. It is merely imposed on Agamemnon as the condition of completing a certain design. It is a temptation indeed, but one which might have been resisted. Agamemnon might have broken up his armament and left Troy to divine vengeance; and the poet several times hints that this would have been the proper course to adopt. But the fatal taint was in his blood, and when the temptation to iniquity came, he fell. From that moment his personal responsibility began. It was increased by his conjugal infidelities in regard to Chryseis and Cassandra, and by the bloodthirsty character of his vengeance upon Troy[1].

Once a man has sinned, then, the mischief tends to propagate itself in his descendants, until in the fulness of time some outrageous act produces the ruin of his race. But to what agency are we to ascribe the first sin of all? In Homeric times it was sufficient to say that 'Zeus took a man's wits away,' or the like. Later ages, seeking for some motive on the part of the Gods, ascribed the fall of princes to a divine jealousy of their prosperity. There was a certain limit of success which no human king might pass with safety, any more than he might journey to the Hyperboreans or sail beyond the pillars of Heracles. This limitation of human capacity was what made a man a man; without it he would have been a God; and the Gods were naturally jealous of their prerogative[2]. Traces of this way of thinking appear in Aeschylus; but where he is speaking most in earnest, where he professes himself at variance with the majority, such a view is evidently repugnant to him[3]. Prosperity by itself, he says, is not sufficient to ruin a race; it is wicked and impious actions which are fatal[4]. But prosperity is dangerous because it affords the temptation and occasion to sin[5]. Similarly great renown is dangerous because it is likely to exalt the heart to presumptuous thoughts and reckless language[6]. From this

[1] vv. 467, 1004, etc.

[2] So Pind. *Ol.* 5. fin. *μὴ ματεύσηι θεὸς γενέσθαι* (advice to a fortunate man), etc.

[3] vv. 749—54. [4] vv. 755—9. [5] vv. 385—97. [6] vv. 474—6.

danger nothing can save a man but a naturally sober mind, 'the greatest gift of God[1].' A mind naturally liable to be spoiled by success is presumably the gift of God also, but the poet does not make this statement with the cheerful indifference of Homer. He loves to trace the misfortunes of a family back to some wild mental impulse in an ancestor, which brings an evil strain into the race, which entails a curse on it, which raises a supernatural avenger to see to its execution. The completion of the train of misfortunes he ascribes to divine agency. But the first inclination to sin appears to arise by itself in the man's own heart; only, like everything which a Greek could not go behind, it tends to be represented as a supernatural possessing power (*παρακοπὰ πρωτοπήμων, πρώταρχος ἄτη, ὄλβος ἄγαν παχυνθείς*)[2]. How this power is related to the general originating power of Zeus, we are not informed. All that is said is, that Zeus sooner or later visits the wicked act with justice. Without sin there could be no justice. But why this or that individual should be destined to be the sinner, upon whom or upon whose race justice is exercised, remains a mystery.

THE CHARACTERS.

In the light of these moral ideas the principal characters of the play are drawn. The fate of Agamemnon, as we have seen, is partly a compensation for his father's crime, partly a punishment for his own. There is an element of misfortune in it, and an element of deserved retribution; and in the presence of these two our reprobation and our sympathy are almost equally divided. He embarks on a selfish and misguided enterprise; but he acts under a natural concern for the wounded honour of his family. He commits an odious crime in pursuit of his end; but he commits it under strong provocation, for the sake of his allies. He is merciless in his vengeance; but the offence was wanton, and the labour of execution prolonged and severe. His language is proud; but his pride is a natural weakness at the moment of his triumph. He is harsh, and

[1] v. 919. [2] vv. 233, 1191, *Theb.* 756.

suspicious; but he has suffered from the insincerity of his friends abroad, and has more than a glimpse of treachery at home. He is suspicious of Heaven also, he is feebly superstitious; but he knows that he is a man, the greatest in the world, the most liable to change. He is an unfaithful husband; but the fault, even when we find it most repugnant[1], is relieved by our knowledge of the infidelity of his wife. In his dignity and his weakness he is every inch a king. While it is impossible to call him an amiable character, we can share in some degree the loyalty which he inspires in the simpler natures of the play, the watchman, the herald, and the elders. When we observe him moving unconsciously to his doom, above all when we see him cut off in the midst of his glory by an ignominious end, our sense of the justice of his fate leaves room for the pity which the bewildered exclamations of his faithful counsellors claim.

To compass the chastisement of the guilty race, the Gods raised up two figures of strange and fearful power, the sisters Helen and Clytaemnestra. The former moves through the background of the drama as a beautiful but fatal presence, the embodiment of wanton sin, the instrument of Heaven for the ruin of the house of Priam, the remoter cause of the catastrophe of the house of Atreus. The latter, who is the direct agent of Agamemnon's fall, presents the same reckless nature armed with the terrible motives of suppressed resentment and vindictive hate. On the portrayal of this grand and appalling figure the poet has concentrated his utmost skill. The two traits which he marks most firmly are her masculine capacity and her unerring duplicity. The first of these, besides being given by the testimony of the other characters, is immediately evident from the situation, in which she appears as adequate to great affairs of state; from the deference with which she is treated by the council of Elders, and from the almost contemptuous manner in which she deals with them; from the tenacity with which she pursues her end, and the promptness and energy with which she executes it. To accomplish her purpose she is ready to defy both Gods and men[2]. The second trait, which cannot of course be directly revealed until the murder is done, is

[1] v. 941.

[2] vv. 965, 1401, etc.

nevertheless conveyed by the prophetic hints of Calchas and Cassandra, and still more by the perpetual irony of her language, which is instinct with the very spirit of deceit. Of the motives which are expressly assigned to her, the most sincerely felt is her anger at the death of Iphigeneia, which has rankled in her bosom for ten long years. She is the lurking avengeress of Agamemnon's crime. Her union with Aegisthus is subordinate; it is a necessary means to her end, a measure for her own protection. Her sense of her husband's infidelities is confined to a passing scoff. But no mere accumulation of motives is sufficient to account for the total effect of her action, its certitude, its self-reliance, its unflagging zest. Only when she declares that she is not Agamemnon's wife, but the incarnation of the 'ancient, bitter Avenger of the cruel feast of Atreus[1],' do we begin to grasp the lines on which her character is conceived. There is something in her beyond the natural capacity of man or woman, something preternatural and daemonic. But if she is not solely sustained by common human motives, neither is she the impassive instrument of justice. She has a cordial relish of wickedness, as appears by the extraordinary gusto with which she dwells on her crime, and by her utter absence of remorse. At the end of the play, what puzzles the Chorus is not the justice of Agamemnon's doom, but the fact that so much wickedness should be allowed to triumph. It is this margin of positive evil which calls for the vengeance of Orestes, a vengeance executed by divine command, and almost contrary to the inclination of the principal actor himself.

In the character of Aegisthus, on the other hand, all is plain. It is not in him that the curse of Thyestes reveals its mystic force. He acts through the natural motives of revenge and ambition. The circumstances of the case compel him to reach his end by treachery; and for all that is said to the contrary, it would appear that this method was itself the most congenial to his nature. By good fortune or by divine decree, he found in Clytaemnestra a nature suited to his purpose; without her he would have been nothing. His ignoble type of cunning, his absence from the scene at the supreme moment, furnish an

[1] v. 1502 f.

effective contrast to the daring hypocrisy and ubiquitous supervision of the queen; as does his overbearing petulance in the hour of success to the few unimpassioned words in which she acknowledges that the work of her life is done.

Cassandra, as Mr Sidgwick observes, is not truly a study of character at all, the interest lies in her situation. She is the victim of events which she clearly foresees, but which, by the condition of her estate, she is powerless to influence. Such a figure, having something improbable in it, requires more than ordinary power for its successful handling; but if successful, none can be more deeply impressive. Aeschylus has omitted no circumstance which could contribute to sink criticism in a flood of absorbing interest. The very silence of Cassandra provokes a disposition to hear her speak. From the first moment that she opens her mouth, curiosity is superseded by sympathy and awe. She is a princess tenderly reared, who, by a fatal mischance, has become an object of derisive contempt to her friends. Her family and her nation are ruined, but she is not permitted to share their fate, being reserved for slavery and death among her foes. She is a prophetess who has a horrible consciousness of the destination to which she has been brought, and an equally horrible prescience of the doom which there awaits her. Her one gleam of consolation is afforded by the fact that she can foresee the vengeance of Orestes. A peculiar poignancy is added to her story by the circumstance that we learn it all from her own lips. At each instant our sensibility to her misery is but the reflexion of her own.

The watchman and the herald are simple characters, such as never fail of effect when mixed up with events, intrigues, and passions greater than themselves. The simplicity of the former is that of the peasant, which includes fidelity to his masters without excluding a shrewd regard for his own safety and interest. The simplicity of the latter is of a different type. It is that of an honest man who has acquired some notion of great affairs by bearing a humble part in them, but whose view is limited to their formal and external side. The transparency of his nature is shown by the uncontrollable vehemence with which he expresses his joys and sorrows. But he does not forget that he is a public officer, and he is almost absurdly anxious to discharge his own particular part in the most becoming manner. His personal delight at the success of the Trojan enterprise is increased by thinking of the high consideration which his master will enjoy in the world. He consoles himself for the sufferings and loss of life at Troy by reflecting what a fine position the army will hold in the esteem of future ages. While he feels it to be his duty to tell the strict truth, he is concerned about the impropriety of joining good and bad news together. The succession or conflict of these various feelings in his simple breast makes his language alternately impetuous, abrupt and circuitous. He is certainly one of the most original and lifelike characters in Tragedy.

[The following MSS. containing the *Agamemnon* either in whole or in part are referred to by their respective symbols in the critical notes:—

M denotes the codex Mediceus (or Laurentianus) XXXII. 9, a parchment MS. of the tenth or eleventh century containing besides the plays of Sophocles and Aeschylus the *Argonautica* of Apollonius. Owing however to the loss of fourteen leaves in the part containing the *Agamemnon*, its evidence is only available for vv. 1—322, 1051—1158. Readings due to the second hand are recorded as m.

a denotes the codex Marcianus 468 (XCI. 4), sometimes known as Ven. 2, and belonging to the thirteenth or fourteenth century. It was formerly owned by Cardinal Bessarion, and in Hermann's edition is distinguished by the compendium Bess. It contains only the first 360 lines of the *Agamemnon*; Franz thought that it was copied from M when that MS. was still entire.

f denotes the codex Florentinus (or Laurentianus) XXXI. 8, a paper MS. written in the earlier part of the fourteenth century. Besides other plays of Aeschylus it contains the *Agamemnon* entire.

g denotes the codex Venetus (or Marcianus) 616 (XCI. 5), a parchment MS. formerly assigned to the thirteenth but now to the fifteenth century. It contains the same plays of Aeschylus as f, but owing to the loss of several leaves is without vv. 46—1079 of the *Agamemnon*.

h denotes the codex Farnesianus (or Neapolitanus) I. E. 5, written in the latter part of the fourteenth century, as is generally believed, by Demetrius Triclinius. It contains the same plays of Aeschylus as f and g, and the *Agamemnon* is complete.

It will be seen that f and h alone contain the whole of the *Agamemnon*, with the support of g in the latter part of the play. Only about a quarter of the text is extant in M.

Corrections due to the editor are denoted by the symbol H.]

ΑΙΣΧΥΛΟΥ

ΑΓΑΜΕΜΝΩΝ

ΑΓΑΜΕΜΝΟΝΟΣ ΥΠΟΘΕΣΙΣ.

Ἀγαμέμνων εἰς Ἴλιον ἀπιὼν τῆι Κλυταιμήστραι, εἰ πορθήσοι τὸ Ἴλιον, ὑπέσχετο τῆς αὐτῆς ἡμέρας σημαίνειν διὰ τοῦ πυρσοῦ. ὅθεν σκοπὸν ἐκάθισεν ἐπὶ μισθῶι Κλυταιμήστρα, ἵνα τηροίη τὸν πυρσόν. καὶ ὁ μὲν ἰδὼν ἀπήγγειλεν, αὐτὴ δὲ τῶν πρεσβυτῶν ὄχλον μεταπέμπεται περὶ τοῦ πυρσοῦ ἐροῦσα· ἐξ ὧν 5 καὶ ὁ χορὸς συνίσταται· οἵτινες ἀκούσαντες παιανίζουσιν. μετ' οὐ πολὺ δὲ καὶ Ταλθύβιος παραγίνεται καὶ τὰ κατὰ τὸν πλοῦν διηγεῖται. Ἀγαμέμνων δ' ἐπὶ ἀπήνης ἔρχεται· εἵπετο δ' αὐτῶι ἑτέρα ἀπήνη, ἔνθα ἦν τὰ λάφυρα καὶ ἡ Κασάνδρα. αὐτὸς μὲν οὖν προεισέρχεται εἰς τὸν οἶκον σὺν τῆι Κλυταιμήστραι, Κασάνδρα δὲ προμαντεύεται, πρὶν εἰς τὰ βασίλεια εἰσελθεῖν, τὸν ἑαυτῆς καὶ 10 τοῦ Ἀγαμέμνονος θάνατον καὶ τὴν ἐξ Ὀρέστου μητροκτονίαν, καὶ εἰσπηδᾶι ὡς θανουμένη, ῥίψασα τὰ στέμματα. τοῦτο δὲ τὸ μέρος τοῦ δράματος θαυμάζεται ὡς ἔκπληξιν ἔχον καὶ οἶκτον ἱκανόν. ἰδίως δὲ Αἰσχύλος τὸν Ἀγαμέμνονα ἐπὶ σκηνῆς ἀναιρεῖσθαι ποιεῖ, τὸν δὲ Κασάνδρας σιωπήσας θάνατον νεκρὰν αὐτὴν ὑπέδειξεν, πεποίηκέν τε Αἴγισθον καὶ Κλυταιμήστραν ἑκάτερον διισχυριζόμενον 15 περὶ τῆς ἀναιρέσεως ἑνὶ κεφαλαίωι, τὴν μὲν τῆι ἀναιρέσει Ἰφιγενείας, τὸν δὲ ταῖς τοῦ πατρὸς Ὀρέστου ἐξ Ἀτρέως συμφοραῖς.

Ἐδιδάχθη τὸ δρᾶμα ἐπὶ ἄρχοντος Φιλοκλέους ὀλυμπιάδι κη̄ ἔτει β̄. πρῶτος Αἰσχύλος Ἀγαμέμνονι, Χοηφόροις, Εὐμενίσι, Πρωτεῖ σατυρικῶι. ἐχορήγει Ξενοκλῆς Ἀφιδνεύς.

16 Ὀρέστου M: Θυέστου Victorius. **17** κη̄ M: ὀγδοηκοστῆι Meursius.

ΤΑ ΤΟΥ ΔΡΑΜΑΤΟΣ ΠΡΟΣΩΠΑ

ΦΥΛΑΞ.
ΧΟΡΟΣ.
[ΑΓΓΕΛΟΣ.]
ΚΛΥΤΑΙΜΗΣΤΡΑ.
[ΤΑΛΘΥΒΙΟΣ] ΚΗΡΥΞ.
ΑΓΑΜΕΜΝΩΝ.
ΚΑΣΑΝΔΡΑ.
ΑΙΓΙΣΘΟΣ.

ΑΓΓΕΛΟΣ et ΤΑΛΘΥΒΙΟΣ del. Stanley.

ΦΥΛΑΞ.

Θεοὺς μὲν αἰτῶ τῶνδ' ἀπαλλαγὴν πόνων
φρουρᾶς ἐτείας μῆκος, ἣν κοιμώμενος
στέγαις Ἀτρειδῶν ἄγκαθεν, κυνὸς δίκην,
ἄστρων κάτοιδα νυκτέρων ὁμήγυριν,
καὶ τοὺς φέροντας χεῖμα καὶ θέρος βροτοῖς 5
λαμπροὺς δυνάστας, ἐμπρέποντας αἰθέρι
ἀστέρας, ὅταν φθίνωσιν, ἀντολάς τε τῶν.
καὶ νῦν φυλάσσω λαμπάδος τὸ σύμβολον,
αὐγὴν πυρὸς φέρουσαν ἐκ Τροίας φάτιν
ἁλώσιμόν τε βάξιν· ὧδε γὰρ κρατεῖ 10
γυναικὸς ἀνδρόβουλον ἐλπίζειν κέαρ.
εὖτ' ἂν δὲ νυκτίπλαγκτον ἔνδροσόν τ' ἔχω
εὐνὴν ὀνείροις οὐκ ἐπισκοπουμένην
ἐμήν· φόβος γὰρ ἀνθ' ὕπνου παραστατεῖ,
τὸ μὴ βεβαίως βλέφαρα συμβαλεῖν ὕπνωι-- 15
ὅταν δ' ἀείδειν ἢ μινύρεσθαι δοκῶ,
ὕπνου τόδ' ἀντίμολπον ἐντέμνων ἄκος,
κλαίω τότ' οἴκου τοῦδε συμφορὰν στένων,
οὐχ ὡς τὰ πρόσθ' ἄριστα διαπονουμένου.
νῦν δ' εὐτυχὴς γένοιτ' ἀπαλλαγὴ πόνων 20
εὐαγγέλου φανέντος ὀρφναίου πυρός.

---

2 ἦν fgh: δ' ἦν M. **11** ἐλπίζειν anon.: ἐλπίζων M.

SCENE: *The palace of Agamemnon at Argos.*

TIME: *Night in the first scene; in the second* (v. 266 sqq.) *dawn. After an interval at* v. 493 *the action is continued on a different day.*

The watchman is discovered on the flat roof of the palace. During the tenth year of the war, in which it had been prophesied that Troy should fall, he had been set to watch for the beacon to be passed from Troy by Agamemnon as the sign of victory. It is now about the setting of the Pleiads (v. 817), *which marked the winter or storm-season* (χειμών, χεῖμα, v. 5).

WATCHMAN.

A whole year's length have I been asking Heaven
Deliverance from this vigil, in the which
Upon the Atridae's roof aloft here stretched
On elbows, watch-dog-fashion, I have learnt
With general congress of the nightly stars
The waning seasons and the rising-times
Of those bright eminent splendid potentates
That bring men storm and summer.
So am I now
Still watching for the signal of a torch,
A fiery gleam with message out of Troy—
News of her fall, her capture—such the faith
Held by the man's mind in a woman's heart.
But while I spend
This restless time of rest abroad by night,
Free to the dews, unvisited by dreams,—
No sleep for me,
I warrant! sentry by my pillow stands
Fear, and forbids
The eyelid closing fast—nay, but as oft
As I would medicine sleep
With antidote of music,—hum a stave
Or whistle,—my voice breaks, my singing turns
To moaning for the fortunes of this House,
Not now so admirably administered
As once it was.—But now at length shine out
The fire with his fair tidings in the gloom
And bring me sweet release!

ὦ χαῖρε λαμπτήρ, νυκτὸς ἡμερήσιον
φάος πιφαύσκων καὶ χορῶν κατάστασιν
πολλῶν ἐν Ἄργει, τῆσδε συμφορᾶς χάριν.
ἰοῦ ἰοῦ· 25
Ἀγαμέμνονος γυναικὶ σημαίνω τορῶς,
εὐνῆς ἐπαντείλασαν ὡς τάχος δόμοις
ὀλολυγμὸν εὐφημοῦντα τῆιδε λαμπάδι
ἐπορθιάζειν, εἴπερ Ἰλίου πόλις
ἑάλωκεν, ὡς ὁ φρυκτὸς ἀγγέλλων πρέπει. 30
αὐτός τ᾽ ἔγωγε φροίμιον χορεύσομαι·
τὰ δεσποτῶν γὰρ εὖ πεσόντα θήσομαι
τρὶς ἓξ βαλούσης τῆσδέ μοι φρυκτωρίας.
γένοιτο δ᾽ οὖν μολόντος εὐφιλῆ χέρα
ἄνακτος οἴκων τῆιδε βαστάσαι χερί. 35
τὰ δ᾽ ἄλλα σιγῶ, βοῦς ἐπὶ γλώσσηι μέγας
βέβηκεν· οἶκος δ᾽ αὐτός, εἰ φθογγὴν λάβοι,
σαφέστατ᾽ ἂν λέξειεν· ὡς ἑκὼν ἐγὼ
μαθοῦσιν αὐδῶ κοὐ μαθοῦσι λήθομαι.

ΧΟΡΟΣ.

δέκατον μὲν ἔτος τόδ᾽ ἐπεὶ Πριάμου 40
μέγας ἀντίδικος,
Μενέλαος ἄναξ ἠδ᾽ Ἀγαμέμνων,
διθρόνου Διόθεν καὶ δισκήπτρου

---

29 ἐπορθιάζειν f g h: ἐπορθριάζειν M. **30** ἀγγέλλων g h: ἀγγέλων M.
40 Πριάμου f g h: πριάμω M.

[*The Beacon presently shines out upon the top of Mount Arachnaeus.*

Hail, O thou blessed Lantern, uttering forth
A daylight in the darkness, to be sign
For many a dance in merry Argos now!

[*calling to* CLYTAEMNESTRA *within.*

Oho! Oho!
Let Agamemnon's consort have clear call
To arise up from her couch and lift up voice
Of jubilant thanksgiving, for as it shows
Plain by the beacon's telling, Troy is taken!

[*Her jubilant cry is heard presently within.*

—I'll lead off with a measure first myself;
My master's fortune will advantage me;
This lucky torch has thrown me sixes three.

[*Dances.—During the interval of time supposed to pass now, sacrifices are lit up throughout the city at the Queen's command and the Elders of the city summoned to her presence.*

Ah well at least God send
The master come safe home, to let me grasp
His friendly hand in mine! Beyond that, I'll
Keep silence; there's an ox
Weighs heavy on my tongue:—only, the house
Itself here, had it but a voice, could tell
Plain tale enough:—I, for my part, keep tales
For those instructed; else,—my memory fails.

[*Exit.—Enter* CHORUS *of* ELDERS *opening with a chant preliminary to their lyric song.*

CHORUS.

Now is here the tenth year
Since Priam's great accusing peer
Prince Menelaus,—and
Prince Agamemnon—brothers twain
And by divine right both to reign

τιμῆς ὀχυρὸν ζεῦγος Ἀτρειδᾶν,
στόλον Ἀργείων χιλιοναύτην 45
τῆσδ' ἀπὸ χώρας
ἦραν, στρατιῶτιν ἀρωγήν,
μέγαν ἐκ θυμοῦ κλάζοντες Ἄρη,
τρόπον αἰγυπιῶν, οἵτ' ἐκπατίοις
ἄλγεσι παίδων ὑπατηλεχέων 50
στροφοδινοῦνται,
πτερύγων ἐρετμοῖσιν ἐρεσσόμενοι,
δεμνιοτήρη
πόνον ὀρταλίχων ὀλέσαντες·
ὕπατος δ' ἀίων ἤ τις Ἀπόλλων 55
ἢ Πὰν ἢ Ζεὺς οἰωνόθροον
γόον ὀξυβόαν
τῶνδε μετοίκων ὑστερόποινον
πέμπει παραβᾶσιν Ἐρινύν.
οὕτω δ' Ἀτρέως παῖδας ὁ κρείσσων 60
ἐπ' Ἀλεξάνδρωι πέμπει ξένιος
Ζεύς, πολυάνορος ἀμφὶ γυναικὸς
πολλὰ παλαίσματα καὶ γυιοβαρῆ
γόνατος κονίαισιν ἐρειδομένου
διακναιομένης τ' ἐν προτελείοις 65
κάμακος θήσων Δαναοῖσιν
Τρωσί θ' ὁμοίως. ἔστι δ' ὅπηι νῦν
ἔστι· τελεῖται δ' ἐς τὸ πεπρωμένον·
οὔθ' ὑποκαίων οὔτ' ἐπιλείβων
ἀπύρων ἱερῶν 70
ὀργὰς ἀτενεῖς παραθέλξει.

---

50 ὑπατηλεχέων H.: ὕπατοι λεχέων M. **69** ὑποκαίων Casaubon: ὑποκλαίων M | οὔτ' ἐπιλείβων Schuetz: οὔθ' ὑπολείβων M. **70** οὔτε δακρύων ante ἀπύρων M, del. Bamberger.

Fast-coupled, one joint rank to share
Of throne and sceptre—since that pair
    Launched from Argive land
A thousand ships in battle-train
    By troops of Argos manned.

With loud War shouted harsh in cries
Of passionate anger in the wise
    Of eagles out they sped,
That lone in solitary woe
For lofty-nested children go
Wheeling round, around, in air
As their beating pinions row,
Lost now all that loving care
    About their infants' bed.

Yet shall there One Above defend
Those in his region denizen'd:
Pan, Zeus, Apollo, from on high
That hears their shrill complaining cry
Shall send his Vengeance by-and-bye
    Upon the felon's head.

The Atridae so doth greater Lord,—
Zeus Guardian of the Stranger's Board,—
    On Alexander send;
For one too common, each man's woman,
Sore fatiguing bouts in common—
Down in dust the knee bowed under
And the spear-shaft knapped asunder
First before the final day—
Meaning both on Troy to lay
And Greece alike:—the matter still
Is where it is, and where Fate's will
    Appoints it, there shall end:—
Unburnt sacrifice will spurn
All softening of a temper stern;
Both oils to pour and coals to burn
    In vain a man shall spend.

ἡμεῖς δ' ἀτίται σαρκὶ παλαιᾶι
τῆς τότ' ἀρωγῆς ὑπολειφθέντες
μίμνομεν ἰσχὺν
ἰσόπαιδα νέμοντες ἐπὶ σκήπτροις. 75
ὅ τε γὰρ νεαρὸς μυελὸς στέρνων
ἐντὸς ἀνάσσων
ἰσόπρεσβυς, Ἄρης δ' οὐκ ἐνὶ χώραι·
τί θ' ὑπέργηρως, φυλλάδος ἤδη
κατακαρφομένης; τρίποδας μὲν ὁδοὺς 80
στείχει, παιδὸς δ' οὐδὲν ἀρείων
ὄναρ ἡμερόφαντον ἀλαίνει.
σὺ δέ, Τυνδάρεω
θύγατερ, βασίλεια Κλυταιμήστρα,
τί χρέος; τί νέον; τί δ' ἐπαισθομένη, 85
τίνος ἀγγελίας
πειθοῖ περίπεμπτα θυοσκεῖς;
πάντων δὲ θεῶν τῶν ἀστυνόμων,
ὑπάτων, χθονίων,
τῶν τε θυραίων τῶν τ' ἀγοραίων, 90
βωμοὶ δώροισι φλέγονται·
ἄλλη δ' ἄλλοθεν οὐρανομήκης
λαμπὰς ἀνίσχει,
φαρμασσομένη χρίματος ἁγνοῦ
μαλακαῖς ἀδόλοισι παρηγορίαις, 95
πελάνωι μυχόθεν βασιλείωι.
τούτων λέξασ' ὅ τι καὶ δυνατὸν
καὶ θέμις αἰνεῖν,

79 *τίθιπεργήρως* M, *τόθιπεργήρως* a f, *τό θ' ὑπέργηρων* h. **82** *ἡμερόφαντον* h: *ἡμεροφάτον* M. **87** *θυοσκεῖς* Turnebus: *θυοσκινεῖς* (*ι* in rasura scr.) M. **90** *τε θυραίων* Enger: *τ' οὐρανίων* M.

But we, that agèd sinews made
Defaulters in the task of aid—
Here on staves at home support
Strength of such a feeble sort
    As infant's may be styled:—
The regent marrow, while his throne
Is youthful in the breast ungrown,
Is but in ancient senior's case,—
Ares lacking from his place:
With Age then, when the green leaf seres,
How is it? Forth abroad his way
Takes he on three feet, yet appears
Wandering like a dream astray,
    As weak as any child.

But thou, our soveran Lady Queen,
What is it thou hast heard or seen,
What stir, event, or new advice
To cause thee raise up sacrifice
    With couriers all our streets around?
Each God that in the township sways,—
God supernal, God infernal,
House-door, market-place or ways,—
Each beholds his altar blaze
    With fresh oblations crowned:
And here and there, anointed well
With all-pure smooth bewitching spell
Of unguent from the royal cell
    The high torch heaven-aspiring towers:—
Resolve me now, so much unfold
As may be or as can be told,

παιών τε γενοῦ τῆσδε μερίμνης,
ἣ νῦν τοτὲ μὲν κακόφρων τελέθει, 100
τοτὲ δ' ἐκ θυσιῶν τὴν θυμοβόρον
φροντίδ' ἄπληστον
φαίνουσ' ἀγάν' ἐλπὶς ἀμύνει.

στρ. κύριός εἰμι θροεῖν ὅδιον τέρας
αἴσιον ἀνδρῶν 105
ἐκτελέων· ἔτι γὰρ
θεόθεν καταπνεύει
πειθώ, μολπᾶν
ἀλκάν, σύμφυτος αἰών·
ὅπως Ἀχαιῶν 110
δίθρονον κράτος, Ἑλλάδος ἥβας
ξύμφρονα ταγάν,
πέμπει σὺν δορὶ καὶ χερὶ πράκτορι
θούριος ὄρνις Τευκρίδ' ἐπ' αἶαν,
οἰωνῶν βασιλεὺς 115
βασιλεῦσι νεῶν,
ὁ κελαινός, ὁ δ' ἐξόπιν ἀργᾶις,
φανέντες ἴκταρ
μελάθρων χερὸς ἐκ δορυπάλτου
παμπρέπτοις ἐν ἕδραισιν, 120
βοσκόμενοι λαγίναν,
ἐρικυμάτα φέρματα, γένναν,

---

101 sqq. *τοτὲ δ' ἐκ θυσιῶν ἀγανὰ φαίνεις | ἐλπὶς ἀμύνει φροντίδ' ἄπλειστον | τὴν θυμοφθόρον λύπης φρένα* M: corr. H. **104** *τέρας* Francken: *κράτος* M. **107** *καταπνέ**ει* (fort. e *καταπνέυει*) M: *καταπνεύει* a f h. **111** *ἥβας* Ar. *Ran.* 1285: *ἥβαν* (corr. ex *ἡβᾶν*) M. **112—114** omiserat M, add. m. **112** *ταγάν* a f h: *τὰν γᾶν* m. **113** *καὶ χερὶ* Ar. *Ran.* 1288: *δίκασ* m. **117** *ἀργᾶις* Thiersch: *ἀργίας* M. **119** *δοριπάλτου* Turnebus. **122** *φέρματα* Hartung: *φέρματι* M.

And medicine for my thoughts declare,
That still malignant aspect wear,
Save that with radiant face benign
From altars Hope doth somewhile shine
And bids avaunt this eating care
That my soul devours.

I 1.

The assuring sign will I tell forth—to me by right belong Strophe.
The warbling measures; vigorous yet the moving spirit strong
Divine force live within me stirs, with valiancy for song—
The sign that on their path befell those twain united Kings,
Joint leaders of the youth of Greece, the sign of warrior wings
That sped them for the Trojan land with fierce avenging spear,—
Shown in a quarter near
Pavilion royal,—sable this, that argent in the rear,—
To Lord of ships the Lord of birds, remarked in place of pride,
Upon the spear-arm side,
On quivering hare's-flesh feeding both, young leverets quick in womb,

βλαβέντα λοισθίων δρόμων.
αἴλινον αἴλινον εἰπέ, τὸ δ' εὖ νικάτω.

ἀντ. κεδνὸς δὲ στρατόμαντις ἰδὼν δύο 125
λήμασι δισσοὺς
Ἀτρεΐδας μαχίμους
ἐδάη λαγοδαίτας
πομπούς τ' ἀρχάς·
οὕτω δ' εἶπε τεράιζων· 130
"χρόνωι μὲν ἀγρεῖ
Πριάμου πόλιν ἅδε κέλευθος,
πάντα δὲ πύργων
κτήνη πρόσθε τὰ δημιοπληθῆ
μοῖρα λαπάξει πρὸς τὸ βίαιον· 135
οἷον μή τις ἄγα
θεόθεν κνεφάσηι
προτυπὲν στόμιον μέγα Τροίας
στρατωθέν· οἴκτωι γὰρ ἐπί-
φθονος Ἄρτεμις ἁγνὰ 140
πτανοῖσιν κυσὶ πατρὸς
αὐτότοκον πρὸ λόχου
μογερὰν πτάκα θυομένοισιν·
στυγεῖ δὲ δεῖπνον αἰετῶν."
αἴλινον αἴλινον εἰπέ, τὸ δ' εὖ νικάτω. 145

ἐπ. τόσον περ εὔφρων, καλά,
δρόσοισι λεπτοῖς μαλερῶν λεόντων

---

136 ἄγα Hermann: ἄτα M. **139** οἴκτωι Scaliger: οἴκωι M. **146** τόσον fh: τόσσων M. **147** δρόσοισι λεπτοῖς Wellauer: δρόσοισιν ἀέλπτοις M | λεόντων Stanley ex *Etym. M.* p. 377, 39: ὄντων M.

Prevented ere the safe last course that might outrun the doom.

Let *Sorrow*, *Sorrow*, a burden sound,—

In Joy prevailing drowned!

I 2.

Antistrophe.

Their sage diviner marking well how twain the tempers were
Of those two brother soldiers, knew the feasters on the hare
For those same captains of the war; and thus did he declare:

"*A prey before this force in time the town of Priam falls;*
When all the general common herd before the castle-walls
Shall be with violent fate consumed:—so be no jealous frown
Above come louring down
And strike the great curb forged to hold the mouth of Ilium town
In tented field,—for pity-struck displeasure sore, I wis,
Hath pure Maid Artemis;
Wroth with her Father's wingèd hounds; foul sacrificers they,
Poor timorous weak enchilded thing, with unborn young to slay!

Let *Sorrow*, *Sorrow*, a burden sound,—

In Joy prevailing drowned!

Epode.

"*Yet O thou Beauteous One, for all*
So tender is thy loving care
To young dew dropping weak and small
In ravenous lion's teeming lair,

πάντων τ' ἀγρονόμων φιλομάστοις
θηρῶν ὀβρικάλοις, εἴπερ τινά,
τούτων αἴνει ξύμβολα κρᾶναι, 150
δεξιὰ μέν, κατάμομφα
δὲ [φάσματα] στρουθῶν.
ἰήιον δὲ καλέω Παιᾶνα,
μή τινας ἀντιπνόους
Δαναοῖς χρονίας ἐχενῇδας ἀπλοίας 155
τεύξηι σπευδομένα θυσίαν
ἑτέραν ἄνομόν τιν', ἄδαιτον,
νεικέων τέκτονα σύμ-
φυτον, οὐ δεισήνορα. μίμνει 160
γὰρ φοβερὰ παλίνορτος
οἰκονόμος δολία,
μνάμων μῆνις τεκνόποινος."
τοιάδε Κάλχας ξὺν
μεγάλοις ἀγαθοῖς ἀπέκλαγξεν 165
μόρσιμ' ἀπ' ὀρνίθων
ὁδίων οἴκοις βασιλείοις
τοῖς δ' ὁμόφωνον
αἴλινον αἴλινον εἰπέ, τὸ δ' εὖ νικάτω.

στρ. α'. Ζεύς, ὅστις ποτ' ἐστίν,—εἰ τόδ' αὐ- 170
τῶι φίλον κεκλημένωι,
τοῦτό νιν προσεννέπω—
οὐκ ἔχω προσεικάσαι

---

149 *ὀβρικάλοις, εἴπερ τινά* H.: *ὀβρικάλοισι τερπνά* M. **150** *αἴνει* Gilbert: *αἰτεῖ* M. **152** *φάσματα* del. H. **165** *ἀπέκλαγξεν* a f h: *ἀπέκλαιξεν* M.

And for the suckling whelps of all
Wild creatures of the wood or field,—
Yet now at our most urgent call
Vouchsafe to yield;
Yield, and fulfil this feathered sign,
The most part good, yet part malign!
Yea and also I pray,
O Healer Apollo, prevent her and stay!
So that she send no contrary wind
With untimely delay
The Greek navy to fetter and bind,
Out of zeal for a sacrifice other and strange,
Without custom or law,
To the feaster unknown,
Bitter enmity working
Betwixt flesh and bone,
Without man-fearing awe,—
For a danger is lurking
In house that abides,
That in subtilty hides
To recoil again, Wrath ever-mindful, a Child will avenge!"

Such fortune for the royal House by sign of omen stored,
Much bane to mix with more of boon, the pealing prophet poured;
Wherewith in just accord
Let *Sorrow, Sorrow,* a burden sound,—
In Joy prevailing drowned!

II i.

1st strophe.

Zeus, whosoe'er indeed he be,—
In that name so it please him hear,—
Zeus, for my help is none but he;—
Conjecture through creation free

πάντ᾿ ἐπισταθμώμενος
πλὴν Διός, εἰ τὸ μάταν 175
ἀπὸ φροντίδος ἄχθος
χρὴ βαλεῖν ἐτητύμως.

ἀντ. α΄. οὗλός τις πάροιθεν ἦν μέγας,
παμμάχωι θράσει βρύων,
οὐδὲ λέξεται, πρὶν ὤν· 180
ὃς δ᾿ ἔπειτ᾿ ἔφυ, τρια-
κτῆρος οἴχεται τυχών·
Ζῆνα δέ τις προφρόνως
ἐπινίκια κλάζων
τεύξεται φρενῶν τὸ πᾶν. 185

στρ. β΄. τὸν φρονεῖν βροτοὺς ὁδώ-
σαντα, τὸν πάθει μάθος
θέντα κυρίως ἔχειν.
στάζει δ᾿ ἔν θ᾿ ὕπνωι πρὸ καρδίας
μνησιπήμων πόνος· 190
καὶ παρ᾿ ἄκοντας ἦλθε σωφρονεῖν.
δαιμόνων δέ που χάρις βίαιος
σέλμα σεμνὸν ἡμένων.

ἀντ. β΄. καὶ τόθ᾿ ἡγεμὼν ὁ πρέσβυς νεῶν Ἀχαιικῶν, 195
μάντιν οὔτινα ψέγων,
ἐμπαίοις τύχαισι συμπνέων,—
εὖτ᾿ ἀπλοίαι κεναγ-

---

175 τὸ Pauw: τόδε M. **178** οὗλός τις H.: οὐδ᾿ ὅστις M. **180** οὐδὲ λέξεται H. L. Ahrens: οὐδὲν λέξαι M. **187** τὸν Schuetz: τῶ M. **192** βίαιος Turnebus: βιαίως M.

I cast, and cannot find his peer;
With this strange load upon my mind
So burdening, only Zeus I find
To lift and fling it sheer.

II 2.

1st antistrophe.

One was that ruled the ring of yore,—
With boisterous challenge big and blown;
Him tell we not, his date is o'er;—
Nay, the next comer is no more,—
Found his outwrestler, and was thrown:—
But Zeus, with heart and voice acclaim
Victorious his triumphal name,
And wisdom is thine own!

III 1.

2nd strophe.

Sing praise; *'Tis he hath guided*, say,
Men's feet in wisdom's way,
Stablishing fast Instruction's rule
That Suffering be her school:—
The heart in time of sleep renews
Aching remembrance of her bruise,
And chastening wisdom enters wills that most refuse;
Stern is the grace and forcèd mercy kind
By Spirits upon their awful bench assigned.

III 2.

2nd antistrophe.

Thus with the elder captain then:—
When all his league of men
Lay weltering in the narrow Sound
Between shores, weatherbound,

γεῖ βαρύνοντ' Ἀχαιικὸς λεώς,
Χαλκίδος πέραν ἔχων παλιρρό- 200
χθοις ἐν Αὐλίδος τόποις·

στρ. γ'. πνοαὶ δ' ἀπὸ Στρυμόνος μολοῦσαι
κακόσχολοι, νήστιδες, δύσορμοι,
βροτῶν ἄλαι,
νεῶν < τε > καὶ πεισμάτων ἀφειδεῖς, 205
παλιμμήκη χρόνον τιθεῖσαι
τρίβῳ κατέξαινον ἄν-
θος Ἀργείων· ἐπεὶ δὲ καὶ
πικροῦ χείματος ἄλλο μῆχαρ
βριθύτερον πρόμοισιν 210
μάντις ἔκλαγξεν προφέρων
Ἄρτεμιν, ὥστε χθόνα βάκτροις
ἐπικρούσαντας Ἀτρείδας
δάκρυ μὴ κατασχεῖν·—

ἀντ. γ'. ἄναξ δ' ὁ πρέσβυς τόδ' εἶπε φωνῶν· 215
"βαρεῖα μὲν κὴρ τὸ μὴ πιθέσθαι,
βαρεῖα δ', εἰ
τέκνον δαΐξω, δόμων ἄγαλμα,
πατρῴους παρθενοσφάγοισιν
χέρας μιαίνων ῥοαῖς 220
πέλας βωμοῦ. τί τῶνδ' ἄνευ
κακῶν; πῶς λιπόναυς γένωμαι

---

200 sq. *παλιρρόχθοις* H. L. Ahrens: *παλιρρόθοις* M. **205** *νεῶν* Pauw: *ναῶν* M | *τε* add. Porson. **216** *πιθέσθαι* Turnebus: *πειθέσθαι* M. **219** sqq. *μιαίνων παρθενοσφάγοισιν* | *ῥεέθροις πατρῴους χέρας* | *βωμοῦ πέλας* M: corr. H. (*ῥοαῖς* Schoemann, *πέλας βωμοῦ* Blomfield). **222** *πῶς λιπόναυς* h: *τί πῶσ λιπόναυστε* M.

With body and spirit well-nigh spent,
Empty, in hard imprisonment
Amid those famed resorbing tides of Aulis pent,—
Without one doubt on prophet cast,
He bowed and drifted with the violent blast.

IV 1.

3rd strophe.

For gales continually from Strymon bore
Lean fast and leisure curst, mooring unstable,
Wildness of wits and waste of ship and cable,
Till the endless weary while with fretting sore
The flower of Argos wore:—
Whereat their prophet, pealing
The dread name *Artemis*,
Cried means of help and healing,—
Such cruel healing this
As heavier still the princes found
Than tempest; hard upon the ground
They beat the sceptre, mute with pain,
Nor tears could they restrain.

IV 2.

3rd antistrophe.

At last the elder uttered voice and cried:
"*Hard cruel fate refusal! Hard and cruel*
The butchery of my child, my own home's jewel!
Father's own hands at the altar crimson dyed
In young pure stricken tide!
Whichever path be taken,
'Tis evil still to choose;
What can I, left forsaken?

ξυμμαχίας ἁμαρτών;
παυσανέμου γὰρ θυσίας
παρθενίου θ' αἵματος ὀργᾶι 225
περιοργῶς ἐπιθυμεῖν
θέμις. εὖ γὰρ εἴη."

στρ. δ'. ἐπεὶ δ' ἀνάγκας ἔδυ λέπαδνον
φρενὸς πνέων δυσσεβῆ τροπαίαν
ἄναγνον, ἀνίερον, τόθεν 230
τὸ παντότολμον φρονεῖν μετέγνω.
βροτοὺς θρασύνει γὰρ αἰσχρόμητις
τάλαινα παρακοπὰ πρωτοπήμων.
ἔτλα δ' οὖν
θυτὴρ γενέσθαι θυγατρός, γυναικοποίνων 235
πολέμων ἀρωγὰν
καὶ προτέλεια ναῶν.

ἀντ. δ'. λιτὰς δὲ καὶ κληδόνας πατρώιους
παρ' οὐδὲν αἰῶνα παρθένειον
ἔθεντο φιλόμαχοι βραβῆς. 240
φράσεν δ' ἀόζοις πατὴρ μετ' εὐχὰν
δίκαν χιμαίρας ὕπερθε βωμοῦ
πέπλοισι περιπετῆ παντὶ θυμῶι
προνωπῆ
λαβεῖν ἀέρδην, στόματός τε καλλιπρώιρου 245
φυλακᾶι κατασχεῖν
φθόγγον ἀραῖον οἴκοις,

---

232 βροτοὺς Spanheim: βροτοῖς M. **239** αἰῶ τε O. Mueller. **246** φυλακᾶι Blomfield: φυλακὰν M.

My league how can I lose?
They press me, furious with desire
For what 'tis lawful to require,
A virgin's blood for calming-spell;—
God send it may be well!"

V 1.

4th strophe.

But under that sore stroke
Once donned the grievous yoke
Of Need compelling, all his thought within
To another quarter veered, set full for sin
And desperate action, to the utmost stretch
Resolved. It is that foul-suggesting wretch
Distraction! With her men's hearts at first
Grow reckless, hence their fatal harms begin,
Ruinous.—Alas, he steeled him to that worst,
Slaying of his child, in sacrifice to speed
War for a woman, sanction to let ships proceed.

V 2.

4th antistrophe.

Her supplications all,
Her oft appealing call
On *Father*, her fresh years of maidenhood,
With umpires clamouring war for nothing stood.
To his ministers her father, after prayer,
Gave the sign—bade them seize her and upbear
Above the altar,—huddling where she lay
Wrapped in her robes, aloft with courage good
Kidwise to hold her, drooping,—and to stay
Those lovely lips with forced impediment,
Bridles with dumb curb muffling utterance, to prevent

στρ. ε'. βίαι χαλινῶν τ' ἀναύδωι μένει·
κρόκου βαφὰς δ' ἐς πέδον χέουσα
ἔβαλλ' ἕκαστον θυτήρων 250
ἀπ' ὄμματος βέλει
φιλοίκτωι,
πρέπουσά θ' ὡς ἐν γραφαῖς, προσεννέπειν
θέλουσ', ἐπεὶ πολλάκις
πατρὸς κατ' ἀνδρῶνας εὐτραπέζους 255
ἔμελψεν· ἁγνᾶι δ' ἀταύρωτος αὐδᾶι
πατρὸς φίλου τριτόσπονδον εὔποτμον
παιᾶνα φίλως ἐτίμα.

ἀντ. ε'. τὰ δ' ἔνθεν οὔτ' εἶδον οὔτ' ἐννέπω·
τέχναι δὲ Κάλχαντος οὐκ ἄκραντοι. 260
Δίκα δὲ τοῖς μὲν παθοῦσιν
μαθεῖν ἐπιρρέπει·
τὸ μέλλον <δ'>
ἐπεὶ γένοιτ', ἂν κλύοις· προχαιρέτω·
ἶσον δὲ τῶι προστένειν· 265
τορὸν γὰρ ἥξει σύνορθρον αὐγαῖς.
πέλοιτο δ' οὖν τἀπὶ τούτοισιν εὔπρα-
ξις, ὡς θέλει τόδ' ἄγχιστον Ἀπίας
γαίας μονόφρουρον ἕρκος.

ἥκω σεβίζων σόν, Κλυταιμήστρα, κράτος· 270
δίκη γάρ ἐστι φωτὸς ἀρχηγοῦ τίειν
γυναῖκ' ἐρημωθέντος ἄρσενος θρόνου.

---

258 *παιᾶνα* Enger (*παιῶνα* Hartung): *αἰῶνα* M. **263** *δ'* add. Elmsley.
264 *ἐπεὶ γένοιτ'* a f h: *ἐπιγένοιτ'* M. **266** *σύνορθρον* Wellauer: *συνορθὸν* M | *αὐγαῖς* Hermann: *αὐταῖς* M.

VI 1.

Curse on his house.—Then, letting raiment fall — 5th strophe.
In saffron to the ground, her slayers all
With eye she smote, the dumb eye's piteous dart
Aimed at each several heart,
Showing as a pictured form, that fain would speak—
How many a time in her dear father's hall
When boards were laden
She had sung before his guests! Unsullied maiden,
Joined in his joyous antheming
At grace with pure note blithe his loving child would sing.

VI 2.

What further was I neither saw nor tell; — 5th antistrophe.
Only, not vain is Calchas' oracle.—
Justice hath willed that knowledge fall inclined
On the tried sufferer's mind,
Learned in the proof: what *shall be* you may hear
Soon as it *is*; before that, fare it well!
'Twere but fore sorrow;
Plain shall it come with the early rays of morrow
Yet good speed now the sequel be,
As here the realm's immediate sole Defence would see.

[*Meaning* CLYTAEMNESTRA *who now approaches.*

ELDER. I am here, O Queen,
In deference to thy rule; when the male Prince
Hath left a vacant throne, due homage then
Belongs unto his consort.—Keep thy counsel now

σὺ δ' εἴτε κεδνὸν εἴτε μὴ πεπυσμένη
εὐαγγέλοισιν ἐλπίσιν θυηπολεῖς,
κλύοιμ' ἂν εὔφρων· οὐδὲ σιγώσῃ φθόνος. 275

ΚΛΥΤΑΙΜΗΣΤΡΑ.

εὐάγγελος μέν, ὥσπερ ἡ παροιμία,
ἕως γένοιτο μητρὸς εὐφρόνης πάρα.
πεύσῃ δὲ χάρμα μεῖζον ἐλπίδος κλύειν·
Πριάμου γὰρ ᾑρήκασιν Ἀργεῖοι πόλιν.
ΧΟ. πῶς φῄς; πέφευγε τοὔπος ἐξ ἀπιστίας. 280
ΚΛ. Τροίαν Ἀχαιῶν οὖσαν· ἦ τορῶς λέγω;
ΧΟ. χαρά μ' ὑφέρπει δάκρυον ἐκκαλουμένη.
ΚΛ. εὖ γὰρ φρονοῦντος ὄμμα σοῦ κατηγορεῖ.
ΧΟ. τί γὰρ τὸ πιστόν; ἔστι τῶνδέ σοι τέκμαρ;
ΚΛ. ἔστιν· τί δ' οὐχί; μὴ δολώσαντος θεοῦ. 285
ΧΟ. πότερα δ' ὀνείρων φάσματ' εὐπιθῆ σέβεις;
ΚΛ. οὐ δόξαν ἂν λάκοιμι βριζούσης φρενός.
ΧΟ. ἀλλ' ἦ σ' ἐπίανέν τις ἄπτερος φάτις;
ΚΛ. παιδὸς νέας ὣς κάρτ' ἐμωμήσω φρένας.
ΧΟ. ποίου χρόνου δὲ καὶ πεπόρθηται πόλις; 290
ΚΛ. τῆς νῦν τεκούσης φῶς τόδ' εὐφρόνης λέγω.
ΧΟ. καὶ τίς τόδ' ἐξίκοιτ' ἂν ἀγγέλων τάχος;
ΚΛ. Ἥφαιστος, Ἴδης λαμπρὸν ἐκπέμπων σέλας.
φρυκτὸς δὲ φρυκτὸν δεῦρ' ἀπ' ἀγγάρου πυρὸς
ἔπεμπεν. Ἴδη μὲν πρὸς Ἑρμαῖον λέπας 295
Λήμνου· μέγαν δὲ πανὸν ἐκ νήσου τρίτον
Ἀθῷον αἶπος Ζηνὸς ἐξεδέξατο,

---

286 εὐπιθῆ Blomfield: εὐπειθῆ (ex εὐπειθεῖ) M. **287** λάκοιμι Karsten: λάβοιμι M. **294** ἀγγάρου Canter ex *Etym. M.* p. 7: ἀγγέλου M. **296** πανὸν Casaubon ex Athen. XV. p. 700 E: φανὸν M.

With all good will;
But I would learn most gladly whether it be
Good news that sets afoot these offerings, or
But happy-tiding hopes.

CLYT. With happy tidings, as the proverb runs,
Come Dawn from Night his Mother! but here is joy
Goes quite beyond all hope,—the Argive arms
Have taken Priam's town.
ELDER. What was this?
It passed believing and escaped me.
CLYT. Troy
In the hands of the Achaeans: am I plain?
ELDER. Such joy steals over me as calls forth tears.
CLYT. The truthful eye bewrays thy sympathy.
ELDER. What warrant is there? Hast thou any proof?
CLYT. Aye surely; unless Heaven hath played us false.
ELDER. Is it the flattering vision of a dream
Hath won thy credence?
CLYT. I should not come crying
The imagination of a drowsing brain.
ELDER. Can it then be some light-winged rumour
Hath fed conceit so high?
CLYT. You rate my wits
As light as a green girl's.
ELDER. What season then
Hath seen the capture made?
CLYT. The self-same night
That now hath given the dawn before us birth.
ELDER. What courier could arrive thus rapidly?
CLYT. Hephaestus; his bright flame from Ida sprang,
And fast in fiery post the beacons flew,
As one dispatched another: Ida first
To Hermes' hill in Lemnos; third the mount
Of Zeus in Athos caught the mighty brand

ὑπερτελής τε, πόντον ὥστε νωτίσαι,
ἰσχὺς πορευτοῦ λαμπάδος πρὸς ἡδονὴν
πεύκη τὸ χρυσοφεγγές, ὥς τις ἥλιος, 300
σέλας παραγγείλασα Μακίστου σκοπάς·
ὃ δ' οὔτι μέλλων οὐδ' ἀφρασμόνως ὕπνωι
νικώμενος παρῆκεν ἀγγέλου μέρος·
ἑκὰς δὲ φρυκτοῦ φῶς ἐπ' Εὐρίπου ῥοὰς
Μεσσαπίου φύλαξι σημαίνει μολόν· 305
οἳ δ' ἀντέλαμψαν καὶ παρήγγειλαν πρόσω
γραίας ἐρείκης θωμὸν ἅψαντες πυρί.
σθένουσα λαμπὰς δ' οὐδέπω μαυρουμένη,
ὑπερθοροῦσα πεδίον Ἀσωποῦ, δίκην
φαιδρᾶς σελήνης, πρὸς Κιθαιρῶνος λέπας 310
ἤγειρεν ἄλλην ἐκδοχὴν πομποῦ πυρός.
φάος δὲ τηλέπομπον οὐκ ἠναίνετο
φρουρά, πλέον καίουσα τῶν εἰρημένων·
λίμνην δ' ὑπὲρ Γοργῶπιν ἔσκηψεν φάος,
ὄρος τ' ἐπ' Αἰγίπλαγκτον ἐξικνούμενον 315
ὤτρυνε θεσμὸν μὴ χρονίζεσθαι πυρός.
πέμπουσι δ' ἀνδαίοντες ἀφθόνωι μένει
φλογὸς μέγαν πώγωνα, καὶ Σαρωνικοῦ
πορθμοῦ κατόπτην πρῶν' ὑπερβάλλειν πρόσω
φλέγουσαν· εἶτ' ἔσκηψεν, εὖτ' ἀφίκετο 320
Ἀραχναῖον αἶπος, ἀστυγείτονας σκοπάς·
κἄπειτ' Ἀτρειδῶν ἐς τόδε σκήπτει στέγος
φάος τόδ' οὐκ ἄπαππον Ἰδαίου πυρός.

---

298 sqq. vitiosa esse liquet. **309** *πεδίον Ἀσωποῦ* f h: *παιδίον ὠποῦ* M.
316 *χρονίζεσθαι* Casaubon: *χαρίζεσθαι* M. **319** *κατόπτην* H.: *κάτοπτρον* M.
320 *εὖτ'* Hermann: *εἶτ'* M. **322** *τόδε* f h: *τόγε* M.

From the island thrown in turn. Then towering high
To clear the broad sea's back, the travelling torch
Shot up to the very sky the courier flame,
In golden glory, like another Sun,
Fame to the far Makistos messaging:
Whose fiery office no defaulting sleep
Or tarrying sloth let fail; his ensign flying
Over the Sound Euripos made aware
Messapion's watchmen of his advent; they
With answering countersign, a kindled stack
Of old gray heather, passed the word along:
Which vigorous lamp with unabated force
Did shining as the bright Moon overleap
Asopus even to Cithaeron's ridge,
There to wake new dispatch; nor being aroused
That watch denied the far-sent missioner;
They burned above their bidding[1], and their light
Went sailing far beyond Gorgopis lake
To the heights of Aegiplanctus, urging still
No dallying in the breathless ordinance.
Whereat with liberal heart aloft they sent
Flame in a great beard streaming, that his flight
Should clean beyond the foreland pass, that looks
O'er the Saronic gulf; nor ever stooped
His pinion ere he gained our neighbouring height,
Arachnae's vigilant peak: alighting thence
Upon the Atridae's roof a gleam there came,
That Ida's fire his ancestor may claim.

[1] *Or* 'beyond the aforesaid.'

τοιοίδε τοί μοι λαμπαδηφόρων νόμοι,
ἄλλος παρ' ἄλλου διαδοχαῖς πληρούμενοι· 325
νικᾶι δ' ὁ πρῶτος καὶ τελευταῖος δραμών.
τέκμαρ τοιοῦτον σύμβολόν τέ σοι λέγω
ἀνδρὸς παραγγείλαντος ἐκ Τροίας ἐμοί.
ΧΟ. θεοῖς μὲν αὖθις, ὦ γύναι, προσεύξομαι·
λόγους δ' ἀκοῦσαι τούσδε κἀποθαυμάσαι 330
διηνεκῶς θέλοιμ' ἄν, ὡς λέγεις, πάλιν.
ΚΛ. Τροίαν Ἀχαιοὶ τῆιδ' ἔχουσ' ἐν ἡμέραι.
οἶμαι βοὴν ἄμεικτον ἐν πόλει πρέπειν.
ὄξος τ' ἄλειφά τ' ἐγχέας ταὐτῶι κύτει
διχοστατοῦντ' ἂν οὐ φίλως προσεννέποις· 335
καὶ τῶν ἁλόντων καὶ κρατησάντων δίχα
φθογγὰς ἀκούειν ἔστι συμφορᾶς διπλῆς·
οἱ μὲν γὰρ ἀμφὶ σώμασιν πεπτωκότες
ἀνδρῶν κασιγνήτων τε καὶ φυτάλμιοι
παίδων γέροντες οὐκέτ' ἐξ ἐλευθέρου 340
δέρης ἀποιμώζουσι φιλτάτων μόρον,
τοὺς δ' αὖτε νυκτίπλαγκτος ἐκ μάχης πόνος
νήστεις πρὸς ἀρίστοισιν ὧν ἔχει πόλις
τάσσει, πρὸς οὐδὲν ἐν μέρει τεκμήριον·
ἀλλ' ὡς ἕκαστος ἔσπασεν τύχης πάλον, 345
ἐν αἰχμαλώτοις Τρωικοῖς οἰκήμασι
ναίουσιν ἤδη, τῶν ὑπαιθρίων πάγων
δρόσων τ' ἀπαλλαχθέντες· ὡς δ' εὐδαίμονες
ἀφύλακτον εὑδήσουσι πᾶσαν εὐφρόνην.

---

324 *τοιοίδε τοί μοι* Schuetz: *τοιοίδ' ἕτοιμοι* a h, *τοιοίδ' ἔτυμοι* f. **331** *λέγοις* f h. **334** *ἐγχέας* Canter: *ἐκχέας* a f h. **339** sqq. *φυταλμίων παῖδες γερόντων* codd.: corr. Weil. **348** *ὡς δ' εὐδαίμονες* Stanley: *ὡς δυσδαίμονες* a f h.

This was the ordering of my torchmen's race,
One from another in succession still
Supplied and plenished; and he that won
Was he *ran first*, though last in all this run.
Here is the proof and warrant of my joy,
Pass'd onward for me by my lord from Troy.

ELDER. Lady, the gods
I will adore hereafter; now I am fain
To satisfy my wonder, might it please you
Discourse again at large.

CLYT. This day the Greeks
Hold Ilium in their hand. O, well I guess
Most ill-according noise is rife within her!
Pour in the same cruse oil and vinegar,
And you shall call them quarrellers, unkind;
Thus differing as their fortunes may be heard
Cries of the vanquish'd and the vanquishers.
Vanquish'd,—upon the several corpses flung
Of children, husbands, brothers,—aged sire,
Wife, sister, from a throat no longer free
Wail for their dear ones dead. The vanquishers
Their after-battle forage
And ranging in the night sets hungry down
Before such breakfasts as the town affords,
By no nice turn of ordered billeting,
But Luck's own lottery has them lodged ere this
In captur'd homes of Troy: there now at length
Delivered from the frosts and from the dews
Of the bleak sky they shelter, and how blest
Shall sleep at ease the whole unguarded night.

εἰ δ᾽ εὐσεβοῦσι τοὺς πολισσούχους θεοὺς 350
τοὺς τῆς ἁλούσης γῆς θεῶν θ᾽ ἱδρύματα,
οὔ τἂν ἑλόντες αὖθις ἀνθαλοῖεν ἄν.
ἔρως δὲ μή τις πρότερον ἐμπίπτηι στρατῶι
πορθεῖν τὰ μὴ χρὴ κέρδεσιν νικωμένους.
δεῖ γὰρ πρὸς οἴκους νοστίμου σωτηρίας, 355
κάμψαι διαύλου θάτερον κῶλον πάλιν.
θεοῖς δ᾽ ἀναμπλάκητος εἰ μόλοι στρατός,
εὐήγορον τὸ πῆμα τῶν ὀλωλότων
γένοιτ᾽ ἄν,—εἰ πρόσπαια μὴ τύχοι κακά.
τοιαῦτά τοι γυναικὸς ἐξ ἐμοῦ κλύεις. 360
τὸ δ᾽ εὖ κρατοίη, μὴ διχορρόπως ἰδεῖν·
πολλῶν γὰρ ἐσθλῶν τὴν ὄνησιν εἱλόμην.

ΧΟ. γύναι, κατ᾽ ἄνδρα σώφρον᾽ εὐφρόνως λέγεις.
ἐγὼ δ᾽ ἀκούσας πιστά σου τεκμήρια
θεοὺς προσειπεῖν αὖ παρασκευάζομαι· 365
χάρις γὰρ οὐκ ἄτιμος εἴργασται πόνων.

Ὦ Ζεῦ βασιλεῦ, καὶ Νὺξ φιλία,
μεγάλων κόσμων κτεάτειρα·
ἥτ᾽ ἐπὶ Τροίας πύργοις ἔβαλες
στεγανὸν δίκτυον, ὡς μήτε μέγαν 370
μήτ᾽ οὖν νεαρῶν τιν᾽ ὑπερτελέσαι
μέγα δουλείας
γάγγαμον, ἄτης παναλώτου.

---

352 οὔ τἂν ἑλόντες Hermann: οὐκ ἀνελόντες a, οὐκ ἂν γ᾽ ἑλόντει fh | ἀνθαλοῖεν Auratus: ἂν θάνοιεν a, αὖ θάνοιεν fh. **358** εὐήγορον H.: ἐγρήγορον codd. **365** αὖ Paley: εὖ codd.

If now they are showing reverence to the Gods
O' the fallen country and their holy shrines,
They shall not spoil then only to be spoiled:
But let no lust be falling on them first
From covetousness to plunder that they should not:—
The backward of the double course is yet
To measure; they must win safe passage home.
But let them only come without offence
Toward Heaven, the grievance of the perished well
May learn fair language,—if no sudden stroke
Of casualty befall.—These are my thoughts,
A woman's; but I pray
Good speed prevail without all counterpoise!
Great are my blessings; I would taste their joys.

ELDER. Thy woman's words, my Lady,
Have all a wise man's judgment: now having heard
Good warrant from thee, I'll address me next
To the praise of Heaven, since to us is given
Ample reward for all that labour done.

O Zeus the king of Heaven! O Night,
With so great splendour and so bright
Possessed, O friendly Night!
On Troy's renowned high towers was cast
Thy snare, a net so close and fast
As neither great nor small
Should leap the immense enslaving woof:
Doom's divine drag-net, huge and proof,
At one sweep took them all!

Δία τοι ξένιον μέγαν αἰδοῦμαι
τὸν τάδε πράξαντ', ἐπ' Ἀλεξάνδρωι 375
τείνοντα πάλαι τόξον, ὅπως ἂν
μήτε πρὸ καιροῦ μήθ' ὑπὲρ ἄστρων
βέλος ἠλίθιον σκήψειεν.

στρ. α'. "Διὸς πλαγὰν ἔχουσιν" εἰπεῖν
πάρεστιν, τοῦτο τ' ἐξιχνεῦσαι· 380
ἔπραξεν ὡς ἔκρανεν. οὐκ ἔφα τις
θεοὺς βροτῶν ἀξιοῦσθαι μέλειν
ὅσοις ἀθίκτων χάρις
πατοῖθ'· ὃ δ' οὐκ εὐσεβής·
πέφανται δ' ἐκτίνουσ' 385
ἀτολμήτων ἀρὴ
πνεόντων μεῖζον ἢ δικαίως,
φλεόντων δωμάτων ὑπέρφευ
ὑπὲρ τὸ βέλτιστον. ἔστω δ' ἀπή-
μαντον ὥστ' ἀπαρκεῖν 390
εὖ πραπίδων λαχόντα.
οὐ γάρ ἐστιν ἔπαλξις
πλούτου πρὸς κόρον ἀνδρὶ
λακτίσαντι μέγαν Δίκας
βωμὸν εἰς ἀφάνειαν. 395

ἀντ. α'. βιᾶται δ' ἁ τάλαινα Πειθώ,
προβούλου παῖς ἄφερτος Ἄτας·

---

379 ἔχουσ' corr. ex ἔχουσαν f. **380** πάρεστιν Hartung: πάρεστι codd. | τοῦτο τ' Boissonade: τοῦτ' f, τοῦτο γ' h. **381** ἔπραξεν Hermann: ὡς ἔπραξεν codd. **385** ἐκτίνουσ' Hartung: ἐγγόνους f, ἐκγόνους h. **386** ἀρὴ H.: ἄρη codd. **394** μέγαν Canter: μεγάλα codd. **397** προβούλου παῖς Hartung: προβουλόπαις codd.

Be Lord Zeus of the Stranger's board
For author of this act adored:
His bolt on Alexander bent
Was aimed so long as neither sent
Over the stars nor early spent
  To light with idle fall.

I 1.

Strophe.

"*Struck by the hand of Zeus!*" ay, truth indeed,
And traceable: 'tis the act of will decreed
And purpose. Under foot when mortals tread
Fair lovely Sanctities, the Gods, one said,
The easy Gods are careless:—'twas profane!
Here are sin's wages manifest and plain,
The sword's work on that swelled presumptuousness,
With affluent mansions teeming in excess,
Beyond Best Measure:—best, and sorrow-free,
The wise well-dowered mind's unharmed Sufficiency!
    The Rich man hath no tower,
    Whose Pride, in Surfeit's hour,
    Kicks against high-enthroned Right
    And spurns her from his sight.

I 2.

Antistrophe.

Child of designing Ate's deadly womb,
The wretch Temptation drives him to his doom.

ἄκος δὲ παμμάταιον· οὐκ ἐκρύφθη,
πρέπει δέ, φῶς αἰνολαμπές, σίνος·
κακοῦ δὲ χαλκοῦ τρόπον 400
τρίβωι τε καὶ προσβολαῖς
μελαμπαγὴς πέλει
δικαιωθείς (ἐπεὶ
διώκει παῖς ποτανὸν ὄρνιν),
πόλει πρόστριμμα θεὶς ἄφερτον· 405
λιτᾶν δ' ἀκούει μὲν οὔτις θεῶν,
τὸν δ' ἐπίστροφον τῶν
φῶτ' ἄδικον καθαιρεῖ.
οἷος καὶ Πάρις ἐλθὼν
ἐς δόμον τὸν Ἀτρειδᾶν 410
ἤισχυνε ξενίαν τράπε-
ζαν κλοπαῖσι γυναικός.

στρ. β'. λιποῦσα δ' ἀστοῖσιν ἀσπίστορας
κλόνους λογχίμους τε καὶ ναυβάτας ὁπλισμούς,
ἄγουσά τ' ἀντίφερνον Ἰλίωι φθοράν, 415
βέβακεν ῥίμφα διὰ πυλᾶν,
ἄτλητα τλᾶσα· πολλὰ δ' ἔστενον
τάδ' ἐννέποντες δόμων προφῆται·
"ἰὼ ἰὼ δῶμα δῶμα καὶ πρόμοι,
ἰὼ λέχος καὶ στίβοι φιλάνορες. 420
πάρεστι σιγὰς ἀτίμους ἀλοιδόρους
. . . . . ἀφημένων ἰδεῖν.

---

401 προσβολαῖς J. Pearson: προβολαῖς codd. **404** ποτανὸν Schuetz: πτανὸν f. **405** ἄφερτον θεὶς f (ἐνθεὶς h): corr. Wilamowitz. **407** τῶν Klausen: τῶνδε codd. **410** τῶν f. **412** κλοπαῖς f. **414** κλόνους τε καὶ λογχίμους ναυβάτας θ' H. L. Ahrens. **417** πολὺ δ' ἀνέστενον f. **418** τάδ' Auratus: τόδ' codd. **421** σιγᾶς ἄτιμος ἀλοίδορος codd.: corr. Hermann. **422** ἄδιστος ἀφεμένων codd.: (ἀφημένων Dindorf).

Then cure is all in vain. The vice he wears
He cannot hide; sinister gleam declares
His mischief; as base metal at the touch
And trial of the stone, he showeth smutch
(This fond man like a child a-chase of wings),
And the awful taint on all his people brings:
To prayers is not an ear in Heaven; one frown
All conversant with such calls guilty and pulls down.
Such Paris was, that ate
Within the Atridae's gate,
And then disgraced the Stranger's bread
By theft of woman wed.

II I.

2nd strophe.

To Argos hurrying tumult, thronging power
Of men-at-arms and men-at-oars bequeathing,—
To Ilium bringing death for her sole dower,—
Ah, tripping it through her gate she's flown,
A crime done!—Then did voices moan,
The secrets of the house in sorrow breathing:

"*The Home, woe, woe, the Home! The Princes, woe!*
The impress where the wedded limbs yet show!
There yonder abject sits, where all may see,
Shamed, unreviling, silent, bowed indignity:

πόθωι δ᾽ ὑπερποντίας
φάσμα δόξει δόμων ἀνάσσειν.
εὐμόρφων δὲ κολοσσῶν 425
ἔχθεται χάρις ἀνδρί,
ὀμμάτων δ᾽ ἐν ἀχηνίαις
ἔρρει πᾶσ᾽ Ἀφροδίτα.

ἀντ. β΄. ὀνειρόφαντοι δὲ πειθήμονες
πάρεισι δόξαι φέρουσαι χάριν ματαίαν· 430
μάταν γάρ, εὖτ᾽ ἂν ἐσθλά τις δοκῶν ὁρᾶν—
παραλλάξασα διὰ χερῶν
βέβακεν ὄψις οὐ μεθύστερον
πτεροῖς ὀπαδοῖς ὕπνου κελεύθων."
τὰ μὲν κατ᾽ οἴκους ἐφ᾽ ἑστίας ἄχη 435
τάδ᾽ ἐστὶ καὶ τῶνδ᾽ ὑπερβατώτερα·
τὸ πᾶν δ᾽ ἀφ᾽ Ἕλλανος αἴας συνορμένοις
πένθει᾽ ἀτλησικάρδιος
δόμων ἑκάστου πρέπει·
πολλὰ γοῦν θιγγάνει πρὸς ἧπαρ· 440
οὓς μὲν γὰρ <τις> ἔπεμψεν
οἶδεν, ἀντὶ δὲ φωτῶν
τεύχη καὶ σποδὸς εἰς ἑκά-
στου δόμους ἀφικνεῖται.

στρ. γ΄ ὁ χρυσαμοιβὸς δ᾽ Ἄρης σωμάτων 445
καὶ ταλαντοῦχος ἐν μάχηι δορὸς

---

429 πειθήμονες Housman: πενθήμονες codd. **434** κελεύθων Karsten: κελεύθοις. **437** Ἕλλανος Bamberger: Ἑλλάδος codd. **438** πένθεια τλησικάρδιος codd.: corr. H. **441** τις add. Porson.

Pined so with his beyond-sea dream
Afar, so lovesick he shall seem
The pale faint ghost of proud authority.

Fair shapely marbles white
Vex the distasting sight,—
Lost in the lack of eyes that shone,
The warm love dead and gone.

II 2.

2nd antistrophe.

"*Dream-shown, in flattering shape, come phantasies,*
With joy—nay, fond illusion all their bringing!
Blissful in vision there when heaven is his—
Ah, vanishing through his arms away
'Tis gone, with never pause or stay,
Fast on the fickle paths where Sleep is winging."

These are the one forlorn home's miseries,
And more exceeding bitter yet than these.
And what at large for all that host of war
Far hence, the general legion sped from Hellas' shore?
Theirs in their several houses due
Is mourning and heart-broken rue—
Cause enough, sure, keen-touching to the core!
From each home once there went
A man forth: him it sent
Each knows; but what are these return?
A little dust, an urn.

III 1.

3rd strophe.

Ares, the Changer—of the Body's coin,
With scales poised—where the spears in battle join,

πυρωθὲν ἐξ Ἰλίου
φίλοισι πέμπει βαρὺ
ψῆγμα δυσδάκρυτον ἀν-
τήνορος σποδοῦ γεμί- 450
ζων λέβητας εὐθέτους.
στένουσι δ' εὖ λέγοντες ἄνδρα τὸν μὲν ὡς μάχης ἴδρις,
τὸν δ' ἐν φοναῖς καλῶς πεσόντ'—
"ἀλλοτρίας διαὶ γυναικός," 455
τάδε σῖγά τις βαΰζει,
φθονερὸν δ' ὑπ' ἄλγος ἕρπει
προδίκοις Ἀτρείδαις.
οἳ δ' αὐτοῦ περὶ τεῖχος
θήκας Ἰλιάδος γᾶς 460
εὔμορφοι κατέχουσιν· ἐχ-
θρὰ δ' ἔχοντας ἔκρυψεν.

ἀντ. γ' βαρεῖα δ' ἀστῶν φάτις σὺν κότωι·
δημοκράντου δ' ἀρᾶς τίνει χρέος.
μένει δ' ἀκοῦσαί τί μου 465
μέριμνα νυκτηρεφές.
τῶν πολυκτόνων γὰρ οὐκ
ἄσκοποι θεοί, κελαι-
ναὶ δ' Ἐρινύες χρόνωι
τυχηρὸν ὄντ' ἄνευ δίκας 470

---

451 *εὐθέτους* Auratus: *εὐθέτου* codd. **455** *διαὶ* Hermann ex Cramer *anecd. Oxon.* I p. 119: *διὰ* f. **458** *προδίκοισιν* f. **464** *δημοκράντου* Porson: *δημοκράτου* codd. **468** *ἀπόσκοποι* f.

Fined in the furnace home from Ilium sends
Dust, heavy dust and sore to weeping friends,—
A live man's worth of ash, full-measured load
In small jars' compass decently bestowed!

Then wail the sorrowing kinsmen, and belaud each man,
This for a perfect soldier, how that fell
Glorious amid the carnage, fighting well—
"*For another's wife!*" the growl comes low,
And sores against their Princes grow,
This process that began.

Others possess their tomb
There, in their beauty's bloom—
Troy's holders, in the land they hold
Graved, beneath hated mould!

III 2.

3rd antistrophe.

A people's talk is dangerous when it storms;
The effect of public curse their wrath performs.
For something cloaked within the night my mind
Stands listening:—the divine eyes are not blind
To men of blood: the man of mere success,
Luck's thriver in defect of Righteousness,

παλιντυχεῖ τριβᾶι βίου
τιθεῖσ᾽ ἀμαυρόν, ἐν δ᾽ ἀΐ-
στοις τελέθοντος οὔτις ἀλκά.
τὸ δ᾽ ὑπερκόπως κλύειν εὖ
βαρύ· βάλλεται γὰρ ὄσσοις 475
Διόθεν κάρανα.
κρίνω δ᾽ ἄφθονον ὄλβον·
μήτ᾽ εἴην πτολιπόρθης,
μήτ᾽ οὖν αὐτὸς ἁλοὺς ὑπ᾽ ἄλλωι βίον κατίδοιμι. 480

πυρὸς δ᾽ ὑπ᾽ εὐαγγέλου
πόλιν διήκει θοὰ
βάξις· εἰ δ᾽ ἐτήτυμος,
τίς οἶδεν;—εἴ τι θεῖόν ἐστι μὴ ψύθος.

τίς ὧδε παιδνὸς ἢ φρενῶν κεκομμένος, 485
φλογὸς παραγγέλμασιν
νέοις πυρωθέντα καρδίαν ἔπειτ᾽
ἀλλαγᾶι λόγου καμεῖν;

γυναικὸς αἰχμᾶι πρέπει
πρὸ τοῦ φανέντος χάριν ξυναινέσαι. 490

πιθανὸς ἄγαν ὁ θῆλυς ἔρος ἐπινέμεται
ταχύπορος· ἀλλὰ ταχύμορον
γυναικογήρυτον ὄλλυται κλέος.

---

471 παλιντυχεῖ Scaliger: παλιντυχῆ (vel -ῆι) codd. **474** ὑπερκόπως Grotius: ὑπερκότως codd. **476** κάρανα Tucker: κεραυνός codd. **480** ἄλλωι H.: ἄλλων codd. **483** ἐτήτυμος Auratus: ἐτητύμως codd. **484** ἢ (ει suprascr.) f, ἢ h | τι Hermann: τοι codd. **489** γυναικὸς Scaliger: ἐν γυναικὸς codd. **491** ἔρος Blomfield: ὅρος codd.

Doomed by the dark Avengers, wanes again at last,
Dwindling, until he fades out where the dim
Lost shadows are; and there, no help for him.—
And Fame, too loudly when she cries,
Is dangerous also; flashing eyes
Of Zeus the proud height blast.

Mine be the happy state
That moves no jealous hate;
No conquest, neither let me see
My own captivity.

AN ELDER. Swift rumour through the city goes
At glorious message blazed in fiery sign:
But whether it tell truth, who knows?
Nay, whether it be not but some guile divine?

ANOTHER. What man so childish or so crazed of wit
To let the tinder of his brain be lit
By news in fire,—and then expire
Extinct at the reverse of it?

ANOTHER. Right woman's giddiness, to a tempting lure
The yielding 'yes' ere present proof assure.

ANOTHER. Feminine assenting, where her wishing lies,
Makes fiery way; with fire's decay
In chaff, so perisheth fame a woman cries!

[*At this point there is an interval lasting some days* (**see Introduction, p. 9**). *At the opening of the new scene the Chorus are alone in the orchestra.*

τάχ᾽ εἰσόμεσθα λαμπάδων φαεσφόρων
φρυκτωριῶν τε καὶ πυρὸς παραλλαγάς, 495
εἴτ᾽ οὖν ἀληθεῖς εἴτ᾽ ὀνειράτων δίκην
τερπνὸν τόδ᾽ ἐλθὸν φῶς ἐφήλωσεν φρένας·
κήρυκ᾽ ἀπ᾽ ἀκτῆς τόνδ᾽ ὁρῶ κατάσκιον
κλάδοις ἐλάιας· μαρτυρεῖ δέ μοι κάσις
πηλοῦ ξύνουρος διψία κόνις τάδε, 500
ὡς οὔτ᾽ ἄναυδος οὔτε σοι δαίων φλόγα
ὕλης ὀρείας σημανεῖ καπνῶι πυρός,
ἀλλ᾽ ἢ τὸ χαίρειν μᾶλλον ἐκβάξει λέγων—
τὸν ἀντίον δὲ τοῖσδ᾽ ἀποστέργω λόγον·
εὖ γὰρ πρὸς εὖ φανεῖσι προσθήκη πέλοι. 505

ὅστις τάδ᾽ ἄλλως τῆιδ᾽ ἐπεύχεται πόλει,
αὐτὸς φρενῶν καρποῖτο τὴν ἁμαρτίαν.

ΚΗΡΥΞ.

ἰὼ πατρῷιον οὖδας Ἀργείας χθονός,
δεκάτου σε φέγγει τῶιδ᾽ ἀφικόμην ἔτους,
πολλῶν ῥαγεισῶν ἐλπίδων μιᾶς τυχών· 510
οὐ γάρ ποτ᾽ ηὔχουν τῆιδ᾽ ἐν Ἀργείαι χθονὶ
θανὼν μεθέξειν φιλτάτου τάφου μέρος.
νῦν χαῖρε μὲν χθών, χαῖρε δ᾽ ἡλίου φάος,
ὕπατός τε χώρας Ζεύς, ὁ Πύθιός τ᾽ ἄναξ,
τόξοις ἰάπτων μηκέτ᾽ εἰς ἡμᾶς βέλη· 515
ἅλις παρὰ Σκάμανδρον ἦσθ᾽ ἀνάρσιος·
νῦν δ᾽ αὖτε σωτὴρ ἴσθι καὶ παιώνιος,

---

509 δεκάτου Iacob: δεκάτωι codd. **516** ἦσθ᾽ margo Askewi: ἦλθ᾽ (ες) f, ἦλθες h.
517 καὶ παιώνιος Dobree: καl παγώνιος f, κἀπαγώνιος h.

[ELDER (*who has been looking out over the plain towards the sea*).

Now presently we shall know
The sober truth of all this cresseting,
Blazing of beacons, handing-on of fire,
Whether it be fact indeed or only some
Delightful dream that flatters and befools:—
A herald yonder from the shore in sight!
Umbraged with olive-branches,—ay, and further,
Mire's consorting sister, thirsty Dust,
Gives me good surety this advertisement
Shall not be voiceless, not a bonfire burned
With smoke of timber on a mountain-top;
His plain word shall establish either joy—
Nay, with aught else I cannot rest content;
Be glad proof present crowned with glad event!

ANOTHER. The man that in that prayer will take no part
Reap the reward of his misguided heart!

[*Enter* HERALD, *worn and broken by ten years' exposure before Troy.*

HERALD.

O Fatherland of mine, sweet home of Argos,
Ten years after on this blessed day
Arrived again at last! One hope hath held,—
One anchor after all those many broken,—
Never could I dream these bones would have
Their own dear Argive soil to rest in happy!
Now hail to thee, O Land, and hail to thee,
Thou bright Sun, and the land's high paramount,
Zeus; and the Lord of Pytho, blest be he,
And shoot his arrows upon us no more!
Scamander showed thee in thy wrath enough;
Preserver be thou, be thou *Healer* now,

ἄναξ Ἄπολλον. τούς τ' ἀγωνίους θεοὺς
πάντας προσαυδῶ, τόν τ' ἐμὸν τιμάορον
Ἑρμῆν, φίλον κήρυκα, κηρύκων σέβας, 520
ἥρως τε τοὺς πέμψαντας, εὐμενεῖς πάλιν
στρατὸν δέχεσθαι τὸν λελειμμένον δορός.
ἰὼ μέλαθρα βασιλέων, φίλαι στέγαι,
σεμνοί τε θᾶκοι, δαίμονές τ' ἀντήλιοι,
εἴ που πάλαι, φαιδροῖσι τοισίδ' ὄμμασιν 525
δέξασθε κόσμωι βασιλέα πολλῶι χρόνωι.
ἥκει γὰρ ὑμῖν φῶς ἐν εὐφρόνηι φέρων
καὶ τοῖσδ' ἅπασι κοινὸν Ἀγαμέμνων ἄναξ.
ἀλλ' εὖ νιν ἀσπάσασθε, καὶ γὰρ οὖν πρέπει,
Τροίαν κατασκάψαντα τοῦ δικηφόρου 530
Διὸς μακέλληι, τῆι κατείργασται πέδον, 531
καὶ σπέρμα πάσης ἐξαπόλλυται χθονός. 533
τοιόνδε Τροίαι περιβαλὼν ζευκτήριον
ἄναξ Ἀτρείδης πρέσβυς εὐδαίμων ἀνὴρ 535
ἥκει, τίεσθαι δ' ἀξιώτατος βροτῶν
τῶν νῦν· Πάρις γὰρ οὔτε συντελὴς πόλις
ἐξεύχεται τὸ δρᾶμα τοῦ πάθους πλέον·
ὀφλὼν γὰρ ἁρπαγῆς τε καὶ κλοπῆς δίκην
τοῦ ῥυσίου θ' ἥμαρτε καὶ πανώλεθρον 540
αὐτόχθονον πατρῶιον ἔθρισεν δόμον,
διπλᾶ δ' ἔτεισαν Πριαμίδαι θἀμάρτια.

ΧΟ. κῆρυξ Ἀχαιῶν χαῖρε τῶν ἀπὸ στρατοῦ.
ΚΗ. χαίρω· τεθναίην δ'· οὐκέτ' ἀντερῶ θεοῖς.

---

525 εἴ που Auratus: ἧπου codd. **532** βωμοὶ δ' ἄϊστοι καὶ θεῶν ἱδρύματα del. Salzmann. **534** τοιοῦδε f. **544** τεθναίην H.: τεθνᾶναι codd. | οὐκέτ' h et schol. 555: οὐκ f.

O Lord Apollo! Greeting unto you,
Ye Gods of Gathering all, with mine own patron,
Hermes, the sweet Herald, that homage hath
From heralds; and O ye Heroes in the earth,
Kind as of old you sped us, now receive
These relics of the spear....
Awake, beloved halls of royalty!
Hail to you! Hail, ye stately judgment-seats!
And hail, ye orient-facing Deities!
If e'er aforetime, O with bright eyes now
Beam after all these days upon the King!
For bringing light in darkness unto you
And all this people, Prince Agamemnon comes.
O give him welcome! 'Tis indeed his due;
He hath digged up Troy with mattock;
Yea, with the mattock of Zeus Justicer
Hath left the whole soil overturned and broke
And her seed rooted out of all the land.
So sore the yoke laid on her caitiff neck
By the elder lord Atrides, who now comes
Blest among men, the worthiest in the world
To be received with honour; for Trojan Paris
Nor all his liable city now can boast
Their trespass to outweigh their punishment:
Convicted both of rape and thievery,
He hath lost his pillage and of House been shorn
With all the land pertaining; he and his
Amerced for crime in twofold penalties!

ELDER. O Herald of the Achaeans from the field,
Best greeting and all joy!
HERALD. I thank you; let me die now! At God's pleasure,
I'll not oppose it longer.

ΧΟ. ἔρως πατρῴας τῆσδε γῆς σ' ἐγύμνασεν. 545

ΚΗ. ὥστ' ἐνδακρύειν γ' ὄμμασιν χαρᾶς ὕπο.

ΧΟ. τερπνῆς ἄρ' ἦτε τῆσδ' ἐπήβολοι νόσου.

ΚΗ. πῶς δή; διδαχθεὶς τοῦδε δεσπόσω λόγου.

ΧΟ. τῶν ἀντερώντων ἱμέρωι πεπληγμένοι.

ΚΗ. ποθεῖν ποθοῦντα τήνδε γῆν στρατὸν λέγεις; 550

ΧΟ. ὡς πόλλ' ἀμαυρᾶς ἐκ φρενός <γ'> ἀναστένειν.

ΚΗ. πόθεν τὸ δύσφρον τοῦτ' ἐπῆν στυγοστράτωι;

ΧΟ. πάλαι τὸ σιγᾶν φάρμακον βλάβης ἔχω.

ΚΗ. καὶ πῶς; ἀπόντων κοιράνων ἔτρεις τινάς;

ΧΟ. ὡς νῦν, τὸ σὸν δή, καὶ θανεῖν πολλὴ χάρις. 555

ΚΗ. εὖ γὰρ πέπρακται. ταῦτα δ' ἐν πολλῶι χρόνωι
τὰ μέν τις ἂν λέξειεν εὐπετῶς ἔχειν,
τὰ δ' αὖτε κἀπίμομφα—τίς δὲ πλὴν θεῶν
ἅπαντ' ἀπήμων τὸν δι' αἰῶνος χρόνον;—
μόχθους γὰρ εἰ λέγοιμι καὶ δυσαυλίας, 560
σπαρνὰς παρείξεις καὶ κακοστρώτους,—τί δ' οὐ
στένοντες οὐ λαχόντες ἤματος μέρος;†
τὰ δ' αὖτε χέρσωι καὶ προσῆν πλέον στύγος·
εὐναὶ γὰρ ἦσαν δηίων πρὸς τείχεσιν·
ἐξ οὐρανοῦ δέ—κἀπὸ γῆς λειμώνιαι 565
δρόσοι—κατεψέκαζον, ἔμπεδον σίνος,
ἐσθημάτων τιθέντες ἔνθηρον τρίχα.
χειμῶνα δ' εἰ λέγοι τις οἰωνοκτόνον,
οἷον παρεῖχ' ἄφερτον Ἰδαία χιών,

---

547 ἴστε f. **549** πεπληγμένοι Tyrwhitt: πεπληγμένος codd. **551** γ' add. Heath. **552** στυγοστράτωι M. Schmidt (στυγόστρατον Pauw): στύγος στρατῶι codd. **554** τυράννων f. **555** ὡς Scaliger: ὧν codd. **557** ἂν Auratus: εὖ codd. **561** παρείξεις H. L. Ahrens: παρήξεις codd. **565** δὲ J. Pearson: γὰρ codd.

ELDER. You have been tried
By sickness for your fatherland?

HERALD. Ay truly;
Mine eyes fill with tears for happiness.

ELDER. Then there was pleasure in the sickness.

HERALD. Pleasure?
Pray you, instruct me.

ELDER. 'Twas a love returned
With love again.

HERALD. For us then your heart yearned
As ours did yearn for home?

ELDER. So much I grieved
That many a sigh my clouded heart hath heaved.

HERALD. What cloudy gloom was this that overhung
Mislikers of our war?

ELDER. A silent tongue
Hath long been my best amulet.

HERALD. Amulet?
In absence of our princes were there any
You stood in fear of, then?

ELDER. Indeed 'twere now,—
Your own phrase,—joy to die.

HERALD. Ay, for it is
A brave success! Though, take the time in all,
With much to cause contentment, there were matters
Also for discontent—but Gods alone
May live unscathed of harm perpetually:—
Troth, were I to recount our miseries,
The toil, the wretched lodging—seldom respite
Snatched on a sorry couch—and all our groans
In the hour of daytime! Then again on shore;
Why there 'twas yet worse hardship; for we lay
Before the enemy's walls, and from the sky,
And from the damp fen, dews with damage dripped
Abiding, that our woolly garments made
All verminous:—or tell again of cold;
How bitter was the snow on Ida made,

ἢ θάλπος, εὖτε πόντος ἐν μεσημβριναῖς 570
κοίταις ἀκύμων νηνέμοις εὕδοι πεσών—
τί ταῦτα πενθεῖν δεῖ; παροίχεται πόνος·
παροίχεται δέ, τοῖσι μὲν τεθνηκόσιν
τὸ μήποτ' αὖθις μηδ' ἀναστῆναι μέλειν.
τί τοὺς ἀναλωθέντας ἐν ψήφωι λέγειν, 575
τὸν ζῶντα δ' ἀλγεῖν χρὴ τύχης παλιγκότου;
καὶ πολλὰ χαίρειν συμφορὰς καταξιῶ.
ἡμῖν δὲ τοῖς λοιποῖσιν Ἀργείων στρατοῦ
νικᾶι τὸ κέρδος, πῆμα δ' οὐκ ἀντιρρέπει.
ὡς κομπάσαι τῶιδ' εἰκὸς ἡλίου φάει 580
ὑπὲρ θαλάσσης καὶ χθονὸς ποτωμένοις·
"Τροίαν ἑλόντες δήποτ' Ἀργείων στόλος
θεοῖς λάφυρα ταῦτα τοῖς καθ' Ἑλλάδα
δόμων ἐπασσάλευσαν ἀρχαίων γάνος."
τοιαῦτα χρὴ κλύοντας εὐλογεῖν πόλιν 585
καὶ τοὺς στρατηγούς· καὶ χάρις τιμήσεται
Διὸς τόδ' ἐκπράξασα. πάντ' ἔχεις λόγον.

ΧΟ. νικώμενος λόγοισιν οὐκ ἀναίνομαι,
ἀεὶ γὰρ ἡβᾶι τοῖς γέρουσιν εὐμαθεῖν·
δόμοις δὲ ταῦτα καὶ Κλυταιμήστραι μέλειν 590
εἰκὸς μάλιστα, σὺν δὲ πλουτίζειν ἐμέ.

ΚΛ. ἀνωλόλυξα μὲν πάλαι χαρᾶς ὕπο,
ὅτ' ἦλθ' ὁ πρῶτος νύχιος ἄγγελος πυρός,
φράζων ἅλωσιν Ἰλίου τ' ἀνάστασιν.
καί τίς μ' ἐνίπτων εἶπε, "φρυκτωρῶν δία 595
πεισθεῖσα Τροίαν νῦν πεπορθῆσθαι δοκεῖς;

---

577 *συμφορὰς* Blomfield: *συμφοραῖς* codd. **584** *δόμων...ἀρχαίων* Hartung: *δόμοις...ἀρχαῖον* codd.

Killing the birds; or sweltering summer's heat,
When slumbering in his noonday drowsiness
Lay without stir the sunk unruffled sea......
What boots it to repine? The pain is past;
Unto the dead so past that no more now
They have any thought or care to rise again:—
Why make, with telling all the lost expense,
The live heart sore at Fate's malevolence?
'Adieu, cross Fortune, fare you well!' say I.
For us, the remnant of the host, our gain
Outweighs the utmost counterpoise of pain:
On Fame's wings flying over land and sea
This glorious day proud boasters we may be:
By the troops of Argos, having taken Troy,
Memorials to the Gods in thankful joy
Throughout all Greece their mansions to adorn
Were pinned these trophies from the Trojans torn.
All those that hear this blazon should applaud
The country and her captains; honour due
Being also done to Zeus, whose hand it is!
You have my tale in full.

ELDER. I am overborne
No more contending; age is never old
For young Instruction.—

[*Turning to* CLYTAEMNESTRA *who enters.*

There should be rich news here,
For me too, but methinks most nearly touching
The House and Clytaemnestra.

CLYT. Some while since
I lifted up my jubilee, already,
When the first messenger, at night, by fire,
Told me the capture and the wrack of Troy.
They chid me then with scorn: *Persuaded so*
By beacons to believe that Troy is taken?

ἦ κάρτα πρὸς γυναικὸς αἴρεσθαι κέαρ."
λόγοις τοιούτοις πλαγκτὸς οὖσ' ἐφαινόμην.
ὅμως δ' ἔθυον· καὶ γυναικείωι νόμωι
ὀλολυγμὸν ἄλλος ἄλλοθεν κατὰ πτόλιν 600
ἔλασκον εὐφημοῦντες ἐν θεῶν ἕδραις
θυηφάγον κοιμῶντες εὐώδη φλόγα.
 καὶ νῦν τὰ μάσσω μὲν τί δεῖ σέ μοι λέγειν;
ἄνακτος αὐτοῦ πάντα πεύσομαι λόγον.
ὅπως δ' ἄριστα τὸν ἐμὸν αἰδοῖον πόσιν 605
σπεύσω πάλιν μολόντα δέξασθαι· τί γὰρ
γυναικὶ τούτου φέγγος ἥδιον δρακεῖν,
ἀπὸ στρατείας ἄνδρα σώσαντος θεοῦ
πύλας ἀνοῖξαι; ταῦτ' ἀπάγγειλον πόσει·
ἥκειν ὅπως τάχιστ' ἐράσμιον πόλει· 610
γυναῖκα πιστὴν δ' ἐν δόμοις εὕροι μολὼν
οἵανπερ οὖν ἔλειπε, δωμάτων κύνα
ἐσθλὴν ἐκείνωι, πολεμίαν τοῖς δύσφροσιν,
καὶ τἄλλ' ὁμοίαν πάντα, σημαντήριον
οὐδὲν διαφθείρασαν ἐν μήκει χρόνου. 615
οὐδ' οἶδα τέρψιν, οὐδ' ἐπίψογον φάτιν,
ἄλλου πρὸς ἀνδρὸς μᾶλλον ἢ χαλκοῦ βαφάς.

ΚΗ. τοιόσδ' ὁ κόμπος,—τῆς ἀληθείας γέμων,
οὐκ αἰσχρὸς ὡς γυναικὶ γενναίαι λακεῖν;

ΧΟ. αὕτη μὲν οὕτως εἶπε, μανθάνοντί σοι, 620
τοροῖσιν ἑρμηνεῦσιν εὐπρεπῶς λόγον.
σὺ δ' εἰπέ, κῆρυξ, Μενέλεων δὲ πεύθομαι,
εἰ νόστιμός τε καὶ σεσωμένος πάλιν
ἥξει σὺν ὑμῖν, τῆσδε γῆς φίλον κράτος.

---

623 τε Hermann: γε codd. | σεσωσμένος codd.

O the right woman's credulous heart on wings!
With such derision was I argued fool:
Yet still kept offering; and throughout the town
Aloud they shouted—after woman's use—
Their jubilant anthem, lulling in the shrines
The hunger of the spice-fed odorous flame.
So now, what need we further circumstance
From *thee*? The King's own mouth shall render us
The tale in full:—but I must give my own
Dear honoured lord the best and soonest welcome—
Soonest and best, for to a woman's eyes
What hour is dearer than the hour when Heaven
Hath saved her husband from the wars, and she
Unbars her gates for him?—Go bid him, then,
Come hither with all speed, the country's darling,
Come with all speed, a faithful wife to find,
Even as he left her, a true hound within,
Still to his foes a foe, to him still kind;
Alike at all parts, every whit the same,
That all this while hath never broke one seal;
Of joys from other—nay, the whispered blame—
I have no more knowledge than of plunging steel!

[*Exit*

HERALD. Valiant protest; with truth in every syllable,
True honest lady need not blush to cry it?

ELDER. We have heard her story,—as you apprehend,
In the ear of judgment, excellent, most plausible.—
But tell me, Herald, our beloved prince
Menelaus, shall we see him safe back with you?

ΚΗ. οὐκ ἔσθ' ὅπως λέξαιμι τὰ ψευδῆ καλὰ 625
ἐς τὸν πολὺν φίλοισι καρποῦσθαι χρόνον.
ΧΟ. πῶς δῆτ' ἂν εἰπὼν κεδνὰ τἀληθῆ τύχοις;
σχισθέντα δ' οὐκ εὔκρυπτα γίγνεται τάδε.
ΚΗ. ἀνὴρ ἄφαντος ἐξ Ἀχαιϊκοῦ στρατοῦ,
αὐτός τε καὶ τὸ πλοῖον. οὐ ψευδῆ λέγω. 630
ΧΟ. πότερον ἀναχθεὶς ἐμφανῶς ἐξ Ἰλίου,
ἢ χεῖμα, κοινὸν ἄχθος, ἥρπασε στρατοῦ;
ΚΗ. ἔκυρσας ὥστε τοξότης ἄκρος σκοποῦ·
μακρὸν δὲ πῆμα συντόμως ἐφημίσω.
ΧΟ. πότερα γὰρ αὐτοῦ ζῶντος ἢ τεθνηκότος 635
φάτις πρὸς ἄλλων ναυτίλων ἐκλῄζετο;
ΚΗ. οὐκ οἶδεν οὐδεὶς ὥστ' ἀπαγγεῖλαι τορῶς,
πλὴν τοῦ τρέφοντος Ἡλίου χθονὸς φύσιν.
ΧΟ. πῶς γὰρ λέγεις χειμῶνα ναυτικῶι στρατῶι
ἐλθεῖν, τελευτῆσαί τε, δαιμόνων κότωι; 640
ΚΗ. εὔφημον ἦμαρ οὐ πρέπει κακαγγέλωι
γλώσσηι μιαίνειν· χωρὶς ἡ τιμὴ θεῶν.
ὅταν δ' ἀπευκτὰ πήματ' ἄγγελος πόλει
στυγνῶι προσώπωι πτωσίμου στρατοῦ φέρηι,
πόλει μὲν ἕλκος ἓν τὸ δήμιον τυχεῖν, 645
πολλοὺς δὲ πολλῶν ἐξαγισθέντας δόμων
ἄνδρας διπλῆι μάστιγι τὴν Ἄρης φιλεῖ,
δίλογχον ἄτην, φοινίαν ξυνωρίδα,—
τοιῶνδε μέντοι πημάτων σεσαγμένον
πρέπει λέγειν παιᾶνα τόνδ' Ἐρινύων· 650
σωτηρίων δὲ πραγμάτων εὐάγγελον

---

627 sq. et sequentia disticha Clytaemnestrae dant codd.: corr. Stanley | τύχοις Porson: τύχης codd. **649** σεσαγμένον Schuetz: σεσαγμένων codd.

HERALD. I have no art to colour falsehood fair
And lend the painting gloss for lasting wear.

ELDER. O might then colour fair be joined with true!
'Tis vain to cloke disjunction of the two.

HERALD. To speak no falsehood then, the prince is vanished
From his companions, together with his ship.

ELDER. Loosing from Ilium in full sight? Or was 't
A general storm that tore him from the rest?

HERALD. You have hit the target with a perfect aim;
And briefly phrased a long sad chronicle.

ELDER. How was his name in current rumour bruited
By the other crews? As yet alive or dead?

HERALD. None can aver by knowledge, save that one
That breeds the increase of the Earth, the Sun.

ELDER. What is your story of the storm? How rose,
And how did close, this angry visitation?

HERALD. It fits not to profane with dolorous tongue
A day of praise: that service and the Gods'
Are twain and separate. When the messenger
Brings gloomy visage and disastrous hap,
An armed host's overthrow—one general wound
Lashed on the country, and her several men
From private home on home driven out with scourge
By curse of Ares with his double thong
Twinned thus for ruin and for slaughter leashed—
When such the load upon the bearer's back,
Why, then 'tis fitting that his anthem sound
The Avengers' tone; but when he comes with news

ἥκοντα πρὸς χαίρουσαν εὐεστοῖ πόλιν,
πῶς κεδνὰ τοῖς κακοῖσι συμμείξω, λέγων
χειμῶν' Ἀχαιοῖς οὐκ ἀμήνιτον θεῶν;
ξυνώμοσαν γάρ, ὄντες ἔχθιστοι τὸ πρίν, 655
πῦρ καὶ θάλασσα, καὶ τὰ πίστ' ἐδειξάτην
φθείροντε τὸν δύστηνον Ἀργείων στρατόν.
ἐν νυκτὶ δυσκύμαντα δ' ὠρώρει κακά.
ναῦς γὰρ πρὸς ἀλλήλαισι Θρήικιαι πνοαὶ
ἤρεικον· αἳ δὲ κεροτυπούμεναι βίαι 660
χειμῶνι Τυφῶ σὺν ζάληι τ' ὀμβροκτύπωι
ᾤχοντ' ἄφαντοι, ποιμένος κακοῦ στρόβωι.
ἐπεὶ δ' ἀνῆλθε λαμπρὸν ἡλίου φάος,
ὁρῶμεν ἀνθοῦν πέλαγος Αἰγαῖον νεκροῖς
ἀνδρῶν Ἀχαιῶν ναυτικοῖς τ' ἐρειπίοις. 665
ἡμᾶς γε μὲν δὴ ναῦν τ' ἀκήρατον σκάφος
ἤτοι τις ἐξέκλεψεν ἢ 'ξῃτήσατο
θεός τις, οὐκ ἄνθρωπος, οἴακος θιγών.
τύχη δὲ σωτὴρ ναῦν θέλουσ' ἐφέζετο,
ὡς μήτ' ἐν ὅρμωι κύματος ζάλην ἔχειν 670
μήτ' ἐξοκεῖλαι πρὸς κραταίλεων χθόνα.
ἔπειτα δ' Ἅιδην πόντιον πεφευγότες,
λευκὸν κατ' ἦμαρ οὐ πεποιθότες τύχηι,
ἐβουκολοῦμεν φροντίσιν νέον πάθος,
στρατοῦ καμόντος καὶ κακῶς σποδουμένου. 675
καὶ νῦν ἐκείνων εἴ τις ἐστὶν ἐμπνέων,
λέγουσιν ἡμᾶς ὡς ὀλωλότας, τί μήν;
ἡμεῖς τ' ἐκείνους ταὔτ' ἔχειν δοξάζομεν.

654 Ἀχαιοῖς...θεῶν Dobree: Ἀχαιῶν...θεοῖς codd. **659** ἀλλήλῃσι f. **660** *κερωτυπούμεναι* codd.: corr. Wasse. **665** *ναυτικῶν τ' ἐριπίων* codd.: corr. Auratus. **677** *τί μήν;* Linwood: *τί μή;* codd.

Of preservation to a country blest
With ease and welfare, how then should I mix
The good with evil, and relate a storm
That ne'er came surely but from angry Gods!
Fire and sea, worst enemies before,
Now sware a covenant, and displayed their pledge
By wrecking all the luckless Argive host.
Trouble of the ocean in the night-time wrought;
The Northern wind grew boisterous, and our ships
Dashed one against the other; which, being rammed
With blast of the hurricane and battering sleet,
By that wild shepherding were lost and vanished.
And when the bright light of the Sun rose up,
Our eyes beheld
The vast Aegean like a field in bloom
With floating carcases of drownèd men
And tattered wrecks of ships. We, with a hull
Still sound, were brought off safe, either by sleight
Or pleading of some Power, had other, sure,
Than human hand, our pilot. Fortune too
Sat Saviour on our deck, vouchsafing us
Neither at mooring in the roads to suffer
Strain of a swelling surge, nor driving split
Upon a rock-bound coast. Then, being at length
From ocean graves delivered, with fair dawn,
The fact scarce crediting, we let our thoughts
Dwell musing on our strange reverse, our fleet
So bruised and buffeted....
Well, they likewise now,
If any be that breathes yet, speak of *us*,
Doubtless, as perished, we meanwhile supposing
Them in the same case:—let us hope the best

γένοιτο δ' ὡς ἄριστα· Μενέλεων γὰρ οὖν
πρῶτόν τε καὶ μάλιστα προσδόκα μογεῖν· 680
εἰ δ' οὖν τις ἀκτὶς ἡλίου νιν ἱστορεῖ
καὶ ζῶντα καὶ βλέποντα, μηχαναῖς Διός,
οὔπω θέλοντος ἐξαναλῶσαι γένος,
ἐλπίς τις αὐτὸν πρὸς δόμους ἥξειν πάλιν.
τοσαῦτ' ἀκούσας ἴσθι τἀληθῆ κλύων. 685

στρ. α'. ΧΟ. τίς ποτ' ὠνόμαζεν ὧδ'
ἐς τὸ πᾶν ἐτητύμως—
μή τις ὅντιν' οὐχ ὁρῶμεν προνοίαισι τοῦ πεπρωμένου
γλῶσσαν ἐν τύχαι νέμων;— 690
τὰν δορίγαμβρον ἀμφινει-
κῆ θ' Ἑλέναν; ἐπεὶ πρεπόντως
ἑλέναυς, ἕλανδρος, ἑλέπτολις,
ἐκ τῶν ἁβροτίμων
προκαλυμμάτων ἔπλευσεν 695
Ζεφύρου γίγαντος αὔραι,
πολύανδροί
τε φεράσπιδες κυναγοὶ
κατ' ἴχνος πλατᾶν ἄφαντον
κελσάντων Σιμόεντος ἀκ-
τὰς ἐπ' ἀεξιφύλλους 700
δι' ἔριν αἱματόεσσαν.

---

680 μογεῖν Sonny: μολεῖν codd. **688** sq. προνοίαισι Pauw: προνοίαις codd. **693** ἑλέναυς Blomfield: ἑλένας codd.

That may be! Menelaus,—in sore plight
Presume him needs you must; yet if the Sun
With any ray descries him hale and quick,
By help of Zeus, then, being loth to see
The race quite blotted out, some hope there is
He yet may come safe home.—You have my story,
And rest assured 'tis absolute verity.

[*Exit.*

CHORUS.

I I.

1st strophe.

Who named her all so truly?
—Was't One beyond our vision,
By glimpse of Order fated
His happy lips who moved?—
This Prize debate-environed,
This Bride with spear to kinsman,
This *Helena*? Most perfect *Helena*?
'Twas *Hell enow* she proved,
When amorous from the silken-tissued
Veils before her bower emerging
Forth to Eastward sail she issued,
Spirit of Earth-born Zephyrus urging—
Forth to Eastward sail,
After her, men with ardour shipped,
Myriads of hunters, all equipped
In arms that harrier-like pursued
Fast on a printless trail of oars
Abeach on Simois' leafy shores,
Full cry, in bloody feud!

ἀντ. α'.

Ἰλίωι δὲ κῆδος ὀρ-
θώνυμον τελεσσίφρων
μῆνις ἤνυσεν, τραπέζας ἀτί-
μωσιν ὑστέρωι χρόνωι 705
καὶ ξυνεστίου Διὸς
πρασσομένα τὸ νυμφότι-
μον μέλος ἐκφάτως τίοντας,
ὑμέναιον, ὃς τότ' ἐπέρρεπεν
γαμβροῖσιν ἀείδειν. 710
μεταμανθάνουσα δ' ὕμνον
Πριάμου πόλις γεραιὰ
πολύθρηνον
μέγα που στένει, κικλήσκου-
σα Πάριν τὸν αἰνόλεκτρον,
τἄμπροσθ' ἦ πολύθρηνον αἰ- 715
ῶν' ἀμφὶ πολιτᾶν
μέλεον αἷμ' ἀνατλᾶσα.

στρ. β'.

ἔθρεψεν δὲ λέοντος ἶ-
νιν δόμοις ἀγάλακτα βού-
τας ἀνὴρ φιλόμαστον, 720
ἐν βιότου προτελείοις
ἅμερον, εὐφιλόπαιδα
καὶ γεραροῖς ἐπίχαρτον.

---

704 sq. ἤνυσεν H.: ἤλασε codd. | ἀτίμωσιν Canter: ἀτίμως ἴν' f, ἀτίμως h. **715** τἄμπροσθ' ἦ (πάμπροσθ' ἦ Hermann) H.: παμπρόσθη codd. **718** sq. λέοντος ἶνιν Conington: λέοντα σίνιν codd. **719** sq. ἀγάλακτα βούτας Wecklein: ἀγάλακτον οὗτος (vel οὕτως) codd.

I 2.

1st antistrophe.

But unbent Wrath abiding
Works her will to render
That so dear alliance
All too dear for Troy;
That scorn of high Zeus guarding
The shared Home's friendly Table
Wrath in her season visits
On all that uttered joy,—
All that once in gay carousal
Bride with *Hymen* fain would honour,
Hymen, when the time of spousal
Bade them heap their praise upon her—
Ah, but at this time,
Though late the lesson, wiser grown
With age-long suffering of her own
Sons' blood so lamentably shed,
That ancient City loud, I ween,
Laments with practice-perfect *Threne,*
'*O Paris evil-wed!*'

II 1.

2nd strophe.

A young babe Lion, still at breast,
Was home once by a Herdsman borne,
Housed beneath roof among the rest
And reared there; in his early morn
And first of age, all gentle, mild,
Youth's darling, the delight of Eld;

πολέα δ’ ἔσχ’ ἐν ἀγκάλαις
νεοτρόφου τέκνου δίκαν 725
φαιδρωπὸν ποτὶ χεῖρα σαί-
νοντα γαστρὸς ἀνάγκαις.

ἀντ. β΄. χρονισθεὶς δ’ ἀπέδειξεν ἦ-
θος τὸ πρὸς τοκέων· χάριν
γὰρ τροφᾶς ἀμείβων 730
μηλοφόνοισιν ἄταις
δαῖτ’ ἀκέλευστος ἔτευξεν·
αἵματι δ’ οἶκος ἐφύρθη,
ἄμαχον ἄλγος οἰκέταις,
μέγα σίνος πολυκτόνον· 735
ἐκ θεοῦ δ’ ἱερεύς τις Ἄ-
τας δόμοις προσεθρέφθη.

στρ. γ΄. πάραυτα δ’ ἐλθεῖν ἐς Ἰλίου πόλιν
λέγοιμ’ ἂν φρόνημα μὲν νηνέμου γαλάνας,
ἀκασκαῖον <δ’> ἄγαλμα πλούτου, 740
μαλθακὸν ὀμμάτων βέλος,
δηξίθυμον ἔρωτος ἄνθος.
παρακλίνασ’ ἐπέκρανεν
δὲ γάμου πικρὰς τελευτάς,
δύσεδρος καὶ δυσόμιλος 745
συμένα Πριαμίδαισιν,
πομπᾶι Διὸς ξενίου,
νυμφόκλαυτος Ἐρινύς.

---

726 sq. φαιδρωπὸν...σαίνοντα Auratus: φαιδρωπὸς...σαίνων τε codd. **728** sq. ἦθος Conington: ἔθος codd. **734** ἄμαχον δ’ f. **737** προσεθρέφθη Heath: προσετράφη codd. **740** δ’ add. Porson.

And ofttimes, like a nursling child,
In arms with happy love was held,
While the weak flesh, demure and bland,
With fawning wooed the fostering hand.

II 2.

2nd antistrophe.

But age grown ripe, his humour showed
The born touch that his parents had;
Thank-offering when his nurture owed,
A banquet, ere the master bade,
With such wild slaughter he prepared,
It sluiced the dwelling foul with gore,
While helpless, all aghast, they stared
Upon that bloody mischief sore:—
Divine Will there had found him room,
Housed, to be Priest of slaughtering Doom.

III 1.

3rd strophe.

Likewise, arriving once in Ilium town
What languorous gentleness was seen!
Tranquillest Pearl to shine in Riches' crown,
With Calm's own soul serene;
Eyes to send arrowy softness winging fire;
Loveliness torturing with the heart's desire.

Then from that Heaven away she fell,
Transformed into a Fiend of Hell:
Launched upon Priam's house to bring
Curse with her sweet companioning;
God's Vengeance, in his conduct led
With ruth about her bridal bed
And tears for widowed wives to shed!

ἀντ. γ΄. παλαίφατος δ᾽ ἐν βροτοῖς γέρων λόγος
τέτυκται, μέγαν τελεσθέντα φωτὸς ὄλβον 750
τεκνοῦσθαι μηδ᾽ ἄπαιδα θνήισκειν,
ἐκ δ᾽ ἀγαθᾶς τύχας γένει
βλαστάνειν ἀκόρεστον οἰζύν.
δίχα δ᾽ ἄλλων μονόφρων εἰ-
μί· τὸ δυσσεβὲς γὰρ ἔργον 755
μετὰ μὲν πλείονα τίκτει,
σφετέραι δ᾽ εἰκότα γένναι·
οἴκων γὰρ εὐθυδίκων
καλλίπαις πότμος αἰεί.

στρ. δ΄. φιλεῖ δὲ τίκτειν Ὕβρις μὲν παλαιὰ νεά- 760
ζουσαν ἐν κακοῖς βροτῶν
Ὕβριν τότ᾽ ἢ τοθ᾽, ὅτε τὸ κύριον μόληι
βαθύσκοτον
δαίμονα τίταν ἄμαχον, ἀπόλεμον,
ἀνίερον θράσος μελαί-
νας μελάθροισιν ἄτας, 765
εἰδομέναν τοκεῦσιν.

ἀντ. δ΄. Δίκα δὲ λάμπει μὲν ἐν δυσκάπνοις δώμασιν,
τὸν δ᾽ ἐναίσιμον τίει·
τὰ χρυσόπαστα δ᾽ ἔδεθλα σὺν πίνωι χερῶν
παλιντρόποις
ὄμμασι λιποῦσ᾽ ὅσια προσέφατο 770
δύναμιν οὐ σέβουσα πλού-
του παράσημον αἴνωι·
πᾶν δ᾽ ἐπὶ τέρμα νωμᾶι.

---

755 δυσσεβὲς γὰρ Pauw: γὰρ δυσσεβὲς codd. **762** ὅτε Klausen: ὅταν codd. **763** βαθύσκοτον (Maehly)...τίταν (Heimsoeth): νεαρὰ φάους κότον...τε τὸν codd. **765** μελάθροις f. **768** τίει βίον codd.: corr. H. L. Ahrens. **769** ἔδεθλα Auratus: ἐσθλὰ codd. **770** προσέφατο Tucker: προσέβα τοῦ codd.

III 2.

3rd antistrophe.

There is an ancient proverb men will preach
As framed by wisdom of old time,
That prosperous Fortune, let him only reach
To full estate and prime,
Hath issue, dies not childless; waxen so,
Weal for his heir begets unsated Woe.

But single in the world I hold
A doctrine different from the old:
Not Weal it is, but Sinful Deed
More sinners after him doth breed
Formed in his image; none the less
Doth lovely offspring always bless
The house that follows Righteousness.

IV 1.

4th strophe.

Old Insolence in the evil sort of men
Young Insolence will gender, then or then,
When dawns the appointed hour, a Fiend of gloom
For penance, violent, unwithstood,
Flushed with such reckless Hardihood
That sin's dark ruinous Doom
In black storm on the roof shall rage,—
The latter offspring like his parentage.

IV 2.

4th antistrophe.

But Righteousness to the upright heart inclines;
Bright beneath smoky rafters her light shines:
Gilt-spangled halls, where hands guilt-spotted are,
Swift with averted eyes forsakes,
Thence to the pure her blessing takes,
To that false lauded star,
The Power of Riches, will not bend,
But guideth all things to their proper end.

ἄγε δή, βασιλεῦ, Τροίας πτολίπορθ',
Ἀτρέως γένεθλον, 775
πῶς σε προσείπω; πῶς σε σεβίζω
μήθ' ὑπεράρας μήθ' ὑποκάμψας
καιρὸν χάριτος;
πολλοὶ δὲ βροτῶν τὸ δοκεῖν εἶναι
προτίουσι δίκην παραβάντες. 780
τῶι δυσπραγοῦντι δ' ἐπιστενάχειν
πᾶς τις ἕτοιμος· δῆγμα δὲ λύπης
οὐδὲν ἐφ' ἧπαρ προσικνεῖται·
καὶ ξυγχαίρουσιν ὁμοιοπρεπεῖς,
ἀγέλαστα πρόσωπα βιαζόμενοι, 785
. . . .
ὅστις δ' ἀγαθὸς προβατογνώμων,
οὐκ ἔστι λαθεῖν ὄμματα φωτός,
τὰ δοκοῦντ' εὔφρονος ἐκ διανοίας
ὑδαρεῖ σαίνει φιλότητι.
σὺ δέ μοι τότε μὲν στέλλων στρατιὰν 790
Ἑλένης ἕνεκ', οὐκ ἐπικεύσω,
κάρτ' ἀπομούσως ἦσθα γεγραμμένος
οὐδ' εὖ πραπίδων οἴακα νέμων,
θάρσος ἑκούσιον
ἀνδράσι θνήισκουσι κομίζων. 795
νῦν δ' οὐκ ἀπ' ἄκρας φρενὸς οὐδ' ἀφίλως
< ἔστιν ἐπειπεῖν >
"εὔφρων πόνος εὖ τελέσασιν."

---

774 πτολίπορθ' Blomfield: πολίπορθ' codd. **782** δῆγμα Stob. *fl.* 112, 12 et h: δεῖγμα f. **785** post hunc versum lacunam indicavit Hermann. **789** σαίνει Casaubon: σαίνειν codd. **791** οὐκ ἐπικεύσω Hermann: οὐ γὰρ ἐπικεύσω codd. **794** θράσος f. **797** ἔστιν ἐπειπεῖν supplevit H.

[*Enter* AGAMEMNON *in a four-wheeled travelling-waggon drawn by mules; followed presently by another containing, among other spoils,* CASSANDRA*; who throughout this scene and through the chorus following it continues motionless and silent but in view.*

CHORUS.

Come O thou conqueror, my King,
What praise, what homage can I bring
Not to be scanty nor outwing
  Thy pleasure with my style?
Too many in this world, we know,
Practise rather outward show,
  Dishonest arts of guile:
All men for a man's distress
Have apt sighs ready,—never smart
Of sorrow going near the heart;
And as rejoiced in happiness
With formal fashion they constrain
  The lips into a smile:—
But him that can discern his flock
The *eyes* that flatter shall not mock,
Fond affection when they feign
  That lukewarm is the while.
Thou, when levying armament
In cause of Helen, didst present—
  I will not cloke it—then
A picture to these aged eyes
Deformed in most unlovely guise,—
The handling of thy helm not wise,
Recovery at such dear expense
To purchase—willing Impudence
  At cost of dying men:—
But now no glozer or false friend
Am I, pronouncing *Happy end*
  Makes happy labourers.

γνώσηι δὲ χρόνωι διαπευθόμενος
τόν τε δικαίως καὶ τὸν ἀκαίρως
πόλιν οἰκουροῦντα πολιτῶν. 800

ΑΓΑΜΕΜΝΩΝ.

πρῶτον μὲν Ἄργος καὶ θεοὺς ἐγχωρίους
δίκη προσειπεῖν, τοὺς ἐμοὶ μεταιτίους
νόστου δικαίων θ' ὧν ἐπραξάμην πόλιν
Πριάμου· δίκας γὰρ οὐκ ἀπὸ γλώσσης θεοὶ
κλύοντες ἀνδροθνῆτας Ἰλίου φθορὰς 805
ἐς αἱματηρὸν τεῦχος οὐ διχορρόπως
ψήφους ἔθεντο· τῶι δ' ἐναντίωι κύτει
ἐλπὶς προσήιει χειρὸς οὐ πληρουμένωι.
καπνῶι δ' ἁλοῦσα νῦν ἔτ' εὔσημος πόλις.
ἄτης θύελλαι ζῶσι· συνθνήισκουσα δὲ 810
σποδὸς προπέμπει πίονας πλούτου πνοάς.
τούτων θεοῖσι χρὴ πολύμνηστον χάριν
τίνειν, ἐπείπερ χἀρπαγὰς ὑπερκόπους
ἐπραξάμεσθα καὶ γυναικὸς εἵνεκα
πόλιν διημάθυνεν Ἀργεῖον δάκος, 815
ἵππου νεοσσός, ἀσπιδηφόρος λεώς,
πήδημ' ὀρούσας ἀμφὶ Πλειάδων δύσιν·
ὑπερθορὼν δὲ πύργον ὠμηστὴς λέων
ἄδην ἔλειξεν αἵματος τυραννικοῦ.

---

805 *φθορᾶς* Dobree. **810** *θυηλαὶ* Hermann. **813** *χἀρπαγὰς* Tyrwhitt: *καὶ πάγας* codd. | *ὑπερκόπους* Heath: *ὑπερκότους* codd. **814** *οὕνεκα* codd. **816** *ἀσπιδηφόρος* Blomfield: *ἀσπιδηστρόφος* f, *ἀσπιδοστρόφος* h.

Thy question in due time shall tell
Among this people which doth well
In stewardship, which errs.

AGAMEMNON.

To Argos first and to the country's Gods
Belongs my duty, that have aided me
To my return and justice we have done
Upon the town of Priam: when they heard
The unvoiced cause in heaven, with one consent
They cast into the urn of blood their votes
For perishing waste of Troy: to the other urn
Hope of the filling hand came ever nigh,—
Unfilled. The city's capture even now
Shows manifest by the smoke; death vigorous yet
In Doom's fierce hurricane[1], the expiring ash
Pants forth his opulent breath in puffs of Wealth.
Behoves us therefore render unto Heaven
Most memorable return, since we have wreaked
Our ample vengeance for an arrogant rape;
A whole town for a woman's sake hath been
Laid desolate in the dust by our fierce brood,
Hatched of a Horse in armed swarm, that sprang
About the sinking of the Pleiades,
And o'er the ramparts like a ravening Lion
Salient hath lapped his fill of soveran blood.

[1] *Or* 'life smouldering yet,
In Doom's burnt sacrifice, ...

θεοῖς μὲν ἐξέτεινα φροίμιον τόδε· 820
τὰ δ' ἐς τὸ σὸν φρόνημα μέμνημαι κλύων,
καὶ φημὶ ταὐτὰ καὶ συνήγορόν μ' ἔχεις·
παύροις γὰρ ἀνδρῶν ἐστι συγγενὲς τόδε,
φίλον τὸν εὐτυχοῦντ' ἄνευ φθόνου σέβειν·
δύσφρων γὰρ ἰὸς καρδίαν προσήμενος 825
ἄχθος διπλοίζει τῶι πεπαμένωι νόσον·
τοῖς τ' αὐτὸς αὑτοῦ πήμασιν βαρύνεται
καὶ τὸν θυραῖον ὄλβον εἰσορῶν στένει.
εἰδὼς λέγοιμ' ἄν, εὖ γὰρ ἐξεπίσταμαι
ὁμιλίας κάτοπτρον, εἴδωλον σκιᾶς 830
δοκοῦντας εἶναι κάρτα πρευμενεῖς ἐμοί.
μόνος δ' Ὀδυσσεύς, ὅσπερ οὐχ ἑκὼν ἔπλει,
ζευχθεὶς ἕτοιμος ἦν ἐμοὶ σειραφόρος·
εἴτ' οὖν θανόντος εἴτε καὶ ζῶντος πέρι
λέγω—τὰ δ' ἄλλα πρὸς πόλιν τε καὶ θεούς, 835
κοινοὺς ἀγῶνας θέντες ἐν πανηγύρει
βουλευσόμεσθα· καὶ τὸ μὲν καλῶς ἔχον
ὅπως χρονίζον εὖ μενεῖ βουλευτέον·
ὅτωι δὲ καὶ δεῖ φαρμάκων παιωνίων,
ἤτοι κέαντες ἢ τεμόντες εὐφρόνως 840
πειρασόμεσθα πῆμ' ἀποστρέψαι νόσου.
νῦν δ' ἐς μέλαθρα καὶ δόμους ἐφεστίους
ἐλθὼν θεοῖσι πρῶτα δεξιώσομαι,
οἵπερ πρόσω πέμψαντες ἤγαγον πάλιν.
νίκη δ' ἐπείπερ ἕσπετ', ἐμπέδως μένοι. 845

---

822 ταὐτὰ Auratus: ταῦτα codd. **824** φθόνου h: φθόνων f: ψόγου Stob. *fl.* 38, 28. **826** πεπαμμενω (-ωι) codd. **841** πῆμ' ἀποστρέψαι νόσου Porson: πήματος τρέψαι νόσον codd.

To Heaven this lengthened preface.—For your thought
(Remembered in my ear), I say the same;
You have me of your counsel; few indeed
Are they with whom 'tis nature to admire
A friend's good fortune with unjealous eyes:
Malignant venom settling at the heart
Distempers, and the sick man's burden makes
Twice heavy; labouring with his own distress
He groans the more for others' blessedness.
By knowledge, proven in companionship's
True mirror, *ghost of a shadow* I can term
Some seeming-absolute devotion to me:—
Only Odysseus, that was loth to sail,
Being harnessed, pulled beside me loyally;
Whether alive he be or whether dead
The while I speak. . . . .
For the rest, as touching
Affairs of policy and of religion,
A congress we shall summon, and debate
In full assemblage. Our debate must be
How what is healthy may persist in health;
Where need appears of wholesome remedies,
We shall endeavour to remove the mischief
By sage employ of knife or cautery.
Now to our palace hearth and home we pass,
First to give salutation to the Gods
That sent us and returned. May Victory
Our firm adherent rest in constancy!

ΚΛ. ἄνδρες πολῖται, πρέσβος Ἀργείων τόδε,
οὐκ αἰσχυνοῦμαι τοὺς φιλάνορας τρόπους
λέξαι πρὸς ὑμᾶς· ἐν χρόνωι δ' ἀποφθίνει
τὸ τάρβος ἀνθρώποισιν. οὐκ ἄλλων πάρα
μαθοῦσ' ἐμαυτῆς δύσφορον λέξω βίον 850
τοσόνδ' ὅσονπερ οὗτος ἦν ὑπ' Ἰλίωι.
τὸ μὲν γυναῖκα πρῶτον ἄρσενος δίχα
ἧσθαι δόμοις ἔρημον ἔκπαγλον κακόν,
πολλὰς κλύουσαν κληδόνας παλιγκότους·
καὶ τὸν μὲν ἥκειν, τὸν δ' ἐπεισφέρειν κακοῦ 855
κάκιον ἄλλο πῆμα λάσκοντας δόμοις.
καὶ τραυμάτων μὲν εἰ τόσων ἐτύγχανεν
ἀνὴρ ὅδ', ὡς πρὸς οἶκον ὠχετεύετο
φάτις, τέτρηται δικτύου πλέω λέγειν.
εἰ δ' ἦν τεθνηκώς, ὡς ἐπλήθυον λόγοι, 860
τρισώματός τἂν Γηρυὼν ὁ δεύτερος
πολλὴν ἄνωθεν—τὴν κάτω γὰρ οὐ λέγω—
χθονὸς τρίμοιρον χλαῖναν ἐξηύχει λαβών,
ἅπαξ ἑκάστωι κατθανὼν μορφώματι.
τοιῶνδ' ἕκατι κληδόνων παλιγκότων 865
πολλὰς ἄνωθεν ἀρτάνας ἐμῆς δέρης
ἔλυσαν ἄλλοι πρὸς βίαν λελιμμένης.
ἐκ τῶνδέ τοι παῖς ἐνθάδ' οὐ παραστατεῖ,
ἐμῶν τε καὶ σῶν κύριος πιστωμάτων,
ὡς χρῆν, Ὀρέστης· μηδὲ θαυμάσηις τόδε. 870
τρέφει γὰρ αὐτὸν εὐμενὴς δορύξενος
Στροφίος ὁ Φωκεύς, ἀμφίλεκτα πήματα

---

854 *κληδόνας* Auratus: *ἡδονὰς* codd. **859** *τέτρηται* H. L. Ahrens: *τέτρωται* codd. **860** *ἐπλήθυον* Porson: *ἐπλήθυνον* codd. **867** *λελιμμένης* Blomfield: *λελημμένης* codd. **869** *πιστωμάτων* Spanheim: *πιστευμάτων* codd. **872** *Στροφίος* habet M in *Cho.* 675: *Στρόφιος* codd.

CLYTAEMNESTRA.

My reverend Elders, worthy citizens,
I shall not blush now to confess before you
My amorous fondness; fear and diffidence
Fade from us all in time. O 'tis not from
Instruction I can tell
The story of my own unhappy life
All the long while my lord lay under Ilium.
First for a woman 'tis a passing trial
To sit forlorn at home with no man present,
Always malignant rumours in her ears,
One bawler tumbling on another's heels
With cruel blows each heavier than the last:—
Wounds! if my lord had got as many wounds
As rumour channelling to us homeward gave him,
He had been more riddled than a net with holes.
Or had his deaths but tallied with all tales!
He might have been a second Geryon,
Three-bodied, with a triple coverture
Of earth above to boast him—never speak
Of that beneath—one for each several corpse.
By reason of
These cross malignant rumours, other hands
Full many a time have set my desperate neck
Free from the hanging noose, recovering me
Against my dearest will.—Hence too it is
We see not present by our side this day
The child, Orestes, in whose person dwell
The pledges of our love; nor wonder at it;
He rests in keeping of our trusty cousin,
Strophius the Phocian, my forewarner oft

ἐμοὶ προφωνῶν—τόν θ' ὑπ' Ἰλίωι σέθεν
κίνδυνον, εἴ τε δημόθρους ἀναρχία
βουλὴν καταρράψειεν, ὥστε σύγγονον 875
βροτοῖσι τὸν πεσόντα λακτίσαι πλέον.
τοιάδε μέντοι σκῆψις οὐ δόλον φέρει.
ἔμοιγε μὲν δὴ κλαυμάτων ἐπίσσυτοι
πηγαὶ κατεσβήκασιν, οὐδ' ἔνι σταγών.
ἐν ὀψικοίτοις δ' ὄμμασιν βλάβας ἔχω, 880
τὰς ἀμφὶ σοὶ κλάιουσα λαμπτηρουχίας
ἀτημελήτους αἰέν. ἐν δ' ὀνείρασιν
λεπταῖς ὑπαὶ κώνωπος ἐξηγειρόμην
ῥιπαῖσι θωύσσοντος, ἀμφὶ σοὶ πάθη
ὁρῶσα πλείω τοῦ ξυνεύδοντος χρόνου. 885
νῦν ταῦτα πάντα τλᾶσ', ἀπενθήτωι φρενὶ
λέγοιμ' ἂν ἄνδρα τόνδ' ἐγὼ σταθμῶν κύνα,
σωτῆρα ναὸς πρότονον, ὑψηλῆς στέγης
στῦλον ποδήρη, μονογενὲς τέκνον πατρὶ
καὶ γῆν φανεῖσαν ναυτίλοις παρ' ἐλπίδα. 890
τοιοῖσδέ τοί νιν ἀξιῶ προσφθέγμασιν. 894
φθόνος δ' ἀπέστω· πολλὰ γὰρ τὰ πρὶν κακὰ 895
ἠνειχόμεσθα· νῦν δέ μοι, φίλον κάρα,
ἔκβαιν' ἀπήνης τῆσδε, μὴ χαμαὶ τιθεὶς
τὸν σὸν πόδ', ὦναξ, Ἰλίου πορθήτορα.
δμωιαί, τί μέλλεθ', αἷς ἐπέσταλται τέλος
πέδον κελεύθου στρωννύναι πετάσμασιν; 900

875 *καταρράψειεν* Scaliger: *καταρρίψειεν* codd. **880** *κλάβας* f. **891** sqq. *κάλλιστον ἦμαρ εἰσιδεῖν ἐκ χείματος,* | *ὁδοιπόρωι διψῶντι πηγαῖον ῥέος·* | *τερπνὸν δὲ τἀναγκαῖον ἐκφυγεῖν ἅπαν* delevit H., vv. 886—893 eiecerat Dindorf. **894** *τοί νιν* Schuetz: *τοίνυν* codd. **898** *ἄναξ* f | *πορθήτορος* Valckenaer ad Eur. *Phoen.* 1518.

Of danger on two scores,—thy jeopardy
At Troy, and fear of popular tumult hatching
Plots in the lack of master, as 'tis common
When the man's down the more to trample on him:
Under which showing lies no trace of guile.
For me, the gushing fountains of my tears
Are e'en dried up, there's not a drop now left;
And my late-rested eyes have suffered hurt
From weeping o'er the lanterns lit for thee
That still were unregarded. If I slept,
The puniest whining of a pulsing gnat
Would rouse me from beholding in my dreams
More accidents to thee than could befall
Within the time that was my bedfellow.
Now, after all this borne, with heart unpined
I hail my lord, safe watchdog of the fold,
Main forestay of the ship, firm-footed pillar
Bearing the roof up, sole-born child vouchsafed
To father, to the wave-tossed seaman, land!
From these my honouring words of courtesy
Envy keep far! The sorrows formerly
Are plenty we have suffered.—Now, dear my lord,
Descend,—but set not on the humble ground
Thy princely foot, this trampler upon Troy.—
Come, women, your best haste, perform your office;
Pave the triumphal path with tapestry!

εὐθὺς γενέσθω πορφυρόστρωτος πόρος,
ἐς δῶμ᾽ ἄελπτον ὡς ἂν ἡγῆται δίκη.
τὰ δ᾽ ἄλλα φροντὶς οὐχ ὕπνωι νικωμένη
θήσει δικαίως, σὺν θεοῖς, θυμάρμενα.
ΑΓ. Λήδας γένεθλον, δωμάτων ἐμῶν φύλαξ, 905
ἀπουσίαι μὲν εἶπας εἰκότως ἐμῆι·
μακρὰν γὰρ ἐξέτεινας· ἀλλ᾽ ἐναισίμως
αἰνεῖν, παρ᾽ ἄλλων χρὴ τόδ᾽ ἔρχεσθαι γέρας.
καὶ τἄλλα μὴ γυναικὸς ἐν τρόποις ἐμὲ
ἅβρυνε, μηδὲ βαρβάρου φωτὸς δίκην 910
χαμαιπετὲς βόαμα προσχάνηις ἐμοί,
μηδ᾽ εἵμασι στρώσασ᾽ ἐπίφθονον πόρον
τίθει· θεούς τοι τοῖσδε τιμαλφεῖν χρεών,
ἐν ποικίλοις δὲ θνητὸν ὄντα κάλλεσιν
βαίνειν ἐμοὶ μὲν οὐδαμῶς ἄνευ φόβου. 915
λέγω κατ᾽ ἄνδρα, μὴ θεόν, σέβειν ἐμέ.
χωρὶς ποδοψήστρων τε καὶ τῶν ποικίλων
κληδὼν ἀυτεῖ· καὶ τὸ μὴ κακῶς φρονεῖν
θεοῦ μέγιστον δῶρον· ὀλβίσαι δὲ χρὴ
βίον τελευτήσαντ᾽ ἐν εὐεστοῖ φίληι. 920
εἶπον τάδ᾽ ὡς πράσσοιμ᾽ ἂν εὐθαρσὴς ἐγώ.
ΚΛ. καὶ μὴν τόδ᾽ εἰπέ, μὴ παρὰ γνώμην, ἐμοί—
ΑΓ. γνώμην μὲν ἴσθι μὴ διαφθεροῦντ᾽ ἐμέ.
ΚΛ. ηὔξω θεοῖς δείσας ἂν ὧδ᾽ ἔρξειν τάδε;
ΑΓ. εἴπερ τις εἰδώς γ᾽ εὖ τόδ᾽ ἐξεῖπεν τέλος. 925
ΚΛ. τί δ᾽ ἂν δοκεῖ σοι Πρίαμος, εἰ τάδ᾽ ἤνυσεν;

---

904 θυμάρμενα H.: εἱμαρμένα codd. **921** εἶπον τάδ᾽ ὡς Weil: εἰ πάντα δ᾽ ὡς codd. **924** ἔρξειν H.: ἔρδειν codd. **925** ἐξεῖπεν Auratus: ἐξεῖπον codd. **926** δοκεῖ Stanley: δοκῆ (δοκῆι) codd.

Straight let a purple road be laid, and so
Let Justice lead him to his undreamed home!
The rest in fashion just with Heaven's consent
Vigilance awake shall order to content.

AGAMEMNON.

Offspring of Leda, guardian of my house,
Thy speech befits our absence,—its proportion
Having been lengthened; but becoming praise,
That is a tribute should proceed from others.
Moreover, womanize me thus no more,
Nor fawn me, as I were an Eastern wight,
With grovelling Oes and clamour; neither strew
Robes on the earth, to call down jealousy.
These are the glorious honours that belong
To Gods; but human feet on broideries—
'Tis in my conscience fearful. Let your homage
Yield to me not the measure of a God,
But of a man; the sound on Rumour's tongue
Rings different far of *mats* and *broideries.*
A modest mind's the greatest gift of Heaven.
The name *felicity*'s to keep till men
Have made an end in blessing.—I have said
How I will act herein to feel no dread.

CLYT. Tell me now, of your honest mind,—

AGAM. My mind
Is fixed, and shall not shake.

CLYT. —in hour of peril
Would you have made performance of this act
A promised vow to Heaven?

AGAM. Aye, had advised
Authority prescribed that holy service.

CLYT. So; and what think you Priamus had done
If this achievement had been his?

ΑΓ. ἐν ποικίλοις ἂν κάρτα μοι βῆναι δοκεῖ.
ΚΛ. μή νυν τὸν ἀνθρώπειον αἰδεσθῆις ψόγον.
ΑΓ. φήμη γε μέντοι δημόθρους μέγα σθένει.
ΚΛ. ὁ δ' ἀφθόνητός γ' οὐκ ἐπίζηλος πέλει. 930
ΑΓ. οὔτοι γυναικός ἐστιν ἱμείρειν μάχης.
ΚΛ. τοῖς δ' ὀλβίοις γε καὶ τὸ νικᾶσθαι πρέπει.
ΑΓ. ἦ καὶ σὺ νίκην τήνδε δήριος τίεις;
ΚΛ. πιθοῦ· κρατεῖς μέντοι παρεὶς ἑκὼν ἐμοί.
ΑΓ. ἀλλ' εἰ δοκεῖ σοι ταῦθ', ὑπαί τις ἀρβύλας 935
λύοι τάχος, πρόδουλον ἔμβασιν ποδός,
καὶ τοῖσδέ μ' ἐμβαίνονθ' ἁλουργέσιν θεῶν
μή τις πρόσωθεν ὄμματος βάλοι φθόνος·
πολλὴ γὰρ αἰδὼς δωματοφθορεῖν ποσὶν
φθείροντα πλοῦτον ἀργυρωνήτους θ' ὑφάς. 940
τοὐμὸν μὲν οὕτω· τὴν ξένην δὲ πρευμενῶς
τήνδ' ἐσκόμιζε· τὸν κρατοῦντα μαλθακῶς
θεὸς πρόσωθεν εὐμενῶς προσδέρκεται·
ἑκὼν γὰρ οὐδεὶς δουλίωι χρῆται ζυγῶι,
αὕτη δὲ πολλῶν χρημάτων ἐξαίρετον 945
ἄνθος, στρατοῦ δώρημ', ἐμοὶ ξυνέσπετο.
ἐπεὶ δ' ἀκούειν σοῦ κατέστραμμαι τάδε,
εἶμ' ἐς δόμων μέλαθρα πορφύρας πατῶν.
ΚΛ. ἔστιν θάλασσα, τίς δέ νιν κατασβέσει;
τρέφουσα πολλῆς πορφύρας ἰσάργυρον 950
κηκῖδα παγκαίνιστον, εἱμάτων βαφάς·

---

928 *αἰδεσθεὶς* f, *αἰδεσθῆς* h. **934** *κρατεῖς…παρείς γ'* Weil, *γ'* del. Wecklein: *κράτος…πάρες γ'* codd. **939** *δωματοφθορεῖν* Schuetz: *σωματοφθορεῖν* codd. **941** *τοὐμὸν* Emperius: *τούτων* codd. **950** *ἰσάργυρον* Salmasius: *εἰς ἄργυρον* codd.

AGAM. Oh, he
Had marched upon embroidered tapestry,
I make no doubt.

CLYT. For *human* censure then
Have never a scruple.

AGAM. Yet the tongues of men
Are potent.

CLYT. He that moves no jealousy
Lies beneath envying.

AGAM. 'Tis not womanly
To thirst for contest!

CLYT. But *felicity*
Is graced in being conquered.

AGAM. And *thine* eyes,
Do *they* account such 'conquest' as a prize?

CLYT. O waive the right and yield! Of your own will
Choose to be vanquished, you are victor still.

AGAM. Well, if you must, let presently be loosed
The shoes that do the service of my feet.

[*A slave unlooses his shoes.*

And as they tread these purple things, I pray,
No jealous eye may strike me from afar!
I have much conscience to be prodigal
In squandering Wealth of silver-purchased woofs.
Thus much for me:—now lead this damsel in

[*Showing Cassandra.*

With kindliness; the eye of Heaven regards
A gentle master with benignity:
None wears the slave's yoke of his will, and she
Comes by the army's tribute in my train
As rarest blossom out of all our spoil.
—So then, being bound and subject to thy pleasure,
Trampling upon purples I will go.

[*He proceeds slowly on the purple path towards the palace.*

CLYT. There is the sea—shall any stanch it up?—
Still breeding, for its worth of silver weight,
Abundant stain, freshly renewable,

οἶκος δ' ὑπάρχει τῶνδε σὺν θεοῖς, ἄναξ,
ἔχειν· πένεσθαι δ' οὐκ ἐπίσταται δόμος.
πολλῶν πατησμὸν δ' εἱμάτων ἂν ηὐξάμην,
δόμοισι προυνεχθέντος ἐν χρηστηρίοις 955
ψυχῆς κόμιστρα τῆσδε μηχανωμένηι.
ῥίζης γὰρ οὔσης φυλλὰς ἵκετ' ἐς δόμους,
σκιὰν ὑπερτείνασα σειρίου κυνός.
καὶ σοῦ μολόντος δωματῖτιν ἑστίαν,
θάλπος μὲν ἐν χειμῶνι σημαίνει μολόν· 960
ὅταν δὲ τεύχηι Ζεύς γ' ἀπ' ὄμφακος πικρᾶς
οἶνον, τότ' ἤδη ψῦχος ἐν δόμοις πέλει
ἀνδρὸς τελείου δῶμ' ἐπιστρωφωμένου.
Ζεῦ Ζεῦ τέλειε, τὰς ἐμὰς εὐχὰς τέλει·
μέλοι δέ τοι σοὶ τῶνπερ ἂν μέλληις τελεῖν. 965

στρ. α'. ΧΟ. τίπτε μοι τόδ' ἔμπεδως
δεῖμα προστατήριον
καρδίας τερασκόπου ποτᾶται,
μαντιπολεῖ δ' ἀκέλευστος ἄμισθος ἀοιδά,
οὐδ' ἀποπτύσας δίκαν 970
δυσκρίτων ὀνειράτων,
θάρσος εὐπειθὲς ἵζει
φρενὸς φίλον θρόνον; χρόνος δ' ἐπεὶ
πρυμνησίων ξυνεμβολὰς
ψαμμὰς ἀκτὰ παρή- 975
φησεν, εὖθ' ὑπ' Ἴλιον
ὦρτο ναυβάτας στρατός.

---

954 δ' εἱμάτων Canter: δειμάτων codd. **956** μηχανωμένηι Abresch: μηχανωμένης codd. **960** σημαίνει Karsten: σημαίνεις codd. | μολόν H. Voss: μολών codd. **961** γ' ἀπ' Stanley: τάπ' f, τ' ἄπ' h. **963** ἐπιστρωφωμένου Victorius: ἐπιστρεφωμένου f, ἐπιστροφωμένου h. **967** δεῖγμα f. **972** εὐπειθὲς Jacob: εὐπιθὲς codd. | ἵζει Scaliger: ἵξει vel ἴξει codd. **974** ξυνεμβολὰς H.: ξυνεμβόλοις codd. **975** sq. ψαμμὰς H. (ψαμμὶς H. L. Ahrens): ψαμμίας codd. | ἀκτὰ (vel ἀγὰ) H. L. Ahrens: ἀκάτα f, ἀκάτας h | παρήφησεν H.: παρήβησεν codd.

For purpling robes withal: nay, Heaven be praised,
The house, my lord, affords us plenty such;
'Tis not acquainted yet with penury.
I had vowed the trampling of a thousand robes,
Had the oracles enjoined it when I sought
Means for recovery of a life so precious!
Still from the living root the mantling green
Against the Dog-star spreads a leafy screen,—
So thou returning to thine hearth and home,
Warmth as in winter cries *Behold me come!*
Aye and when mellowing Zeus makes ripe and sweet
Wine from the young grape's bitter, cool in heat
Reigns within walls where moves the man complete:—

[*As Agamemnon goes in.*

O Zeus Completer, now complete my prayer,
Completion of thy plans be now thy care!

[*Exit.*

CHORUS.

I 1.

1st strophe.

Still not shifting:—wherefore yet
Hovereth so persistent set
Before my boding heart this haunting fear?
While ever in mine ear
Music unbid sounds a prophetic drone:
What ails me that I cannot say,
As to a riddling dream, '*Away!*'
And seat Assurance firm upon my bosom's throne?

The time is past, and fully past,
  When seaward from the sandy shore
  Came following home with furrowed score
The long ropes' mooring-cast,
When from the land our gathered host
Loosed for the war and Ilium's coast.

ἀντ. α'. πεύθομαι δ' ἀπ' ὀμμάτων
νόστον, αὐτόμαρτυς ὤν·
τὸν δ' ἄνευ λύρας ὅμως ὑμνῳδεῖ 980
θρῆνον Ἐρινύος αὐτοδίδακτος ἔσωθεν
θυμός, οὐ τὸ πᾶν ἔχων
ἐλπίδος φίλον θράσος.
σπλάγχνα δ' οὔτοι ματάιζει,
πρὸς ἐνδίκοις φρεσὶν τελεσφόροις 985
δίναις κυκώμενον κέαρ.
εὔχομαι δ' ἐξ ἐμᾶς
ἐλπίδος ψύθη πεσεῖν
ἐς τὸ μὴ τελεσφόρον.

στρ. β'. μάλα γάρ τοι τᾶς πολλᾶς ὑγιείας 990
ἀκόρεστον τέρμα. νόσος γὰρ
γείτων ὁμότοιχος ἐρείδει·
καὶ πότμος εὐθυπορῶν
ἀνδρὸς ἔπαισεν < ἄφνω
δυστυχίας πρὸς > ἄφαντον ἕρμα.
καὶ πρὸ μέν τι χρημάτων 995
κτησίων ὄκνος βαλὼν
σφενδόνας ἀπ' εὐμέτρου—
οὐκ ἔδυ πρόπας δόμος
πημονᾶς γέμων ἄγαν,

---

980 *ὅμως* Auratus: *ὅπως* codd. **981** *Ἐρινύος* Porson: *ἐριννὺς* codd. **986** *κυκώμενον* H.: *κυκλούμενον* codd. **988** *ψύθη* Stephanus: *ψύδη* codd. **991** *γὰρ* <*ἀεὶ*> Blomfield. **994** *ἄφνω πολλάκι δὴ πρὸς* postea *ἄφνω δυστυχίας* lacunae explendae causa supplevit H. L. Ahrens. **995** *πρὸ μέν τι* Enger: *τὸ μὲν πρὸ* codd. **999** *πημονᾶς* Victorius: *πημονὰς* codd.

I 2.

1st antistrophe.

Now by mine own eyes I learn,
Mine own witness, their return;
Yet none the less my soul within me still
With all-unprompted skill
Dolorous her descant endless doth intone,
Murmuring in the dismal gloom
Dirge of angry Spirits' doom,
And cannot call sweet Hope's fair confidence her own.
And Truth is in this troubled sea;
  The heart within my bosom whirled
  Is tossed with Omen, dashes hurled
Ashore on Verity!—
God send that all may false my thought
And be to unfulfilment brought!

II 1.

2nd strophe.

Health, to largeness growing, will not rest
Safe within limit; yet the verge is pressed
  By neighbour Sickness, one thin wall between:
Ships in full career and fates alike
In prosperous weather unawares will strike
  Upon a reef unseen.
Yet if but Caution scrupulous fling
Wealth by the board with timely swing
Of Measure's tempered sling,—
With harm-fraught overcharge unfilled,
No foundering of the fabric's build;

οὐδ' ἐπόντισε σκάφος· 1000
πολλά τοι δόσις ἐκ Διὸς ἀμφιλαφής τε καὶ ἐξ ἀλόκων ἐπετειᾶν
νῆστιν ἤλασεν νόσον.

ἀντ. β'. τὸ δ' ἐπὶ γᾶν πεσὸν ἅπαξ θανάσιμον
πρόπαρ ἀνδρὸς μέλαν αἷμα τίς ἂν 1005
πάλιν ἀγκαλέσαιτ' ἐπαείδων;
οὐδὲ τὸν ὀρθοδαῆ
τῶν φθιμένων ἀνάγειν
Ζεὺς ἀπέπαυσεν ἐπ' ἀβλαβείαι;
εἰ δὲ μὴ τεταγμένα 1010
μοῖρα μοῖραν ἐκ θεῶν
εἶργε μὴ πλέον φέρειν,
προφθάσασα καρδία
γλῶσσαν ἂν τάδ' ἐξέχει·
νῦν δ' ὑπὸ σκότωι βρέμει, 1015
θυμαλγής τε καὶ οὐδὲν ἐπελπομέ-
να ποτὲ καίριον ἐκτολυπεύσειν
ζωπυρουμένας φρενός.

ΚΛ. εἴσω κομίζου καὶ σύ, Κασάνδραν λέγω·
ἐπεί σ' ἔθηκε Ζεὺς ἀμηνίτως δόμοις 1020
κοινωνὸν εἶναι χερνίβων, πολλῶν μετὰ
δούλων σταθεῖσαν κτησίου βωμοῦ πέλας,
ἔκβαιν' ἀπήνης τῆσδε, μηδ' ὑπερφρόνει.
καὶ παῖδα γάρ τοι φασὶν Ἀλκμήνης ποτὲ
πραθέντα τλῆναι δουλίας μάζης βίαι. 1025

1003 *ἤλασεν* Schuetz: *ὤλεσεν* codd. **1004** *πεσὸν* Auratus: *πεσόνθ'* codd.
1009 *ἀπέπαυσεν* Hartung: *αὔτ' ἔπαυσ'* codd. | *ἐπ' αὐλαβειαι* f, *ἐπ' ἀβλαβείαι γε* h.
1025 *δουλείας...βία* f (*καὶ ζυγῶν θίγειν βίαι* h).

The walls ride out the perilous day;
Largess of Heaven with ample yield
From one year's furrowing of the field
Shall forthwith drive the fasting plague away.

II 2.

2nd antistrophe.

Aye, but on the earth let mortal fall
A man's red lifeblood, who shall then recall
With art of warbling verse the life once dropt?
One there was that had that proper skill
To raise up from the dead, but hindered will
Of Zeus the wizard stopped.
Appointed portions God-ordained
Curb each other, each refrained
From undue vantage gained;
Else to the light, outstripping tongue,
Heart of her own self all had flung,
That now frets passioning in the dark,
Frenzied, without all hope to find
In mazes of the fevered mind
One thread of help, one clew to reach her mark.

Enter CLYTAEMNESTRA.

CLYT. Get thee within, thou also, thou, Cassandra:
Since God hath mercifully appointed thee
To take thy place among our troop of slaves
By the altar of Possession, there to stand
Partaker in our holy laving-water,
Come step down from the wain and be not proud;
Alcmena's own son condescended once,
They say, to bondage, spite of the slave's fare.

εἰ δ' οὖν ἀνάγκη τῆσδ' ἐπιρρέποι τύχης,
ἀρχαιοπλούτων δεσποτῶν πολλὴ χάρις·
οἳ δ' οὔποτ' ἐλπίσαντες ἤμησαν καλῶς,
ὠμοί τε δούλοις πάντα καὶ παρὰ στάθμην.
ἔχεις παρ' ἡμῶν οἷάπερ νομίζεται. 1030
ΧΟ. σοί τοι λέγουσα παύεται σαφῆ λόγον.
ἐντὸς δ' ἂν οὖσα μορσίμων ἀγρευμάτων
πείθοι' ἄν, εἰ πείθοι'· ἀπειθοίης δ' ἴσως.
ΚΛ. ἀλλ' εἴπερ ἐστὶ μὴ χελιδόνος δίκην
ἀγνῶτα φωνὴν βάρβαρον κεκτημένη, 1035
ἔσω φρενῶν λέγουσα πείθω νιν λόγωι.
ΧΟ. ἕπου· τὰ λῶιστα τῶν παρεστώτων λέγει.
πιθοῦ λιποῦσα τόνδ' ἁμαξήρη θρόνον.
ΚΛ. οὔτοι θυραίαν τήνδ' ἐμοὶ σχολὴν πάρα
τρίβειν· τὰ μὲν γὰρ ἑστίας μεσομφάλου 1040
ἕστηκεν ἤδη μῆλα πρὸς σφαγὰς πάρος,
ὡς οὔποτ' ἐλπίσασι τήνδ' ἕξειν χάριν.
σὺ δ' εἴ τι δράσεις τῶνδε, μὴ σχολὴν τίθει·
εἰ δ' ἀξυνήμων οὖσα μὴ δέχηι λόγον,
σὺ δ' ἀντὶ φωνῆς φράζε καρβάνωι χερί. 1045
ΧΟ. ἑρμηνέως ἔοικεν ἡ ξένη τοροῦ
δεῖσθαι· τρόπος δὲ θηρὸς ὡς νεαιρέτου.
ΚΛ. ἦ μαίνεταί γε καὶ κακῶν κλύει φρενῶν,
ἥτις λιποῦσα μὲν πόλιν νεαίρετον
ἥκει, χαλινὸν δ' οὐκ ἐπίσταται φέρειν, 1050
πρὶν αἱματηρὸν ἐξαφρίζεσθαι μένος.
οὐ μὴν πλέω ῥίψασ' ἀτιμασθήσομαι.

1029 παραστάθμων f. **1030** ἕξεις Auratus. **1032** δ' ἀλοῦσα C. G. Haupt. **1038** πιθοῦ Blomfield: πείθου codd. **1039** σχολὴν Dobree: σχολῇ codd. **1041** πάρος Musgrave: πυρός codd.

And should that portion be assigned by force,
At least there is much comfort in a master
Whose wealth is ancient heritage; your sudden harvesters
Are still excessive to their slaves and harsh.
Expect from us our usage customary.

ELDER *to* CASSANDRA.

She pauses for thee:—damsel, it was plain,
To thee.—Being taken in the toils of Fate,
Be swayed an if thou wilt; perhaps thou wilt not.

CLYT. Well, if she be not, like a cheeping swallow,
Possessed of some unknown outlandish tongue,
My words must penetrate and speak persuasion.

ELDER. Go with her; 'tis well as may be, what she saith;
Be ruled, and leave thy session in this carriage.

CLYT. I have no leisure to be tarrying here
Abroad; already by the central hearth
The beasts are waiting for the sacrifice,
Thank-offering for our so unhoped-for joy:
Thou then, if aught herein
Thou wilt, make no delays; or if thou hast
No speech or understanding, then let e'en
Thine uncouth hand make signal.

ELDER. An interpreter,
Methinks, the lady needs; her ways are as
A wild creature's made captive.

CLYT. Sooth, she is mad,
And swayed by some curst mood, when she hath left
A land made captive thus, yet cannot brook
To endure the bridle till she first foam off
Her passionate rage in blood.—But I'll not waste
More words to be disdained.

[*She flings in.*

ΧΟ. ἐγὼ δ', ἐποικτίρω γάρ, οὐ θυμώσομαι·
ἴθ', ὦ τάλαινα, τόνδ' ἐρημώσασ' ὄχον,
εἴκουσ' ἀνάγκηι τῆιδε καίνισον ζυγόν. 1055

ΚΑΣΑΝΔΡΑ.

στρ. α'. ὀτοτοτοτοῖ ποποῖ δᾶ.
ὤπολλον ὤπολλον.
ΧΟ. τί ταῦτ' ἀνωτότυξας ἀμφὶ Λοξίου;
οὐ γὰρ τοιοῦτος ὥστε θρηνητοῦ τυχεῖν.

ἀντ. α'. ΚΑ. ὀτοτοτοτοῖ ποποῖ δᾶ. 1060
ὤπολλον ὤπολλον.
ΧΟ. ἣ δ' αὖτε δυσφημοῦσα τὸν θεὸν καλεῖ
οὐδὲν προσήκοντ' ἐν γόοις παραστατεῖν.

στρ. β'. ΚΑ. Ἄπολλον Ἄπολλον
ἀγυιᾶτ' ἀπόλλων ἐμός· 1065
ἀπώλεσας γὰρ οὐ μόλις τὸ δεύτερον.
ΧΟ. χρήσειν ἔοικεν ἀμφὶ τῶν αὑτῆς κακῶν.
μένει τὸ θεῖον δουλίαι περ ἐν φρενί.

ἀντ. β'. ΚΑ. Ἄπολλον Ἄπολλον
ἀγυιᾶτ' ἀπόλλων ἐμός. 1070
ἆ ποῖ ποτ' ἤγαγές με; πρὸς ποίαν στέγην;
ΧΟ. πρὸς τὴν Ἀτρειδῶν. εἰ σὺ μὴ τόδ' ἐννοεῖς,
ἐγὼ λέγω σοι· καὶ τάδ' οὐκ ἐρεῖς ψύθη.
ΚΑ. [ἆ ἆ]

1055 εἴκουσ' Robortellus: ἑκοῦσ' M. **1068** περ ἐν Schuetz: παρ' ἐν M.
1074 ἆ ἆ omittunt f h.

ELDER. And I feel rather
Pity and will not be anger'd: come, sad lady,
Leave thy carriage void; yield to necessity
And take this yoke upon thee.

I 1.

CASS. O woe, woe, woe, O Earth!
Apollo, O Apollo!

1st strophe.

ELDER. How now?
What means this in Apollo's case? His nature
Is not to have dirges for him.

I 2.

CASS. O woe, woe, woe, O Earth!
Apollo, O Apollo!

1st antistrophe.

ELDER. There again,
Crying upon Apollo thus, when grief
Is profanation to his presence.

II 1.

CASS. Apollo, O Apollo!
Thou God of Ways, Apollo mine, Destroying name,
Proved on me in verity this second time!

2nd strophe.

ELDER. She will be prophesying of her own distresses;
The spirit abides yet though the mind be slaved.

II 2.

CASS. Apollo, O Apollo!
Thou God of Ways, Apollo mine, Destroying name,
Whither hast thou made my way! what House is this!

2nd antistrophe.

ELDER. The Atridae's; if you understand not that,
Learn it of me; you shall not find it false.

στρ. γ'. μισόθεον μὲν οὖν, πολλὰ συνίστορα 1075
αὐτοφόνα κακὰ καὶ ἄρταμα,
ἀνδροσφαγεῖον καὶ πεδορραντήριον.
ΧΟ. ἔοικεν εὔρις ἡ ξένη κυνὸς δίκην
εἶναι, ματεύει δ' ὧν ἀνευρήσει φόνον.

ἀντ. γ'. ΚΑ. μαρτυρίοισι γὰρ τοῖσδ' ἐπιπείθομαι· 1080
κλαιόμενα τάδε βρέφη σφαγὰς
ὀπτάς τε σάρκας πρὸς πατρὸς βεβρωμένας.
ΧΟ. τὸ μὲν κλέος σοῦ μαντικὸν πεπυσμένοι
ἦμεν, προφήτας δ' οὔτινας ματεύομεν.

στρ. δ'. ΚΑ. ἰὼ πόποι, τί ποτε μήδεται; 1085
τί τόδε νέον ἄχος μέγα
μέγ' ἐν δόμοισι τοῖσδε μήδεται κακὸν
ἄφερτον φίλοισιν,
δυσίατον; ἀλκὰ δ'
ἑκὰς ἀποστατεῖ. 1090
ΧΟ. τούτων ἄϊδρίς εἰμι τῶν μαντευμάτων.
ἐκεῖνα δ' ἔγνων· πᾶσα γὰρ πόλις βοᾶι.

ἀντ. δ'. ΚΑ. ἰὼ τάλαινα, τόδε γὰρ τελεῖς;
τὸν ὁμοδέμνιον πόσιν
λουτροῖσι φαιδρύνασα—πῶς φράσω τέλος; 1095
τάχος γὰρ τόδ' ἔσται,
προτείνει δὲ χεὶρ ἐκ
χερὸς ὀρεγομένα.
ΧΟ. οὔπω ξυνῆκα· νῦν γὰρ ἐξ αἰνιγμάτων
ἐπαργέμοισι θεσφάτοις ἀμηχανῶ. 1100

1076 *καὶ ἄρταμα* (vel *ἀρταμάς*) H. (*κἀρτάμου* Emperius, *κἄρταμα* H. L. Ahrens): *καρτάναι* codd. **1077** *ἀνδροσφαγεῖον* Dobree (*ἀνδροσφάγιον* Casaubon): *ἀνδρὸσ σφάγιον* M. **1079** *ἀνευρήσει* Porson: *ἂν εὑρήσῃ* M. **1080** *μαρτυρίοισι* Pauw: *μαρτυρίοισ* M | *τοῖσδ' ἐπιπείθομαι* Abresch: *τοῖσδε πεπείθομαι* M. **1083** *τὸ μὲν* H.: *ἦμεν* / *ἤμην* M.

III 1.

CASS. Nay, 'tis abominable! 't hath known within it
Murder unnatural, butchery, limbs dissevered—
A human shambles, floor with horror spersing!

3rd strophe.

ELDER. 'Tis a keen-scented hound; she hunts, she hunts,
And on this track will presently see killing.

III 2.

CASS. Ha!
There are the witnesses I build my trust on—
Yonder, behold there, babes for slaughter plaining,
Plaining for roasted flesh, a father's eating!

3rd antistrophe.

ELDER. Truly, we were acquainted with your fame
In soothsaying, but we seek no prophets here.

IV 1.

CASS. O God, what is this thing!
What awful, horrible thing!
Designed within these walls, what heinous act!
No art shall cure, nor love endure . . . .
And all help far aloof.

4th strophe.

ELDER. What she divines now is unknown to me;
The first I saw, because the whole city rings it.

IV 2.

CASS. O monster, wilt thou so!
The partner of thy bed,
After his laving—How declare the end?
'Tis near—apace with hurrying reach
Hand upon hand, it comes!

4th antistrophe.

ELDER. Beyond me still; dark riddle enough before;
Now 'tis obscure and purblind oracle.

στρ. ε΄. ΚΑ. ἒ ἒ παπαῖ παπαῖ,
τί τόδε φαίνεται;
ἦ δίκτυόν τί γ' Ἅιδου;
ἀλλ' ἄρκυς ἡ ξύνευνος, ἡ ξυναιτία
φόνου. στάσις δ' ἀκόρετος γένει 1105
κατολολυξάτω
θύματος λευσίμου.

ΧΟ. ποίαν Ἐρινὺν τήνδε δώμασιν κέληι
ἐπορθιάζειν; οὔ με φαιδρύνει λόγος.
ἐπὶ δὲ καρδίαν ἔδραμε κροκοβαφὴς 1110
σταγών, ἅτε καὶ δορὶ πτωσίμοις
ξυνανύτει βίου
δύντος αὐγαῖς. ταχεῖ-
α δ' ἄτα πέλει.

ἀντ. ε΄. ΚΑ. ἆ ἆ, ἰδοὺ ἰδού· 1115
ἄπεχε τῆς βοός·
τὸν ταῦρον ἐν πέπλοισιν
μελάγκερωι λαβοῦσα μηχανήματι
τύπτει· πίτνει δ' <ἐν> ἐνύδρωι τεύχει.
δολοφόνου λέβη- 1120
τος τύχαν σοι λέγω.

ΧΟ. οὐ κομπάσαιμ' ἂν θεσφάτων γνώμων ἄκρος
εἶναι, κακῶι δέ τωι προσεικάζω τάδε.
ἀπὸ δὲ θεσφάτων τίς ἀγαθὰ φάτις
βροτοῖς τέλλεται; κακῶν γὰρ διὰ 1125
πολυεπεῖς τέχναι
θεσπιωιδὸν φόβον
φέρουσιν μαθεῖν.

1105 ἀκόρετος Bothe: ἀκόρεστος M. **1111** δορὶ πτωσίμοις Casaubon: δορία πτώσιμος M. **1119** ἐν addidit Schuetz. **1125** τέλλεται Emperius: στέλλεται M | διαὶ Hermann.

V 1.

CASS. O Heavens, what should this be? Some devilish net? 5th strophe.
—But she's a net that shares the bed, that shares
Murder! Uplift, ye ravenous haunting Pack,
Your jubilant hymn for sacrifice, O damnable!

ELDER. Avenging Spirit to raise her triumph-shout
Over this House? The words appal my cheer.

VI 1.

The ruddy drops run yellow back to my heart,
Such pallor as when
Men faint of a mortal stroke, such pallor as times
With the sunset rays of life when the fatal end is nigh.

V 2.

CASS. Ah ware, beware, away! Keep clear of the Cow! 5th antistrophe.
The Bull . . . . . in cloak . . . . . with horned engine, see,
Felled! In a vessel of water prone he falls......
This is the tale of a Caldron's murderous treachery!

ELDER. I cannot boast to be a master-judge
Of oracles, but I spell some mischief here.

VI 2.

But when from divinations ever hath come
One message of good?
'Tis matter of evil still, some lesson of fear
Is ever the drift of all their multitudinous words.

στρ. ϛʹ. ΚΑ. ἰὼ ἰὼ ταλαίνας
κακόποτμοι τύχαι— 1130
τὸ γὰρ ἐμὸν θροῶ
πάθος ἐπεγχύδαν—
ποῖ δή με δεῦρο τὴν τάλαιναν ἤγαγες;
οὐδέν ποτ' εἰ μὴ ξυνθανουμένην. τί γάρ;

ΧΟ. φρενομανής τις εἶ θεοφόρητος, ἀμ- 1135
φὶ δ' αὑτᾶς θροεῖς
νόμον ἄνομον, οἷά τις ξουθὰ
ἀκόρετος βοᾶς, φεῦ,
ταλαίναις φρεσὶν
Ἴτυν Ἴτυν στένουσ' ἀμφιθαλῆ κακοῖς 1140
ἀηδὼν βίον.

ἀντ. ϛʹ. ΚΑ. ἰὼ ἰὼ λιγείας
μόρον ἀηδόνος·
περέβαλόν γέ οἱ
πτεροφόρον δέμας 1145
θεοὶ γλυκύν τ' αἰῶνα κλαυμάτων ἄτερ·
ἐμοὶ δὲ μίμνει σχισμὸς ἀμφήκει δορί.

ΧΟ. πόθεν ἐπισσύτους θεοφόρους ἔχεις
ματαίους δύας,
τὰ δ' ἐπίφοβα δυσφάτωι κλαγγᾶι 1150
μελοτυπεῖς ὁμοῦ τ' ὀρ-
θίοις ἐν νόμοις;
πόθεν ὅρους ἔχεις θεσπεσίας ὁδοῦ
κακορρήμονας;

1132 ἐπεγχύδαν H.: ἐπεγχέασα M. **1138** ἀκόρετος Ald.: ἀκόρεστος M. **1143** μόρον ἀηδόνος Hermann: ἀηδόνος μόρον M. **1144** περέβαλόν γέ οἱ Enger: περεβάλοντο γὰρ οἱ M. **1146** αἰῶνα γρ. m: ἀγῶνα M. **1148** θεοφόρους τ' M: corr. Hermann.

VII 1.

CASS. O sorrowful doom of me— 6th strophe.
Aye, *me*, for the bowl I crown
With mine own fate—Ah whither hast brought me, then,
Only to share, yes, only to share in death!

VIII 1.

CHORUS. Thou art brainsick, heaven-distraught,
For thine own case lamenting
In lawless measures, like the brown sad nightingale,
That *Ityn*, *Ityn* calleth still-unhushed through all
Her sorrow-plenished life.

VII 2.

CASS. Ah fate of the nightingale; 6th antistrophe.
Sweet singer, the Gods round her
Put wings, put life, save only for wailing, sweet;
For me 'tis cleaving soon with a two-edged blade!

VIII 2.

CHORUS. These wild and passionate throes,
Whence rush they on thee thronging?
Such terrors wherefore shape in uncouth dismal song,
Yet clarion-high? What is it guides thy boding lips
On their ill-uttering path?

στρ. ζ´. ΚΑ. ἰὼ γάμοι γάμοι Πάριδος ὀλέθριοι 1155
φίλων. ἰὼ Σκαμάνδρου πάτριον ποτόν·
τότε μὲν ἀμφὶ σὰς ἀϊόνας τάλαιν᾽
ἠνυτόμαν τροφαῖς·
νῦν δ᾽ ἀμφὶ Κωκυτόν τε κἀχερουσίους
ὄχθους ἔοικα θεσπωιδήσειν τάχα. 1160
ΧΟ. τί τόδε τορὸν ἄγαν ἔπος ἐφημίσω;
νεογνὸς ἀνθρώπων μάθοι.
πέπληγμαι δ᾽ ἅπερ δάκει φοινίωι
δυσαλγεῖ τύχαι μινυρὰ θρεομένας,
θραύματ᾽ ἐμοὶ κλύειν. 1165

ἀντ. ζ´. ΚΑ. ἰὼ πόνοι πόνοι πόλεος ὀλομένας
τὸ πᾶν. ἰὼ πρόπυργοι θυσίαι πατρὸς
πολυκανεῖς βοτῶν ποιονόμων· ἄκος δ᾽
οὐδὲν ἐπήρκεσαν
τὸ μὴ <οὐκ ἔχειν> πόλιν μὲν ὥσπερ οὖν ἔχει· 1170
ἐγὼ δὲ θερμόνους τάχ᾽ ἐμπελῶ βόλωι
ΧΟ. ἑπόμενα προτέροις τάδ᾽ ἐφημίσω,
καί τίς σε κακοφρονῶν τίθησι δαίμων ὑπερβαρὴς ἐμπίτνων
μελίζειν πάθη γοερὰ θανατοφόρα· 1175
τέρμα δ᾽ ἀμηχανῶ.

ΚΑ. καὶ μὴν ὁ χρησμὸς οὐκέτ᾽ ἐκ καλυμμάτων
ἔσται δεδορκὼς νεογάμου νύμφης δίκην,

1162 *νεογνὸς ἂν αἰων* Karsten. **1163** *ἅπερ* Franz: *ὑπὸ* f g, *ὑπαὶ* h | *δάκει* Hermann: *δήγματι* codd. **1164** *δυσαλγεῖ* Canter: *δυσαγγεῖ* codd. | *μινυρὰ* Schuetz: *μινύρα κακὰ* codd. **1170** *οὐκ ἔχειν* addidit Stadtmueller | *ἔχειν παθεῖν* f g, *ἔχει παθεῖν* h. **1171** *ἐμπελῶ βόλωι* H.: *ἐμπέδωι βαλῶ* codd., *ἐν πέδωι* Casaubon. **1172** *ἐπεφημίσω* Paley. **1173** *κακοφρονῶν* Schuetz: *κακοφρονεῖν* codd.

IX 1.

CASS. O bridal, bridal of Paris, ruin of home! 7th strophe.

Scamander river whereof my people drank!

By thy dear beaches once was I nursed and throve, but now

My place of prophecy is like to be

Cocytus and the shores of Acheron.

X 1.

CHORUS. Ah, what is this thou hast uttered all too plain!

A babe might understand .....

Compassion wounds me in the flesh with fangs

At thy sore agonizing plaintive wail,

Harrowing my soul to hear.

IX 2.

CASS. O labour, labour of Ilium utterly lost! 7th antistrophe.

O slaughter lavish of kine my father made

For her proud rampired walls! Yet it would not serve—
no cure;

Her case is even as it is, and I

Shall in a fever soon dash into the snare.

X 2.

CHORUS. Still in the former strain thine utterance goes;

It is some Spirit malign

Whose heavy spite upon thee tunes thy song

To things of dole and sorrow, telling of death;

And the end I cannot see.

CASS. No more now with a newly-wedded bride's

Dim vision from a veil shall peep my oracle—

λαμπρὸς δ' ἔοικεν ἡλίου πρὸς ἀντολὰς
πνέων ἐσάιξειν, ὥστε κύματος δίκην 1180
κλύζειν πρὸς αὐγὰς τοῦδε πήματος πολὺ
μεῖζον· φρενώσω δ' οὐκέτ' ἐξ αἰνιγμάτων.
καὶ μαρτυρεῖτε συνδρόμως ἴχνος κακῶν
ῥινηλατούσηι τῶν πάλαι πεπραγμένων.
τὴν γὰρ στέγην τήνδ' οὔποτ' ἐκλείπει χορὸς 1185
ξύμφθογγος οὐκ εὔφωνος· οὐ γὰρ εὖ λέγει.
καὶ μὴν πεπωκώς γ', ὡς θρασύνεσθαι πλέον,
βρότειον αἷμα κῶμος ἐν δόμοις μένει,
δύσπεμπτος ἔξω, συγγόνων Ἐρινύων.
ὑμνοῦσι δ' ὕμνον δώμασιν προσήμεναι 1190
πρώταρχον ἄτην· ἐν μέρει δ' ἀπέπτυσαν
εὐνὰς ἀδελφοῦ, τῶι πατοῦντι δυσμενεῖς.
ἥμαρτον, ἢ θηρῶ τι τοξότης τις ὥς;
ἢ ψευδόμαντίς εἰμι θυροκόπος φλέδων;
ἐκμαρτύρησον προυμόσας τό μ' εἰδέναι 1195
λόγωι παλαιὰς τῶνδ' ἁμαρτίας δόμων.

ΧΟ. καὶ πῶς ἂν ὅρκου πῆγμα γενναίως παγὲν
παιώνιον γένοιτο; θαυμάζω δέ σου,
πόντου πέραν τραφεῖσαν ἀλλόθρουν πόλιν
κυρεῖν λέγουσαν, ὥσπερ εἰ παρεστάτεις. 1200

ΚΑ. μάντις μ' Ἀπόλλων τῶιδ' ἐπέστησεν τέλει.

ΧΟ. μῶν καὶ θεός περ ἱμέρωι πεπληγμένος;

ΚΑ. προτοῦ μὲν αἰδὼς ἦν ἐμοὶ λέγειν τάδε.

ΧΟ. ἁβρύνεται γὰρ πᾶς τις εὖ πράσσων πλέον.

1180 ἐσάιξειν Bothe: ἐς ἥξειν codd. **1181** κλύζειν Auratus: κλύειν codd. **1193** θηρῶ Canter: τηρῶ codd., κυρῶ H. L. Ahrens. **1197** ὅρκου πῆγμα Auratus: ὅρκος πῆμα codd. **1202, 1203** inverso ordine praebent codd., transposuit Hermann.

I feel the spirit
Upon me rushing, like a mighty wind
To the sunrise blowing clear: now presently
Rolled up against the orient light shall wash
Disaster huger far! I'll monish you
No more in riddles; come, attest me, run
My pace now while I scent the traces out
Of acts done long ago.
Within these walls
There haunts a Quiring Band, that sings one tune,
But not sounds tuneful—'tis not sweet, their theme.
Aye, to more riotous courage well caroused
With human blood, within this House abides,
And will not be sent forth, a Rout of wassailers,
Kindred-Avengers, that besetting keep
Fast by the chambers, chanting; and their chant
Is Deadly Primal Sin:—anon they sicken,—
A Brother's bed their fierce abhorrence, cursing
The abuser—Have I missed the target now,
Or will you cry me aim? Am I indeed
Mere *babbler, knocker at the doors* with lies
And trickery? On your oath, confess the long
Bad history of this House my knowledge!

ELDER. Nay,
Let oath be ne'er so well and truly plighted,
It cannot medicine:—but I marvel at thee,
To have lived thy life beyond the seas, and yet
Of alien people to speak sure as though
Thou hadst been a witness present.

CASS. It was the seer
Apollo made me mistress of this power.

ELDER. His Godhead smitten with love?

CASS. I was ashamed,
The time was, to speak of it.

ELDER. Aye, brighter days
Make daintier niceness ever.

ΚΑ. ἀλλ' ἦν παλαιστὴς κάρτ' ἐμοὶ πνέων χάριν. 1205
ΧΟ. ἦ καὶ τέκνων εἰς ἔργον ἠλθέτην νόμωι;
ΚΑ. ξυναινέσασα Λοξίαν ἐψευσάμην.
ΧΟ. ἤδη τέχναισιν ἐνθέοις ἡιρημένη;
ΚΑ. ἤδη πολίταις πάντ' ἐθέσπιζον πάθη.
ΧΟ. πῶς δῆτ' ἄνατος ἦσθα Λοξίου κότωι; 1210
ΚΑ. ἔπειθον οὐδέν' οὐδέν, ὡς τάδ' ἤμπλακον.
ΧΟ. ἡμῖν γε μὲν δὴ πιστὰ θεσπίζειν δοκεῖς.
ΚΑ. ἰοὺ ἰού, ὢ ὢ κακά.
ὑπ' αὖ με δεινὸς ὀρθομαντείας πόνος
στροβεῖ ταράσσων φροιμίοις.... 1215
ὁρᾶτε τούσδε τοὺς δόμοις ἐφημένους
νέους, ὀνείρων προσφερεῖς μορφώμασιν;
παῖδες, θανόντες ὡσπερεὶ πρὸς τῶν φίλων,
χεῖρας κρεῶν πλήθοντες, οἰκείας βορᾶς,
σὺν ἐντέροις τε 'σπλάγχν', ἐποίκτιστον γέμος, 1220
πρέπουσ' ἔχοντες, ὧν πατὴρ ἐγεύσατο.
ἐκ τῶνδε ποινὰς φημὶ βουλεύειν τινὰ
λέοντ' ἄναλκιν ἐν λέχει στρωφώμενον,
οἰκουρόν, οἶμαι, τῶι μολόντι δεσπότηι
ἐμῶι· φέρειν γὰρ χρὴ τὸ δούλιον ζυγόν. 1225
νεῶν τ' ἄπαρχος Ἰλίου τ' ἀναστάτης
οὐκ οἶδεν οἷα γλῶσσα μισητῆς κυνὸς
λέξασα κἀκτείνασα φαιδρόνους, δίκην
ἄτης λαθραίου, τεύξεται κακῆι τύχηι.

1206 *ἠλθέτην* Elmsley: *ἦλθετον* codd. **1210** *ἄνατος* Canter: *ἄνακτος* codd. **1211** *οὐδέν'* Canter: *οὐδὲν* codd. **1215** *ἐφημένους* post *φροιμίοις* habent codd., eiecit Butler. **1224** *οἶμαι* Paley: *οἴμοι* codd. **1226** *νεῶν δ'* G. Voss | *ἔπαρχος* Canter. **1228** *κἀκτείνασα* Canter: *καὶ κτείνασα* codd.

CASS. O but he strove
Ardent with favour for me.
ELDER. And so in course
Came you to the act of kind?
CASS. I did consent
With Loxias, and then failed him.
ELDER. Being possessed
Already with divining spirit?
CASS. Already
I showed my own folk all that should befall them.
ELDER. Yet without suffering from Apollo's wrath?
CASS. After that sin I never might have credit.
ELDER. Thy art seems credible enough to us.

CASSANDRA *moaning*.

Oh, oh, oh, my pain . . . . . again comes on me
The agony of clear vision, racks me at first
With dizzying whirl . . . . . anguish . . . . .
There, see now
Those yonder, seated at the House . . . . . young forms
Like phantoms of a dream . . . . . children, as 'twere,
Slain by their own kindred . . . . . their hands filled
With flesh, familiar meat . . . . . aye, they show now
Visible,—the inward parts, a rueful burden,
Tasted of by their father!
For these things
Vengeance is plotted by a faint soft Lion,
Wallowing the while in bed,—forsooth to keep it
Warm and safe against the Master's coming!
My master—the slave's yoke must be endured.
High admiral, proud vanquisher of Troy,
He dreams not, he,
After the fawning speeches long drawn out
By lecherous hound's false tongue, what act it is
With smiling Ate's treachery she designs

τοιάδε τόλμα· θῆλυς ἄρσενος φονεὺς 1230
ἔστιν. τί νιν καλοῦσα δυσφιλὲς δάκος
τύχοιμ' ἄν; ἀμφίσβαιναν; ἢ Σκύλλαν τινὰ
οἰκοῦσαν ἐν πέτραισι, ναυτίλων βλάβην;
θύουσαν Ἅιδου μητέρ' ἄσπονδόν τ' Ἄρη
φίλοις πνέουσαν—ὡς δ' ἐπωλολύξατο, 1235
ἡ παντότολμος, ὥσπερ ἐν μάχης τροπῆι·
δοκεῖ δὲ χαίρειν νοστίμωι σωτηρίαι.
καὶ τῶνδ' ὅμοιον εἴ τι μὴ πείθω· τί γάρ;
τὸ μέλλον ἥξει. καὶ σύ μ' ἐν τάχει παρὼν
ἄγαν ἀληθόμαντιν οἰκτίρας ἐρεῖς. 1240
ΧΟ. τὴν μὲν Θυέστου δαῖτα παιδείων κρεῶν
ξυνῆκα καὶ πέφρικα, καὶ φόβος μ' ἔχει
κλύοντ' ἀληθῶς οὐδὲν ἐξῃκασμένα·
τὰ δ' ἄλλ' ἀκούσας ἐκ δρόμου πεσὼν τρέχω.
ΚΑ. Ἀγαμέμνονός σέ φημ' ἐπόψεσθαι μόρον. 1245
ΧΟ. εὔφημον, ὦ τάλαινα, κοίμησον στόμα.
ΚΑ. ἀλλ' οὔτι παιὼν τῶιδ' ἐπιστατεῖ λόγωι.
ΧΟ. οὔκ, εἴπερ ἔσται γ'· ἀλλὰ μὴ γένοιτό πως.
ΚΑ. σὺ μὲν κατεύχηι, τοῖς δ' ἀποκτείνειν μέλει.
ΧΟ. τίνος πρὸς ἀνδρὸς τοῦτ' ἄγος πορσύνεται; 1250
ΚΑ. ἦ κάρτα . . . . . παρεκόπης χρησμῶν ἐμῶν.
ΧΟ. τοῦ γὰρ τελοῦντος οὐ ξυνῆκα μηχανήν.
ΚΑ. καὶ μὴν ἄγαν γ' Ἕλλην' ἐπίσταμαι φάτιν.

1230 τόλμα H. L. Ahrens: τολμᾶ (τολμᾶι) codd. **1234** Ἄρη Franz (Ἄρην anon. ap. Blomfield): ἀρὰν codd. **1239** μ' ἐν Auratus: μὴν codd. **1240** ἄγαν Bothe: ἄγαν γ' codd. **1241** παιδίων codd.: corr. Schuetz. **1248** εἴπερ ἔσται Schuetz: εἰ παρέσται codd. **1250** ἄγος Auratus: ἄχος codd. **1251** κάρτ' ἄρ' ἂν παρεσκόπεις (παρεσκόπης) codd., κάρτα τἄρα παρεκόπης Hartung.

For deed in cursed hour! Such monstrous doing,—
The female slayer of the male! What beast
Most loathsome shall I call her? *Amphisbaena?*
—Or rather *Scylla,* dweller in the rocks,
Housed there for seaman's ruin! A Mother wild
With Hell's own bacchanal rage, whose heart breathes war
To the death against her own! With jubilant cry
The monster, how she shouted, as men's triumph
Shouts when the battle breaks,—while safe return
Would seem her gladness . . . . .
Credit me now or not,
'Tis all one; for what skills it? What must be
Will be; and you shall soon behold, and pity,
And call me all too true a prophetess.

ELDER. Thyestes' banquet on his children's flesh
I understand and shudder,—nothing feigned,
No fable, terrible truth; but for the rest
I lose the track and wander.

CASS. You shall see
The death of Agamemnon.

ELDER. Hush, good words!
Calm thine unhappy lips.

CASS. Nay, what offence?
There is none in presence here with *Healing* office,
In the case I tell of!

ELDER. Not if it is to be,
But Heaven avert it!

CASS. While you stand and pray
They are busy there with killing.

ELDER. What man's hand
Must bring this crime about?

CASS. O wide then truly
You have wandered from my warning!

ELDER. I cannot see
The means whereby the doer should compass it.

CASS. Yet am I well instructed in the tongue
Of Hellas,—all too well.

ΧΟ. καὶ γὰρ τὰ πυθόκραντα· δυσμαθῆ δ' ὅμως.

ΚΑ. παπαῖ, οἷον τὸ πῦρ· ἐπέρχεται δέ μοι. 1255

ὀτοτοῖ, Λύκει' Ἄπολλον, οἲ ἐγὼ ἐγώ.

αὕτη δίπους λέαινα συγκοιμωμένη

λύκωι λέοντος εὐγενοῦς ἀπουσίαι

κτενεῖ με τὴν τάλαιναν· ὡς δὲ φάρμακον

τεύχουσα κἀμοῦ μισθὸν ἐνθήσει κότωι 1260

ἐπεύχεται, θήγουσα φωτὶ φάσγανον,

ἐμῆς ἀγωγῆς ἀντιτείσασθαι φόνον.

τί δῆτ' ἐμαυτῆς καταγέλωτ' ἔχω τάδε,

καὶ σκῆπτρα καὶ μαντεῖα περὶ δέρηι στέφη;

σὲ μὲν πρὸ μοίρας τῆς ἐμῆς διαφθερῶ. 1265

ἴτ' ἐς φθόρον πέσοντ', ἐγὼ δ' ἅμ' ἕψομαι.

ἄλλην τιν' ἄτης ἀντ' ἐμοῦ πλουτίζετε.

ἰδοὺ δ' Ἀπόλλων αὐτὸς ἐκδύων ἐμὲ

χρηστηρίαν ἐσθῆτ', ἐποπτεύσας δέ με

κἀν τοῖσδε κόσμοις καταγελωμένην μετὰ 1270

φίλων ὑπ' ἐχθρῶν οὐ διχορρόπως μάτην—

καλουμένη δὲ "φοιτάς," ὡς ἀγύρτρια

πτωχός, τάλαινα, λιμοθνής, ἠνεσχόμην—

καὶ νῦν ὁ μάντις μάντιν ἐκπράξας ἐμὲ

ἀπήγαγ' ἐς τοιάσδε θανασίμους τύχας. 1275

βωμοῦ πατρῴου δ' ἀντ' ἐπίξηνον μένει,

θερμὸν κοπέντος φοινίωι προσφάγματι.

οὐ μὴν ἄτιμοί γ' ἐκ θεῶν τεθνήξομεν,

ἥξει γὰρ ἡμῶν ἄλλος αὖ τιμάορος,

μητροκτόνον φίτυμα, ποινάτωρ πατρός· 1280

1254 δυσμαθῆ Stephanus: δυσπαθῆ codd. **1257** δίπους Victorius: δίπλους codd. **1260** ἐνθήσειν (ν finali post adscripto) h | ποτῶι Auratus. **1266** ἐγὼ δ' Heath, ἅμ' ἕψομαι Hermann: ἀγαθῷ δ' ἀμείψομαι codd., πεσόντα θ' ὧδ' ἀμείψομαι Verrall. **1276** ἀντεπίξηνον codd. **1277** θερμὸν Schuetz: θερμῶι codd. | κοπέντος H.: κοπείσης codd.

ELDER. Why, so are the oracles
From Pytho, yet they are hard enough withal.

CASS. Ah! the fire, coming upon me ..... how it burns,
O Slayer Apollo, O!

[*Groaning.*

This human Lioness yonder couching with
A Wolf in absence of the generous Lion,
Will take my wretched life—as 'twere a poison
She were compounding, to the venomous brew
Vows she will add my wages,—while she whets
Her blade for man, vows for my bringing here
To take revenge in blood.
Why keep I then,
Only to be mockery of myself, these baubles—
Wands and prophetic wreaths about my neck?
You shall perish first before my hour:

[*She flings off the sacred symbols of her office and then tramples on them,—fillet and golden wand and gold-embroidered robe.*

So:
Lie there; go to perdition,—I shall follow:
Endow some other with your fatal Wealth!
—Why, 'tis Apollo that himself now strips
My prophet's raiment off—that even in this,
His livery, let his eyes behold me laughed,
By friends and foes indifferently, to scorn:
—I suffered, like a vagrant mountebank,
Like some poor starveling wretch, the name of *Wanderer*,—
And now the Seer hath made a seer of me
To bring me to this bloody end! Here waits,
Here for my father's altar waits a block,
Hot with the red stream from another's neck.
Yet shall we fall
Not unavenged of Heaven, for there shall come
A Champion of our cause, an Offspring born
To Mother's death and Father's recompense;

φυγὰς δ' ἀλήτης τῆσδε γῆς ἀπόξενος
κάτεισιν, ἄτας τάσδε θριγκώσων φίλοις·
ὀμώμοται γὰρ ὅρκος ἐκ θεῶν μέγας,
ἄξειν νιν ὑπτίασμα κειμένου πατρός.
τί δῆτ' ἐγὼ κάτοικτος ὧδ' ἀναστένω; 1285
ἐπεὶ τὸ πρῶτον εἶδον Ἰλίου πόλιν
πράξασαν ὡς ἔπραξεν, οἳ δ' εἷλον πόλιν
οὕτως ἀπαλλάσσουσιν ἐν θεῶν κρίσει,
ἰοῦσα πράξω, τλήσομαι τὸ κατθανεῖν.
Ἅιδου πύλας δὲ τάσδ' ἐγὼ προσεννέπω· 1290
ἐπεύχομαι δὲ καιρίας πληγῆς τυχεῖν,
ὡς ἀσφάδαστος, αἱμάτων εὐθνησίμων
ἀπορρυέντων, ὄμμα συμβάλω τόδε.

ΧΟ. ὦ πολλὰ μὲν τάλαινα, πολλὰ δ' αὖ σοφὴ
γύναι, μακρὰν ἔτεινας. εἰ δ' ἐτητύμως 1295
μόρον τὸν αὑτῆς οἶσθα, πῶς θεηλάτου
βοὸς δίκην πρὸς βωμὸν εὐτόλμως πατεῖς;

ΚΑ. οὐκ ἔστ' ἄλυξις, οὔ, ξένοι, χρόνωι πλέω.

ΧΟ. ὁ δ' ὕστατός γε τοῦ χρόνου πρεσβεύεται.

ΚΑ. ἥκει τόδ' ἦμαρ· σμικρὰ κερδανῶ φυγῆι. 1300

ΧΟ. ἀλλ' ἴσθι τλήμων οὖσ' ἀπ' εὐτόλμου φρενός.

ΚΑ. οὐδεὶς ἀκούει ταῦτα τῶν εὐδαιμόνων.

ΧΟ. ἀλλ' εὐκλεῶς τοι κατθανεῖν χάρις βροτῶι.

ΚΑ. ἰὼ πάτερ σοῦ σῶν τε γενναίων τέκνων.

1283 post **1289** habent codd., huc transtulit Hermann | *ἄραρε γὰρ ὅρκος ἐκ θεῶν μέγας* Cramer *Anecd. Ox.* I p. 88. **1285** *κάτοικτος* Scaliger: *κάτοικος* codd. **1287** *εἷλον* Musgrave: *εἶχον* codd. **1290** *τάσδ' ἐγὼ* Auratus: *τὰς λέγω* codd. **1294** *δὲ σοφὴ* f g. **1304** *σῶν* Auratus: *τῶν* codd.

An exile and a stranger from the land,
A wanderer shall return
To set the last crown on this pile of doom:
In Heaven above there is a great oath sworn
His father's outstretched corpse shall bring him home.
Why stand I then lamenting? Once I have seen
My town of Ilium in her present case,
While those that led her captive, under God's
High judgment, so come off,—I will go too
Forthwith and face my fortune—to my death.

[*She goes up to the palace-gates.*

The Gates of Death, I hail you! I pray only
To get a mortal wound, that I may close
These eyes without a struggle, my life's blood
Ebbing to an easy death.

ELDER. Sad lady,
Of so much sorrow and withal so wise,
Thou art long in thy discoursing:
But if thou verily knowest thine own fate,
What means it, like the heaven-appointed ox,
Moving so patiently to the altar?

CASS. Sirs,
There is no avoidance, none, by time deferred.

ELDER. Yet latest is the best.

CASS. The day is come;
Little shall I gain by flight.

ELDER. Well, thou hast truly
A fortitude in sufferance.

CASS. Those are terms
Bright fortune never hears.

ELDER. Well, there is comfort
In death that comes with honour.

CASS. O my father,
Thou and thy noble children!

[*In entering the palace-doors she suddenly recoils with horror.*

ΧΟ. τί δ' ἐστὶ χρῆμα; τίς σ' ἀποστρέφει φόβος; 1305
ΚΑ. φεῦ φεῦ.
ΧΟ. τί τοῦτ' ἔφευξας; εἴ τι μὴ φρενῶν στύγος.
ΚΑ. φόνον δόμοι πνέουσιν αἱματοσταγῆ.
ΧΟ. καὶ πῶς; τόδ' ὄζει θυμάτων ἐφεστίων.
ΚΑ. ὅμοιος ἀτμὸς ὥσπερ ἐκ τάφου πρέπει. 1310
ΧΟ. οὐ Σύριον ἀγλάϊσμα δώμασιν λέγεις.
ΚΑ. ἀλλ' εἶμι κἀν δόμοισι κωκύσουσ' ἐμὴν
Ἀγαμέμνονός τε μοῖραν· ἀρκείτω βίος.
ἰὼ ξένοι,
οὔτοι δυσοίζω θάμνον ὡς ὄρνις φόβωι 1315
ἄλλως· θανούσηι μαρτυρεῖτέ μοι τόδε,
ὅταν γυνὴ γυναικὸς ἀντ' ἐμοῦ θάνηι,
ἀνήρ τε δυσδάμαρτος ἀντ' ἀνδρὸς πέσηι·
ἐπιξενοῦμαι ταῦτα δ' ὡς θανουμένη.
ΧΟ. ὦ τλῆμον, οἰκτίρω σε θεσφάτου μόρου. 1320
ΚΑ. ἅπαξ ἔτ' εἰπεῖν ῥῆσιν ἢ θρῆνον θέλω
ἐμὸν τὸν αὐτῆς. ἡλίωι δ' ἐπεύχομαι
πρὸς ὕστατον φῶς τοῖς ἐμοῖς τιμαόροις
ἐχθροὺς φόνευσιν τοὺς ἐμοὺς τίνειν ὁμοῦ,
δούλης θανούσης, εὐμαροῦς χειρώματος. 1325
ΧΟ. ἰὼ βρότεια πράγματ'· εὐτυχοῦντα μὲν
σκιά τις ἂν πρέψειεν· εἰ δὲ δυστυχοῖ,
βολαῖς ὑγρώσσων σπόγγος ὤλεσεν γραφήν.
καὶ ταῦτ' ἐκείνων μᾶλλον οἰκτίρω πολύ.

1316 ἄλλως Hermann: ἀλλ' ὡς codd. **1322** ἡλίου Jacob. **1324** ἐχθροὺς . . τοὺς ἐμοὺς J. Pearson, φόνευσιν Bothe: ἐχθροῖς φονεῦσι τοῖς ἐμοῖς codd. **1326** sqq. Cassandrae continuant codd.: corr. Weil. **1327** ἂν πρέψειεν Boissonade: ἀντρέψειεν codd. | δυστυχοῖ Blomfield: δυστυχῆ codd.

ELDER. What is the matter? what is it affrights thee?
CASS. Faugh, faugh!
ELDER. Faugh, faugh? Wherefore so?
Unless it be some sickening in the spirit.
CASS. Blood! the air is full of weltering blood!
ELDER. Nay, nay; it is nothing but the smell of sacrifice
Offering upon the hearth.
CASS. 'Tis such a reek
As issues from a tomb.
ELDER. Well, truly that
Were most un-Syrian odour.
CASS. I will go in
To finish there my wailing for my own
And Agamemnon's fate: life, content me!
—O think not, sirs,
I am as a bird that startles at a bush
In idle terror: when I am dead, confirm me,
When for this woman here a woman dies,
And slain a man for man ill-mated lies:—
I crave this of you as at point of death.
ELDER. Poor soul, with death foreknown, I pity thee.
CASS. Yet once more will I speak, one speech, or dirge
Over my own death:—O thou Sun in heaven,
I pray to thee, before thy latest light,
That, when my champion comes, my enemies
May pay the same time then for murdering this
Poor slave, an easy victim!

[*She passes into the palace.*

ELDER. O sad vanity
Of human fortunes! Their best happiness
Faint as a pencil'd shadow; once unhappy,—
Dashed with a wet sponge at a sweep clean out!
This, to my thinking, pitiable far more.

τὸ μὲν εὖ πράσσειν ἀκόρεστον ἔφυ 1330
πᾶσι βροτοῖσιν· δακτυλοδείκτων δ'
οὔτις ἀπειπὼν εἴργει μελάθρων,
"μηκέτ' ἐσέλθηις," τάδε φωνῶν.
καὶ τῶιδε πόλιν μὲν ἑλεῖν ἔδοσαν
μάκαρες Πριάμου· 1335
θεοτίμητος δ' οἴκαδ' ἱκάνει·
νῦν δ' εἰ προτέρων αἷμ' ἀποτείσει
καὶ τοῖσι θανοῦσι θανὼν ἄλλων
ποινὰς θανάτων ἐπικρανεῖ,
τίς ἂν ἐξεύξαιτο βροτῶν ἀσινεῖ 1340
δαίμονι φῦναι τάδ' ἀκούων;

ΑΓ. ὤμοι, πέπληγμαι καιρίαν πληγὴν ἔσω.
ΧΟ. σῖγα· τίς πληγὴν ἀυτεῖ καιρίως οὐτασμένος;
ΑΓ. ὤμοι μάλ' αὖθις, δευτέραν πεπληγμένος.
ΧΟ. τοὔργον εἰργάσθαι δοκεῖ μοι βασιλέως οἰμώγμασιν·
ἀλλὰ κοινωσώμεθ' εὖ πως ἀσφαλῆ βουλεύματα. 1346
α'. ἐγὼ μὲν ὑμῖν τὴν ἐμὴν γνώμην λέγω,
πρὸς δῶμα δεῦρ' ἀστοῖσι κηρύσσειν βοήν.
β'. ἐμοὶ δ' ὅπως τάχιστά γ' ἐμπεσεῖν δοκεῖ
καὶ πρᾶγμ' ἐλέγχειν σὺν νεορρύτωι ξίφει. 1350
γ'. κἀγὼ τοιούτου γνώματος κοινωνὸς ὢν
ψηφίζομαί τι δρᾶν· τὸ μὴ μέλλειν δ' ἀκμή.
δ'. ὁρᾶν πάρεστι· φροιμιάζονται γὰρ ὡς
τυραννίδος σημεῖα πράσσοντες πόλει.

1331 βροτοῖσιν Pauw: βροτοῖς codd. **1333** μηκέτ' ἐσέλθηις Hermann: μηκέτι δ' εἰσέλθῃς codd. **1339** fort. ἐπικράνειεν. **1340** ἐξεύξαιτο Schneidewin: εὔξαιτο codd. **1346** εὖ Donaldson: ἂν codd.

CHORUS.

With all on earth insatiate is
Good Fortune; while she wooes the door
Of gazed and gorgeous palaces,
None warns her from it, bars ingress
With *Enter here no more!*
Here is a man the Gods let burn
The town of Priam; safe return
He finds, with Heaven-awarded bliss:—
If now for others' blood-guilt he
Must pay the forfeit, his death be
For deaths of old the crowning fee,—
Who may boast harmless destiny
His birthright, hearing this?

AGAMEMNON *within the palace.*

O I am hurt! wounded, a mortal wound.

ELDER. Peace, hark! Whose voice is that cries out a hurt, a mortal wound?

AGAM. O God! wounded again, another.

ELDER. To judge by groaning of the king, the deed should e'en be done;
Come let us join debate and take safe counsel as we may.

FIRST ELDER. I give you my opinion,—sound alarm
And summon rescue to the palace hither.

SECOND. And I say, burst in now immediately
And prove the matter with the naked sword.

THIRD. Holding the same opinion, I would vote
For acting somehow; there's no tarrying here.

FOURTH. 'Tis gross and palpable; their opening act
Shows ominous of usurping tyranny.

ε΄. χρονίζομεν γάρ· οἱ δὲ τῆς Μελλοῦς κλέος 1355
πέδοι πατοῦντες οὐ καθεύδουσιν χερί.
ϛ΄. οὐκ οἶδα βουλῆς ἧστινος τυχὼν λέγω.
τοῦ δρῶντός ἐστι καὶ τὸ βουλεῦσαι πέρι.
ζ΄. κἀγὼ τοιοῦτός εἰμ', ἐπεὶ δυσμηχανῶ
λόγοισι τὸν θανόντ' ἀνιστάναι πάλιν. 1360
η΄. ἦ καὶ βίον τείνοντες ὧδ' ὑπείξομεν
δόμων καταισχυντῆρσι τοῖσδ' ἡγουμένοις;
θ΄. ἀλλ' οὐκ ἀνεκτόν, ἀλλὰ κατθανεῖν κρατεῖ·
πεπαιτέρα γὰρ μοῖρα τῆς τυραννίδος.
ι΄. ἦ γὰρ τεκμηρίοισιν ἐξ οἰμωγμάτων 1365
μαντευσόμεσθα τἀνδρὸς ὡς ὀλωλότος;
ια΄. σάφ' εἰδότας χρὴ τῶνδε θυμοῦσθαι πέρι·
τὸ γὰρ τοπάζειν τοῦ σάφ' εἰδέναι δίχα.
ιβ΄. ταύτην ἐπαινεῖν πάντοθεν πληθύνομαι,
τρανῶς Ἀτρείδην εἰδέναι κυροῦνθ' ὅπως. 1370

ΚΛ. πολλῶν πάροιθεν καιρίως εἰρημένων
τἀναντί' εἰπεῖν οὐκ ἐπαισχυνθήσομαι.
πῶς γάρ τις ἐχθροῖς ἐχθρὰ πορσύνων, φίλοις
δοκοῦσιν εἶναι, πημονὴν ἀρκύστατον
φράξειεν ὕψος κρεῖσσον ἐκπηδήματος; 1375
ἐμοὶ δ' ἀγὼν ὅδ' οὐκ ἀφρόντιστος πάλαι
νείκης παλαιᾶς ἦλθε, σὺν χρόνωι γε μήν·
ἕστηκα δ' ἔνθ' ἔπαισ' ἐπ' ἐξειργασμένοις.
οὕτω δ' ἔπραξα, καὶ τάδ' οὐκ ἀρνήσομαι,

1355 μελλοῦς Trypho (*Rhet.* VIII p. 741 Waltz, III p. 196 Spengel): μελλούσης codd. **1356** πέδοι Hermann: πέδον codd. **1361** τείνοντες Canter: κτείνοντες codd. **1367** θυμοῦσθαι E. A. I. Ahrens: μυθοῦσθαι codd. **1374** πημονῆς Auratus | ἀρκύσταт' ἂν Elmsley. **1377** νείκης Heath: νίκης codd.

FIFTH. Because we dally! while the lauded name
Of *Tarrying* is as dirt beneath their feet.

SIXTH. I have no counsel or advice to give;
Counsel is Action's own prerogative.

SEVENTH. I am of that same mind; it passes me
To raise the dead again with only words.

EIGHTH. Even to prolong our lives shall we bow down
Under these foul disgracers of the House?

NINTH. It is not to be borne, 'twere better die;
Death were a milder lot than tyranny!

TENTH. What, shall we then conjecture of his death
By divination of mysterious groans?

ELEVENTH. We should be certified before we passion;
Surmise is one thing, certitude another.

TWELFTH. I am multiplied on all sides for that course,
Plainly to assure us of the King's condition.

[*As* THE ELDERS *are about to enter the palace, the bodies of Agamemnon and Cassandra are exposed, with* CLYTAEMNESTRA *standing over them.*

CLYT. All my politic speeches heretofore
Shall nowise make me blush now to confess
The truth and contrary:—how else indeed
When studying hate's act for a hated foe
Supposed friend—how else pitch the toils of Doom
To a height beyond o'erleaping? 'Twas not sudden;
For me, 'twas but
The test and trial of an ancient feud,
Long thought on, and at last in time arrived:—
I stand here now triumphant, where I struck!
And so contrived it also—I'll avow it—

ὡς μήτε φεύγειν μήτ᾽ ἀμύνεσθαι μόρον. 1380
ἄπειρον ἀμφίβληστρον, ὥσπερ ἰχθύων,
περιστιχίζω, πλοῦτον εἵματος κακόν.
παίω δέ νιν δίς· κἀν δυοῖν οἰμώγμασιν
μεθῆκεν αὑτοῦ κῶλα· καὶ πεπτωκότι
τρίτην ἐπενδίδωμι, τοῦ κατὰ χθονὸς 1385
Διὸς νεκρῶν Σωτῆρος εὐκταίαν χάριν.
οὕτω τὸν αὑτοῦ θυμὸν ὁρμαίνει πεσών·
κἀκφυσιῶν ὀξεῖαν αἵματος σφαγὴν
βάλλει μ᾽ ἐρεμνῆι ψακάδι φοινίας δρόσου,
χαίρουσαν οὐδὲν ἧσσον ἢ διοσδότωι 1390
γάνει σπόρητος κάλυκος ἐν λοχεύμασιν.
ὡς ὧδ᾽ ἐχόντων, πρέσβος Ἀργείων τόδε,
χαίροιτ᾽ ἄν, εἰ χαίροιτ᾽, ἐγὼ δ᾽ ἐπεύχομαι.
εἰ δ᾽ ἦν πρεπόντων ὥστ᾽ ἐπισπένδειν νεκρῶι,
τάδ᾽ ἂν δικαίως ἦν, ὑπερδίκως μὲν οὖν· 1395
τοσῶνδε κρατῆρ᾽ ἐν δόμοις κακῶν ὅδε
πλήσας ἀραίων αὐτὸς ἐκπίνει μολών.

ΧΟ. θαυμάζομέν σου γλῶσσαν, ὡς θρασύστομος,
ἥτις τοιόνδ᾽ ἐπ᾽ ἀνδρὶ κομπάζεις λόγον.

ΚΛ. πειρᾶσθέ μου γυναικὸς ὡς ἀφράσμονος· 1400
ἐγὼ δ᾽ ἀτρέστωι καρδίαι πρὸς εἰδότας
λέγω—σὺ δ᾽ αἰνεῖν εἴτε με ψέγειν θέλεις
ὅμοιον—οὗτός ἐστιν Ἀγαμέμνων, ἐμὸς
πόσις, νεκρὸς δὲ τῆσδε δεξιᾶς χερὸς
ἔργον, δικαίας τέκτονος. τάδ᾽ ὧδ᾽ ἔχει. 1405

1380 ἀμύνεσθαι Victorius: ἀμύνασθαι codd. **1382** περιστοιχίζων f, περιστιχίζων g. **1386** Διὸς Enger: ἅιδου codd. **1387** ὀρυγάνει Hermann. **1390** sq. διοσδότωι γάνει Porson: διὸς νότω γᾶν εἰ codd.

As neither should he scape me nor resist:
I wreathed around him, like a fishing-net,
Swathing in a blind maze,—deadly Wealth of robe,—
And struck two blows; and with a groan for each
His limbs beneath him slacked; and as he lay,
I gave him yet a third, for grace of prayer
To God Safe-keeper—of the dead below.
With that he lay still, panting his own life out:
And as the gory jets he blasted forth,
Rain of the sanguine drench bespattered me,
Rejoicing, as in balm of heaven rejoices
Cornland when the teeming ear gives birth!
  The case then standing thus,
My reverend Elders, you may find herein
What gladness you may find,—but I do glory!
Yea, and upon the body could we pour
Drink-offerings of the proper substance, then
Those offerings had been just, past measure just!
Drink-offering from the bowl of harm and bane
Brimmed for his home, which here his own lips drain!

ELDER. We are astonished at thy tongue's audacity,
Such glorying over thine own wedded man.

CLYT. You practise on me
As I were a thoughtless woman:
With heart unshook I tell you what you know,—
And praise me or dispraise me as you please,
'Tis all one,—this is Agamemnon; my
Husband; a corpse; the work of this right hand,
Whose workmanship was just. That is the case.

στρ. ΧΟ. τί κακὸν, ὦ γύναι,
χθονοτρεφὲς ἐδανὸν ἢ ποτὸν
πασαμένα ῥυτᾶς ἐξ ἁλὸς ὄρμενον
τόδ' ἐπέθου θύος δημοθρόους τ' ἀράς;
ἀπέδικες, ἀπέταμες—ἀπόπολις δ' ἔσηι— 1410
μῖσος ὄβριμον ἀστοῖς.

ΚΛ. νῦν μὲν δικάζεις ἐκ πόλεως φυγὴν ἐμοὶ
καὶ μῖσος ἀστῶν δημόθρους τ' ἔχειν ἀράς,
οὐδὲν τότ' ἀνδρὶ τῶιδ' ἐναντίον φέρων·
ὃς οὐ προτιμῶν, ὡσπερεὶ βοτοῦ μόρον, 1415
μήλων φλεόντων εὐπόκοις νομεύμασιν,
ἔθυσεν αὑτοῦ παῖδα, φιλτάτην ἐμοὶ
ὠδῖν', ἐπωιδὸν Θρηικίων ἀημάτων.
οὐ τοῦτον ἐκ γῆς τῆσδε χρῆν σ' ἀνδρηλατεῖν,
μιασμάτων ἄποιν'; ἐπήκοος δ' ἐμῶν 1420
ἔργων δικαστὴς τραχὺς εἶ. λέγω δέ σοι
τοιαῦτ' ἀπειλεῖν, ὡς παρεσκευασμένης
ἐκ τῶν ὁμοίων, χειρὶ νικήσαντ' ἐμοῦ
ἄρχειν· ἐὰν δὲ τοὔμπαλιν κραίνηι θεός,
γνώσηι διδαχθεὶς ὀψὲ γοῦν τὸ σωφρονεῖν. 1425

ἀντ. ΧΟ. μεγαλόμητις εἶ,
περίφρονα δ' ἔλακες. ὥσπερ οὖν
φονολιβεῖ τύχαι φρὴν ἐπιμαίνεται,
λίπος ἐπ' ὀμμάτων αἵματος εὖ πρέπειν·
ἀτίετον ἔτι σὲ χρὴ στερομέναν φίλων 1430
τύμμα τύμματι τεῖσαι.

1408 ῥυτᾶς Stanley: ῥύσας vel ῥυσᾶς codd. | ὄρμενον Abresch: ὀρώμενον (ὀρ- h) codd. **1410** ἀπόπολις Seidler: ἄπολις codd. **1411** ὄμβριμον codd. **1414** τότ' I. Voss: τόδ' codd. **1418** ἀημάτων Canter: τε λημμάτων codd. **1419** χρῆν Porson: χρή codd. **1429** πρέπειν E. A. I. Ahrens: πρέπει codd. **1431** τύμματι I. Voss: τύμμα codd.

CHORUS *clamouring.*

Woman, what poisonous herb of the earth hast eaten — Strophe.
Or sorcerous liquor sprung from the running sea
To bring this slaughter upon thee and curse of the land?
Having stricken off, shorn off, cut off thyself shalt be,
With general hatred banned!

CLYT. Your sentence *now* is banishment for me
And execration and the people's curse,
Though never did you *then* the least advance
Objection against *him*, that never recked
No more than a beast's death, one lost from all
The abundance of the fleecy multitude,
But slaughtered his own child, my dearest travail,
To charm a wind from Thracia! Was't not right
In recompense of that polluted act
To banish *him* the land? Yet now you hear
My doing, you are a harsh judge. But I warn you,
If thus you mean to menace, be advised
That I am well prepared, conditions equal,
If you shall vanquish me by force, to own
Your rule;—but if God will the contrary,
Then lessoning you shall have, though late, in wisdom!

CHORUS.

Lofty in arrogant vaunt as wicked of spirit! — Antistrophe.
Mind being then so mad with shedding of gore,
On the eye should answering gore in a blood-fleck show;
Disgraced, abhorred, unowned, thou hast yet thy doom in
store,
To pay with blow for a blow!

ΚΛ. καὶ τήνδ' ἀκούεις ὁρκίων ἐμῶν θέμιν·
μὰ τὴν τέλειον τῆς ἐμῆς παιδὸς Δίκην,
Ἄτην Ἐρινύν θ', αἷσι τόνδ' ἔσφαξ' ἐγώ,
οὔ μοι Φόβου μέλαθρον Ἐλπὶς ἐμπατεῖ, 1435
ἕως ἂν αἴθηι πῦρ ἐφ' ἑστίας ἐμῆς
Αἴγισθος, ὡς τὸ πρόσθεν εὖ φρονῶν ἐμοί.
οὗτος γὰρ ἡμῖν ἀσπὶς οὐ σμικρὰ θράσους.
κεῖται γυναικὸς τῆσδε λυμαντήριος,
Χρυσηίδων μείλιγμα τῶν ὑπ' Ἰλίωι, 1440
ἥ τ' αἰχμάλωτος ἥδε καὶ τερασκόπος,
καὶ κοινόλεκτρος τοῦδε θεσφατηλόγος
πιστὴ ξύνευνος, ναυτίλων δὲ σελμάτων
ἰσοτριβής.—ἄτιμα δ' οὐκ ἐπραξάτην.
ὁ μὲν γὰρ οὕτως· ἡ δέ τοι, κύκνου δίκην 1445
τὸν ὕστατον μέλψασα θανάσιμον γόον,
κεῖται, φιλήτωρ τοῦδ', ἐμοὶ δ' ἐπήγαγεν,
εὐνῆς παροψώνημα τῆς ἐμῆς, χλιδήν.

στρ. α'. ΧΟ. φεῦ, τίς ἂν ἐν τάχει, μὴ περιώδυνος,
μηδὲ δεμνιοτήρης, 1450
μόλοι τὸν αἰεὶ φέρουσ' ὁμιλεῖν
Μοῖρ' ἀτέλευτον ὕπνον, δαμέντος
φύλακος εὐμενεστάτου,
πολλὰ τλάντος γυναικὸς διαί·
πρὸς γυναικὸς δ' ἀπέφθισεν βίον. 1455

1432 fort. ἀκούσηι γ'. **1436** ἐμῆς Porson: ἐμὰς codd. **1444** ἰσοτριβής Pauw: ἱστοτρίβης codd. **1447** φιλήτως f. **1448** χλιδήν Auratus: χλιδῆς codd. **1451** ὁμιλεῖν H.: ἐν ἡμῖν codd. **1453** καὶ post εὐμενεστάτου habent codd., delevit Franz.

CLYT. Hear then the sanction of my solemn oath:—
By Justice, taken in fulness for my child,
By Ate, and Erinys, unto whom
I slew that sacrifice, in the House of Fear
My spirit sets no foot! so long as fire
Is kindled on my hearth by my good friend
Aegisthus, true and kind as heretofore:
Him find we no slight shield of confidence.
Low lies the wronger of his wedded wife,
Solace of every Chryseid under Troy,—
With her, his bondservant and soothsayer,
His fortune-telling concubine, his true
Bedfellow, practised equally with him
In lore of the bench on shipboard.—But the pair
Have got their merits: his condition, thus;
While she, after her swan's last dying wail,
This lover of *him*, lies there; to me this slight
Side-morsel to the wedded feast, this toy,
To *me* brings only the dear sweet of triumph!

CHORUS.

I 1.

O for a Fate might bring me swift,
Without sore-agonizing pain
Or lingering bed, her blessed gift
Of sleep, that world-without-end sleep,
Converse with me still to keep,
That would not wake again!
My kind Protector, he that bore
In woman's cause a toil so sore,
By woman's hand extinguished!

1st strophe.

ἰὼ <ἰὼ> παράνους Ἑλένα
μία τὰς πολλάς, τὰς πάνυ πολλὰς
ψυχὰς ὀλέσασ' ὑπὸ Τροίαι.
νῦν δὲ τελείαν πολύμναστον ἐπηνθίσω
δι' αἷμ' ἄνιπτον, εἴ τις ἦν ποτ', ἐν δόμοις 1460
ἔρις ἐρίδματος, ἀνδρὸς οἰζύς.

ΚΛ. μηδὲν θανάτου μοῖραν ἐπεύχου
τοῖσδε βαρυνθείς·
μηδ' εἰς Ἑλένην κότον ἐκτρέψηις, 1465
ὡς ἀνδρολέτειρ', ὡς μία πολλῶν
ἀνδρῶν ψυχὰς Δαναῶν ὀλέσασ'
ἀξύστατον ἄλγος ἔπραξεν.

ἀντ. α'. ΧΟ. δαῖμον, ὃς ἐμπίτνεις δώμασι καὶ διφυί-
οισι Τανταλίδαισιν, 1470
κράτος <τ'> ἰσόψυχον ἐκ γυναικῶν
καρδιόδηκτον ἐμοὶ κρατύνεις.
ἐπὶ δὲ σώματος δίκαν
κόρακος ἐχθροῦ σταθεῖσ' ἐννόμως
ὕμνον ὑμνεῖν ἐπεύχεται 1475

ΚΛ. νῦν ὤρθωσας στόματος γνώμην,
τὸν τριπάχυντον
δαίμονα γέννης τῆσδε κικλήσκων.

1456 ἰὼ addidit Blomfield | παράνους Hermann: παρανόμους codd. **1460** sq. εἴ τις ἦν ποτ' H. (εἴ τις ποτ' Karsten): ἥτις ἦν τότ' codd. **1465** ἐκτρέχῃς f. **1467** ὀλέσαν fg. **1469** sq. ἐμπίτνεις Canter: ἐμπίπτεις codd. | διφυίοισι Hermann: διφυεῖσι codd. **1471** τ' add. Hermann. **1472** καρδιόδηκτον Abresch: καρδίᾳ δηκτὸν codd. **1473** μοι post δίκαν habent codd., del. Dindorf. **1474** ἐκνόμως h: fort. ἐκνόμοις. **1475** fort. ἐπεύχεται νόμοις. **1476** νῦν δ' codd.: corr. H. **1477** τριπάχυντον Bamberger: τριπάχυιον codd.

O Helena, thou cause insane
    That all those many lives hath lost,
    Lives untold for thy sole cost
Upon the Trojan plain!
But now thou hast crowned complete that hecatomb
    In blood past all remission
With one full-perfect, memorable indeed
As e'er the world hath seen,—thou bitter seed
Of enmity, firm-planted in man's home
    To man's perdition!

CLYTAEMNESTRA.

Nay sink not so, be not so broke
Death for your portion to invoke,
    Nor yet your wrath divert
On Helena, that her sole guilt
All those many lives hath spilt
    With such deep yawning hurt.

CHORUS.

I 2.

1st antistrophe.

O Spirit of haunting Doom that bears
    The House down, O how sore thou art
On Tantalus' twain soveran heirs!
In woman too twain weapon, steel'd
Of equal temper, thy hands wield,—
    A poignard in my heart!
Feet planted on his corse, the proud
Foul raven, uttering harsh and loud
    His chant of joy triumphant!

CLYTAEMNESTRA.

Ah, now you set your verdict right;—
The Spirit of all our race indite,
    So gross with o'ergrown flesh!

ἐκ τοῦ γὰρ ἔρως αἱματολοιχὸς
νειριτροφεῖται, πρὶν καταλῆξαι 1480
τὸ παλαιὸν ἄχος, νέος ἶχαρ.

στρ. β΄. ΧΟ. ἦ μέγαν οἴκοις τοῖσδε
δαίμονα καὶ βαρύμηνιν αἰνεῖς,
φεῦ φεῦ, κακὸν αἶνον ἀτη-
ρᾶς τύχας ἀκορέστου· 1485
ἰὼ ἰή, διαὶ Διὸς
παναιτίου πανεργέτα.
τί γὰρ βροτοῖς ἄνευ Διὸς τελεῖται;
τί τῶνδ' οὐ θεόκραντόν ἐστιν;

ἰὼ ἰὼ βασιλεῦ βασιλεῦ, 1490
πῶς σε δακρύσω;
φρενὸς ἐκ φιλίας τί ποτ' εἴπω;
κεῖσαι δ' ἀράχνης ἐν ὑφάσματι τῶιδ'
ἀσεβεῖ θανάτωι βίον ἐκπνέων.
ὤμοι μοι κοίταν τάνδ' ἀνελεύθερον 1495
δολίωι μόρωι δαμεὶς
ἐκ χερὸς ἀμφιτόμωι βελέμνωι.

ΚΛ. αὐχεῖς εἶναι τόδε τοὔργον ἐμόν;
μηδ' ἐπιλεχθῆις
Ἀγαμεμνονίαν εἶναί μ' ἄλοχον· 1500
φανταζόμενος δὲ γυναικὶ νεκροῦ
τοῦδ' ὁ παλαιὸς δριμὺς ἀλάστωρ
Ἀτρέως χαλεποῦ θοινατῆρος
τόνδ' ἀπέτεισεν
τέλεον νεαροῖς ἐπιθύσας. 1505

1480 νειριτροφεῖται H.: νείρει τρέφεται codd. **1481** ἶχαρ H.: ἰχώρ codd.
1482 τοῖσδε corruptum. **1487** πανεργάταν fg.

'Tis he still fosters in the maw
This bloodthirst hungering for the raw,
With lickerish craving, ere last bite
Have well ceased aching, fresh!

CHORUS.

II I.

2nd strophe.

Huge of a truth his bloated mass
And fierce wrath never-bated:
Story of ruthless Doom, alas,
With harm unsated.
By will of Zeus did this befall,
Sole author and sole cause of all;
Can aught without him come to pass?
Herein was aught not fated?

O my King, my King,
Tears enough I cannot bring,
Words enough I cannot find
To voice my loving mind:
Thus to lie by murderous death
In that spider-web entangled,
Gasping out thy breath,
On so churlish bed, ay me,
With slaughtering weapon slain and mangled
By the hand of treachery!

CLYTAEMNESTRA.

Suppose you it was mine, this act?
Conceive not e'en that here in fact
'Tis Agamemnon's wife you see!
Mere semblance of her, she:
The fierce ancestral Ghost of him
That Atreus made a feast so grim
Hath made this man the price;
Heaped him this man upon his own
Young firstlings offered yet ungrown,
Full perfect sacrifice!

ἀντ. β'. ΧΟ. ὡς μὲν ἀναίτιος εἶ
τοῦδε φόνου τίς ὁ μαρτυρήσων;
πῶ πῶ; πατρόθεν δὲ συλλή-
πτωρ γένοιτ' ἂν ἀλάστωρ.
βιάζεται δ' ὁμοσπόροις 1510
ἐπιρροαῖσιν αἱμάτων
μέλας Ἄρης, ὅποι δίκας προβαίνων
πάχναι κουροβόρωι παρέξει.

ἰὼ ἰὼ βασιλεῦ βασιλεῦ,
πῶς σε δακρύσω; 1515
φρενὸς ἐκ φιλίας τί ποτ' εἴπω;
κεῖσαι δ' ἀράχνης ἐν ὑφάσματι τῶιδ'
ἀσεβεῖ θανάτωι βίον ἐκπνέων.
ὤμοι μοι κοίταν τάνδ' ἀνελεύθερον
δολίωι μόρωι δαμεὶς 1520
ἐκ χερὸς ἀμφιτόμωι βελέμνωι.

ΚΛ. οὐδὲ γὰρ οὗτος δολίαν ἄτην
οἴκοισιν ἔθηκ'; 1525
ἀλλ' ἐμὸν ἐκ τοῦδ' ἔρνος ἀερθέν,
πολυκλαύτην Ἰφιγένειαν,
ἄξια δράσας ἄξια πάσχων
μηδὲν ἐν Ἅιδου μεγαλαυχείτω,
ξιφοδηλήτωι 1530
θανάτωι τείσας ἅπερ ἦρξεν.

1512 *δίκας* Martin (*δίκην* Butler): *δὲ καὶ* codd. | *προβαίνων* Canter: *προσβαίνων* codd. **1522** sq. *οὔτ' ἀνελεύθερον οἶμαι θάνατον* | *τῶιδε γενέσθαι* damnavit Seidler. **1527** *τὴν πολύκλαυτόν τ'* codd., *τὴν* delevit Meineke, *πολυκλαύτην* coniecit Porson. **1528** *ἀνάξια δράσας* codd.: corr. Hermann. **1531** *ἔρξεν* Spanheim.

CHORUS.

II 2.

2nd antistrophe.

'Not guilty'? Then support that plea:
  Whose witness can be cited?
Go to:—yet such a Ghost might be
  In aid united;
Onward it rolls in kindred blood,
Red Slaughter's torrent, flood on flood,
Till Babes' flesh fed-upon shall see
  Its firm stain full requited!

O my King, my King,
Tears enough I cannot bring,
Words enough I cannot find
To voice my loving mind:
Thus to lie by murderous death
In that spider-web entangled,
Gasping out thy breath,
On so churlish bed, ay me,
With slaughtering weapon slain and mangled
By the hand of treachery!

CLYTAEMNESTRA.

Of treachery! Dealt not he then too
  This House a treacherous blow?
But what he wrought that branch that grew
  From me, that he made grow,
My sore-wept own beloved maid,
With equal penance hath he paid;
Slain for it even as he slew,
  He need not boast below!

στρ. γ'. ΧΟ. ἀμηχανῶ φροντίδος στερηθεὶς
εὐπάλαμον μέριμναν,
ὅπαι τράπωμαι, πίτνοντος οἴκου.
δέδοικα δ' ὄμβρου κτύπον δομοσφαλῆ 1535
τὸν αἱματηρόν· ψεκὰς δὲ λήγει.
Δίκαι δ' ἐπ' ἄλλο πρᾶγμα θήγεται βλάβης
πρὸς ἄλλαις θηγάναισι μοῖρα.

ἰὼ γᾶ γᾶ, εἴθε μ' ἐδέξω,
πρὶν τόνδ' ἐπιδεῖν ἀργυροτοίχου 1540
δροίτης κατέχοντα χαμεύνην.
τίς ὁ θάψων νιν; τίς ὁ θρηνήσων;
ἦ σὺ τόδ' ἔρξαι τλήσηι, κτείνασ'
ἄνδρα τὸν αὑτῆς ἀποκωκῦσαι
ψυχῆι τ' ἄχαριν χάριν ἀντ' ἔργων 1545
μεγάλων ἀδίκως ἐπικρᾶναι;
τίς δ' ἐπιτύμβιος αἶνος ἐπ' ἀνδρὶ θείωι
σὺν δακρύοις ἰάπτων
ἀλαθείαι φρενῶν πονήσει;

ΚΛ. οὐ σὲ προσήκει τὸ μέλημ' ἀλέγειν 1550
τοῦτο· πρὸς ἡμῶν
κάππεσε, κάτθανε, καὶ καταθάψομεν—
οὐχ ὑπὸ κλαυθμῶν τῶν ἐξ οἴκων,

1533 *εὐπάλαμνον* codd.: corr. Porson. **1537** *δίκη* f, *δίκα* (η supra α) g | *θήγεται* Emperius: *θήγει* codd. **1538** *θηγάναις* codd. **1545** *ψυχῆι τ'* E. A. I. Ahrens: *ψυχὴν* codd. **1550** *μέλημ' ἀλέγειν* Karsten: *μέλημα λέγειν* codd.

CHORUS.

III 1.

3rd strophe

Thought fails me; in a maze I grope
And find no means of help or hope,
  While the very House is quaking:
Under this crashing rain of gore
'Twill sink—'tis early drip no more.
—Yet other whetstones rest, whereon
Justice for other work undone
  Her weapon sharp is making!

O Earth, O Earth, would thou hadst been
My shroud, ere I my lord had seen
Here in a silvern coffer spread,
That kingly head
Laid on such a lowly bed!

Who shall bury him? who make moan?
Wilt *thou* add sin to sin,—thine own
Man's blood upon thy hands, proceed
Then with a mockery to atone,—
With funeral dole for his dead soul
To salve thy heinous deed?

And how should mourning o'er him dart
The hero's praise with tears of ruth?
How should it bear that heavy part
With heart-felt sorrow's truth?

CLYTAEMNESTRA.

That care is no concern for thee;
  Beneath *our* hand he fell,
Down beneath *us* lay dead; and *we*
  Beneath will speed him well:—
But not with household from his gates
  To wail behind his bier—

ἀλλ' Ἰφιγένειά νιν ἀσπασίως
θυγάτηρ, ὡς χρή, 1555
πατέρ' ἀντιάσασα πρὸς ὠκύπορον
πόρθμευμ' ἀχέων
περὶ χεῖρα βαλοῦσα φιλήσει.

ἀντ. γ'. ΧΟ. ὄνειδος ἥκει τόδ' ἀντ' ὀνείδους,
δύσμαχα δ' ἔστι κρῖναι. 1560
φέρει φέροντ', ἐκτίνει δ' ὁ καίνων.
μένει δὲ μίμνοντος ἐν θρόνωι Διὸς
παθεῖν τὸν ἔρξαντα· θέσμιον γάρ.
τίς ἂν γονὰν ἀραῖον ἐκβάλοι δόμων;
κεκόλληται γένος πρὸς ἄται. 1565

ΚΛ. ἐς τόνδ' ἐνέβης ξὺν ἀληθείαι
χρησμόν. ἐγὼ δ' οὖν
ἐθέλω δαίμονι τῶι Πλεισθενιδῶν
ὅρκους θεμένη τάδε μὲν στέργειν,
δύστλητά περ ὄνθ', ὃ δὲ λοιπόν, ἰόντ' 1570
ἐκ τῶνδε δόμων ἄλλην γενεὰν
τρίβειν θανάτοις αὐθένταισιν.
κτεάνων τε μέρος
βαιὸν ἐχούσηι πανεπαρκὲς ἔμοιγ'
ἀλληλοφόνους 1575
μανίας μελάθρων ἀφελούσηι.

1554 Ἰφιγένειά νιν Auratus: Ἰφιγένειαν· ἶν' codd. **1558** φιλήσει Stanley: φιλήσηι codd. **1562** θρόνωι Schuetz: χρόνω (χρόνωι) codd. **1564** ἀραῖον Hermann: ῥᾶον codd. **1565** πρὸς ἄται Blomfield: προσάψαι codd. **1566** ἐνέβης Canter: ἐνέβη codd. **1574** πανεπαρκὲς ἔμοιγ' H.: πᾶν ἀπόχρη μοι δ' codd.

His *daughter* at the Doleful Straits
  Below stands waiting near:
Her love, her duty she shall bring,
Her arms about his neck shall fling,
  And kiss her *Father dear*!

CHORUS.

III 2.

3rd antistrophe.

Thrust by counterthrust is foiled;
Judgment is hard,—the spoiler spoiled,
  The price for bloodshed yielded.
While Zeus upon his throne shall reign,
For wrong done, *penance* must remain
Commandment:—How shall forth be cast
The seed of Curse? To Ruin fast
  The race is glued and welded.

CLYTAEMNESTRA.

Ah, justly now you leave your taunts
  For God's most firm decrees.—
I say now to the Spirit that haunts
  The House of Pleisthenes:
"I am ready—let an oath be sworn—
To bear, though heavy to be borne,
  Thus much: but now begin
New order; quit this House outworn;
Henceforth some other race be torn
  By own blood shed within.
If such within these halls the price,
For me small riches will suffice
Once having rid them of their vice,
  The frenzy murdering kin!"

ΑΙΓΙΣΘΟΣ.

ὦ φέγγος εὖφρον ἡμέρας δικηφόρου.
φαίην ἂν ἤδη νῦν βροτῶν τιμαόρους
θεοὺς ἄνωθεν γῆς ἐποπτεύειν ἄγη,
ἰδὼν ὑφαντοῖς ἐν πέπλοις Ἐρινύων 1580
τὸν ἄνδρα τόνδε κείμενον φίλως ἐμοί,
χερὸς πατρῴας ἐκτίνοντα μηχανάς.
Ἀτρεὺς γὰρ ἄρχων τῆσδε γῆς, τούτου πατήρ,
πατέρα Θυέστην τὸν ἐμόν, ὡς τορῶς φράσαι,
αὑτοῦ δ' ἀδελφόν, ἀμφίλεκτος ὢν κράτει, 1585
ἠνδρηλάτησεν ἐκ πόλεώς τε καὶ δόμων.
καὶ προστρόπαιος ἑστίας μολὼν πάλιν
τλήμων Θυέστης μοῖραν ηὗρετ' ἀσφαλῆ,
τὸ μὴ θανὼν πατρῷιον αἱμάξαι πέδον
αὐτοῦ· ξένια δὲ τοῦδε δύσθεος πατὴρ 1590
Ἀτρεύς, προθύμως μᾶλλον ἢ φίλως, πατρὶ
τὠμῶι, κρεουργὸν ἦμαρ εὐθύμως ἄγειν
δοκῶν, παρέσχε δαῖτα παιδείων κρεῶν.
τὰ μὲν ποδήρη καὶ χερῶν ἄκρους κτένας
. . . .
ἔθρυπτ' ἄνωθεν ἀνδρακὰς καθήμενος 1595
ἄσημ'· ὃ δ' αὐτῶν αὐτίκ' ἀγνοίαι λαβὼν
ἔσθει βορὰν ἄσωτον ὡς ὁρᾶις γένει.
κἄπειτ' ἐπιγνοὺς ἔργον οὐ καταίσιον
ᾤμωξεν, ἀμπίπτει δ' ἀπὸ σφαγὴν ἐρῶν,
μόρον δ' ἄφερτον Πελοπίδαις ἐπεύχεται, 1600

1579 ἄγη Auratus: ἄχη codd. **1585** αὑτοῦ δ' Elmsley: αὐτοῦ τ' codd. Post **1594** lacunam indicavit Hermann. **1595** fort. ἔνθρυπτ'. **1596** ἄσημ'· ὃ δ' Dindorf: ἄσημα δ' codd. **1599** ἀμπίπτει Canter: ἄν· πίπτει codd. | σφαγὴν Auratus: σφαγῆς codd.

[*Enter* AEGISTHUS *attended by a body-guard of spearmen.*

AEGISTHUS.

O welcome dawning of the day of judgment!
Now will I say the Gods above look down
With eyes of justice on the sins of earth,
When I behold this man, to my dear pleasure,
In woven raiment from the loom of Vengeance
Paying for the foul craft of his father's hands.
  Atreus was his father, reigning here
In Argos; and his right being questioned by
Thyestes—understand,
My father and his brother—he drove out
Thyestes from the house and from the land.
Returning then
Suppliant in sacred form petitionary,
Safety so far did poor Thyestes find
As not to perish there upon the spot
And spill his life-blood where his fathers trod:
But mark what entertainment this dead man's
Ungodly father makes the sacred guest;
With welcoming
Most *hearty* but scarce *kind*, feigning a day
Of cheer and sacrifice and flesh-killing,
He served a feast up of his children's flesh.
The foot-parts and the fringes of the hands
He kept aside concealed; the rest in messes
Gave him to eat, obscure; he straightway took of it
Unwitting, and made banquet, as you see,
Most thriftless for this House! Then being aware
Of that enormous deed, he groaned, he reeled
Backward, spewing up the butchery, and invoked
An awful doom upon the House of Pelops,

λάκτισμα δείπνου ξυνδίκως τιθεὶς ἀρᾶι,
οὕτως ὀλέσθαι πᾶν τὸ Πλεισθένους γένος.
ἐκ τῶνδέ σοι πεσόντα τόνδ' ἰδεῖν πάρα,
κἀγὼ δίκαιος τοῦδε τοῦ φόνου ῥαφεύς·
τρίτον γὰρ ὄντα μ' ἐπὶ δύ' ἀθλίωι πατρὶ 1605
συνεξελαύνει τυτθὸν ὄντ' ἐν σπαργάνοις·
τραφέντα δ' αὖθις ἡ δίκη κατήγαγεν.
καὶ τοῦδε τἀνδρὸς ἡψάμην θυραῖος ὤν,
πᾶσαν συνάψας μηχανὴν δυσβουλίας.
οὕτω καλὸν δὴ καὶ τὸ κατθανεῖν ἐμοί, 1610
ἰδόντα τοῦτον τῆς δίκης ἐν ἕρκεσιν.

ΧΟ. Αἴγισθ', ὑβρίζειν ἐν κακοῖσιν οὐ σέβω.
σὺ δ' ἄνδρα τόνδε φῂς ἑκὼν κατακτανεῖν,
μόνος δ' ἔποικτον τόνδε βουλεῦσαι φόνον·
οὔ φημ' ἀλύξειν ἐν δίκηι τὸ σὸν κάρα 1615
δημορριφεῖς, σάφ' ἴσθι, λευσίμους ἀράς.

ΑΙ. σὺ ταῦτα φωνεῖς νερτέραι προσήμενος
κώπηι, κρατούντων τῶν ἐπὶ ζυγῶι δορός;
γνώσηι γέρων ὢν ὡς διδάσκεσθαι βαρὺ
τῶι τηλικούτωι σωφρονεῖν εἰρημένον. 1620
δεσμὸς δὲ καὶ τὸ γῆρας αἵ τε νήστιδες
δύαι διδάσκειν ἐξοχώταται φρενῶν
ἰατρομάντεις. οὐχ ὁρᾶις ὁρῶν τάδε;
πρὸς κέντρα μὴ λάκτιζε, μὴ πταίσας μογῆις.

ΧΟ. γύναι, σὺ τοὺς ἥκοντας ἐκ μάχης νέον 1625
οἰκουρὸς εὐνὴν ἀνδρὸς αἰσχύνων ἅμα
ἀνδρὶ στρατηγῶι τόνδ' ἐβούλευσας μόρον;

1602 ὀλέσθαι Tzetzes: ὀλέσθη codd. **1605** ἐπὶ δύ' Emperius: ἐπὶ δέκ' codd. **1613** τόνδε φῂς Pauw: τόνδ' ἔφης codd. **1624** πταίσας Butler: πήσας codd., παίσας schol. Pind. *Pyth.* II 173. **1626** αἰσχύνων Keck: αἰσχύνουσ' codd.

Thus, with a kick to aid his curse, and dashing
The table down,
Thus perish all the seed of Pleisthenes!
Hence comes it in your sight a corpse lies he,
And I the just contriver of his death.
A third-born living child, a third last hope,
In my unhappy father's banishment
He drave me out a babe in swaddling-clothes,
And Justice now hath brought the grown man back.
While yet without I touched him, hit my man,
For this dark subtle train was all my plan.
My hour is ripe for death now when he lies
In toils of Justice caught before these eyes.

ELDER. Aegisthus, to insult upon distress
I like not.—So thou sayest that wilfully
Thou hast compassed the man's death, alone devised
This woful tragedy? Thine own head then,
I say, shall not scape justice; thou shalt feel
The pelting volleys of a people's curse!

AEGISTH. Thou talk so, sirrah, from the lower bench,
When on the main thwart sits authority!
The task is wisdom, and grey hairs will find
At these years how 'tis grievous to be put
To school; but prison and the pangs of hunger
Are your most excellent doctors to instruct
The hoariest head in wisdom. Hast thou eyes
And seest not? Kick not thus
Against the goad or thou mayst hurt thy feet.

ELDER. Vile woman, thou to deal with soldiers thus
Come newly from the field! Home-keeping, and
Dishonouring the man's bed, to plot this death
Against a man and captain of the war!

ΑΙ. καὶ ταῦτα τἄπη κλαυμάτων ἀρχηγενῆ.
Ὀρφεῖ δὲ γλῶσσαν τὴν ἐναντίαν ἔχεις·
ὁ μὲν γὰρ ἦγε πάντ᾽ ἀπὸ φθογγῆς χαρᾶι, 1630
σὺ δ᾽ ἐξορίνας νηπίοις ὑλάγμασιν
ἄξηι· κρατηθεὶς δ᾽ ἡμερώτερος φανῆι.

ΧΟ. ὡς δὴ σύ μοι τύραννος Ἀργείων ἔσηι,
ὃς οὐκ, ἐπειδὴ τῶιδ᾽ ἐβούλευσας μόρον,
δρᾶσαι τόδ᾽ ἔργον οὐκ ἔτλης αὐτοκτόνως; 1635

ΑΙ. τὸ γὰρ δολῶσαι πρὸς γυναικὸς ἦν σαφῶς·
ἐγὼ δ᾽ ὕποπτος ἐχθρὸς ἢ παλαιγενής.—
ἐκ τῶν δὲ τοῦδε χρημάτων πειράσομαι
ἄρχειν πολιτῶν· τὸν δὲ μὴ πειθάνορα
ζεύξω βαρείαις—οὔτι μὴ σειραφόρον 1640
κριθῶντα πῶλον· ἀλλ᾽ ὁ δυσφιλεῖ σκότωι
λιμὸς ξύνοικος μαλθακόν σφ᾽ ἐπόψεται.

ΧΟ. τί δὴ τὸν ἄνδρα τόνδ᾽ ἀπὸ ψυχῆς κακῆς
οὐκ αὐτὸς ἠνάριζες, ἀλλά νιν γυνή,
χώρας μίασμα καὶ θεῶν ἐγχωρίων, 1645
ἔκτειν᾽; Ὀρέστης ἆρά που βλέπει φάος,
ὅπως κατελθὼν δεῦρο πρευμενεῖ τύχηι
ἀμφοῖν γένηται τοῖνδε παγκρατὴς φονεύς.

ΑΙ. ἀλλ᾽ ἐπεὶ δοκεῖς τάδ᾽ ἔρδειν καὶ λέγειν, γνώσηι τάχα—
εἶα δή, φίλοι λοχῖται, τοὔργον οὐχ ἑκὰς τόδε. 1650

ΧΟ. εἶα δή, ξίφος πρόκωπον πᾶς τις εὐτρεπιζέτω.

ΑΙ. ἀλλὰ κἀγὼ μὴν πρόκωπος οὐκ ἀναίνομαι θανεῖν.

ΧΟ. δεχομένοις λέγεις θανεῖν σε· τὴν τύχην δ᾽ αἱρούμεθα.

1631 *νηπίοις* Jacob: *ἠπίοις* codd. **1637** *ἢ* Porson: *ἡ* codd. **1638** *ἐκ τῶνδε* codd.: corr. Jacob. **1641** *δυσφιλεῖ σκότωι* Scaliger: *δυσφιλὴς κότωι* codd. **1644** *νιν* Spanheim: *σὺν* codd. **1650** choro dant codd.: corr. Stanley. **1653** *αἱρούμεθα* Auratus: *ἐρούμεθα* codd.

AEGISTH. Progenitors of tears are these words too:—
The very counter thine to Orpheus' tongue!
He with his ravishing voice did all things hale;
Thou, with a foolish yelp exasperating,
Shalt see thyself
Haled, and thine own breast by compulsion tamed.

ELDER. Thou to be despot over Argive men!
When after plotting murder of this one
Thou durst not venture thine own hand to do it.

AEGISTH. The cozening clearly was the woman's part;
I was a suspect foe hereditary.
—However,
With help of this man's treasure I will essay
To rule here, and the disobedient colt
With heavy yoke will break—no courser running
In traces, crammed with corn! 'tis hunger lodged
In loathsome darkness that shall humble his flesh.

ELDER. Ah, why then didst thou with a craven's heart
Not slay the man thyself, but take a woman,
Stain to her country and her country's Gods,
To do the killing? O doth somewhere look
Orestes on the light, that Fortune's grace
May give him good speed home again to be
Victorious executioner of these both!

AEGISTH. O well then, sirrah,
If thus you mean with act and word, you soon shall understand—
What ho! my trusty men-at-arms! Your work lies here to hand.

[*The Guard advance.*

ELDER. What ho! let each his sword well-gripped be now prepared to ply.

AEGISTH. Well, I too with my sword well-gripped will not refuse to die.

ELDER. *To die!* An omen! Be it so; content, content, am I.

ΚΛ. μηδαμῶς, ὦ φίλτατ' ἀνδρῶν, ἄλλα δράσωμεν κακά,
ἀλλὰ καὶ τάδ' ἐξαμῆσαι πολλά, δύστηνον θέρος· 1655
πημονῆς δ' ἅλις γ' ὑπάρχει μηδὲν ἡιματωμένοις.
στείχετ' αἰδοῖοι γέροντες πρὸς δόμους, πεπρωμένοις,
πρὶν παθεῖν, εἴξαντες ὥραι· χρῆν τάδ' ὡς ἐπράξαμεν.
εἰ δέ τοι μόχθων γένοιτο τῶνδ' ἅλις, δεχοίμεθ' ἄν,
δαίμονος χηλῆι βαρείαι δυστυχῶς πεπληγμένοι. 1660
ὧδ' ἔχει λόγος γυναικός, εἴ τις ἀξιοῖ μαθεῖν.

ΑΙ. ἀλλὰ τούσδ' ἐμοὶ ματαίαν γλῶσσαν ὧδ' ἀπανθίσαι
κἀκβαλεῖν ἔπη τοιαῦτα δαίμονος πειρωμένους,
σώφρονος γνώμης θ' ἁμαρτεῖν τὸν κρατοῦντ' ἀ<ρνου-
μένους>.

ΧΟ. οὐκ ἂν Ἀργείων τόδ' εἴη, φῶτα προσσαίνειν κακόν.

ΑΙ. ἀλλ' ἐγώ σ' ἐν ὑστέραισιν ἡμέραις μέτειμ' ἔτι. 1666

ΧΟ. οὔκ, ἐὰν δαίμων Ὀρέστην δεῦρ' ἀπευθύνηι μολεῖν.

ΑΙ. οἶδ' ἐγὼ φεύγοντας ἄνδρας ἐλπίδας σιτουμένους.

ΧΟ. πρᾶσσε, πιαίνου, μιαίνων τὴν δίκην· ἐπεὶ πάρα.

ΑΙ. ἴσθι μοι δώσων ἄποινα τῆσδε μωρίας χρόνωι. 1670

ΧΟ. κόμπασον θαρσῶν, ἀλέκτωρ ὥστε θηλείας πέλας.

ΚΛ. μὴ προτιμήσηις ματαίων τῶνδ' ὑλαγμάτων· ἐγὼ
καὶ σὺ θήσομεν κρατοῦντε τῶνδε δωμάτων καλῶς.

1654 *δράσωμεν* Victorius: *δράσομεν* codd. **1655** *θέρος* Schuetz: *ὁ ἔρως* codd. **1656** *ὑπάρχει* Scaliger: *ὕπαρχε* codd. | *ἡιματωμένοις* Hermann: *ἡματώμεθα* codd. **1657** sq. *στείχετ' αἰδοῖοι* H. L. Ahrens: *στείχετε δ' οἱ* codd. | *πεπρωμένοις...εἴξαντες* Madvig: *πεπρωμένους τούσδε...ἔρξαντες* (*ἔρξαντα* g h) codd. | *ὥραι* H. (*ὥραν* Housman): *καιρόν* codd. **1659** *δέχοιμεθ'* Martin: *γ' ἐχοίμεθ'* codd. **1663** *δαίμονος* Casaubon: *δαίμονας* codd. **1664** *θ'* Stanley: *δ'* f h | *ἁμαρτεῖν τὸν* Casaubon: *ἁμαρτῆτον* f h, om. g | *ἀρνουμένους* supplevit H. **1670** *χρόνωι* Wecklein: *χάριν* codd. **1671** *θαρρῶν* codd.: corr. Porson | *ὥστε* Scaliger: *ὥσπερ* codd. **1672** sq. *ἐγὼ* et *καλῶς* om. codd., ex schol. suppleverunt Canter et Auratus.

CLYTAEMNESTRA, *interposing.*

Nay nay forbear, my dearest lord, let us no mischief more;
The harvest here already reaped is plenty and full sore;
We have surely suffered harms enough without the waste of gore.—
Most reverend Elders, get you home; yield now to Fate's decree,
Betimes, before you suffer; Fate's executor were we.
But should this heavy chastening prove enough, we will submit,
So hard by our familiar Spirit with his fierce talon smit:
A woman's counsel here you have, will any stoop to it.

AEGISTHUS, *fuming still.*

But these to let their tongue run wild and wanton at this rate,
And fling such whirling words abroad in tempting of their fate,
And be so reft of all advice, their master thus to brave!

ELDER. 'Twas never yet the Argive way to cringe before a knave.

AEGISTH. Ah well, I'll have my vengeance of you yet in days to come!

ELDER. Thou shalt not, if but Heaven direct Orestes' footsteps home.

AEGISTH. O, well I know how banished men will feed on husks of hope.

ELDER. Do, do; with fatness gross defile God's law; 'tis in thy scope.

AEGISTH. The day will come; I warn thee, thou shalt rue this folly then!

ELDER. O bravely now the cock may crow and strut beside his hen!

CLYTAEM. These idle yelpings prithee hold in slight regard; we two
Will be the masters in this House, and our dispose will do.

NOTES

4 ff. The Watchman has been watching for the greater part of a whole year—not longer, because according to God's prophecy through Calchas Troy was only to fall in the tenth year and not before: see Homer B 329. The ἀστέρες are of course the constellations whose risings and settings were the signs of seasons (*P.V.* 473 f. ἀντολὰς ἐγὼ ἄστρων ἔδειξα τάς τε δυσκρίτους δύσεις), and the Watchman has had time to learn the signs of Winter or Storm-season—the same word expresses both in Greek—for it is now past the autumnal equinox, the time when χειμέριαι δύνουσι Πελειάδες (Hes. fr. 44), and the setting of the Pleiades proverbially marked the season most dangerous of all at sea. In this allusion therefore an ominous note is heard at once; and presently confirmed, for the capture, as we are duly informed in v. 817, has taken place 'about the sinking of the Pleiades,' and Agamemnon has set sail for home immediately, committing the rash act against which Neoptolemus in Quint. 7. 298–311 is expressly warned by Lycomedes. His rashness was followed by the disastrous storm in the Aegean.—The construction ὅταν φθίνωσιν in v. 7 is idiomatic for *watching, observing, marking* (φυλάττειν, τηρεῖν) *the time when*; Herodas 3. 55 is an example, νοεῦνθ' ὁκῆμος παιγνίην ἀγινῆτε. Dem. 4. 31 Φίλιππος φυλάξας τοὺς ἐτησίας ἢ τὸν χειμῶνα ἐπιχειρεῖ ἡνίκ' ἂν ἡμεῖς μὴ δυναίμεθα ἐκεῖσε ἀφικέσθαι.—δυνάστας is an astrological word: see Proclus on Plat. *Rep.* in Schoell and Studemund *Anecdota* ii. p. 26; in sense, synonymous with more familiar terms such as κρατήτωρ, δεσπόζειν, οἰκοδεσποτεῖν, *tyrannus Hesperiae Capricornus undae* (Hor. *C.* ii. 17. 19).

ἀστέρας repeats in plain words the preceding metaphorical description. This is a common feature of Tragic style, and as such is burlesqued by Xenarchus (Ath. 63 f) κοὔτε βυσαύχην θεᾶς Δηοῦς σύνοικος, γηγενὴς βόλβος. Further Aeschylean examples will be found *inf.* 500, 816, *Pers.* 615, *Theb.* 191, 476, 717, 926, *P. V.* 7, 374, 829, 956, 1054, *Supp.* 231.

8. **καὶ νῦν** answers to μὲν in v. 1, which is itself intended to qualify φρουρᾶς ἐτείας μῆκος: *as throughout the year...so now.* Similarly *inf.* 592 ἀνωλόλυξα μὲν πάλαι (for πάλαι μὲν ἀνωλόλυξα)...603 καὶ νῦν, *Theb.* 21 καὶ νῦν μὲν ἐς τόδ' ἦμαρ (for καὶ νῦν ἐς μὲν τόδ' ἦμαρ) εὖ ῥέπει θεός· νῦν δέ

κ.τ.λ., Soph. *Phil.* 617 οἴοιτο μὲν μάλισθ' (for οἴοιτο μάλιστα μὲν) ἑκούσιον λαβών, εἰ μὴ θέλοι δ', ἄκοντα, *Ant.* 327 ἀλλ' εὑρεθείη μὲν μάλιστ', ἐὰν δέ τοι ληφθῆι τε καὶ μή...Aesch. fr. 36 εὐοδίαν μὲν πρῶτον, Soph. fr. 807.

10 f. 'For so a woman's manlike spirit is sanguine to expect,' *ita enim sperare valet.* The MS. gives ἐλπίζων with ο written above ω, meaning ἐλπίζον, an obvious conjecture which naturally has not contented scholars. The correction ἐλπίζειν I find from Wecklein had been proposed before by an anonymous critic in 1834, but I have never seen it even mentioned. For the infinitive after κρατεῖν, expressing what your superiority or predominance enables you to do, cf. Thuc. iv. 104 κρατοῦντες τῶι πλήθει ὥστε μὴ αὐτίκα τὰς πύλας ἀνοίγεσθαι. vi. 74 ἐν ὅπλοις ὄντες ἐπεκράτουν μὴ δέχεσθαι τοὺς Ἀθηναίους. Eur. *Hel.* 1639 ΘΕ. ἀρχόμεσθ' ἄρ', οὐ κρατοῦμεν. ΧΟ. ὅσια δρᾶν, τὰ δ' ἔκδικ' οὔ. For ἀνδρόβουλον cf. Soph. fr. 857 κατ' ὀρφανὸν γὰρ οἶκον ἀνδρόφρων γυνή.

12 ff. **εὖτ' ἂν δὲ** is resumed by **ὅταν δ'** (16) after the interruption caused by the explanatory γάρ-clause. For similar instances of a resumptive δέ cf. *Cho.* 988, 1024, Plat. *Apol.* 34 D εἰ δή τις ὑμῶν οὕτως ἔχει,—οὐκ ἀξιῶ μὲν γὰρ ἔγωγε· εἰ δ' οὖν κ.τ.λ., *Gorg.* 480 E ἐὰν μόνον μὴ αὐτὸς ἀδικῆται ὑπὸ τοῦ ἐχθροῦ· τοῦτο μὲν γὰρ εὐλαβητέον· ἐὰν δὲ ἄλλον ἀδικῆι ὁ ἐχθρός...Pausan v. 25. 8, 9 τῶν δὲ ἐπὶ τῶι Ἕκτορι κληρουμένων ἀριθμὸν ὄντων ὀκτώ, τὸν γὰρ ἔνατον..., τῶν δὲ ὀκτὼ τούτων κ.τ.λ.

15. **τὸ μὴ...συμβαλεῖν** depends on φόβος παραστατεῖ—a favourite construction in Aeschylus. Cf. *Pers.* 294 ὑπερβάλλει γὰρ ἥδε συμφορὰ τὸ μήτε λέξαι μήτ' ἐρωτῆσαι πάθη, *P. V.* 891 μίαν δὲ παίδων ἵμερος θέλξει τὸ μὴ κτεῖναι σύνευνον.

16. **μινυρίζειν**: cf. Max. Tyr. 7. 7 ἤδη τις καὶ ὑπὸ αὐλημάτων ἀνὴρ ἄμουσος διετέθη μουσικῶς, καὶ τὰ ὦτα ἔναυλος ὢν διαμέμνηται τοῦ μέλους, καὶ μινυρίζει πρὸς αὐτόν.

27. **εὐνῆς ἐπαντείλασαν** is a reverent phrase, suggested by a comparison with the rising of the sun or stars. Lucian i. 474 applies it in the same way to a great man dawning on the clients waiting in his ante-chambers till he rises: ὁ δὲ μόγις ἄν ποτε ἀνατείλας αὐτοῖς πορφυροῦς τίς ἢ περίχρυσος ἢ διαποικίλος· εὐδαίμονας ὤιετο καὶ μακαρίους ἀποφαίνειν τοὺς προσειπόντας ἢν τὸ στῆθος ἢ τὴν δεξιὰν προτείνων δοίη καταφιλεῖν. In the *Bacchae* 747 a messenger wishes to say 'the flesh was torn from their limbs before you could wink' (πρὶν μύσαι, πρὶν καταμύσαι), but feeling this is too familiar to a king, he turns it θᾶσσον δὲ διεφοροῦντο σαρκὸς ἐνδυτὰ ἢ σὺ ξυνάψαις βλέφαρα βασιλείοις κόραις 'than you could close your eyelids on your royal eyes.' οὐδ' εὖ πραπίδων οἴακα νέμων, applied by the Chorus to the King in v. 793, is another such respectful phrase.

28. **ὀλολυγμός** is the 'lulu', 'ullaloo', familiar to us now from Africa, the shrill cry of *women* either for joy and triumph, or in sorrow and mourning. For its association with the παιάν cf. Bacchyl. xvi. 124 ff. ἀγλαόθρονοί τε κοῦραι σὺν εὐθυμίαι νεοκτίτωι ὠλόλυξαν...ἠίθεοι δ' ἐγγύθεν νέοι παιάνιξαν, Aesch. *Theb.* 254 ὀλολυγμὸν ἱερὸν εὐμενῆ παιώνισον. For the dative λαμπάδι cf. Eur. *I. A.* 1467 ὑμεῖς δ' ἐπευφημήσατ', ὦ νεάνιδες, παιᾶνα τῆμῆι συμφορᾶι.

32 f. **τὰ δεσποτῶν...φρυκτωρίας.** The metaphor is taken from the game of πεσσοί, *Tables* or *Backgammon*, in which the moves of the pieces were determined or limited by the throws (βάλλειν, βόλος), or falls (πίπτειν, πτώσεις) of the dice. τίθεσθαι is applied to the skill of the player, whose opportunities are so conditioned: cf. Soph. fr. 861 στέργειν τε τἀκπεσόντα καὶ θέσθαι πρέπει | σοφὸν κυβευτήν, ἀλλὰ μὴ στένειν τύχην. Plat. *Rep.* 604 C ὥσπερ ἐν πτώσει κύβων, πρὸς τὰ πεπτωκότα τίθεσθαι τὰ αὑτοῦ πράγματα. This is referred to by Plut. *Mor.* 467 A where he says κυβείαι γὰρ ὁ Πλάτων τὸν βίον ἀπείκασεν, ἐν ὧι καὶ βάλλειν δεῖ τὰ πρόσφορα, καὶ βαλόντα χρῆσθαι καλῶς τοῖς πεσοῦσι. Stob. *Flor.* 124. 41 πεττείαι τινι ἔοικεν ὁ βίος, καὶ δεῖ, ὥσπερ ψῆφόν τινα, τίθεσθαι τὸ συμβαῖνον. οὐ γὰρ ἔστιν ἄνωθεν βαλεῖν, οὐδ' ἀναθέσθαι τὴν ψῆφον ('to make another throw or withdraw the move'). [Plat.] *Hipparch.* 229 E ὥσπερ πεττεύων, ἐθέλω σοι ἐν τοῖς λόγοις ἀναθέσθαι ὅτι βούλει τῶν εἰρημένων. Plut. *Pyrrh.* 26 ὅθεν ἀπείκαζεν αὐτὸν ὁ Ἀντίγονος κυβευτῆι πολλὰ βάλλοντι καὶ καλά, χρῆσθαι δὲ οὐκ ἐπισταμένωι τοῖς πεσοῦσι. Hor. *C.* i. 9. 14 *quem sors dierum cunque dabit, lucro appone.* Hence expressions like Dem. 23. 134 πρὸς τὸ καλῶς ἔχον τίθεσθαι, Eur. fr. 287 ἀλλ' οὑντυγχάνων τὰ πράγματ' ὀρθῶς ἂν τιθῆι, πράσσει καλῶς. But that εὖ belongs to πεσόντα is shown by Eur. *Or.* 603, *El.* 1101, etc.

43 f. **δισκήπτρου τιμῆς**: *Eum.* 629 διοσδότοις σκήπτροισι τιμαλφούμενον, Hom. A 278 ἐπεὶ οὔ ποθ' ὁμοίης ἔμμορε τιμῆς σκηπτοῦχος βασιλεύς.

48. **κλάζοντες** introduces the following simile: Hom. Π 428 οἳ δ' ὥστ' αἰγυπιοὶ γαμψώνυχες ἀγκυλοχεῖλαι πέτρηι ἐφ' ὑψηλῆι μεγάλα κλάζοντε μάχωνται, Hes. *Scut.* 405, Eur. *Tro.* 146 μάτηρ δ' ὡσεί τις πτανοῖς κλαγγὰν ὄρνισιν, ὅπως ἐξάρξω.

49. **ἐκπατίοις.** Criticism here has wavered between the MS. ἐκπατίοις and ἐκπάγλοις the conjecture of Blomfield. ἐκπάγλοις ἄλγεσι 'exceeding anguish' would of course be perfectly natural in language; but ἐκπατίοις is better rhythmically, and better sustains the figure. Other poets are content with transitory metaphors, and that is one way of writing; no one but Aeschylus has his habitual practice—no one, perhaps, but Pindar had his power—of pursuing a similitude, of carrying a figure through. This passage is a very fine example. Eagles always represented Kings, but the Kings here—for the two are closely coupled,

and one's quarrel is the other's (vv. 42–44)—whose high bed has been robbed are compared to eagles whose high bed has been robbed, ἄλγεσι παίδων ὑπατηλεχέων, δεμνιοτήρη πόνον ὀλέσαντες. As the Kings launch forth in ships, so fly the eagles πτερύγων ἐρετμοῖσιν ἐρεσσόμενοι—this need not be pressed, but still it happily maintains the parallel. And then the likeness is pursued; the eagles in their lofty haunts are conceived as denizens (μέτοικοι) in the region of the loftiest-dwelling Gods,—Apollo, Pan, or Zeus; and as μέτοικοι when wronged appealed at Athens to their προστάται or 'patrons,' so the eagles will appeal to these; One above will surely hear their cry and will defend their right. 'And thus,' continues Aeschylus, 'the Atridae are sent by a greater lord, Ζεὺς ξένιος, against Alexander.'

It is in the manner of Aeschylus, then, to choose an epithet which will bear out his comparison. Now eagles and vultures were notoriously remote and solitary; so of course, from the nature of their high degree, were Kings—all Kings, though the more ἀπρόσιτοι they were, the more marked was the resemblance: Horapoll. *Hieroglyph.* ii. 56 βασιλέα ἰδιάζοντα καὶ μὴ ἐλεοῦντα ἐν τοῖς πταίσμασι βουλόμενοι σημῆναι, ἀετὸν ζωγραφοῦσιν· οὗτος γὰρ ἐν τοῖς ἐρήμοις τόποις ἔχει τὴν νεοσσιὰν καὶ ὑψηλότερος πάντων τῶν πετεινῶν ἵπταται.

50. **ἄλγεσι παίδων ὑπατηλεχέων**, 'in exceeding anguish for their lofty-cradled children.' As you could say ἀλγεῖν τινος (*inf.* 576, Eur. *Hec.* 1256), so you could say ἄλγος τινός: *Pers.* 837, Eur. *Hel.* 202, *Suppl.* 807, 1117 παίδων ὑπὸ πένθους, *Phoen.* 1578 ἄχει δὲ τέκνων.—Mr Housman (*Journ. Phil.* xvi. 247) first pointed out that ὕπατοι λεχέων (see cr. n.) could not mean 'high above their eyries.' ὕπατος means ὕψιστος, and is always a *superlative*: ὕπατε κρειόντων Hom. Θ 31, σὸν δὲ κράτος πάντων ἐσθ' ὕπατον Theogn. 376, θεῶν ὕπατον Ap. Rhod. iv. 146, Δία τὸν πάντων ὕπατον, hymn. ap. Aristid. i. 452, ὕπατον παίδων Pind. *P.* x. 9. The genitive is of the partitive nature, as in ἄντυξ ἣ πυμάτη θέεν ἀσπίδος Hom. Z 118, τὸν δ' ὕστατον εὗρεν ὁμίλου ἑσταότα N 459, οἴακος ὑστάτου νεώς Aesch. *Supp.* 725, ὁ δ' ὕστατός γε τοῦ χρόνου *inf.* 1299, ἐσχάτῃ χθονός *P. V.* 872, ἤδη γὰρ ἕδραι Ζεὺς ἐν ἐσχάτηι θεῶν; Soph. fr. 821: so ὕπατός τε χώρας Ζεύς *inf.* 514 means 'supreme in the land,' as Pind. *O.* xiii. 24 ὕπατ' εὐρυανάσσων Ὀλυμπίας, and in Tim. Locr. 100 A ὡς τἆλλα μέρεα ὑπηρετεῖν τούτωι καθάπερ ὑπάτωι τῶ σκάνεος ἅπαντος, translate it as you may, it will be seen that ὑπάτωι is still superlative, and τῶ σκάνεος a partitive genitive; and this is the sense which is impossible in ὕπατοι λεχέων. I believe that the MS. reading is the corruption of a compound, to be added to the many adjectives in -λεχής, as πρωτολεχής, μουνο-, κοινο-, αἰνο-, δεινο-, ἀπειρο-, εὐ-, ἱππο-, ὀρει-, γη-, χαμαι-. The formation would first be ὑπατολεχέων, and in Epic the

λ might merely be doubled in pronunciation, as πολύλλιστος Hom., μονόλλυκος Arat. 1124; but the usual plan for metrical purposes or for euphony was to substitute η for ο, as θανατηφόρος, αἱματηφόρος, θεσφατηλόγος, ἐλαφηβόλος, πολεμηδόκος, ξενηδόκος, γλαυκηπόρος, ὀμφαλητόμος, νεήφατος, νεηθαλής, and countless others, to which I will only add ὀφιηβοσίη from the *Inscriptions of Cos*, p. 113. The whole subject is treated with his unique learning by Lobeck, *Phryn.* p. 633–713.

55. εἴ τις Ἀπόλλων would be easier to support than the MS. ἤ τις: see on 149, 1461.—For τις ('Apollo, it may be') cf. Antiphanes fr. 129 (ii. 63 K.) θαλάττιον μὲν οὗτος οὐδὲν ἐσθίει | πλὴν τῶν παρὰ γῆν, γόγγρον τιν' ἢ νάρκην τιν' ἢ κτέ., Alexis fr. 108 (ii. 334 K.) ὁ μὲν οὖν ἐμὸς υἱός... τοιοῦτος γέγονεν, Οἰνοπίων τις ἢ Μάρων τις ἢ Κάπηλος ἢ <τις> Τιμοκλῆς, Lucian iii. p. 14 ἀλλ' εἴ τις ἢ Τιτυός, ἢ Ὦτος, ἢ Ἐφιάλτης, ὑπὲρ ἐκείνους, ii. p. 60 μὴ πρὸς ἓν μέρος ὁράτω...εἰ μὴ Βρασίδας τις εἴη προπηδῶν ἢ Δημοσθένης ἀνακόπτων τὴν ἐπίβασιν.

65. ἐν προτελείοις, before the issue is decided. προτέλεια, as representing the ceremonies previous to the consummation of marriage, was metaphorically used for *preliminaries* to the completion, perfection, accomplishment of anything—of a voyage in v. 237, of mature age in v. 721, and often in later authors.

70. ἀπύρων ἱερῶν. ἄπυρα, far from being abnormal, were a distinct class of offerings, roughly parallel with ἔμπυρα and λοιβαί, but not needing dedication by fire, as when in an ordinary sacrifice the worshipper shared his meal with the gods. They might be offered to the Olympians as a means of propitiation; but as a rule these deities were invited to fire-sacrifices. The mistake of the Rhodians in Pind. *O.* vii. 88 was that they established a worship of Athena with ἄπυρα, whereas, being an Olympian, she should have been honoured with fire. The regular offerings to the subterranean powers were ἄπυρα, partly because intended to sink into the earth instead of ascending to Heaven, and partly because their worship in general involves propitiation rather than communion. The scholiast rightly recognises the customary character of such offerings: τῶν θυσιῶν τῶν Μοιρῶν καὶ τῶν Ἐρινύων, ἃ καὶ νηφάλια καλεῖται. So Eur. fr. 904 mentions the offering of θυσίαν ἄπυρον παγκαρπείας to a deity who may be either Zeus or Hades: Ζεὺς εἴτ' Ἀίδης ὀνομαζόμενος στέργεις. Other instances of ἄπυρα, given in Gardner and Jevons' *Manual of Antiquities*, p. 238, are coins, locks of hair, horses driven into the sea and so forth. Of course neither the kindling of fire nor the pouring of libations would make ἄπυρα effective; and the Chorus cannot mean by ὑποκαίων and ἐπιλείβων (Apoll. Rhod. i. 1132 πολλὰ δὲ τήνγε λιτῇσιν ἀποστρέψαι ἐριώλας | Αἰσονίδης γουνάζετ' ἐπιλλείβων ἱεροῖσιν | αἰθομένοις) that somebody might seek so to appease divine anger

aroused by another regular kind. It is clearly their intention to express that by no sort of offering, neither by ἔμπυρα nor by λοιβαί nor by ἄπυρα will anyone appease the stubborn anger of Zeus (or of Μοῖρα Διός implied in τὸ πεπρωμένον, which comes to the same thing), whose intention is to cause many woes to Greeks and Trojans alike. Thus, 'the stern temper of unburnt sacrifices' represents the fixed mood of Fate, in relation to which all sacrifice is useless: Verg. *Aen.* vi. 376 *desine fata deum flecti sperare precando.* Moschion fr. 2 (*F. T. G.* p. 812) ὦ καὶ θεῶν κρατοῦσα καὶ θνητῶν μόνη | μοῖρ', ὦ λιταῖς ἄτρεπτε (see *Class. Rev.* xviii. p. 430) δυστήνων βροτῶν, | πάντολμ' ἀνάγκη. Manetho p. 92 Koechly τίπτε μάτην, ἄνθρωπε, θυηπολέεις μακάρεσσιν; | τίπτε μάτην τρισέλικτος ἀν' οὐρανὸν ἤλυθε κνῖσα; | ἴσχεο, οὐ γὰρ ὄνειαρ ἐν ἀθανάτοιο θυηλαῖς (ἐν ἀθανάτοισι θυηλῆς). | οὐ γάρ τις δύναται γένεσιν μετατρεψέμεν ἀνδρῶν, | ἥθ' ἅμα νηπιάχοις συγγίγνεται ἀνθρώποισιν, | εὐθύ τε Μοιράων εἱλίσσεται ἀμφὶ μίτοισιν, | κλώσμασιν ἀρρήκτοισι σιδηρείοισι τ' ἀτράκτοις.

71. **παραθέλξει** without τις is strange: perhaps we should read παραθέλξεις.

72. **ἀτῖται** means 'insolvent,' 'defaulters,' 'bankrupt,' unable to pay the debt of military service to the State (χρέος τόδε *Theb.* 20). Hesych. ἀτίτην: ἄπορον. ἄτιμον. τὸν μὴ ἔχοντα ἀποτῖσαι, and τίται: εὔποροι, 'men of means.'

76 ff. **ὅ τε γὰρ νεαρὸς μυελὸς στέρνων ἐντὸς ἀνάσσων ἰσόπρεσβυς·... τί θ' ὑπέργηρως; ...παιδὸς οὐδὲν ἀρείων**: as the marrow in its nonage is as feeble and unfit for war as in old age, so conversely in extreme old age it is as feeble and unwarlike as a child's,—a pathetic expansion of the saying δὶς παῖδες οἱ γέροντες, 'old age is second childhood.' The marrow is the measure of the whole bodily vigour: in fact a familiar name for it was αἰών, 'the life,' as in Pind. fr. 111 αἰὼν δὲ δι' ὀστέων ἐραίσθη. **ἀνάσσων** is appropriate to the marrow, regent in its frame of bone and dominating vital functions (Tim. Locr. 100 A, Plat. *Tim.* 73 B), and should not be changed to ἀνᾴσσων, *shooting up* like a beanstalk! See also Plin. *N. H.* xi. 37, 67.—These lines prepare us for the βουλαὶ γερόντων which we find instead of ἔργα at the crisis. Euripides would have apologised at the crisis itself.

79. **τί θ' ὑπέργηρως; κτέ.** For the question cf. Pind. *P.* viii. 95 ἐπάμεροι· τί δέ τις; τί δ' οὔ τις; σκιᾶς ὄναρ ἄνθρωπος.

87. See cr. n. The corruption is due to the tendency of the copyists to remove paroemiacs.

90. **τῶν τε θυραίων τῶν τ' ἀγοραίων** appears to be the right antithesis, viz. that of the shrines of all deities in the public places of the town and of those in each several and private place,—at the street-door of each house. The title θυραῖος is assigned to Apollo in Macrob. *Sat.* i. 9. 6.

For the similar practice of the Jews see Isaiah 57. 8 'Behind the doors also and the posts hast thou set up thy remembrance.' 1 Maccabees 1. 55 'And at the doors of the houses and in the streets they burnt incense.'

96. **βασιλείωι.** The appellation 'royal' often connotes choiceness of quality: Athen. 64 b (*βολβοί*) *οἱ βασιλικοὶ λεγόμενοι, οἳ καὶ κρείσσονες τῶν ἄλλων εἰσί*, id. 54 b, 76 f.

97 f. **ὅ τι καὶ δυνατὸν καὶ θέμις αἰνεῖν.** Cf. Eur. *Ion* 233 *πάντα θεᾶσθ' ὅτι καὶ θέμις ὄμμασι.*

99. **τε γενοῦ.** The sentence begins as though another *τε* were to follow, but it never does, because the intervening relative clauses are supposed to have put it out of mind; a parenthesis usurps the place of the main sentence. Cf. *Supp.* 490 *κλάδους τε τούτους αἶψ' ἐν ἀγκάλαις λαβὼν κτἑ.* It is studied carelessness to resemble the irregularity of actual speech, like the 'nominativus pendens,' which Aeschylus is so fond of using.

101 ff. See cr. n. The words, I think, were transposed to show the construction, *i.e.* in order to bring *ἐκ θυσιῶν—ἀγανὰ φαίνουσ'* together, and *τὴν θυμοφθόρον λύπης φρένα* was an explanation of *τὴν θυμοβόρον φροντίδα.* In reading *φαίνουσ'* I follow f and Triclinius. *ἀγανὰ φαίνουσα* is like Theocr. ii. 10 *ἀλλὰ Σελάνα, φαῖνε καλόν*: so now the reason is apparent why we find *ἀγανὰ*, not *ἀγανή*: it was not feminine but neuter plural.

106. **ἐκτελέων**, 'men of prime': which, however, would be more naturally contrasted with immaturity than with the aged Elders' own decay. *ἐντελέων* (Hermann al.) would be 'men in power.'

108. **πειθώ** should possibly be *πειθοῖ* (Heller), 'inspires me by divine impulse with puissance in song.' The general sense is 'though I am now too weak to fight, I am still strong enough to sing,' as the old shepherd says in *A. P.* vi. 73 *εἰσέτι γὰρ σύριγγι μελίσδομαι, εἰσέτι φωνὰ ἄτρομος ἐν τρομερῷ σώματι ναιετάει.* The passage has echoes of Pind. *O.* i. 104—112, and seems to me to be itself echoed in Eur. *Phaethon* fr. 774. 44 *κοσμὸν δ' ὑμεναίων δεσποσύνων | ἐμὲ καὶ τὸ δίκαιον ἄγει καὶ ἔρως | ὑμνεῖν· δμωσὶν γὰρ ἀνάκτων | εὐαμερίαι προσιοῦσαι | μολπᾶν θράσος αἴρουσ' | ἐπὶ χάρμασιν* (as I emend *χάρματ'*).

113. See cr. n. *δίκας* was a gloss on *πράκτορι*, and *καὶ χερὶ* was no doubt lost owing to the recurring final syllable.

121 ff. The kings subduing Troy with her teeming multitude inside are typified by eagles. Aeschylus, I suspect, was thinking of that remarkable passage—Hesiodic or Orphic in character rather than Ionic —about *Ἄτη* and the *Λιταί*: Hom. I 505 *ἡ δ' Ἄτη σθεναρή τε καὶ ἀρτίπος, οὕνεκα πάσας πολλὸν ὑπεκπροθέει, φθάνει δέ τε πᾶσαν ἐπ' αἶαν βλάπτουσ' ἀνθρώπους*, with *βλαφθεὶς* in 512. So *inf.* 406, when *Ἄτη* has her way, λιτᾶν ἀκούει οὐδεὶς θεῶν. For the significance of βλαβέντα λοισθίων δρόμων, 'prevented from her final course,' as applied to the hare, see Platt in *Class. Rev.* xi. p. 94. For the accusative after βοσκόμενοι cf. Eur. *Med.* 826 φερβόμενοι κλεινοτάταν σοφίαν, Cratinus (i. 57 K.) ap. Athen. 99 f. ἧσθε πανημέριοι χορταζόμενοι γάλα λευκόν. The order of the words (λαγίναν...γένναν), common in Latin, is rare in Greek, although Lucian has it.

125 f. The principle that in Greek the emphatic words are placed first, and the unemphatic follow after, is the key to the understanding of this sentence. All critics have assumed that λήμασι δισσούς go together; then, seeing that δισσούς is unsuitable, some have substituted other words, as Lobeck πιστούς, Dindorf ἴσους. The truth is that the words which go together are δύο λήμασι: 'seeing the twain warrior sons of Atreus two in temper.' What enables the sage prophet to identify the pair of eagles with the pair of princes is that the birds are royal warriors, but one κελαινός and the other ἐξόπιν ἀργᾶς—in common language μελανάετος and πύγαργος (Arist. 618 b 18). These represent characters which correspond to those of Agamemnon and Menelaus. The taunt of spiritlessness or κακία so often aimed at Menelaus (largely based, one may suppose, on the lost Epic and Lyric literature) seems to be hinted at in v. 420—424; οὐ γὰρ εἰκός, says Pindar fr. 81, τῶν ἐόντων ἁρπαζομένων παρά θ' ἑστίαι καθῆσθαι καὶ κακὸν ἔμμεν. Menelaus is called by Apollo in the guise of Asiades (Hom. P 588) μαλθακὸς αἰχμητής, and of him Orestes says (Eur. *Or.* 754) οὐ γὰρ αἰχμητὴς πέφυκεν, ἐν γυναιξὶ δ' ἄλκιμος, Electra (*Or.* 1201) οὔτε γὰρ θρασὺς οὔτ' ἄλκιμος πέφυκεν, Helen (Colluthus 314) οἶσθα γὰρ ὡς Μενέλαος ἀνάλκιδός ἐστι γενέθλης. Add Quint. vi. 30—43. δισσοὶ Ἀτρεῖδαι is the common phrase, Eur. *Hec.* 510, *Or.* 818, Soph. *Ai.* 57, 947, and similarly 390, 960, *Phil.* 793, 1024, *sup.* 43.

131. ἀγρεῖ recalls the ἄγρα of the eagles.

134. κτήνη is not κτήματα, but means 'beasts, cattle.' There is a double meaning, as the language suggests to the audience the herd of the Greek forces.

136 ff. οἶον μή...κνεφάσηι means μόνον φράζεσθαι or φυλακτέον μή... and this is the saving clause which it appears from some amusing parodies was proper to a prophecy: *A. P.* xi. 163 a wrestler, a pentathlete, and a runner come to find out from a μάντις which will win. 'πάντες' ἔφη 'νικᾶτε· μόνον μή τις σε παρέλθηι, καὶ σε καταστρέψηι, καὶ σε παρατροχάσηι.' In xi. 365 a farmer consults an astrologer on his prospects. 'If it rains enough,' is the response, 'and not too much, and the furrows are not spoilt by frost, nor young shoots crushed by hail, nor the crop devoured by deer, and nothing else unfavourable befalls

from earth or air, I foretell you a good harvest—*μούνας δείδιθι τὰς ἀκρίδας*.'—**στόμιον...στρατωθέν**, 'the great embattled bit that should hold the mouth of Troy.' *στρ.* is an epithet 'limiting' the metaphor. **προτυπέν**, as by lightning.

139. **οἴκτωι**: cf. Philipp. Thess. *A. P.* ix. 22 *ἡ θεὸς ὠδίνων γὰρ ἐπίσκοπος, οὐδ' ἐδίκαζεν τικτούσας κτείνειν, ἃς ἐλεεῖν ἔμαθεν.*

143. **θυομένοισιν** glances at Iphigeneia.

146. We should probably read *τόσον περ εὔφρων* <*δέ*>, *καλά*, or *τόσον περ εὔφρων, ἀκαλά*, 'thou gentle one' (so Platt in *C. R.* xi. 95). That at any rate should be the metre. *καλά*, if sound, is the well-known epithet of Artemis [more often *καλλίστη*: but see Ar. *Ran.* 1359 and other evidence quoted by Gruppe, *Gr. Myth.* p. 1271, n. 1], used here after the usual custom to flatter and conciliate the goddess. *τόσσων* of M is an epicism, due to the familiarity of Homer to the copyists.

147. **λεόντων**. The *lion*, which is common on Lydian coins and still extant on the ancient gates of Mycenae, was probably the badge of the Lydian dynasty of Pelops. That seems to be the reason why the term is applied to various members of that family, Agamemnon in v. 1258, him or his army in v. 818, Clytaemnestra in v. 1257, Aegisthus in v. 1223; and as the lion's offspring is a type of Helen in v. 718, so it appears here to mean Iphigeneia.

149. **ὀβρικάλοις, εἴπερ τινά**: see crit. n. '*Consent to ratify, if ever any, the portents of these fowls.*' The alteration involves the writing of ΟΒΡΙΚΑΛΟΙϹΙΠΕΡΤΙΝΑ for ΟΒΡΙΚΑΛΟΙϹΙΤΕΡΠΝΑ, by which means we obtain the usual formula of invocation, justifying (as in no other way it can be justified) the emphatic place of *τούτων*, and abolishing the superfluous and inappropriate *τερπνά* which had been already bracketed by Paley. The form of appeal is 'if ever before, so now,' that is 'no occasion was ever more urgent than the present'; *e.g.* Dem. 32. 3 *δέομαι δ' ὑμῶν πάντων, εἴπερ ἄλλωι τινὶ πώποτε πράγματι τὸν νοῦν προσέσχετε, καὶ τούτωι προσέχειν*: Isae. 8. 5 *εἴ τινι οὖν καὶ ἄλληι πώποτε δίκηι προσέσχετε τὸν νοῦν, δέομαι ὑμῶν καὶ ταύτηι προσέχειν ὁμοίως*: for other examples see Blomfield on *inf.* 503 (525 W.) *εἴ που πάλαι, φαιδροῖσι τοισίδ' ὄμμασιν δέξασθε*, 'with bright eyes now,' Blaydes on Ar. *Nub.* 356, *Thesm.* 1157, Leaf on Hom. Ω 704, Stat. *Achill.* I. 509 *si quando, auidissimus hauri.*

151. **κατάμομφα**: since after all they are not wholly favourable to us, not satisfactory altogether (*ἀψεγῆ*, Soph. *El.* 496), but with elements in them which portend us evil too.

159. **σύμφυτον**, 'cleaving,' is used in the same way as *ξύμφυτος αἰών* (v. 109).

165. **ἀπέκλαγξεν**, like *ἔκλαγξεν inf.* 211, expresses the loud and

excited tone of voice which marked the spiritual exaltation of the *μάντις*. This is the explanation of other words applied to the delivery of oracles, as *ἰάχειν* and *κέλαδος* and those which are technical of them, *λακεῖν*, *ὀρθιάζειν*. *λακεῖν* does not mean 'to say,' or, as L. and S. suppose, 'to noise abroad,' but 'to utter with a wild, confused, and half-articulate cry,' such as comes from the victims of a *nightmare*. Compare for instance *Cho.* 35, 533, *inf.* 287.

170 ff. How could Agamemnon, so plainly warned, commit this fatal crime? Because he is an example of the general law laid down by Zeus that man shall learn wisdom, not by foresight or prophetic admonition, but after the event by experience and reflexion on his own past actions. Experience teaches by memory revisiting us in dreams or by unnoticed working.

175. μάταν, 'causeless,' 'unaccountable,' 'unwarranted.' *μάταν*, as often, is used like the adjective *μάταιος*.

178. οὖλός τις: see cr. n. I am aware that *ὅστις* may be argued for, but probability is very much against it, and when we find the sentence beginning with *οὐδ' ὅστις*, suspicion is considerably increased. For what is certain is that *οὐδ' ὅστις πάροιθεν* or *οὐδ' ὃς τοῖς πάροιθεν* could only mean 'not even he that was great aforetime,' the stress being on *πάροιθεν*. That is pointless here. The only plausible conjecture I have seen is *οἶδ' ὅστις* (Pauw). For ΟΥΔΟϹΤΙϹ I write ΟΥΛΟϹΤΙϹ, 'a violent one was great of old, swelling with boisterous puissance.' The metaphor throughout is of a combat—*τριακτῆρος* and *παμμάχωι*, a word which it will be seen in the *Thesaurus* was properly used of the pancratiast. *οὖλος*, the epithet applied by Homer to Ares and Achilles, is eminently suitable to this turbulent swasher.

180. οὐδὲ λέξεται: 'but shall not be reckoned, being one of the past.' Cf. Eur. *Alc.* 322 *ἀλλ' αὐτίκ' ἐν τοῖς μηκέτ' οὖσι λέξομαι*, *Hec.* 905 *σὺ μέν, ὦ πατρὶς Ἰλιάς, τῶν ἀπορθήτων πόλις οὐκέτι λέξηι*. For the sense cf. Timotheus ap. Athen. 122 d (fr. 21 Wil.) *νέος ὁ Ζεὺς βασιλεύει· τὸ πάλαι δ' ἦν Κρόνος ἄρχων. ἀπίτω μοῦσα παλαιά.*

181. τριακτῆρος: an allusion to the myth, probably of Orphic origin, of the wrestling-match between Cronos and Zeus at Olympia. Pausanias, in his account of Olympia (v. 7. 10) refers to it: "Some say that Zeus here wrestled with Cronos himself; others that he held the games in honour of his victory over Cronos." See also viii. 2. 2.

185. τεύξεται φρενῶν τὸ πᾶν is the opposite of *ἁμαρτήσεται φρενῶν*.

186 ff. It was in this way, I believe, that Prometheus became reconciled to Zeus. For the proverb *Instruction by Suffering* see Hom. P 32 *ῥεχθὲν δέ τε νήπιος ἔγνω*, Hes. *Op.* 218 *παθὼν δέ τε νήπιος ἔγνω*, Hdt. i. 207 *τὰ δέ μοι παθήματα ἐόντα ἀχάριτα μαθήματα ἐγεγόνεε*, Plat. *Symp.* 222 B *κατὰ τὴν παροιμίαν ὥσπερ νήπιον παθόντα γνῶναι.*

189 ff. **ἔν θ' ὕπνωι...καὶ** is an instance of the common idiom, according to which τε...καί serve rather to subordinate than to co-ordinate: 'when...then...' Cf. Soph. fr. 234. 5 εἶτ' ἦμαρ αὔξει μέσσον ὄμφακος τύπον, | καὶ κλίνεταί τε κἀποπερκοῦται βότρυς, 'and as it declines the grape reddens.' *Antig.* 1186. Hdt. iv. 181, 199, ii. 93, vi. 41 Stein. Xen. *Anab.* iv. 2. 12, vii. 4. 12, *Eq.* 5. 10 οὐ φθάνει τε ἐξαγόμενος ὁ ἵππος καὶ.... Aristid. i. 492, 511. Lucian ii. 584. Timocles (Ath. 407 d) καὶ ταῦτά τε | εἴρητο (Porson for εἴρηται) καὶ.... Heliod. viii. 8, v. 18 ἀλλ' ἅμ' ἥλιός τε ἀνίσχε καὶ ἡμεῖς ἄγκυραν καθίεμεν. Plat. *Phaedr.* 254 B καὶ πρός τ' αὐτῶι ἐγένοντο καὶ εἶδον τὴν ὄψιν κτέ.—**στάζει** is rightly explained by Dr Verrall: 'The admonitory recollection of experience is compared to a wound which long afterwards will ache at times and even break out again, reminding the sufferer of the original hurt.' I cannot go with him further in his reading and explanation; but the root of the idea is a sore that oozes, bleeds, breaks out again. And ἐν ὕπνωι is a most important part of it. Bodily disease may be unfelt in the activity of day, but will disturb the sick man's rest upon his bed: Dio Chrys. ii. p. 169 R. οὐδὲ γὰρ νόσημα οὐδὲν οὕτως ἀναίσθητον τοῖς ἔχουσιν ὡς μηδέποτε βλάψαι μηδὲ ἐμποδὼν γενέσθαι μηδεμιᾶς πράξεως, ἄλλα κἂν ἐγρηγορότι καὶ βαδίζοντι μὴ σφόδρα ἐνοχλῆι, εἴς γε τὴν κοίτην ἀπήντησε καὶ διασπᾶι καὶ διαφθείρει τὸν ὕπνον. And as it is with bodily diseases, so it is with the sufferings of a wounded spirit, which are eloquently described by Achilles Tatius i. 6 ὡς δ' εἰς τὸ δωμάτιον παρῆλθον, ἔνθα μοι καθεύδειν ἔθος ἦν, οὐδ' ὕπνου τυχεῖν ἠδυνάμην. ἔστι μὲν γὰρ φύσει καὶ τἄλλα νοσήματα καὶ τὰ τοῦ σώματος τραύματα ἐν νυκτὶ χαλεπώτερα καὶ ἐπανίσταται μᾶλλον ἡμῖν ἡσυχάζουσι καὶ ἐρεθίζει τὰς ἀλγηδόνας· ὅταν γὰρ ἀναπαύηται τὸ σῶμα, τότε σχολάζει τὸ ἕλκος νοσεῖν· τὰ δὲ τῆς ψυχῆς τραύματα μὴ κινουμένου τοῦ σώματος πολὺ μᾶλλον ὀδυνᾶι. ἐν ἡμέραι μὲν γὰρ ὀφθαλμοὶ καὶ ὦτα πολλῆς γεμιζόμενα περιεργίας ἐπικουφίζει τῆς νόσου τὴν ἀκμήν, ἀντιπεριάγοντα τὴν ψυχὴν τῆς εἰς τὸ πονεῖν σχολῆς· ἐὰν δ' ἡσυχίαι τὸ σῶμα πεδηθῆι, καθ' ἑαυτὴν ἡ ψυχὴ γενομένη τῶι κακῶι κυμαίνεται· πάντα γὰρ ἐξεγείρεται τότε τὰ τέως κοιμώμενα· τοῖς πενθοῦσιν αἱ λῦπαι, τοῖς μεριμνῶσιν αἱ φροντίδες, τοῖς κινδυνεύουσιν οἱ φόβοι, τοῖς ἐρῶσι τὸ πῦρ. Conscience also 'chastens in the night-season,' as they say in the Old Testament, from which many illustrations could be drawn; the best, perhaps, are Job 33. 14. *For God speaketh once, yea twice, in a dream, in a vision of the night, when deep sleep falleth upon men, in slumberings upon the bed; then he openeth the ears of men, and sealeth their instruction, that he may withdraw man from his purpose, and hide pride from man; he keepeth back man from the pit, and his life from perishing by the sword. He is chastened also with pain upon his bed, and with continual strife in his bones*: and so on; such act of God is a χάρις βίαιος—whom he loveth he chasteneth—to make man repent and deliver his soul from going into the pit: 5. 17 *Happy is the man whom God correcteth; therefore despise not thou the chastening of the Almighty: for he maketh sore, and bindeth up: he woundeth, and his hands make whole.* Psalm 16. 7 *I will bless the Lord who hath given me counsel: yea, my reins instruct me in the night seasons.* συμφέρει, as we are told in the *Eumenides* v. 523, σωφρονεῖν ὑπὸ στένει, under the deterrent influence of fear; and when fear was sent divinely to a man, it was commonly in the time of rest upon his bed, in dreams (Job 4. 12—17, 30. 15—17, *Wisdom of Solomon* 17 and 18. 17—19); and such fears, in the Greek view, came by the agency of δαίμονες, black spirits (*e.g. Cho.* 282—8): thus were theologised the twinges of a guilty conscience, which Plato in *Rep.* 330 D—E describes as torturing a man upon his death-bed with the fear of Hell, and causing him to start up, like a frightened child, from sleep: he had ridiculed such myths before, but now they rack him with the apprehension that they may be true—whether it be merely from the weakness of old age, or because he really sees those terrors plainer, being nearer to them. It was in dream that the divine part of us waked and saw; εὕδει δέ, says Pindar in fr. 231, πρασσόντων μελέων, it lies dormant while the limbs are active, but becomes prophetic while we are asleep. Aeschylus can hardly not have shared in the Pythagorean doctrine, and must, I think, include allusion to it here; it is his brevity in allusion to familiar doctrine that makes his lyrics difficult. μνησιπήμων, like μνησιστέφανος ἀγών in Pindar, means 'putting in mind of suffering,' and could mean both 'reminding of the past' and 'warning of the future.'—πρὸ καρδίας is 'at the seat of consciousness,' cf. 967, *Cho.* 390, *Eum.* 103.

192 f. δαιμόνων δέ που χάρις κ.τ.λ. The particles δέ που ('and I suppose,' *P. V.* 848, Plat. *Phaedr.* 270 E, *Legg.* 650 B) are often used of some presumption that may be entertained about *divinities.* See *Pers.* 726 γνώμης δέ πού τις δαιμόνων ξυνήψατο. Bacchyl. v. 91 τὰ δέ που Παλλάδι ξανθᾶι μέλει. Plat. *Rep.* 517 B θεὸς δέ που οἶδεν εἰ ἀληθὴς οὖσα τυγχάνει. Soph. *Ai.* 489 θεοῖς γὰρ ὧδ' ἔδοξέ που.—It might, however, be suggested that the purpose of the lines is to contrast the gentle and spiritual mode of correction existing under the reign of Zeus with the turbulent rule of Ouranos and Cronos. For how, the poet would then conclude, should man be grateful to and adore a deity who ruled the world by main force? Thus, with ποῦ and βιαίως retained, 'whereas where is there any joy of deities who sit upon their awful seat violently?'

194. καὶ τότε means 'so it was then,' as καὶ νῦν means 'so it is on this occasion'; in other words, both phrases are employed to mark a particular example of a general principle: Pind. *P.* iii. 29 κλέπτει τέ *νιν οὐ θεὸς οὐ βροτὸς ἔργοις οὔτε βουλαῖς. καὶ τότε γνοὺς Ἴσχυος Εἰλατίδα ξεινίαν κοίταν....* Agamemnon acted hastily, yielding without critical enquiry (*παθὼν ἔγνω* gives the contrast to *μάντιν ψέγων*), and so is described as *ἐμπαίοις τύχαισι συμπνέων*, 'letting his spirit yield to violent circumstance,' which is the same thing as *φρενὸς πνέων δυσσεβῆ τροπαίαν* in v. 229.

197 ff. συμπνέων. Cf. Schol. Pind. *N.* vi. 90 (55) *ἢ ζάκοτόν φησι κατὰ μετουσίαν τοῦ φέροντος καὶ αὐτὸ συμπνέον τῆι ὀργῆι ἀπὸ τῶν παρ' Ὁμήρωι* (A 573 f.).—The lyric method is to begin at the crisis and to jot in points of description or narrative without regard to their logical sequence.—**κεναγγεῖ,** *famishing*, is a Hippocratean word: lit. emptying the vessel of the stomach. [Cf. *ἀγγεῖον* as used by Empedocles (A 74 Diels).]

211. προφέρων: cf. *inf.* 955 *δόμοισι προυνεχθέντος ἐν χρηστηρίοις.*

212 f. χθόνα βάκτροις ἐπικρούσαντας. The action shows their emotion: see Hom. A 245, *β* 80.

219. πατρῴους κ.τ.λ. See cr. n. The reading of the MS. arises through *τὸ ἑξῆς*, *i.e.* the tendency of the scribes to simplify the order of the words, with *ῥεέθροις* substituted for *ῥοαῖς*.

228 ff. ἐπεὶ δ' ἀνάγκας ἔδυ λέπαδνον...τόθεν τὸ παντότολμον φρονεῖν μετέγνω: once he had persuaded himself that he was yielding to Necessity, from that point he abandoned himself in desperation and resolved to stick at nothing. This was a familiar idea, that *ἀνάγκη* (of poverty or love, for instance) drives a man to do or suffer anything: Theognis 195 *ἐπεὶ κρατερή μιν ἀνάγκη ἐντύει, ἥ τ' ἀνδρὸς τλήμονα θῆκε νόον.* 384 *πενίην μητέρ' ἀμηχανίης ἔλαβον, τὰ δίκαια φιλεῦντες, ἥ τ' ἀνδρῶν παράγει θυμὸν ἐς ἀμπλακίην, βλάπτουσ' ἐν στήθεσσι φρένας κρατερῆς ὑπ' ἀνάγκης· τολμᾶι δ' οὐκ ἐθέλων αἴσχεα πολλὰ φέρειν, χρημοσύνηι εἴκων, ἣ δὴ κακὰ πολλὰ διδάσκει, ψεύδεά τ' ἐξαπάτας τ' οὐλομένας τ' ἔριδας, ἄνδρα καὶ οὐκ ἐθέλοντα.* Antiphon 121. 12, *P. V.* 16, Sappho 2. 17. Hence *πάντολμος* became a regular epithet of *ἀνάγκη*: *A. P.* ix. 11 *πάντα δὲ ταῦτ' ἐδίδαξε πικρὴ πάντολμος ἀνάγκη.* xvi. 15. 7 *ἀσχήμων ἔνδεια καὶ ἁ πάντολμος ἀνάγκα.* Moschion, *Telephus* fr. 2 N. *ὦ καὶ θεῶν κρατοῦσα καὶ θνητῶν μόνη Μοῖρ', ὦ λιταῖς ἄτρεπτε δυστήνων βροτῶν πάντολμ' ἀνάγκη, στυγνὸν ἣ κατ' αὐχένων ἡμῶν ἐρείδεις τῆσδε λατρείας ζυγόν.* The parenthesis *βροτοὺς θρασύνει γὰρ αἰσχρόμητις τάλαινα παρακοπὰ πρωτοπήμων* describes the process by which *ἀνάγκη* produces this state of mind: he is at his wits' end; *ἀμηχανίη* drives him to distraction (*παρακοπά*), *βλάπτουσ' ἐν στήθεσσι φρένας κρατερῆς ὑπ' ἀνάγκης*, as Theognis says; he abandons the restraint (*σωφροσύνη*) which had hitherto kept him in check, and gives himself up wholly to *θράσος*, the spirit of bad audacity, bold recklessness and sin. *Ἀνάγκη*, therefore, acts in the same way as Ἄτη βλαψίφρων, who makes a man φρενοβλαβῆ and leads him astray into ἀνιερὸν θράσος (v. 764).

The words δυσσεβῆ, ἄναγνον, ἀνιερόν mean 'wicked,' 'sinful against God': ἄναγνος or δύσαγνος always means 'polluted' by sacrilege or bloodshed.

When used in a bad sense, τόλμα is much the same as θράσος, and expresses 'criminal wickedness' or 'crime' in general; and παντότολμος or πάντολμος is the strongest term of condemnation that can be applied to man or woman, 'ready to commit any crime without restraint of conscience.' This is the meaning of ὑπέρτολμον φρόνημα and παντόλμους ἔρωτας in *Cho.* 591, 595 and ἄτολμον *ib.* 628 is the opposite. τλᾶν and τλήμων are sometimes used to the same effect, as τλάμονι καὶ πανούργωι χειρί in *Cho.* 383: just as ἀτολμήτων in v. 385 implies a 'wicked sin,' so ἄτλητα τλᾶσα in v. 417 means in English 'committing a crime.' Similarly ἔτλα in v. 234 is equivalent to ἐτόλμησεν in the sense indicated.

230. **τόθεν**, 'from that moment,' might also be relative, picked up by ἔτλα δ' οὖν after the parenthesis: but in any case it refers to ἀνάγκας, as has been shown in the previous note.

232. See cr. n. The copyist assumed that γὰρ must be the second word, and therefore punctuated after βροτούς, the explanation offered in the schol. being ὅθεν ἔγνω πάντας τοὺς ἀνθρώπους τολμᾶν. It was probably another groping at a sense that produced the reading of M. Similarly, the right reading (Heath) in Eur. *H. F.* 1126 is ἀρκεῖ σιωπὴ γὰρ μαθεῖν ὃ βούλομαι; but γάρ was assumed to be the second word; a stop accordingly was placed after ἀρκεῖ, and then to get a sense the ὃ was changed to οὐ: so that we find ἀρκεῖ· σιωπὴ (or σιωπῇ) γὰρ μαθεῖν οὐ βούλομαι.

237. **προτέλεια.** It is possible that, as in Eur. *I. A.* 433 Ἀρτέμιδι προτελίζουσι τὴν νεάνιδα, there is an allusion to the pretended marriage with Achilles.

239. [Mueller's correction was provisionally adopted. For the form see the commentators on *Cho.* 349.]

243. **περιπετῆ**: the adj. is passive corresponding to περιβάλλω τινὰ πέπλοις. 'Where she lay, wrapt in her robes.'

246. **φυλακᾶι.** If the MS. reading is kept, it should be treated as subject to κατασχεῖν. In Eur. *Tro.* 194 τὰν παρὰ προθύροις φυλακὰν κατέχουσ' the sense is 'to keep watch.' Cf. Pind. *P.* iv. 75 τὸν μονοκρήπιδα πάντως ἐν φυλακᾶι σχεθέμεν μεγάλαι.

257 f. **τριτόσπονδον...παιᾶνα.** Cf. Harmodius ἐν τῶι περὶ τῶν κατὰ Φιγάλειαν νομίμων, ap. Athen. iv. 149 C μετὰ δὲ τὸ δεῖπνον σπονδὰς ἐποιοῦντο...ἀπὸ δὲ τῶν σπονδῶν παιὰν ἄιδεται.

265. ἴσον. So Eur. *Or.* 426 τὸ μέλλον δ' ἴσον ἀπραξίαι λέγω.—τὸ δὲ προκλύειν added by m to 263 was a gloss on this word.

266. σύνορθρον αὐγαῖς, 'full clear with the rays of morning'—a vague but ominous reference.

268 f. τόδ' ἄγχιστον κ.τ.λ. refers to Clytaemnestra. ἄγχιστον describes her relation to the throne, which is expressly stated in the verses following (Schuetz). It was the almost invariable practice of the Greek stage for a character on the first appearance to be *announced* and described for the information of the audience. So *inf.* 590.

ἕρκος is used several times in Homer of persons: so ἔρυμα (*Eum.* 704), πύργος, ἕρμα and the like.

276. εὐάγγελος μέν. The tenor of the answer with its repetition of εὐάγγελος from the previous speech corresponds exactly to *Supp.* 381 ἄγος μὲν...ὑμῖν δ' ἀρήγειν...

282. Cf. Plut. *Camill.* 30 δακρύοντες ἀπιστίαι τῆς παρούσης ἡδονῆς.

283. εὖ γὰρ φρονοῦντος ὄμμα σοῦ κατηγορεῖ. For an explanation of the full force contained in these words we must look to the records of Physiognomy. In that science, so much studied in the East, it is the eyes that give the most important signs and are the windows of the soul: *Script. Physiogn.* i. p. 305 Foerster τὰ δὲ πολλὰ τῶν σημείων καὶ τὰ σύνολα τοῖς ὀφθαλμοῖς ἐνίδρυται καὶ ὥσπερ διὰ πυλῶν τούτων ἡ ψυχὴ διαφαίνεται. *ib.* ii. 17, 409. 1 Samuel 16. 7 'for man looketh on the outward appearance, but the Lord looketh on the eyes,' that is, 'the heart.' Leon. Tar. *A. P.* vii. 661 φυσιγνώμων ὁ σοφιστής, δεινὸς ἀπ' ὀφθαλμοῦ καὶ τὸ νόημα μαθεῖν. Eur. *Med.* 215. There are other passages in this play which are explained by the same notion; see notes on 786 and 1427. **κατηγορεῖν,** 'to argue,' 'prove,' belongs to the physiognomical vocabulary (see Foerster's Index ii. p. 394—5), having been used, doubtless, by old Ionic writers on the subject and retained as technical; hence it appears in other writers often when they speak of what is indicated, whether good or evil, by such outward signs. See Eur. fr. 690 τό γ' εἶδες αὐτὸ σοῦ κατηγορεῖ σιγῶντος ὡς εἴης ἄν..., Philostr. *Imag.* 29 ὠκύτητα κατηγορεῖ τοῦ κυνός, *Vit. Soph.* i. 17 πειθὼ κατηγορεῖ τοῦ ἀνδρός (ii. p. 19 and p. 380 Kayser), *Heroic.* p. 303 = 698, Aelian *N. A.* i. 5, Heliod. iii. 5, Plut. *Mor.* 695 D, Schol. *Theb.* 109: there are also some examples in the Dictionaries which should be classed under this head.

287. λάκοιμι is Karsten's correction of the MS. λάβοιμι, which cannot bear the sense attributed to it here—'I would not accept the mere fancy of a slumbering mind'; that would be οὐδ' ἂν δεχοίμην δόξαν εὐδούσης φρενός. But δόξαν λαβεῖν is used only in the following senses: (1) *to get reputation*, with or without an epithet, or with a genitive *repu-*

tation of or *for*; as λαβεῖν αἰτίαν, ἔπαινον, ψόγον, ὄνειδος, εὔκλειαν, διαβολήν, φθόνον, αἰσχύνην, γέλωτα etc., (2) *to conceive a notion* (*of*), *entertain a conception* (*of*), as λαβεῖν ἔννοιαν, φαντασίαν, νόησιν. But δόξαν or δόκησιν λέγειν is *to state mere opinion* as opposed to knowledge (Eur. *I. T.* 1164, *Bacch.* 628, *Heracl.* 395, Soph. *Trach.* 426, Hdt. vii. 185): λάκοιμι is a stronger synonym of λέγοιμι (see on 619), and now the emphasis falls where it should, on δόξαν.

288. The old men assume that she has only ordinary woman's reasons, dream or rumour, as in Eur. *Hel.* 1190 πότερον ἐννύχοις πεπεισμένη στένεις ὀνείροις ἢ φάτιν τιν' οἴκοθεν κλύουσα;—**ἐπίανεν** is a heightened synonym of ἔθρεψεν: Bacchyl. iii. 67 ὅστις μὴ φθόνωι πιαίνεται, Plut. *Mor.* 516 D ἡ ψυχή...βόσκουσα καὶ πιαίνουσα τὸ κακόηθες. Similar is the use of αὔξειν: Ath. 782 d αὔξει γὰρ καὶ τρέφει μεγαλύνει τε τὴν ψυχὴν ἡ ἐν τοῖς ποτοῖς διατριβή, Pind. *N.* iii. 58 ἐν ἀρμένοισι πᾶσι θυμὸν αὔξων, Bacchyl. i. 52 ἐθέλει δ' αὔξειν φρένας ἀνδρός (*sc.* πλοῦτος). So ἐλπίδι τρέφεσθαι is varied by βόσκεσθαι, σιτεῖσθαι (*inf.* 1668), φέρβεσθαι: see *Class. Rev.* xv. p. 102.—**ἄπτερος φάτις**, of which fantastic explanations have been given, means a *winged*, or metaphorically a *wing-swift* rumour. Φήμη, *fama*, was a thing that flew: Hdt. ix. 100, 101, Telestes (Ath. 616 f), Orph. *Arg.* 596; *fama uolat.* It should be observed that when the phrase τῆι δ' ἄπτερος ἔπλετο μῦθος occurs in the *Odyssey*, it seems always to denote a certain obscurity in the speaker's words, which causes them to fall short of the hearer's intelligence. Thus in *Od.* 17. 57, when Penelope has questioned Telemachus about the result of his voyage to Pylus, and Telemachus, who has just recognised his father at the swineherd's hut and been commanded to keep silence, has made an evasive reply, the meaning is that the full intention of his speech was hidden from her. In *Od.* 19. 29 Telemachus makes no direct answer to Eurycleia's question about the torch-bearer who would be required, and it is implied that his words had a hidden import in reference to his father which failed to reach her. In *Od.* 21. 386 Eurycleia failed to understand that the slaying of the suitors was implied in the speech of the swineherd. In *Od.* 22. 398 Eurycleia, when invited to enter, beholds to her joyful amazement the bloody corpses of the suitors lying on the ground.

However this may be, the old poetical word ἄπτερος was used by later writers of things which *though wingless* are *swift as with wings*, *wing-swift*, like the Flying Dutchman. And in this sense ἀπτέρωι τάχει was a favourite phrase (fully illustrated by Nauck, *F. T. G.*² p. 922): we find πτηνῶι τάχει sometimes used instead. In the same sense—the usual explanation of the grammarians is ταχέως or αἰφνιδίως—was used the adverb ἀπτέρως, or ἀπτερέως (lengthened like ἀψοφέως for the purpose of dactylic verse). ἄπτερος or ἀπτέρως should probably be read in *P. V.* 707: see *Journ. Phil.* xx. p. 296, where further illustrations are quoted.

298. πόντον ὥστε νωτίσαι may be either 'to put the ocean at his back' or 'to skim the broad back of ocean.' The passage is incomplete, and the line which follows cannot be explained with any certainty. [The translation favours Weil's view that the gloss of Hesychius, προσαιθρίζουσα πόμπιμον φλόγα, which Dindorf wished to substitute for πλέον καίουσα τῶν εἰρημένων in 313, formed part of a passage which has been lost here.]

299. It is possible that there is an allusion to Ischys, the son of Elatus (pitch-pine), who intrigued with Coronis, daughter of Phlegyas, when she was with child by Apollo.

305. σημαίνει μολόν may mean 'signified his arrival,' as translated (cf. 960); or simply 'arrived, giving signal,' [as in Soph. *Ant.* 1208.]

316. μὴ χρονίζεσθαι: see cr. n. So in 1670 χρόνωι and χάριν are confused.

318. πώγωνα: so πωγωνίας in familiar use of a comet.

319. κατόπτην: see cr. n. This is the form which analogy supports: cf. fr. 304 τοῦτον δ' ἐπόπτην ἔποπα τῶν αὑτοῦ κακῶν, *sup.* 299 πορευτοῦ λαμπάδος, Ar. *Au.* 57 τὸν πότην λύχνον. See also Stat. *Silu.* ii. 2. 3 *celsa Dicarchei speculatrix uilla profundi.* In *Theb.* 631 cod. Viteb. has ἄνδρα τευχιστὸν for ἄνδρα τευχηστήν, and in *Anacreont.* 40. 10 φθόνον οὐκ οἶδα δαϊκτόν Pauw restored δαϊκτήν.

320. ἔσκηψεν: *tum demum terrae incubuit cum ad Arachnaeum montem uenit.*

321. For mt. Arachnaeus see Pausan. ii. 25. 10, Steph. Byzant. p. 110, 4 Ἀραχναῖον· ὄρος Ἄργους.

322. ἐς τόδε: see cr. n. In *Eum.* 755 M has ὅγ' where ὅδ' is preserved by the other copies, and in Soph. *O. C.* 860 F has τόν γ' for τόνδ'.

326. πρῶτος δραμεῖν, though it could mean 'to start first,' usually meant 'to finish first,' and the play of words (which may have been familiar in the case of torch-running) depends upon this ambiguity. The light from Ida ran both first and last, as starting first and ending last; the light from Mount Arachnaeus ran both first and last, as starting last and ending first.

331. ὡς λέγεις, 'your version of this tale': see cr. n. Perhaps we should read ἕως λέγοις (the optative following θέλοιμ' ἄν), as ἕως ἄν is now read for ὡς ἄν in Soph. *Phil.* 1330, *Ai.* 1117, *O. C.* 1361: this would be 'so long as you should speak.' For the optative see Goodw. *M. T.* § 531, who quotes Plat. *Theaet.* 155 A.

335. οὐ φίλως might appear to belong to προσεννέποις (Soph. *El.* 1471 προσηγορεῖν φίλως, *O. C.* 758 τήνδε τὴν πόλιν φίλως εἰπών, Eur. *Hipp.* 793 εὐφρόνως προσεννέπειν), but sense requires that it should be joined to διχοστατοῦντε 'unfriendly separated.' Many editors accept Auratus' διχοστατοῦντ' ἄν, οὐ φίλω 'separated, and not friends,' which may well be right.

348. ἀπαλλαχθέντες is corrupted to ἀπαλλαγέντες fh. So for κρυφθείς we get κρυφείς and even κρυβείς. See also on 737.—ὡς δ' εὐδαίμονες, 'and how blest!' exclamatory, as in 1235 ὡς δ' ἐπωλολύξατο. This use of ὡς and ὅσος, in combination with δέ, is very common in Greek verse, but sometimes escapes critics because Greek does not use the note of exclamation. Cf. Ar. *Eq.* 269 ὡς δ' ἀλαζών, ὡς δὲ μάσθλης, Dem. 21. 209 τὸν δὲ βάσκανον, τὸν δὲ ὄλεθρον, τοῦτον δὲ ὑβρίζειν ἀναπνεῖν δέ, Lucian i. 552 ὅσον δὲ καὶ ἀποπνεῖ μύρων, ὡς δὲ καὶ σφαλερὸν βαδίζει. So the text is quite sound in Eur. *Supp.* 901 πολλοὺς δ' ἐραστὰς κἀπὸ θηλειῶν ὅσας ἔχων, ἐφρούρει μηδὲν ἐξαμαρτάνειν, where Canter conjectured ἴσας, which would be correct if instead of πολλούς a definite number had been named. Liban. iv. 116. 11 μετὰ τοὺς πολλοὺς πολέμους, μετὰ τὰς πολλὰς μάχας καὶ ἀριστείας καὶ τρόπαια, καὶ θάλατταν ὅσην, '*and all that sea!*' Tzetzes, *Chil.* vii. 39 ἵππων τε τοῖς ἀρδεύμασι τοὺς ποταμοὺς ξηράνας ἄλλα τε πόσα βάρβαρα δράσας εἰς ἐπιπλήξεις. Damoxenus fr. 3 (iii. 353 K.) ἡ δ' εὐρυθμία τό τ' ἦθος ἡ τάξις θ' ὅση.

It was a commonplace in praise of Peace that you could sleep the whole night long and were not wakened by the trumpet in the morning just when sleep is sweetest: Bacchylides fr. 2. 9 J.

> χαλκεᾶν δ' οὐκ ἔστι σαλπίγγων κτύπος,
> οὐδὲ συλᾶται μελίφρων ὕπνος ἀπὸ βλεφάρων
> ἀῷιος ὃς θάλπει κέαρ.

Polyb. iii. 433, Schweighäuser δεῖν ἀναμνησθῆναι τοὺς συνέδρους διότι κοιμωμένους τὸν ὄρθρον ἐν μὲν τῷ πολέμῳ διεγείρουσιν αἱ σάλπιγγες, κατὰ δὲ τὴν εἰρήνην οἱ ὄρνιθες, a saying quoted by Plut. *Nic.* 9. So ἀφύλακτον = 'without a watch to keep.'

350. εὐσεβοῦσι need not be altered to εὖ σέβουσι (Scaliger). In Lyric you would say εὖ σέβειν (εὐσεβοῦντες in *Eum.* 1020 is perhaps an exception), εὖ λέγειν, εὖ θαρσεῖν: elsewhere εὐλογεῖν etc. The edd. unnecessarily restore εὖ θαρσεῖτε in *Theb.* 34, and Cobet wrongly rejects κατηφεῖς in Eur. *Med.* 1012.

352. οὔ τἂν ἑλόντες αὖθις ἀνθαλοῖεν ἄν: the combination is proverbial. Zenob. i. 35, Diogen. i. 33 αἱροῦντες ἡιρήμεσθα, Suid. *s.v.* αἱρήσω τάχα, Ael. *N. H.* i. 29 αἱρεῖ τοὺς ὀρνιθοθήρας ἡιρημένη, Opp. *Hal.* ii. 133 ὀλλύμενοι δ' ὀλέκουσι καὶ οὓς πέφνουσι φονῆας, Xen. *Cyr.* vi. 3. 20 εἰ οἱ κυκλούμενοι

κυκλωθεῖεν, *A. P.* ix. 14 εἷλε δ' ἁλούς, Soph. *O. C.* 1025 ἔχων ἔχει, καί σ' εἷλε θηρῶνθ' ἡ τύχη: such phrases for 'the biter bit,' 'turning the tables,' or 'catching a Tartar' are favourite in Greek and Latin.

353 f. She is still imagining the scene. μὴ ἐμπίπτηι could not refer to the future; we must have had μὴ ἐμπέσηι, as in *Pers.* 128. So above εἰ εὐσεβοῦσι can only mean 'if they are reverencing.'

357 ff. θεοῖς δ' ἀναμπλάκητος εἰ μόλοι στρατός,
εὐήγορον τὸ πῆμα τῶν ὀλωλότων
γένοιτ' ἄν,—εἰ πρόσπαια μὴ τύχοι κακά.

This is somewhat darkly worded for the sake of double meanings. To their intelligence she says: 'The only danger to be apprehended now is that they may commit some sacrilege, which would bring the vengeance of the gods upon them; otherwise, if they arrive without having offended against Heaven, the human discontent at home caused by the losses in an unpopular war is likely to be reconciled, to hush its murmuring voice and welcome the returning Princes with good words; there is nothing to be apprehended here, unless some accident should happen to them.' τὸ πῆμα τῶν ὀλωλότων, 'the grievance of the lost'—the wound that each home suffers for the loss of its dead kinsman, the growls under the breath at the unworthiness of the cause, the festering resentment against the Princes growing under the surface like a spreading gangrene, and the grave danger that the angry murmurs of the people may result in insurrection, are the theme on which the Elders dwell in the succeeding chorus (455 ff.):

'ἀλλοτρίας διαὶ γυναικός,'
τάδε σῖγά τις βαΰζει,
φθονερὸν δ' ὑπ' ἄλγος ἕρπει
προδίκοις Ἀτρείδαις.

. . . . . .

βαρεῖα δ' ἀστῶν φάτις σὺν κότωι,
δημοκράντου δ' ἀρᾶς τίνει χρέος.

However, as Clytaemnestra anticipates, this bitter feeling has abated by the time the King arrives; εὔφρων πόνος εὖ τελέσασιν is the note of his reception, 'good ends make all amends' (v. 797).

But the covert meaning for herself is that her own sore πῆμα—the word she uses with the same concealed significance in v. 856—her own grievance for the loss of Iphigeneia will know how to put on fawning and effusive welcome, as of course it does when the time comes; her daughter's death she does not even mention—but a 'sudden stroke' may fall upon him unawares!

It is for the sake of this that she selects the word εὐήγορον (Eubul. 'Οδ. 1), a synonym of εὔφημον, as εὐαγορία (Callim. *Lau. Pall.* 139) of εὐφημία. She anticipates her own long-drawn smiling welcome and laudation, εὔφροσιν δέξεται λόγοις, *inf.* 1227 οἷα γλῶσσα...λέξασα κἀκτείνασα φαιδρόνους ..τεύξεται; which is what the Chorus hint to Agamemnon in 779—800, and what he understands, 821—831. The MS. reading is supposed to mean 'And (*even*) if they came without offence towards Heaven, (*yet*) the soreness of the slain might become wide-awake, even supposing no sudden accident befel them'; except that ἐγρηγορὸς γένοιτ' ἂν is usually slurred over and taken as though it were ἐγρηγορὸς εἴη, 'would be on the watch.' But some word of favourable sense appears to be demanded by the order of the words. ἐπήγορον...γένοιτ' ἄν, if we read it, would be 'might turn accuser'; the φθονερὸν ἄλγος of the Argives on account of their bereavements (457) might give its discontentment voice; but my objection to that sense is still the same, that the Greek should then have been εἰ δὲ καὶ θεοῖς ἀναμπλάκητος μόλοι στρατός, ἀλλὰ τῶν γ' ὀλωλότων ἐπήγορον (or ἐγρηγορὸς) γένοιτ' ἂν τὸ πῆμα.—The last clause is added like an afterthought, correcting a too confident expression, as Hom. A 60, Soph. *O. T.* 969, *O. C.* 1450, *Trach.* 586.

361. **τὸ δ' εὖ κρατοίη**: *Supp.* 985 εἴη δὲ τὰ λῷστα, Dem. 4. 51 νικῴη δ' ὅ τι πᾶσιν ὑμῖν μέλλει συνοίσειν.

362. **τὴν ὄνησιν**, 'the due fruit.' Cf. Soph. fr. 533 ἀλλὰ τῶν πολλῶν καλῶν τίς χάρις; 'The blessings are many: what I want is their enjoyment.'

365. **θεοὺς προσειπεῖν αὖ παρασκευάζομαι**: so Ar. *Au.* 226 οὔποψ μελῳδεῖν αὖ παρασκευάζεται, *Thesm.* 99 σίγα· μελῳδεῖν αὖ παρασκευάζεται. They never said θεοὺς εὖ προσειπεῖν, but used the verb alone, προσειπεῖν, προσαυδᾶν, προσφωνεῖν, προσεννέπειν, προσαγορεύειν. Observe that in Soph. *Trach.* 229 ἀλλ' εὖ μὲν ἵγμεθ', εὖ δὲ προσφωνούμεθα there is a special reason for the addition of the adverb. In Eur. *H.F.* 599 Paley was wrong in taking καλῶς with πρόσειπε.

368. **κόσμων.** The Pythagoreans called the stars κόσμοι [Aët. ii. 13. 15, Diels, *Doxogr.*, p. 343, 7].

374 ff. **Δία τοι ξένιον**: 'It is Zeus Hospitable, I say, who is the author of this act; if the vengeance has been long in coming, let that cause no doubt; it has only been deferred in order that the stroke might fall the surer.' Such is the connexion with the following lyric, where the sentiment is taken up and developed: ἔπραξεν ὡς ἔκρανεν. There is a strong stress on Δία τοι as there is with σύ τοι, σέ τοι, which is only one case of a more general use. τοι makes an appeal to the knowledge or conscience of the hearer and so is often used in *assertion*, as οὔτοι in negation, to lay stress upon the word it goes with. Examples are *inf.* 913, 1031, 1039, *Cho.* 913, *Supp.* 375, 545, *Eum.* 758,

Soph. *El.* 582, 624, 773, *Phil.* 1095, Pind. *P.* v. 122: so in ἐκ τῶνδέ τοι '*this* is the reason,' *inf.* 867, 1603, *Cho.* 1054.

379. 'Διὸς πλαγὰν ἔχουσιν' κ.τ.λ. The lyric takes up the preceding declaration and confirms it: '*It is the stroke of Zeus that they have felt* may safely be pronounced, and if we follow out the sequence of events, the act and its motive can be traced to him. It was his act, and his act was the execution of a determined purpose. It has been said that the gods do not concern themselves to visit sin: an irreligious lie! Here is a manifest proof that they do visit it; for the destruction of Troy is evidently punishment for the presumptuous sin of Paris. This is the reward of those who are made insolent with riches and righteousness.'

There is a chorus in the *Hercules Furens* of Euripides precisely to the same effect as this passage, and closely resembling it in language. It is sung after the triumph of Heracles over the murderous usurper Lycus: his dying cry is heard within, ὦ πᾶσα Κάδμου γαῖ', ἀπόλλυμαι δόλωι: and then the Chorus rejoin:

747 καὶ γὰρ διώλλυς· ἀντίποινα δ' ἐκτίνων
τόλμα, διδούς γε τῶν δεδραμένων δίκην.—
τίς θεοὺς ἀνομίαι χραίνων θνητὸς ὢν
ἄφρονα λόγον οὐρανίων μακάρων
κατέβαλ' ὡς ἄρ' οὐ σθένουσιν θεοί;—
γέροντες, οὐκέτ' ἔστι δυσσεβὴς ἀνήρ.

773 θεοὶ θεοὶ τῶν ἀδίκων
μέλουσι καὶ τῶν ὁσίων ἐπάιειν.
ὁ χρυσὸς ἅ τ' εὐτυχία
φρενῶν βροτοὺς ἐξάγεται
δύνασιν ἄδικον ἐφέλκων,

but Justice shatters them in time.

802 πιστόν μοι τὸ παλαιὸν ἤδη
λέχος, ὦ Ζεῦ, τὸ σὸν οὐκ
ἐπ' ἐλπίδι φάνθη,
λαμπρὰν δ' ἔδειξ' ὁ χρόνος
τὰν Ἡρακλέος ἀλκάν.

809 κρείσσων μοι τύραννος ἔφυς
ἢ δυσγένει' ἀνάκτων,
ἃ νῦν ἐσορῶντι φαίνει
ξιφηφόρων ἐς ἀγώνων
ἅμιλλαν εἰ τὸ δίκαιον
θεοῖς ἔτ' ἀρέσκει.

'The base-born usurper affords manifest proof, when you regard the issue of the contest, that Righteousness is still pleasing in the sight of Heaven.'

Blomfield pointed out that πλαγὰν ἔχουσιν must be taken together: but few have heeded. πληγήν, ἕλκος (Herod. iv. 60), τραῦμα, ἔχειν are regular expressions for 'to be wounded,' ἔχειν serving to form a passive as in αἰτίαν ἔχω, etc. εἰπεῖν πάρεστιν is 'that judgment may be pronounced indeed'; as in *Theb.* 906 παρέστι δ' εἰπεῖν ἐπ' ἀθλίοισιν ὡς ἐρξάτην... and Philemon, fr. 108 'καλὸν τὸ θνήισκειν ἔστιν ἐπὶ τούτωι λέγειν.'—For ἐξιχνεῦσαι cf. *Supp.* 89 Διὸς ἵμερος οὐκ εὐθήρατος ἐτύχθη.

381. See cr. n. The first ὡς was inserted to explain the construction. Cf. Schol. *Supp.* 441 λείπει τὸ ὅτι.—οὐκ ἔφα τις. It has been supposed (Jebb on Soph. *Ant.* 620) that Diagoras of Melos is referred to, and the allusion suits the reason for his atheism given in Sext. Emp. *Math.* ix. 53, that the guilty are not punished: ἀδικηθεὶς ὑπό τινος ἐπιορκήσαντος καὶ μηδὲν ἕνεκα τούτου παθόντος. [But it is very doubtful if he can be placed so early: see *e.g.* Gomperz, *Greek Thinkers*, E. tr. i. p. 577.]

385 f. The MS. reading (see cr. n.) is meaningless. We can quickly clear the ground; for a little reflection will admit what Karsten and Weil have pointed out, that there is no place here either for ἐκγόνους or for Ἄρη πνεόντων: Paris, who is the sinner (v. 409), has paid for his sin in his own person; and the subject of the passage is the retribution following sin that comes through a spirit made insolent with riches; whereas Ἄρη πνεόντων μείζον' ἢ δικαίως would condemn him for a spirit *over-bellicose*! Hartung's reading therefore, ἐκτίνουσα τόλμα τῶν Ἄρη πνεόντων κτἑ., besides giving an unparalleled caesura, is untenable for sense: nevertheless the chief part of the credit is due to him for ἐκτίνουσα. For ἄρη I merely restore ἀρή, *havoc, destruction by the sword*, a word used by Aeschylus in *Supp.* 86. No accusative is now required with ἐκτίνουσα, because ἀρή is itself the penalty—a turn of phrase exactly paralleled in v. 1512 Ἄρης δίκας πάχναι κουροβόρωι παρέξει. There is the same conception in 760—6 (δαίμονα τίταν) and in *Cho.* 643 (τίνειν μύσος).

389 ff. ὑπὲρ τὸ βέλτιστον, *i.e.* 'beyond due Measure' (ὑπὲρ τὸ μέτρον). But it is not necessary to read with Weil μέτρον τὸ βέλτιστον, though that is in any case the meaning: see *Paroem.* ii. p. 80—2 Leutsch, for the proverb πάντων μέτρον ἄριστον, Lucian i. 756, and Aristotle, *Index s.v.* μέσος for βέλτιστον. The reference to Troy is illustrated by Homer N 621 Τρῶες ὑπερφίαλοι, Bacchyl. xii. 158 ἢ μεγάλαις ἐλπίσιν πνείοντες ὑπερφίαλον...Τρῶες ἱππευταί. In the following words the definition of τὸ μέτρον is laid down as '*Sufficience, clear of harm, with an ample endowment of understanding* (σύνεσις),' as Pythagoras μήκιστον πραπίδων ἐκτήσατο πλοῦτον according to Empedocles (fr. 129, 2 Diels); or 'sufficience for one well-endowed with sense.' ἀπήμαντον ἀπαρκεῖν means ἔχειν ὅσον ἀποζῆν ἀβλαβῶς (Theognis 1153), as ἐξαρκέων κτεάτεσσι in Pind. *O.* v. 24, ζώειν τ' ἀπ' οἰκείων ἔχει Bacchyl. i. 57, Solon 5. 1 δήμωι μὲν γὰρ ἔδωκα τόσον κράτος, ὅσσον ἐπαρκεῖ.

395. **εἰς ἀφάνειαν**: that is ὅταν τὴν δίκην τις ἀφανίσηι. Cf. Trag. fr. in Stob. *Ecl.* i. 3. 45 (fr. adesp. 418 N.) ἄφρονες δ' ὁπόσοι τὸ δίκαιον ἄγουσ' ὑπὸ τᾶς ἀδίκου βιοτᾶς ἀφανές. Max. Tyr. 31. 2 ὁμολογίαν εἶναι δεῖ ἔργου καὶ λόγου, καὶ μήτε τὰ ἔργα εἰς ἀφάνειαν κομιδῆι ξυνεληλάσθαι κτέ.

396. **βιᾶται δ' ἁ τάλαινα Πειθώ**: [for the significance of Persuasion in connexion with ὕβρις, ἄτη, and ἐλπίς, see *Cambridge Praelections*, p. 115 ff.].

397. The reading of the MS. (see cr. n.) is not a metrical line at all, apart from strophic correspondence. **προβούλου παῖς** (Hartung) is right: Soph. fr. 533 ποικιλομήτιδες ἆται, *Cho.* 645 τέκνον δ' ἐπεισφέρει δόμοις αἱμάτων παλαιτέρων τίνειν μύσος χρόνωι κλυτὰ βυσσόφρων Ἐρινύς, like Hecate in *Macbeth*, 'the close contriver of all harms.' πρόβουλοσ παῖσ was probably the first stage in the error.

398 f. **ἄκος** recalls Hesiod's νήκεστον ἀασθῆι quoted on v. 469.—**σίνος**, *mischief*, is a synonym of ἄτη or βλάβη: for Ἄτη βλάπτουσ' ἀνθρώπους see Hom. I 505, T 91.

404. **ποτανὸν ὄρνιν** is an allusion to ἐλπίς: πτηνὰς διώκεις, ὦ τέκνον, τὰς ἐλπίδας Eur. fr. 271. In Soph. *Ant.* 615 ἐλπίς is ἁ πολύπλαγκτος. Hope of wrongful gain, Ambition, is a stage on the road to ruin: Thuc. iii. 45 ἥ τε ἐλπὶς καὶ ὁ ἔρως ἐπὶ παντὶ πλεῖστα βλάπτουσι, v. 103 ἐλπὶς δέ, κινδύνωι παραμύθιον οὖσα, τοὺς μὲν ἀπὸ περιουσίας χρωμένους αὐτῆι κἂν βλάψηι, οὐ καθεῖλε· τοῖς δὲ ἐς ἅπαν τὸ ὑπάρχον ἀναρριπτοῦσι (δάπανος γὰρ φύσει) ἅμα τε γιγνώσκεται σφαλέντων, καὶ ἐν ὅτωι ἔτι φυλάξεταί τις αὐτὴν γνωρισθεῖσαν, οὐκ ἐλλείπει. Plut. *Pyrrh.* 26 οὕτω μὲν ἐξέπεσε τῶν Ἰταλικῶν καὶ Σικελικῶν ὁ Πύρρος ἐλπίδων, νομισθεὶς ἃ ταῖς πράξεσιν ἐκτᾶτο ταῖς ἐλπίσιν ἀπολλύναι, δι' ἔρωτα τῶν ἀπόντων οὐδὲν εἰς ὃ δεῖ θέσθαι τῶν ὑπαρχόντων φθάσας. Pind. *P.* iii. 19 ἀλλά τοι | ἤρατο τῶν ἀπεόντων· οἷα καὶ πολλοὶ πάθον· | ἔστι δὲ φῦλον ἐν ἀνθρώποισι ματαιότατον, | ὅστις αἰσχύνων ἐπιχώρια παπταίνει τὰ πόρσω, | μεταμώνια θηρεύων ἀκράντοις ἐλπίσιν. | ἔσχε τοιαύταν μεγάλαν αὐάταν | καλλιπέπλου λῆμα Κορωνίδος. Thuc. iv. 17 μὴ παθεῖν ὅπερ οἱ ἀήθως τι ἀγαθὸν λαμβάνοντες τῶν ἀνθρώπων· ἀεὶ γὰρ τοῦ πλέονος ἐλπίδι ὀρέγονται διὰ τὸ καὶ τὰ παρόντα ἀδοκήτως εὐτυχῆσαι.

405. See cr. n. What the MS. gives is merely a case of *simplex ordo*, as explained in my paper on Transposition of Words, *Class. Rev.* xvi. p. 243.—**πρόστριμμα** suggests βάσανος (401): Max. Tyr. 20. 3 τὸν μὲν γὰρ χρυσὸν βασανίζει λίθος προστριβόμενον αὐτῆι.

418. **δόμων προφῆται** 'spokesmen of the house' are members of Menelaus' household whose gossip voiced abroad the condition of affairs within; gave whispered utterance to the private and domestic

grief of the deserted husband. These revelations they convey in guarded language like the Chorus in the *Choephori*, 45—82, not mentioning names, but saying πρόμοι, ἀφημένων, ὑπερποντίας, ἀνδρί, τις. For πρ. with the genitive cf. Athen. 187 b, ὁ δ' Ἐπίκουρος ἅπαντας εἰσήγαγε προφήτας ἀτόμων.

421. See cr. nn. The reading of the MSS. is neither sense nor metre: with **σιγὰς ἀτίμους ἀλοιδόρους** Hermann restored both. The corruption was introduced by some scribe who failed to perceive the construction of πάρεστιν ἰδεῖν—thought that it required a nominative. Just the same thing happened in Eur. *Tro.* 36 τὴν δ' ἀθλίαν τήνδ' εἴ τις εἰσορᾶν θέλει, πάρεστιν, Ἑκάβην κειμένην πυλῶν πάρος: where inferior MSS. give πάρεστιν Ἑκάβη κειμένη. What **ἄδιστος** should be is uncertain. **ἀφημένων**, 'sitting apart': of Achilles sulking in his tent in Hom. Ο 106 ὁ δ' ἀφήμενος οὐκ ἀλεγίζει οὐδ' ὄθεται (with which Leaf compares Θ 207, Λ 81). Add Hdt. iv. 66 ἠτιμωμένοι ἀποκατέαται. Mourners are constantly said to *sit* moping, *e.g.* Hom. κ 497, ξ 41, π 145, Epictet. ii. 16. 33 κλαύσεις καθήμενος ὡς τὰ παιδία; so ii. 24. 25 τί οὖν ἐκεῖνον (Achilles) ὠφελεῖ ταῦτα, ὅταν καθήμενος κλαίηι διὰ τὸ κορασίδιον; iii. 13. 9 μέλλω καθήμενος κλαίειν, ὅτι μόνος ἀπελείφθην καὶ ἔρημος; iii. 24. 8 ἂν δέ τις ἀποδημήσηι τῶν συνήθων, καθήμενοι κλαίωμεν; see κάθημαι in Upton's index. So 'By the waters of Babylon we sat down and wept, remembering Zion.'

424. **δόξει.** Attic puts δόξειεν ἂν where the Ionic writers say ἐρεῖς or the like: so Herodas, *e.g.* iv. 31.

427. **ὀμμάτων δ' ἐν ἀχηνίαις ἔρρει πᾶσ' Ἀφροδίτα** is precisely like an Orphic line quoted by Lobeck, *Aglaophamus*, p. 951 χειρῶν δ' ὀλλυμένων ἔρρεν πολυεργὸς Ἀθήνη, 'with the destruction of hands, Athena, the goddess of handicraft, was clean gone': and so all spirit of love, love-sense, is departed in the lack of eyes, which are the channels of desire (ἵμερος), and were created, according to Empedocles, by Aphrodite (frs. 86, 87 Diels).

429. **πενθήμονες** of the MSS. is contrary to the sense: πειθήμονες Housman ('si dicerentur πειθήμονες, intelligerem' Karsten) rightly: v. 286 ὀνείρων φάσματ' εὐπιθῆ. Tryphiod. 456 (Aphrodite) προσέφη πειθήμονι φωνῆι.

431. This line has caused much trouble because the sentence has no finite verb; yet δοκῶν ὁρᾶι, the most plausible of the conjectures, cannot be right, because Greek never said δοκῶν ὁρῶ, always δοκῶ ὁρᾶν. The verb is in fact *omitted*, with dramatic effect: 'For oft, as dreaming that he beholds his joy, *he would embrace*.' This is quite common in Greek writing: Semon. Amorg. 7. 110 κεχηνότος γὰρ ἀνδρός— οἱ δὲ γείτονες χαίρουσ' ὁρῶντες, Philem. 126 μῦς λευκός, ὅταν αὐτήν τις—

ἀλλ' αἰσχύνομαι λέγειν—κέκραγε... 4. 15, Xenarch. 4. 16, Theocr. i. 105 οὐ λέγεται τὰν Κύπριν ὁ βουκόλος— ; Lucian i. 242 ἐγὼ δὲ ἤδη ποτὲ τὴν Ἀφροδίτην—ἀλλ' οὐ χρὴ αὐχεῖν, iii. 178, i. 232, 274, *A.P.* v. 34, 184. 5, 128, *Priap.* 82. 6, Verg. *Ecl.* iii. 8, Ar. *Vesp.* 1178 Blaydes. Soph. *O.T.* 1288 τὸν πατροκτόνον, τὸν μητρός—αὐδῶν ἀνόσι' οὐδὲ ῥητά μοι, Lucian iii. 296 πολὺ τὸ 'ἐὰν ὁ πατήρ—καὶ κύριος γένωμαι τῶν πατρώιων, [καὶ] πάντα σά,' Ov. *Heroid.* xiii. 164. Cf. *inf.* 503 (as Ar. *Lys.* 33, 37), 1095, *Cho.* 193, 1030, Eur. *Tro.* 713.

To the passages already cited in general illustration may be added Lycophr. 112—4, Eur. *Hel.* 35, Meleag. *A.P.* xii. 125, Hor. *C.* iv. 1. 37, Theocr. xxx. 22, Eur. *Alc.* 348—356.

ἐσθλά here and elsewhere = the Attic ἀγαθά.

434. **κελεύθοις** of the MSS. was an easy error for **κελεύθων** (see cr. n.): when there was the choice, Aeschylus can hardly have preferred to make the sense less lucid by an assonance less pleasant to the ear. For the sense cf. Lucian ii. 711 (of the Dream) πτηνὸς ὤν, ὥς φασι, καὶ ὅρον ἔχων τῆς πτήσεως τὸν ὕπνον.—Milton must have been thinking of this passage when he wrote (*Il Penseroso*, 6—10):

> And *fancies fond* with gaudy shapes possess
> As thick and numberless
> As the gay motes that people the sunbeams,
> Or *likest hovering dreams*,
> *The fickle pensioners of Morpheus' train.*

436. **ὑπερβατώτερα**, or ὑπερφατώτερα as Herwerden proposed. It is an extremely easy alteration, and so would be ὁ πολύφατός τ' ἀγὼν βροτῶν in *Theb.* 759, if not in Pind. fr. 75: cf. *P.* xi. 47. Hom. β 50 and the oracle in Hdt v. 78.—ὑπέρβαρτον in Aesch. fr. 99. 21 may be for ὑπέρφατον or ὑπέρβατον.

437 ff. τὸ πᾶν δ' ἀφ' Ἕλλαδος αἴας συνορμένοις of the MSS. is impossible rhythm here: it would be a single unrepeated logaoedic figure in a stanza of quite different rhythm. See cr. n. From the private grief of Menelaus while he sat at home we pass now to the general multitude at large, the warriors across the sea at Troy and their kinsmen, whom they left at home in Greece: what of the warriors? In their homes too the due and fitting behaviour towards them is mourning. **πρέπει** governs the dative **συνορμένοις**: for a victor, acclamation is the proper tribute, Pind. *N.* iii. 67 βοὰ δὲ νικαφόρωι σὺν Ἀριστοκλείδαι πρέπει; the proper tribute to the dead is (also praise, but in the shape of) regretful lamentation. And **γοῦν** depends on πρέπει: well, they may, there is reason enough, surely, why their houses should behave so.

ἀτλησικάρδιος is 'broken-hearted,' as ἀτλησίφρων (Hesych. ἀτλησίφρων:

οὐδεμιᾶς τόλμης ἔννοιαν ἔχων). The MSS. give πένθεια τλησικάρδιος, the opposite of the sense, and a contradiction in terms: *P.V.* 169 τίς ὧδε τλησικάρδιος θεῶν ὅτωι τάδ' ἐπιχαρῆ; τίς οὐ συνασχαλᾶι κακοῖς τεοῖσι; 'who is so *hard-hearted* as to feel no grief or indignation?' But Hesychius also records τλασίφρονα: ὑπομονητικόν, '*patient*,' '*long-suffering*,' '*stout-hearted*.' Hom. I 3 πένθεϊ δ' ἀτλήτωι βεβολήατο (T 367 ἄτλητον ἄχος, Apoll. Rhod. ii. 858 κῆδος), E 382 τέτλαθι...καὶ ἀνάσχεο κηδομένη περ, Y 18 τέτλαθι δή, κραδίη· καὶ κύντερον ἄλλο ποτ' ἔτλης, Ω 48 ἀλλ' ἤ τοι κλαύσας καὶ ὀδυράμενος μεθέηκεν· τλητὸν γὰρ μοῖραι θυμὸν θέσαν ἀνθρώποισι. *inf.* 886 τλᾶσ' ἀπενθήτῳ φρενί. *A.P.* vii. 335 τλῆθι πένθος, εὔνασον. Archilochus 9. 5—10 ending τλῆτε, γυναικεῖον πένθος ἀπωσάμενοι.

443. τεύχη may mean 'arms.'

445 ff. ὁ χρυσαμοιβὸς δ' Ἄρης κτέ. This is a fine example of the power that Aeschylus has of developing an image and sustaining it: The God of War is like a money-changer who gives gold for bulkier metal; but his dealing is in flesh and blood; he has his scales like the money-changer, but they are the scales of battle; he receives a human body, a man's bulk, and what he gives back for it in exchange is like the merchant's gold-dust (ψῆγμα), *fined in the fire* (πυρωθέν), and *heavy*, for it causes heaviness; and packed in vessels which are εὔθετοι, a word covering two senses,—'handy,' *habiles*, and 'decently disposed,' *bene compositi*, applied to a corpse: Bekker *Anecd.* 40. 23 εὐθετεῖν νεκρόν: τὸ εὖ κοσμεῖν ἐν τάφοις νεκρόν.

455. In a similar spirit, as reported by Eur. *Tro.* 374 ff., Cassandra argues that the sorrows of Argos were worse than those of Troy:

> ἐπεὶ δ' ἐπ' ἀκτὰς ἤλυθον Σκαμανδρίους,
> ἔθνῃσκον, οὐ γῆς ὅρι' ἀποστερούμενοι
> οὐδ' ὑψίπυργον πατρίδ'· οὓς δ' Ἄρης ἕλοι,
> οὐ παῖδας εἶδον, οὐ δάμαρτος ἐν χεροῖν
> πέπλοις συνεστάλησαν, ἐν ξένῃι δὲ γῆι
> κεῖνται. τὰ δ' οἴκοι τοῖσδ' ὅμοι' ἐγίγνετο·
> χῆραί τ' ἔθνῃσκον, οἱ δ' ἄπαιδες ἐν δόμοις
> ἄλλως τέκν' ἐκθρέψαντες, οὐδὲ πρὸς τάφοις
> ἔσθ' ὅστις αὐτῶν αἷμα γῆι δωρήσεται.

The consequence of discontent at home formed the subject of well-known stories referred to by Plat. *Legg.* 682 D: οὐκοῦν ἐν τούτωι τῶι χρόνωι, ὅντι δεκέτει, ὃν τὸ Ἴλιον ἐπολιορκεῖτο, τὰ τῶν πολιορκούντων ἑκάστων οἴκοι κακὰ πολλὰ ξυνέβαινε γιγνόμενα περὶ τὰς στάσεις τῶν νέων, οἳ καὶ ἀφικομένους τοὺς στρατιώτας εἰς τὰς αὑτῶν πόλεις τε καὶ οἰκίας οὐ καλῶς οὐδ' ἐν δίκηι ὑπεδέξαντο, ἀλλ' ὥστε θανάτους τε καὶ σφαγὰς καὶ φυγὰς γενέσθαι παμπόλλας;

461 **εὔμορφοι.** So Homer X 370 (the Greeks gathering round the corpse of Hector) οἳ καὶ θηήσαντο φυὴν καὶ εἶδος ἀγητὸν Ἕκτορος.

463. **βαρεῖα,** *dangerous*, is answered by βαρύ in 475.

464. **δημοκράντου**: popular indignation is as effectual as a curse officially pronounced (Dem. 18. 130 οὐδὲ γὰρ ὧν ἔτυχεν ἦν, ἀλλ' οἷς ὁ δῆμος καταρᾶται, id. 19. 70): it may lead to a rising and the stoning of its object.—**χρέος** is anything *required*; in prose confined to a debt of money, but in poetry any function, service, obligation. ἀπαιτεῖν is to demand, **τίνειν** to fulfil the requirement.

469. Another image, developed out of the word ἀμαυρόν: Hesiod had said that when a man is prosperous unrighteously, his estate is *minished and brought low*: *Op.* 321

εἰ γάρ τις καὶ χερσὶ βίηι μέγαν ὄλβον ἕληται,
ἢ ὅγ' ἀπὸ γλώσσης ληΐσσεται, οἷά τε πολλὰ
γίγνεται, εὖτ' ἂν δὴ κέρδος νόον ἐξαπατήσηι
ἀνθρώπων, αἰδῶ δέ τ' ἀναιδείη κατοπάζηι·
ῥεῖα δέ μιν μαυροῦσι θεοί, μινύθουσι δὲ οἶκοι
ἀνέρι τῶι, παῦρον δέ τ' ἐπὶ χρόνον ὄλβος ὀπηδεῖ.

and again 282:

ὃς δέ κε μαρτυρίηισιν ἑκὼν ἐπίορκον ὀμόσσας
ψεύσεται, ἐν δὲ δίκην βλάψας νήκεστον ἀασθῆι,
τοῦ δέ τ' ἀμαυροτέρη γενεὴ μετόπισθε λέλειπται·
ἀνδρὸς δ' εὐόρκου γενεὴ μετόπισθεν ἀμείνων.

471. **παλιντυχεῖ τριβᾶι βίου** has not been understood: τριβᾶι means *attrition*; as Fortune caused him to wax great unrighteously, so the Erinyes cause him eventually to wane again and *dwindle*, minishing him to a faint shadow, till at last he disappears in Hell. The working of a curse, of which the Erinyes are the embodiment, upon the conscience of the victim is more fully pictured in the *Eumenides*: they suck his blood, until they have worn him away to a shadow (264–7, 302, 360, 371, 938), and then drag him down to Hell (267), from which there is no escape (175, 341).

476. **κάρανα.** The construction of the sentence corresponds to Athen. 523 b ἐξ οὐρανοῦ βαλλόμενοι πυρὶ καὶ χαλκῶι.

The MS. reading βάλλεται γὰρ ὄσσοις Διόθεν κεραυνός has received the following interpretations: (1) 'for a thunderbolt is hurled from Zeus upon the eyes (of the too-famous man).' Even if the construction be allowed to pass, this is excluded, because Greek never spoke of hurling a thunderbolt on a man's eyes; it would convey no meaning. The eyes are plainly the jealous eyes of Zeus. (2) 'for a thunderbolt is hurled by the eyes of Zeus (upon the too-famous man).' But though lightning may be flashed from his eyes, the thunderbolt was always wielded in his hand. On these grounds I am convinced that Prof. Tucker (*Class. Rev.* vii. p. 340) is right in regarding κεραυνός as an error and in substituting κάρανα: that is precisely what the sentence wants.

477. **ἄφθονος ὄλβος**: there is a pun on the double meaning of ἄφθονος, of which some early moralist must have taken advantage.

484. **εἴ τι...ψύθος** is added as an afterthought: see on 359.

487 ff. The phrases of the Chorus are mockingly borrowed from the fire, **πυρωθέντα** καρδίαν and in 491 πιθανὸς ἄγαν ὁ θῆλυς ἔρος ἐπινέμεται —for there were two things ἐπινέμεσθαι was so commonly applied to that the original metaphor from grazing cattle was forgotten in their case and became appropriated to themselves,—the ravages of *fire* or of *disease* (Thuc. ii. 54, 58). There is a playful application of the word in Plut. *Mor.* 415 F ὁρῶ τὴν Στωικὴν ἐκπύρωσιν ὥσπερ τὰ Ἡρακλείτου καὶ Ὀρφέως ἐπινεμομένην ἔπη οὕτω καὶ τὰ Ἡσιόδου καὶ συνεξάπτουσαν: and what the Elders mean (with an undercurrent of allusion to her amorous intrigue and protestations) is that a woman is ready to accept good news upon the slightest warrant (*quo rumorem reconciliationis afficeret, acciperetque Agrippina, facili feminarum credulitate ad gaudia*, Tac. *Ann.* xiv. 4), without waiting for proof visible and palpable, πρὸ τοῦ φανέντος: such premature rejoicing is presently apt to be extinct as the fire among the thorns.—The MS. reading ὅρος ἐπινέμεται cannot be interpreted as 'the boundaries of a woman's mind are encroached upon' (ἐπινέμεται passive). To cross a limit was ὑπερβαίνειν (ὑπερπηδᾶν, ὑπερθορεῖν) ὅρον: but no Greek ever said ἐπινέμεσθαι ὅρον.—For the general sense cf. Plut. *Artox.* 28 καθόλου μὲν οὖν ἴσως, τὸ Σοφόκλειον, 'ταχεῖα πειθὼ τῶν κακῶν ὁδοιπορεῖ·' (fr. 714) λεία γάρ τις ἡ πορεία καὶ κατάντης ἐπὶ τὸ βουλόμενον. For χάριν ξυναινέσαι, 'to yield assent to pleasure,' cf. Pind. *P.* iv. 139 f. ἐντὶ μὲν θνατῶν φρένες ὠκύτεραι κέρδος αἰνῆσαι πρὸ δίκας δόλιον.

500. **κόνις**. The dust is an indication of speed: *Theb.* 60 χωρεῖ κονίει. Lucian i. 623 οὐχ ὁρᾷς δὲ καὶ τὸν Ἑρμῆν αὐτὸν ἱδρῶτι ῥεόμενον καὶ τὼ πόδε κεκονιμένον καὶ πνευστιῶντα; μεστὸν γοῦν ἄσθματος αὐτῷ τὸ στόμα. τί ταῦτα, ὦ Ἑρμῆ, ἡ σπουδή; The speed of the Herald shows that he comes with a definite message: *Pers.* 249 ἀλλ', ἐμοὶ δοκεῖν, τάχ' εἴσῃ πάντα νημερτῆ λόγον· τοῦδε γὰρ δράμημα φωτὸς Περσικὸν πρέπει μαθεῖν· καὶ φέρει σαφές τι πρᾶγος ἐσθλὸν ἢ κακὸν κλύειν. *Theb.* 356 ὁ τοι κατόπτης, ὡς ἐμοὶ δοκεῖ, στρατοῦ πευθώ τιν' ἡμῖν, ὦ φίλαι, νέαν φέρει, σπουδῆι διώκων πομπίμους χνόας ποδῶν. Eur. *Hec.* 216 καὶ μὴν Ὀδυσσεὺς ἔρχεται σπουδῆι ποδός, Ἑκάβη, νέον τι πρὸς σε σημανῶν ἔπος. *Hel.* 602 λέγ', ὡς φέρεις τι τῆιδε τῆι σπουδῆι νέον. *Med.* 1118 καὶ δὴ δέδορκα τόνδε τῶν Ἰάσονος στείχοντ' ὀπαδῶν· πνεῦμά τ' ἠρεθισμένον δείκνυσιν ὥς τι καινὸν ἀγγελεῖ κακόν. *Christ. Pat.* 98, 125, 1858. Lucian ii. 681 ἀλλὰ τίς ὁ

σπουδῆι προσιὼν οὗτός ἐστιν; ἤ πού τι ἐκ γῆς νεώτερον ἀπαγγέλλεις. ΕΡΜ. ὑπέρμεγα, ὦ Ζεῦ, καὶ μυρίας τῆς σπουδῆς δεόμενον.

501. **σοι.** The dative belongs to both clauses, and must be taken after σημανεῖ. Cf. *Eum.* 36 ὡς μήτε σωκεῖν μήτε μ' ἀκταίνειν βάσιν, *Theb.* 651, Soph. *O.T.* 1455.

504. **ἀποστέργω** always means 'I fall out of love with,' 'I cease to care for': thus here the thought implied is that anything less than glad news explicitly told will leave the speaker *dissatisfied.* Hence γάρ in v. 505: what has appeared is so good that any addition which is otherwise will be disappointing. For the force of ἀπό in composition cf. ἀπεσθίειν = *to leave off eating*, as illustrated in Athen. 649 b. So ἀπαλγήσαντας τὰ ἴδια in Thuc. ii. 61.

509. **δεκάτου**: see cr. n. Some modern editors retain the MS. error δεκάτωι, as though the Herald said he had returned on the tenth day of the year, for it could not mean anything else.

510. **ῥαγεισῶν**: hopes were *anchors* or *cables* to a Greek: Eur. *Hel.* 277 ἄγκυρα δ' ἥ μοι τὰς τύχας ὤχει μόνη, πόσιν ποθ' ἥξειν καί μ' ἀπαλλάξειν κακῶν, οὗτος τέθνηκεν, οὗτος οὐκέτ' ἔστι δή. Heliod. v. 19 Χαρίκλειά μοι βίος ἦν, ἐλπὶς καὶ διαδοχὴ τοῦ γένους· Χαρίκλεια μόνη παραψυχὴ καί, ὡς εἰπεῖν, ἄγκυρα. καὶ ταύτην ὑπετέμετο καὶ παρήνεγκεν ὅτι ποτ' ἐστὶ τὸ εἰληχός με δαιμόνιον. For ῥαγεισῶν cf. *spem abrumpere* (Tac. *Ann.* iv. 50 etc.).

516. **ἦλθες** (see cr. n.) was perhaps an explanation of a false reading ἤισθα.

518. **ἀγωνίους**: gods of assembly, as in *Supp.* 195, where Zeus, Apollo, Poseidon, and Hermes are subsequently singled out for mention: so *ib.* 248. Probably they were the twelve chief gods of the tribes who worshipped at the games. As gods of meeting they are also ἀγοραῖοι: Schol. Hom. Ω 1 παρὰ δὲ Βοιωτοῖς ἀγὼν ἡ ἀγορά... ὅθεν καὶ ἀγωνίους θεοὺς Αἰσχύλος τοὺς ἀγοραίους.

521. **ἥρως**: cf. Xen. *Cyr.* ii. 1. 1 προσευξάμενοι θεοῖς καὶ ἥρωσι τοῖς τὴν Περσίδα γῆν κατέχουσιν ἵλεως καὶ εὐμενεῖς πέμπειν σφᾶς, Plut. *Arist.* 11 οἱ μὲν γὰρ ἥρωες, οἷς ἐκέλευε θύειν, ἀρχηγέται Πλαταιέων ἦσαν.

525. **εἴ που**, 'if perchance' (*puta*).... Cf. Ar. *Eq.* 347 εἴ που δικίδιον εἶπας εὖ κατὰ ξένου μετοίκου, *Supp.* 405 εἴ που τι μὴ τοῖον τύχοι. The prayer is of the same form as Hom. E 116 εἴ ποτέ μοι καὶ πατρὶ φίλα φρονέουσα παρέστης δηίωι ἐν πολέμωι, νῦν αὖτ' ἐμὲ φῖλαι, Ἀθήνη. Apoll. Rhod. iv. 757 νῦν, εἴ ποτ' ἐμὰς ἐτέλεσσας ἐφετμάς, εἰ δ' ἄγε. Sappho i. 5 ἀλλὰ τυῖδ' ἔλθ', αἴποτα κἀτέρωτα...ἔκλυες. 25 ἔλθε μοι καὶ νῦν. Ar. *Ach.* 405 ὑπάκουσον, εἴπερ πώποτ' ἀνθρώπων τινί. We expect καὶ νῦν, but that is here expressed by τοισίδε, which has been a great puzzle to critics: 'with bright eyes now.' Else we should only have had τοῖσιν (which h writes), as Alciphron i. 38 ἡ δὲ οὐκέτι φαιδροῖς τοῖς ὄμμασιν ὄψεται μειδιῶσα.

530 ff. There are certain images in Isaiah which this passage recalls: 14. 23 'I will sweep it (Babylon) with the besom of destruction, saith the Lord of hosts.' 30. 28 The breath of the Lord shall reach 'to sift the nations with the sieve of vanity.' Aeschylus in his characteristic way sustains his image. In the MSS. however it is interrupted by a line interpolated from the margin (*Pers.* 813) βωμοὶ δ' ἄϊστοι δαιμόνων θ' ἱδρύματα, which had been quoted to illustrate the devastation of the land. In the *Persae* the verse is spoken by the ghost of King Darius, who has been raised from the dead to give advice to the Persians after their defeat at Salamis: on being informed of Xerxes' expedition he condemns it, and prophesies the crowning disaster of Plataea, v. 809

οὗ σφιν κακῶν ὕψιστ' ἐπαμμένει παθεῖν,
ὕβρεως ἄποινα κἀθέων φρονημάτων·
οἳ γῆν μολόντες Ἑλλάδ' οὐ θεῶν βρέτη
ᾐδοῦντο συλᾶν οὐδὲ πιμπράναι νεώς,
βωμοὶ δ' ἄϊστοι, δαιμόνων θ' ἱδρύματα
πρόρριζα φύρδην ἐξανέστραπται βάθρων.
τοιγὰρ κακῶς δράσαντες οὐκ ἐλάσσονα
πάσχουσι, τὰ δὲ μέλλουσι, κοὐδέπω κακῶν
κρηνὶς ἀπέσβηκ' ἀλλ' ἔτ' ἐκπιδύεται.

There in store abides
The crown of all their ills, in recompense
For their presumptuous and ungodly sin,
That in the land of Hellas made no conscience
Either to spoil the images of the gods
Or burn the temples; the altars are clean gone,
The shrines of deities torn up by the roots
And overturned and swept from their foundations.
Therefore for their ill-doing, ills no less
They have in suffering, and yet more shall have;
The fount of sorrow is not stanched yet
But still comes welling forth.

That is his denunciation of those barbarous and irreligious acts of desecration which Herodotus records (viii. 33, 53, 109, ix. 42) and which had impressed the Greek imagination with such deep and lasting horror (see *e.g.* Isocr. 4. 155). The passage in the *Persae* must have been familiar to all that heard the *Agamemnon*, and the acts themselves—including the burning of the temples on the Acropolis at Athens—must have been within the memory of many. Is it conceivable that Aeschylus before this audience, or any Greek at any time, could have put this statement as a proud boast in the mouth of a religious herald? See also Eur. *Hec.* 802—5.

The destruction of sacred buildings had no significance in the story of the Sack of Troy. If it happened, it was because in the burning of the town it was inevitable.

Quint. xiii. 432 speaks of the fire raging round: ὁμοῦ καίοντο δὲ πάντα Ἀντιμάχοιο μέλαθρα, καταίθετο δ' ἄσπετος ἄκρη Πέργαμον ἀμφ' ἐρατὴν περί θ' ἱερὸν Ἀπόλλωνος νηόν τε ζάθεον Τριτωνίδος ἀμφί τε βωμὸν Ἑρκείου· θάλαμοι δὲ κατεπρήθοντ' ἐρατεινοὶ υἱωνῶν Πριάμοιο· πόλις δ' ἀμαθύνετο πᾶσα: and in Seneca, *Agam.* 653 the Chorus lament *templa deos super usta suos.* But this is nowhere mentioned as having brought them retribution; and indeed for the Greeks to commit this act deliberately would have been impossible; there was no religious enmity; the Trojan gods were their gods. This is quite a different matter from the particular acts of sacrilege that were committed by individuals: Eur. *Tro.* 15 Poseidon complains ἔρημα δ' ἄλση καὶ θεῶν ἀνάκτορα φόνωι καταρρεῖ· πρὸς δὲ κρηπίδων βάθροις πέπτωκε Πρίαμος: and in describing the massacre Tryphiodorus 598 says: οὐδὲ θεῶν ὄπιν εἶχον ἀθεσμοτάτης ὑπὸ ῥιπῆς, ἀθανάτων δ' ἔχραινον ἀπενθέας αἵματι βωμούς. οἰκτρότατοι δὲ γέροντες ἀτιμοτάτοισι φόνοισιν οὐδ' ὀρθοὶ κτείνοντο, χαμαὶ δ' ἱκετήσια γυῖα τεινάμενοι πολιοῖσι κατεκλίνοντο καρήσιν.

537. **συντελής**, sharing the same privileges and so involved in the same liabilities.

539. **κλοπῆς**: Hdt. ii. 114 ἥκει ξεῖνος, γένος μὲν Τευκρός, ἔργον δὲ ἀνόσιον ἐν τῆι Ἑλλάδι ἐξεργασμένος· ξείνου γὰρ τοῦ ἑωυτοῦ ἐξαπατήσας τὴν γυναῖκα, αὐτήν τε ταύτην ἄγων ἥκει καὶ πολλὰ κάρτα χρήματα, *ib.* 118, 119.

543. **τῶν ἀπὸ στρατοῦ**, *returned from the field* = ἀπὸ στρατείας (608).

544. The form τεθνᾶναι was long ago rejected by Hermann. Against all such conjectures as retain τεθνάναι οὐκ ἀντερῶ it is sufficient to point out that ἀντιλέγω θανεῖν could not possibly mean 'I refuse to die'; still less could ἀντιλέγω τεθνάναι. Hartung's χαίρω· θανεῖν ἂν δ' οὐκέτ' ἀντερῶ θεοῖς would mean 'I will not urge against the gods that I would die'; and Kayser's χαίρω· θανεῖν δέ μ' οὐκέτ' ἀντερῶ θεοῖς 'I will not urge against the gods that I died.' The only conjecture that approaches the meaning aimed at is Schneidewin's χαίρω· τὸ τεθνάναι δ' οὐκέτ' ἀντερῶ θεοῖς, if rendered, 'as to dying, I will no more oppose the gods.' The general idea is doubtless the same as that in Hom. η 225 (first cited by Butler) ὡς κ' ἐμὲ τὸν δύστηνον ἐμῆς ἐπιβήσετε πάτρης | καίπερ πολλὰ παθόντα· ἰδόντα με καὶ λίποι αἰὼν | κτῆσιν ἐμὴν δμῶάς τε καὶ ὑψερεφὲς μέγα δῶμα. Add *h. Aphrod.* 154 βουλοίμην κεν ἔπειτα, γύναι εἰκυῖα θεῇσιν, σῆς εὐνῆς ἐπιβάς, δῦναι δόμον Ἄιδος εἴσω. Aesch. *Cho.* 437

ἔπειτ' ἐγὼ νοσφίσας ὀλοίμαν. Callim. fr. 219 τεθναίην ὅτ' ἐκεῖνον ἀποπνεύσαντα πυθοίμην. Eur. *El.* 281 θάνοιμι μητρὸς αἷμ' ἐπισφάξασ' ἐμῆς. *Or.* 1116 καὶ μὴν τόδ' ἔρξας δὶς θανεῖν οὐχ ἅζομαι. Musaeus 79 αὐτίκα τεθναίην λεχέων ἐπιβήμενος Ἡροῦς. Plat. *Apol.* 28 D, Synes. *Epist.* 107, Plut. *Mor.* 1094 A οὐδ' εὔξατό τις ἐμπλησθεὶς ὄψων ἢ πεμμάτων βασιλικῶν εὐθὺς ἀποθανεῖν, Aristid. i. p. 709. 20 Dind., *inf.* 1610. Cic. 2 *Phil.* 119 *mihi uero, patres conscripti, iam etiam optanda mors est, perfuncto rebus iis*, etc. Guided by these passages I read as in the text. Cf. *Othello* ii. 1. 187 If it were now to die, | 'Twere now to be most happy; for I fear, | My soul hath her content so absolute | That not another comfort like to this | Succeeds in unknown fate.

χαίρω γε, read by Enger and others, cannot be right, as this is the answer to χαίρεις; not to χαῖρε.

551. When it is seen that this line is the answer to a question (as Heath took it), it is plain that the natural supplement is γ', 'Aye,' which is besides most easily omitted. For similar instances see Eur. *Or.* 1122, *Phoen.* 1344, *Cycl.* 217, *El.* 667, Ar. *Nub.* 469.

552. **στυγοστράτωι**: see cr. n. The corruption is an example of a very common form of error, which has been illustrated in *Class. Rev.* xv. p. 17 f.

555. **τὸ σὸν** refers to his τεθναίην in v. 544. Cf. Strabo, p. 793 ὥστε νῦν, τὸ τοῦ ποιητοῦ, 'ἐξ ἑτέρων ἕτερ' ἐστίν.' Aristid. ii. 164, Dind. καλῶς γε ποιῶν, ὦ ἑταῖρε, τὸ σὸν δὴ τοῦτο, καὶ τἀληθῆ λέγων.

561. **παρείξεις** (from παρείκω as εἶξις from εἴκω), 'opportunities,' or 'relaxations.' See cr. n. The schol. has σπανίους. καὶ τούτου γὰρ οὐ συνεχῶς ἀπηλαύομεν.—**κακοστρώτους**: Chionides ἥρωες fr. 1 (i. 4 K.) πολλοὺς ἐγῷδα κοὐ κατὰ σὲ νεανίας φρουροῦντας ἀτεχνῶς (? ἀτενὲς K.) κἂν σάμακι κοιμωμένους.

562 is corrupt. For οὐ λαχόντες, οὗ λάχοι τις might be suggested. Margoliouth's ἀσχάλλοντας would require a second negative.

563. **καὶ προσῆν πλέον στύγος** is perhaps a case of *simplex ordo* (see *Class. Rev.* xvi. p. 244), and we should read καὶ πλέον προσῆν στύγος.

565. **δέ.** For the corruption into γάρ see Porson on *Med.* 34, 1083, *On editing Aeschylus*, p. 119.—The words κἀπὸ...δρόσοι are parenthetic, which accounts for the gender of τιθέντες (Verrall). Cf. 616 f. οὐδ' οἶδα τέρψιν—οὐδ' ἐπίψογον φάτιν—ἄλλου πρὸς ἀνδρός.

566 f. 'Causing mildew and making the hair or wool of our garments verminous,' ἔνθηρον,—for θηρίον was applied in more or less humorous horror to the smallest creatures. No one who has served a campaign—in South Africa or elsewhere—will dispute the truth of the description. Plut. *Mor.* 352 F, speaking of the linen garments

worn by the Egyptian priests, remarks that linen is ἥκιστα φθειροποιόν, ὡς λέγουσι.

This in any case is the meaning of ἔνθηρον, which is applied to a festering wound in Soph. *Phil.* 698; and the rhythm is in favour of the punctuation adopted in the text. The usual arrangement

δρόσοι κατεψέκαζον, ἔμπεδον σίνος
ἐσθημάτων, τιθέντες ἔνθηρον τρίχα,

moves haltingly and throws the unemphatic τιθέντες into an abnormal place at the beginning of a clause. Sophocles, however, would appear to have read it so and taken τρίχα to mean the hair of the head: in the *Ajax* he makes his sailors before Troy complain as follows:—

600 ἐγὼ δ' ὁ τλάμων παλαιὸς ἀφ' οὗ χρόνος
Ἰδαῖα μίμνων λειμώνι' ἄποινα μηνῶν
ἀνήριθμος αἰὲν εὐνῶμαι.

1206 κεῖμαι δ' ἀμέριμνος οὕτως
ἀεὶ πυκιναῖς δρόσοις τεγγόμενος κόμας,
λυγρᾶς μνήματα Τροίας.

577. The sense is ἔρρετ' ἀνῖαι *A. P.* v. 72, *ualete curae.* **χαίρειν καταξιῶ** is merely one of the many variations of the phrase χαίρειν λέγω or κελεύω, which meant 'I say to you χαῖρε,' 'I bid you hail,' or 'I bid farewell to you,' 'I say good-bye to you.' Instead of these words poetical or humorous language indulged in a great variety of substitutes: χαῖρε προσείπας Kaibel, *Epig.* 256. προσείπας χαίρειν 781. αὐδήσαντες χαίρειν 205. ἔννεπε χαίρειν 103. ἐνέπω κλαίειν μακρά Archestratus (Ath. 117 a). χαίρειν προυννέπω Soph. *Trach.* 227. χαίρειν ἐφίεμαι *Ai.* 112. ἄρτι δὲ χαίρειν τοῖσι τεοῖς προθύροις ἐπιτέλλομαι Theocr. xix. 26. ἀείσας χαίρειν Kaibel, *Epig.* 237. χαίρειν κελεύων πολλά Ar. *Ach.* 200. πολλὰ χαίρειν φράσας: ἀποταξάμενος Hesych. μακρὰ χαίρειν λέγων Lucian ii. 614, ἐῶν i. 714, φράσαντες ii. 820. ἐρρῶσθαι λέγων Antiphanes 88. ἐρρῶσθαι φράσας πολλὰ Dem. 19. 248, Lucian ii. 861. κλαίειν ἄνωγα Eur. *Cycl.* 340, 701. κλαίειν ἀγορεύω Plat. Com. 173. οἰμώζειν παραγγείλαντες Lucian i. 422.

583. **θεοῖς...τοῖς καθ' Ἑλλάδα**: Soph. fr. 871 νὴ τοὺς ἐν Ἄργει καὶ κατὰ Σπάρτην θεούς.

585. **εὐλογεῖν**: see on 350.

589. **εὐμαθεῖν**, 'teachableness,' as δυσμαθεῖν (*Cho.* 224) from δυσμαθής, ὀψιμαθεῖν, φιλομαθεῖν. 'It is never too late to learn.'

591. **σὺν δὲ πλουτίζειν ἐμέ**: *Cho.* 820 πλεῖ τάδ' εὖ· ἐμὸν ἐμὸν κέρδος αὔξεται τόδ'· ἄτα δ' ἀποστατεῖ φίλων.

592. **ἀνωλόλυξα μὲν πάλαι** is equivalent to πάλαι μὲν ἀνωλόλυξα (see note on v. 8), and πάλαι μὲν is taken up by καὶ νῦν in 603.

595. **καί τις μ' ἐνίπτων** reproduces the language of the Elders in vv. 481 ff., which Clytaemnestra had not heard. But the Chorus merely expressed the general sense of Argos, and the queen must have become acquainted with this in the interval implied in πάλαι (592).

602. **κοιμῶντες** perhaps means 'extinguishing with wine at the end of the rite.'

609. **πύλας ἀνοῖξαι.** Similarly Eur. *Cycl.* 502 θύραν τίς οἴξει μοι; Eupolis fr. 220 ἣν οὐκ ἀνέωιξα πώποτ' ἀνθρώποις ἐγώ. Ar. *Eccl.* 962, 990. Nicet. Eugen. 4. 245, 268, 6. 528.

614. **σημαντήριον.** Oppian *Hal.* iii. 361 κτῆσιν ἀεὶ κείροντες ἀσημάντοιο δόμοιο—an orphan's unprotected home. It was the common practice to seal up store-rooms and other treasuries, *e.g.* Eur. *Or.* 1108, Plat. *Legg.* 954 AB, Ar. *Thesm.* 414 ff., *Lys.* 1199, Diog. L. iv. 59, Hdt. ii. 121 *β*, Plaut. *Cas.* 144, *Amphitr.* 773, Stob. *Flor.* 6. 33 (so here σημαντήριον includes the seal of chastity).

616 f. **ἄλλου πρὸς ἀνδρὸς** belongs to **τέρψιν** and has no connexion with the intervening words **οὐδ' ἐπίψογον φάτιν.** So Theogn. 461 μή ποτ' ἐπ' ἀπρήκτοισι νόον ἔχε, μηδὲ μενοίνα, χρήμασι, τῶν ἄνυσις γίνεται οὐδεμία. [For fuller discussions of this idiom, which Bergk (*P. L. G.* ii. p. 159) unnecessarily doubts, see Tyrrell in *C. R.* ii. p. 140 f., Kaibel on Soph. *El.* 1358 (p. 279[1]).]—It is most natural to understand **χαλκοῦ βαφάς** (with the schol.) as poetical for σιδήρου βαφάς, which is often mentioned, the tempering of iron, to harden it or to soften it. The illustration is chosen of course for the double meaning.

618 ff. The MS. gives 618—9 to the Herald; most critics follow Hermann now in giving them to Clytaemnestra; Dr Verrall thinks they are spoken by a 'Conspirator.' Many commentators render **τοιόσδ' ὁ κόμπος,** '*talis quidem sui iactatio*,' '*a boast like this*,' '*that sort of boast*,' as though it were τοιόσδε κόμπος; but it can only mean '*such is the boast*,' and unless it is corrupt—which is improbable, for corruption would rather be the other way—our explanation must allow it its due meaning. **μανθάνω** means *intellego*, '*I see*,' '*I understand*,' '*I take your meaning*'; μανθάνεις, 'do you see?' Examples are abundant in Comedy and Plato: Eur. *Or.* 1129 ΠΥ. εἶτ' αὐτὸ δηλοῖ τοὔργον οἷ τείνειν χρεών. ΟΡ. Ἑλένην φονεύειν· μανθάνω τὸ σύμβολον. ΠΥ. ἔγνως. Ar. *Ran.* 64 ΔΙ. ἆρ' ἐκδιδάσκω τὸ σαφές, ἢ 'τέραι φράσω; ΗΡ. μὴ δῆτα περὶ ἔτνους γε· πάνυ γὰρ μανθάνω. And μανθάνεις accordingly means '*you understand*,' *rem tenes*, as Lucian i. 564 ΑΓΟ. οὐκοῦν...δῆλον ὅτι μόνος ὁ σπουδαῖος μισθὸν ἐπὶ τῆι ἀρετῆι λήψεται; ΧΡΥΣ. μανθάνεις. This is implied by a participle in *Cho.* 112 ΗΛ. ἐμοί τε καὶ σοὶ τἄρ' ἐπεύξωμαι τάδε; ΧΟ. αὐτὴ σὺ ταῦτα μανθάνουσ' ἤδη φράσαι, *i.e.* μανθάνεις: and the same is implied here by **μανθάνοντί σοι**: '*Her* speech is thus, as you understand.' The person addressed, therefore, must have shown the Elder that he understands; and it follows that the previous remark cannot have been made by Clytaemnestra: seeing no reason to believe in Dr Verrall's Conspirator, I conclude that the MS. is right in assigning 618—9 to the Herald. **αὕτη μὲν οὕτως εἶπε** is a formula dismissing *her* case, as 941 τοὐμὸν μὲν οὕτω, *Eum.* 556, *Theb.* 409, 1003, *Supp.* 513; they jot in μανθάνοντί σοι, and add a plainer explanation in the following line, of which the natural interpretation is 'in the judgment of good critics—those who can read between the lines—only very specious words.' Then σὺ δ' εἰπέ, κῆρυξ, is the antithesis to αὕτη μὲν οὕτως, 'now for *your* story further.' **λακεῖν** is an invidious word; it means 'to scream' or 'cry aloud without reserve or self-control' (αὔειν, λακάζειν, σωφρόνων μισήματα *Theb.* 169, *Supp.* 884): it is used contemptuously by Clytaemnestra of the bawling news-bringers in 856, and her γυναικείωι νόμωι ὀλολυγμὸν ἔλασκον in 601 is a retort, quoting the contemptuous judgments passed on her supposed impetuous behaviour; in 1427 περίφρονα ἔλακες is used of her by the Chorus (as κομπάζεις in 1399) to rebuke her vaunting menaces, but a woman of her character would never, I think, apply it to herself: see n. on 287.—But the most important phrase is **ὡς γυναικὶ γενναίαι**, in which ὡς after an adjective should have a limiting or qualifying force; not, as Peile takes it, 'particularly for a noble lady,' but 'for such a person as a noble lady,' 'considering that a noble lady is the speaker.' Examples are familiar, as Soph. *O. T.* 1118 πιστὸς ὡς νομεὺς ἀνήρ, 'trusty as any, in his shepherd's place,' *O. C.* 20 μακρὰν γὰρ ὡς γέροντι προυστάλης ὁδόν, 'a long way for an old man,' *Ai.* 395 ἔρεβος ὦ φαεννότατον, ὡς ἐμοί, Plat. *Sophist.* 226 C ταχεῖαν, ὡς ἐμοί, σκέψιν ἐπιτάττεις, 'a rapid process of thought for such as I am,' *Parmen.* 136 D πολὺ ἔργον προστάττεις ὡς τηλίκωιδε, Dio Chrys. ii. p. 267 R. δριμὺν <μὲν> καὶ δόλιον ὡς ἐν τοῖς τότε, πολὺ δὲ ἀπέχοντα τῆς νῦν κακοηθείας, Thuc. v. 43 ἡλικίαι μὲν ἔτι τότε ὢν νέος ὡς ἐν ἄλληι πόλει, iv. 84 ἦν δὲ οὐδὲ ἀδύνατος, ὡς Λακεδαιμόνιος, εἰπεῖν. The meaning then should be that such unabashed avowals, though brim-full of truth, are surely *indecorous*, unbecoming a true gentlewoman. If the punctuation is made interrogative, this is exactly what the Herald says.—The Chorus are well aware of Clytaemnestra's hypocrisy; therefore I do not think 618—9 would be said by one of them; but the Herald, who knows nothing, is surprised and unfavourably impressed, thinking that noble ladies do not usually proclaim their fidelity and affection in such terms (cf. Plut. *Mor.* 768 B ἡ δὲ γενναία γυνὴ πρὸς ἄνδρα νόμιμον συγκραθεῖσα δι' Ἔρωτος ἄρκτων ἂν ὑπομείνειε καὶ δρακόντων περιβολὰς μᾶλλον ἢ ψαῦσιν ἀνδρὸς ἀλλοτρίου καὶ συγκατάκλισιν); thinking perhaps that there is some indecency in her saying 'that I may give my honoured lord the best and soonest welcome—for to a woman's eyes what hour is dearer than ἀπὸ στρατείας ἀνδρί, σώσαντος θεοῦ, πύλας ἀνοῖξαι (v. 608 f., where see n.)?' Clytaemnestra here of course is merely overacting; but in Sophocles her true behaviour is such that Electra refuses her the character of γενναία γυνή: *El.* 287 αὕτη γὰρ ἡ λόγοισι γενναία γυνὴ φωνοῦσα τοιάδ' ἐξονειδίζει κακά· ὦ δύσθεον μίσημα, σοὶ μόνηι πατὴρ τέθνηκεν; κτέ. It is true that Sir R. Jebb renders, 'this woman, in professions so noble'; but I incline to the other interpretation, 'this so-called noble lady,' as in Eur. *El.* 326 Aegisthus is to Electra τῆς ἐμῆς μητρὸς πόσις ὁ κλεινός, ὡς λέγουσιν. *Or.* 17 ὁ κλεινός, εἰ δὴ κλεινός, Ἀγαμέμνων.

623. **σεσωμένος.** [In support of this form Wecklein, *Curae epigr.* p. 60 quotes Photius, p. 507, 22 σέσωται καὶ σεσωμένος οἱ παλαιοὶ ἄνευ τοῦ σ̄...οἱ δὲ νεώτεροι σέσωσμαι, and Suid. *s.v.* σέσωται, and concludes 'librarios peccauisse addendo σ̄ ex posteriore dicendi consuetudine.']

631. **ἀναχθεὶς ἐμφανῶς ἐξ Ἰλίου** points to the form of the legend according to which Menelaus quarrelled with Agamemnon after the sack of Troy, and set sail before him: see Hom. γ 136 ff., Soph. fr. 479, Pausan. x. 25. 3.

641 ff. **εὔφημον ἦμαρ οὐ πρέπει κακαγγέλωι γλώσσηι μιαίνειν· χωρὶς ἡ τιμὴ θεῶν...(653) πῶς κεδνὰ τοῖς κακοῖσι συμμείξω;** These are all religious phrases. In the *Ion* 1017 Creusa has two drugs with different virtues, one wholesome and the other—venom from the Gorgon's serpents—deadly, and is asked εἰς ἓν δὲ κραθέντ' αὐτὸν ἢ χωρὶς φέρεις; She replies χωρίς· κακῶι γὰρ ἐσθλὸν οὐ συμμείγνυται. See further Paley's note on *Ion* 246, and compare Plat. *Legg.* 800 B—E, Plut. *Aem. Paul.* 35 τὴν ὠμότητα τῆς τύχης, ὡς οὐκ ἠιδέσατο πένθος τοσοῦτον εἰς οἰκίαν ζήλου καὶ χαρᾶς καὶ θυσιῶν γέμουσαν εἰσάγουσα καὶ καταμιγνύουσα θρήνους καὶ δάκρυα παιᾶσιν ἐπινικίοις καὶ θριάμβοις. The words χωρὶς ἡ τιμὴ θεῶν are a brief proverbial expression of familiar doctrine—'*that ceremony is apart from the Gods of Heaven*': see Plat. *Legg.* 828 C ἔτι δὲ καὶ τὸ τῶν χθονίων καὶ ὅσους αὖ θεοὺς οὐρανίους ἐπονομαστέον καὶ τὸ τῶν τούτοις ἑπομένων οὐ ξυμμεικτέον, ἀλλὰ χωριστέον κτέ., *Tim.* 69 D σεβόμενοι μιαίνειν τὸ θεῖον, ὅ τι μὴ πᾶσα ἦν ἀνάγκη, χωρὶς ἐκείνου κατοικίζουσιν εἰς ἄλλην τοῦ σώματος οἴκησιν τὸ θνητόν, Plut. *Mor.* 361 B θεοί and ἀθάνατοι are often used in discrimination from the χθόνιοι δαίμονες: Apollodor. i. 33 Wagner, Persephone was compelled to remain the third part of the year μετὰ Πλούτωνος, τὸ δὲ λοιπὸν παρὰ τοῖς θεοῖς: frequently by Aeschylus in the *Eumenides*, 109, 352, 363, 414, who have λάχη θεῶν διχοστατοῦντα 389. But each form of worship is *fitting* in its proper place, and πρέπει is the word habitually used: the true paean should be sung at banquets, ἀνδρείων παρὰ δαιτυμόνεσσι πρέπει παιᾶνα κατάρχειν Alcman fr. 22: praise and honour are the fitting tributes (πρέπει) to a

conqueror or benefactor, *sup.* 437, 529, Pind. fr. 121, *O.* ii. 50, iii. 9, *P.* v. 43, *N.* iii. 67 βοὰ δὲ νικαφόρωι σὺν Ἀριστοκλείδαι πρέπει: praise also is the fitting memorial of the dead, only in their case it takes the form of lamentation—πρέπει λέγειν παιᾶνα τόνδ' Ἐρινύων.

645 ff. 'News of the double wound inflicted by the double scourge that Ares uses—one the general public wound felt by the whole country, the other that felt severally by each home in private for the loss of a loved man.' The notion of a wound suggests a scourge; the notion of a scourge leads Aeschylus to conceive these lost men as driven out from their houses *banned and excommunicate* beneath the curse of War; because polluted men banned by the people's execration were expelled ἀγηλάτωι μάστιγι as Lycophron calls it, v. 436, which would seem to have been the original reading in *Cho.* 288 διώκεσθαι πόλεως | ἀγηλάτωι μάστιγι λυμανθὲν δέμας where the MS. has χαλκηλάτωι πλάστιγγι. This one may suppose was the reason why Christ used a *scourge* in driving out the money-changers from the Temple (John 2. 15) as defilers and polluters of it. See also *Cho.* 374 ἀλλὰ διπλῆς γὰρ τῆσδε μαράγνης | δοῦπος ἱκνεῖται· τῶν μὲν ἀρωγοὶ | κατὰ γῆς ἤδη· τῶν δὲ κρατούντων | χέρες οὐχ ὅσιαι, where, as in the present passage, the two lashes are the clauses marked by μέν and δέ. Both passages have been misinterpreted, but would not have been if critics had remembered that when the items signified by Greek words meaning *two* or *double* are specifically named, it was regular to indicate them by the particles μέν and δέ, or τε and τε, or τε and καί: examples near at hand are v. 337, 826, 872, *Supp.* 1020, *Pers.* 168, *Theb.* 769, Eur. *Andr.* 516. Here, instead of preceding as is usual, the word διπλῆι follows the two items, as in Pind. *N.* v. 52, Eur. *Supp.* 332, Soph. *El.* 1078, *A. P.* ix. 40. 5, Ov. *Trist.* iii. 8. 33. δίλογχον ἄτην and φοινίαν ξυνωρίδα introduce new metaphors, and δίλογχον no more refers to the μάστιξ than ξυνωρίδα: it is derived from the common practice of carrying a pair of spears.

654. οὐκ ἀμήνιτον θεῶν refers to the crime and punishment of Aias the Locrian: see Schol. AD on Hom. N 66.

656. πῦρ καὶ θάλασσα. This in the usual story was regarded as a compact struck between Poseidon and Athena (privileged to employ her father's lightning: *Eum.* 830), who had previously been on opposite sides. The opening of the *Troades* of Euripides shows them making this agreement.

659. See cr. n. It is impossible to say whether f's reading is an epicism introduced by the copyists or whether the Attic poets really used such forms; nor do inscriptions give any help.

661. σὺν ζάλῃι τ' ὀμβροκτύπωι. In descriptions of storms at sea ὄμβρος, rain, is a constant detail. [Thus Eur. *Tro.* 78 (referring to this particular storm) καὶ Ζεὺς μὲν ὄμβρον καὶ χάλαζαν ἄσπετον πέμψει.] Greek ships, we must remember, were undecked and had no bilge-pumps; all the baling must be done by hand.

667 f. **ἤτοι τις ἐξέκλεψεν ἢ 'ξῃτήσατο, κτἑ.** 'We were either spirited away θεῶν κλοπαῖς (Eur. *Or.* 1497) or saved by the intercession of some divinity who begged us off,' ἐξῃτήσατο, as Apollo, for example, ἐξῃτήσατο Ἄδμητον from the Fates, schol. Eur. *Alc.* 12. παῦροι δὲ φύγον μόρον οὓς ἐσάωσεν ἢ θεὸς ἢ δαίμων, says Quintus of this, xiv. 627. Gods often save from shipwreck: Apoll. Rhod. iii. 323 θεὸς δέ τις ἄμμ' ἐσάωσεν, 328 Ζηνὸς νόος ἠέ τις αἶσα. iv. 930 Thetis steers the Argo between the Shifting Rocks, ἡ δ' ὄπιθεν πτέρυγος θίγε πηδαλίοιο. Val. Flacc. ii. 48. Ach. Tat. iii. 5 δαίμων τις ἀγαθὸς περιέσωσεν ἡμῖν τῆς πρώιρας μέρος. Lucian i. 652 sailors narrate τοὺς Διοσκούρους ἐπιφαινομένους ἤ τιν' ἄλλον ἐκ μηχανῆς θεὸν ἐπὶ τῶι καρχησίωι καθεζόμενον ἢ πρὸς τοῖς πηδαλίοις ἑστῶτα καὶ πρός τινα ἠϊόνα μαλακὴν ἀπευθύνοντα τὴν ναῦν.

670. **ἐν ὅρμωι** refers to the danger of a rising swell when the ship is at anchor. Cf. *Supp.* 774 οὐδ' ἐν ἀγκυρουχίαις θαρσοῦσι ναῶν ποιμένες παραυτίκα, ἄλλως τε καὶ μολόντες ἀλίμενον χθόνα ἐς νύκτ', *sup.* 203 πνοαὶ δύσορμοι. Such was the position of the Athenians at Pylos: Thuc. iv. 26 τῶν νεῶν οὐκ ἐχουσῶν ὅρμον...οἱ δὲ μετέωροι ὥρμουν...ῥᾶιον γὰρ τὴν φυλακὴν τῶν τριήρων ἐλάνθανον, ὁπότε πνεῦμα ἐκ πόντου εἴη· ἄπορον γὰρ ἐγίγνετο περιορμεῖν. The correction ἁρμῶι should mean *in compagibus*—in the seams or frame of the ship. But that would be ἐν ἁρμοῖς.

676 ff. **καὶ νῦν ἐκείνων**: he endeavours to suggest grounds for hoping the best. The connexion of thought is as follows:—'All we know for certain is that Menelaus and the rest have disappeared; but after all, we do not know that they have perished: we conjecture it; but *they*, no doubt—if there are any among them that survive—are now conjecturing the same of *us*; and it is possible that our conjecture may be equally mistaken. So we need not quite despair. Let us hope for the best in a bad business. For the truth is you must expect that Menelaus is most probably in great distress; but still, wherever he may be, if only he is alive, there is some hope yet that he may manage to get home again.'—**γένοιτο δ' ὡς ἄριστα**: 'as well as may be.'—**πρῶτόν τε καὶ μάλιστα** is opposed to εἰ δ' οὖν ('if, however') in the same way as the ordinary phrase μάλιστα μέν may be followed by ἔπειτα (*e.g.* Heliod. i. 15 μάλιστα μὲν εἰκὸς σχολάσειν τὸν ἔρωτα· εἰ δ' ἐναπομείνειεν,...), πρῶτον being neuter and adverbial: Plut. *Mor.* 574 E μάλιστα μὲν καὶ πρῶτον..., δεύτερον δέ.... Isaeus ii. 20 μάλιστα μὲν ὑπὸ τῆς ἐρημίας ἐπείσθη, δεύτερον δὲ διὰ.... So Iambl. ii. 416. Diog. Laert. ix. 66 διαγωνίζεσθαι δ' ὡς οἷόν τε πρῶτον μὲν τοῖς ἔργοις πρὸς τὰ πράγματα, εἰ δὲ μή, τῶι λόγωι. 'Though your

first and chiefest expectation—the great probability—must be that he is in sore straits, still there is some hope.' Aristid. i. 810 μάλιστα μὲν δὴ καὶ πρῶτον..., ἔτι δέ. Hdt. ii. 59 μάλιστα μὲν καὶ προθυμότατα..., δεύτερα.... πρῶτον might also be masculine, although that is less likely here: Ath. 524 d μάλιστα δὴ καὶ πρῶτοι. Plat. *Amat.* 136 D μή μοι, εἶπον ἐγώ, ἀμφοτέρους λέγε, ἀλλ' ὁπότερον μᾶλλόν τε καὶ πρότερον. οὐδεὶς ἄν, ἔφη, τοῦτό γ' ἀμφισβητήσειεν, ὡς οὐχὶ τὸν ἰατρὸν καὶ μᾶλλον καὶ πρότερον. Dio Chrys. i. 180 πρώτωι καὶ μάλιστα αὐτῶι.—**οὖν** merely adds emphasis to the other particles it is combined with: *O. T.* 834 ἡμῖν μέν, ὦναξ, ταῦτ' ὀκνήρ'· ἕως δ' ἂν οὖν πρὸς τοῦ παρόντος ἐκμάθηις, ἔχ' ἐλπίδα, '*but still* have hope.' δ' οὖν is a more emphatic δέ. εἰ δ' οὖν is the same as εἰ δέ, but a little stronger. It introduces the alternative, to which πρῶτόν τε καὶ μάλιστα is opposed.—**μογεῖν**: see cr. n. Tzetz. *Antehom.* 140 κεῖνοι γάρ τε μέγα πέλαγος Τύρων περόωντες | ἄστυ Τρώιον ἴδον, ὅλον λυκάβαντα μογεῦντες.

696. **Ζεφύρου γίγαντος αὖραι**: the reason for this epithet is to suggest that Zephyrus, the Spring-wind, lent his influence as the wind of Love; because according to one legend the father of Ἔρως was Ζέφυρος γίγας: Lydus *de mens.* p. 117, *de ostent.* p. 282 ὁμοίως δὲ καὶ Τύχηι ἐφόρωι (ηὔχοντο) Σωφροσύνηι τε καὶ Ἔρωτι, ὃν οἱ μυθικοὶ Ζεφύρου τοῦ γίγαντος εἶναι παῖδα ἀξιοῦσιν, ὥς φησιν Εὔρυτος ὁ Λακεδαιμόνιος ὁ μελοποιός· ἄρχεται δὲ οὕτως· 'ἀγλαομειδὲς Ἔρως.' See Bergk, *Poet. Lyr. Gr.* iii. p. 639. [Alcaeus fr. 13 calls Eros δεινότατον θεῶν <τὸν> γέννατ' εὐπέδιλλος Ἶρις χρυσοκόμαι Ζεφύρωι μιγεῖσα.]

697. **πολύανδροι**: she is always πολυάνωρ γυνή (v. 62), but the swarms of men pursuing her in hot quest now are in a different temper.

702 ff. **κῆδος ὀρθώνυμον τελεσσίφρων μῆνις ἤνυσεν** (that is, ἐτέλεσεν, ἐτελείωσεν, ἐξέπραξεν): 'thought-executing Wrath brought the κῆδος to fulfilment in the true meaning of the term,' as *Antig.* 1178 ὦ μάντι, τοὔπος ὡς ἄρ' ὀρθὸν ἤνυσας. Cf. *O. C.* 454 παλαίφαθ' ἁμοὶ Φοῖβος ἤνυσέν ποτε, *O. T.* 166 ἠνύσατ' ἐκτοπίαν φλόγα, Hom. τ 567 οἵ ῥ' ἔτυμα κραίνουσιν, *Theb.* 870 ἀληθῆ...ἐπέκρανεν. This transformation is the subject of the following passage to v. 717, which describes how the Doom of Ζεὺς ξένιος was at last effected, how Helen παρακλίνασ' ἐπέκρανεν γάμου πικρὰς τελευτάς, and how joy was changed to sorrow. κῆδος means both 'relationship by marriage' and 'mourning' (the due office of relations); and there is no single word in English that will cover the two senses. Cf. Eur. *Andr.* 103 Ἰλίωι αἰπεινᾶι Πάρις οὐ γάμον ἀλλά τιν' ἄταν ἀγάγετ' εὐναίαν ἐς θαλάμους Ἑλέναν. The MS. reading κῆδος ἤλασε would mean 'drove away,' 'dispelled,' as in Orph. *hymn.* 73. 7 πολύστονα κήδε' ἐλάσσας. In Eur. *Heracl.* 788 Reiske substituted διήνυσεν for διήλασεν.

707 f. **τὸ νυμφότιμον μέλος ἐκφάτως τίοντας**: Troy, in the person of the bridegroom's kinsmen (γαμβροί), to whom fell the singing of the wedding-chorus, *honoured* (that is, *celebrated*, as εὔποτμον παιᾶνα φίλως ἐτίμα in v. 258) the Hymenaeus sung in *honour* of the guilty bride and bridegroom, slighting and *dishonouring* thereby the Stranger's Table. But if it was all joy and merry-making then, it is all sorrow now and lamentation; ὑμέναιος has been changed to θρῆνος.—That being an εὔφημος ὕμνος changed to a δύσφημος, it is very likely that ἐκφάτως is a mistake for εὐφάτως meaning εὐφήμως, as δυσφάτωι κλαγγᾶι in v. 1150 means δυσφήμωι. If ἐκφάτως is sound, it means 'outspokenly,' in loud and bold avowal. The sentence is turned artificially in order to make all these antithetical points in a brief compass with the telling words in telling places. The change of the ὑμέναιος to the θρῆνος was a commonplace: Eur. *Alc.* 922 νῦν δ' ὑμεναίων γόος ἀντίπαλος, Soph. *O. T.* 420 ff. βοῆς δὲ τῆς σῆς...ὅταν καταίσθηι τὸν ὑμέναιον, ὃν δόμοις ἄνορμον εἰσέπλευσας, εὐπλοίας τυχών.

712. **γεραιά**, *i.e.* all too late: *inf.* 1425 γνώσηι διδαχθεὶς ὀψὲ γοῦν τὸ σωφρονεῖν. It must be joined with μεταμανθάνουσα (cf. ὀψιμαθής).

718 ff. **ἔθρεψεν δὲ λέοντος ἶνιν δόμοις ἀγάλακτα βούτας ἀνὴρ φιλόμαστον**: throughout this simile we must remember that the Lion-cub means Helen and the Herdsman Paris, and observe how carefully the touches are designed to correspond. It does not seem unlikely that λέοντος ἶνιν would be specially appropriate to Helen as a member by marriage of the Pelopid House; see my note on v. 147: but Paris who carried her off and kept her in his house was of course habitually called βούτας ἀνὴρ (Eur. *Hec.* 646) or βουκόλος or *pastor*,—which confirms the truth of the corrected reading. As Wecklein has pointed out, without this word we should not know what μηλοφόνοισι (v. 731) meant. For the evidence of the wider sense of μῆλον see *On editing Aeschylus*, p. 137. Yet Wilamowitz in *C. R.* xx. 446 speaks as if μηλοφόνοισι were fatal to βούτας, and had been overlooked. ἀγάλακτα (from ἀγάλαξ) means ὁμογάλακτα, 'foster-brother'; for as yet it is an unweaned suckling, φιλόμαστος.

723. **γεραροῖς ἐπίχαρτον** calls to mind the famous passage in the *Iliad*, Γ 149 ff., where the aged councillors at the Scaean gate are entranced by the sight of Helen's beauty. The late Epic writers describe the spell of her beauty in similar terms: Quint. xiv. 58, Tzetz. *Antehom.* 141.

724 ff. **πολέα δ' ἔσχ' ἐν ἀγκάλαις...φαιδρωπὸς ποτὶ χεῖρα σαίνων τε γαστρὸς ἀνάγκαις** (see cr. n.) could only mean, as Dr Verrall takes it, the young lion 'got many a thing, when embraced it wooed the hand with radiant visage under stress of appetite'; but as ἐν ἀγκάλαις ἔχειν

was the regular phrase for holding a child or a pet-creature in one's arms, I incline to read with Auratus what I have translated, φαιδρωπὸν ποτὶ χεῖρα σαίνοντα γαστρὸς ἀνάγκαις. Which we take of these two readings matters little, but if we read σαίνοντα we must also read φαιδρωπόν—whether masculine or neuter used adverbially with σαίνοντα—because both these words belong to the description of the lion-cub. The point is that he, or Helen whom he typifies, began by fawning with a smile *like treacherous Ate*, who σαίνει φιλόφρων or φαιδρόνους as I shall show on v. 1226. This is clear when we compare the corresponding final lines of the antistrophe, ἐκ θεοῦ δ' ἱερεύς τις Ἄ|τας δόμοις προσεθρέφθη.

729. **χάριν.** 'As grace to his maintainers owed': because it was the custom for children on coming of age to make their parents and nurses a symbolic thank-offering (θρέπτρα Hom. Δ 478, θρεπτήρια, τροφεῖα) in return for their bringing-up.—By the slaughter of the cattle we are to imagine the carnage in the streets of Troy.

731. **μηλοφόνοισιν ἄταις.** As a point is elsewhere reinforced by the insistent repetition of a word, by πολύθρηνον for example in vv. 713, 715, and by ἄτας following ἄταις in v. 736, so, when the comparison is expounded, the conclusion is that Helen proved a νυμφόκλαυτος Ἐρινύς (748). This recalls the language of Soph. fr. 519 ἡ δ' ἄρ' ἐν σκότωι λήθουσά με ἔσαιν' Ἐρινύς. For the words cf. *Pers.* 655 οὔτε γὰρ ἄνδρας ποτ' ἀπώλλυ πολεμοφθόροισιν ἄταις.

737. **προσεθρέφθη**: see cr. n. In Eur. *Hec.* 600 for θρεφθῆναι L. has τραφῆναι: and in MSS. generally the heavier first aorist forms tend to be wrongly ousted by the weaker second aorists (*On editing Aeschylus*, p. 104 ff.).—**ἐκ θεοῦ** = θεόθεν, 'by the will of the gods' (*Theb.* 311 ὑπ' ἀνδρὸς Ἀχαιοῦ θεόθεν περθομέναν). So *Theb.* 23 καλῶς τὰ πλείω πόλεμος ἐκ θεῶν κυρεῖ, and see the examples quoted in *On editing Aeschylus*, p. 107.

739. **φρόνημα μὲν νηνέμου γαλάνας**: the idea this would suggest is smiling and seductive Calm, who tempts men to embark, but in seeming innocence treacherously lures them to disaster,—just as Ἄτη does, whose wrath is elsewhere likened to a storm (v. 810). *A. P.* vii. 668 οὐδ' εἴ μοι γελόωσα καταστορέσειε γαλήνη κύματα,...νηοβάτην μ' ὄψεσθε. Lucian iii. 197 ὅτι μὲν γὰρ καὶ ἡ θάλαττα ἱκανὴ προκαλέσασθαι καὶ εἰς ἐπιθυμίαν ἐπισπάσασθαι ἐν γαλήνηι φανεῖσα, ἴστε, κἂν μὴ εἴπω· ὅτε εἰ καὶ παντάπασιν ἠπειρώτης καὶ ἀπειρόπλους τις εἴη, πάντως ἂν ἐθελήσειε καὶ αὐτὸς ἐμβῆναι καὶ περιπλεῦσαι καὶ πολὺ ἀπὸ τῆς γῆς ἀποσπάσαι. Lucret. ii. 556: wrecks are a warning to mankind

> *infidi maris insidias uirisque dolumque*
> *ut uitare uelint, neue ullo tempore credant,*
> *subdola cum ridet placidi pellacia ponti*

and again, v. 1004

> *nec poterat quemquam placidi pellacia ponti*
> *subdola pellicere in fraudem ridentibus undis,*
> *improba naucleri ratio cum caeca iacebat.*

Meleager, *A. P.* v. 156:

> ἁ φίλερως χαροποῖς Ἀσκληπιὰς οἷα Γαλήνης
> ὄμμασι συμπείθει πάντας ἐρωτοπλοεῖν.

> Such glittering Calm of sunlit weather
> In her bright eyes hath she,
> Fair Amoret! all men's hearts together
> Launch upon Love's alluring sea.

Simonides quoted by Plut. *Mor.* 798 D (where I adopt Hermann's παρέπεισαν for the MS. παρήισαν):

> λευκᾶς καθύπερθε γαλάνας
> εὐπρόσωποί σφας παρέπεισαν ἔρωτες ναίας
> κλαΐδος χαραξιπόντου δαιμονίαν ἐς ὕβριν,

the result of which is ὄλεθρος or ἄτη.

γαλήνη *calm* and γέλως *smile* are in fact the same in origin, γαληνής and γελανής merely different forms of the same word: γελανώσας θυμόν Bacchyl. v. 80, διαγαληνίσας πρόσωπον Ar. *Eq.* 646, γαληνοῦ μειδιάματος Themist. 282 A, μειδιᾶι τῆς θαλάσσης γαληνιώσης χαριέστερον Alciphr. iii. 1. Aristotle, *Physiogn.* p. 811 b 37 οἱ κύνες ἐπειδὰν θωπεύωσι, γαληνὲς τὸ πρόσωπον ἔχουσιν. ἐπειδὴ οὖν ἥ τε συννεφὴς ἕξις αὐθάδειαν ἐμφαίνει ἥ τε γαληνὴ κολακείαν, ἡ μέση ἂν τούτων ἕξις εὐαρμόστως ἔχοι. Philostratus, *Imag.* ii. 1 says of the ὑμνήτριαι singing before Aphrodite that their gestures prove that they have risen from the sea, τὸ μειδίαμα δ' αὐτῶν γαλήνης ἐστὶν αἴνιγμα.

740. **ἀκασκαῖον δ' ἄγαλμα πλούτου,** 'a jewel in the crown of Wealth.' In *P. V.* 482 he applies the phrase to horses, bred by the wealthy for the race-course, ἵππους, ἄγαλμα τῆς ὑπερπλούτου χλιδῆς, 'the lustre of luxurious affluence'; and Meredith in *Beauchamp's Career* c. 15, doubtless with both these passages in mind, very happily makes a double application of it: 'As the yacht, so the mistress: things of wealth, owing their graces to wealth, devoting them to wealth—splendid achievements of art both!...Did Beauchamp at all desire to have those idly lovely adornments of riches, the Yacht and the Lady, swept away?' Thucyd. vi. 41 speaks of ἵπποις καὶ ὅπλοις καὶ τοῖς ἄλλοις οἷς ὁ πόλεμος ἀγάλλεται, 'all the pride and pomp of war,' and in Philostr. *Heroic.* p. 791 Ajax, for his strength and beauty, is called ἄγαλμα πολέμου. In Thuc. ii. 44 Pericles asks the Athenians to regard their houses and their lands as κηπίον καὶ ἐγκαλλώπισμα πλούτου, the mere pleasance

for wealth to display its graces in. ἀγλάϊσμα is used in the same way: Achill. Tat. ii. 1 of the rose, γῆς ἐστι κόσμος, φυτῶν ἀγλάϊσμα, ὀφθαλμὸς ἀνθέων. Heliod. iii. 6 εἶδες τὸ ἀγλάϊσμα ἐμόν τε καὶ Δελφῶν, Χαρικλείαν. ἀκασκαῖον, 'gentle,' expresses 'languid, delicate': Hesych. ἄκασκα· ἡσύχως, μαλακῶς, βραδέως. Cratinus ap. Bekk. *Anecd.* p. 371, 1 σκήπτροισιν ἄκασκα προβῶντες.

This passage affords a remarkable instance of a common formula of description, in which the details are accumulated without any connecting particles. The mannerism has been imitated by Milton, *Paradise Regained* ii. 156 More like to goddesses | Than mortal creatures, graceful and discreet, | Expert in amorous arts, enchanting tongues | Persuasive, virgin majesty with mild | And sweet allayed, yet terrible to approach, | Skilled to retire, and in retiring draw | Hearts after them, tangled in amorous nets. So Ach. Tat. i. 3 ἐφίσταταί δέ μοι γυνὴ φοβερὰ καὶ μεγάλη, τὸ πρόσωπον ἀγρία, ὀφθαλμὸς ἐν αἵματι, βλοσυραί παρειαί, ὄφεις αἱ κόμαι· ἅρπην ἐκράτει τῆι δεξιᾶι, δᾶιδα τῆι λαιᾶι. i. 4 τοιαύτην εἶδον ἐγώ ποτ' ἐπὶ ταύρωι γεγραμμένην Σελήνην· ὄμμα γοργὸν ἐν ἡδονῆι· κόμη ξανθή, τὸ ξανθὸν οὖλον· ὀφρῦς μέλαινα, τὸ μέλαν ἄκρατον· λευκὴ παρειά, τὸ λευκὸν εἰς μέσον ἐφοινίσσετο καὶ ἐμιμεῖτο πορφύραν, οἵαν εἰς τὸν ἐλέφαντα Λυδία βάπτει γυνή· τὸ στόμα ῥόδων ἄνθος ἦν, ὅταν ἄρχηται τὸ ῥόδον ἀνοίγειν τῶν φύλλων τὰ χείλη. ὡς δ' εἶδον, εὐθὺς ἀπωλώλειν· κάλλος γὰρ ὀξύτερον τιτρώσκει βέλους καὶ διὰ τῶν ὀφθαλμῶν εἰς τὴν ψυχὴν καταρρεῖ· ὀφθαλμὸς γὰρ ὁδὸς ἐρωτικῶι τραύματι. viii. 12 παρθένος ἦν εὐειδής, ὄνομα Ῥοδῶπις, κυνηγίων ἐρῶσα καὶ θήρας· πόδες ταχεῖς, εὔστοχοι χεῖρες, ζώνη καὶ μίτρα καὶ ἀνεζωσμένος εἰς γόνυ χιτών, καὶ κατ' ἄνδρας κουρὰ τριχῶν. Antiphanes Ἀντ. *fr.* 33 (ii. 23 K.) A. ὦ 'τάν, κατανοεῖς τίς ποτ' ἐστὶν οὑτοσὶ | ὁ γέρων; B. ἀπὸ τῆς μὲν ὄψεως Ἑλληνικός· | λευκὴ χλανίς, φαιὸς χιτωνίσκος καλός, | πιλίδιον ἁπαλόν, εὔρυθμος βακτηρία, | βεβαία τράπεζα—τί μακρὰ δεῖ λέγειν; ὅλως | αὐτὴν ὁρᾶν γὰρ τὴν Ἀκαδημίαν δοκῶ. Ter. *Phorm.* 104 *uidemus: uirgo pulchra: et quo magis diceres,* | *nil aderat adiumenti ad pulchritudinem:* | *capillus passus, nudus pes, ipsa horrida,* | *lacrumae, uestitus turpis.* Aesch. *Theb.* 611 γέροντα τὸν νοῦν, σάρκα δ' ἡβῶσαν φύει, | ποδώκες ὄμμα, χεῖρα δ' οὐ βραδύνεται. Eur. *Supp.* 867 φίλοις τ' ἀληθὴς ἦν φίλος παροῦσί τε | καὶ μὴ παροῦσιν· ὧν ἀριθμὸς οὐ πολύς· | ἀψευδὲς ἦθος, εὐπροσήγορον στόμα, | ἄκραντον οὐδὲν οὔτ' ἐς οἰκέτας ἔχων | οὔτ' ἐς πολίτας. *ib.* 904 οὐκ ἐν λόγοις ἦν λαμπρὸς ἀλλ' ἐν ἀσπίδι | δεινὸς σοφιστὴς πολλά τ' ἐξευρὼν σοφά, | γνώμηι δ' ἀδελφοῦ Μελεάγρου λελειμμένος | ἴσον παρέσχεν ὄνομα διὰ τέχνης δορός, | εὑρὼν ἀκριβῆ μουσικὴν ἐν ἀσπίδι· | φιλότιμον ἦθος πλούσιον, φρόνημα δὲ | ἐν τοῖσιν ἔργοις, οὐχὶ τοῖς λόγοις ἔχων. Verg. *Aen.* xi. 338 *largus opum et lingua melior, sed frigida bello* | *dextera, consiliis habitus non futilis auctor,* | *seditione potens.* So in Aesch.

Supp. 577 βοτὸν ἐσορῶντες δυσχερὲς μειξόμβροτον, | τὰ μὲν βοός, τὰ δ' αὖ γυναικός, he might have said τὰ μὲν βοῦν, τὰ δὲ γυναῖκα or τὰ μὲν βοὸς ἔχουσαν, τὰ δὲ γυναικός, but it was as easy and more elegant to introduce τὰ μὲν βοός without construction. The earliest example is Semonid. Amorg. 7. 71 τὴν δ' ἐκ πιθήκου· τοῦτο δὴ διακριδὸν | Ζεὺς ἀνδράσιν μέγιστον ὤπασεν κακόν. | αἴσχιστα μὲν πρόσωπα· τοιαύτη γυνὴ | εἶσιν δι' ἄστεος πᾶσιν ἀνθρώποις γέλως· | ἐπ' αὐχένα βραχεῖα, κινεῖται μόγις, | ἄπυγος, αὐτόκωλος. In this passage the word κινεῖται enables me to see that the Physiognomic writers were the source from which this manner of description was derived.

748. **νυμφόκλαυτος Ἐρινύς.** So in describing Hecuba's dream of the birth of Paris, Pind. fr. *Paean.* viii. 30 (*Ox. Pap.* v. p. 65) ἔδοξε δὲ τεκεῖν πυρφόρον Ἐρινύν. According to Stasinus, the author of the *Cypria*, Helen was the daughter of Zeus and Nemesis: Athen. viii. 334 c d, Eratosth. *Catast.* 25.

749 ff. There is an important passage in an earlier and remarkable writer with which this, I believe, has not been brought into comparison: Ezekiel 18. 1 *The word of the Lord came unto me again, saying, What mean ye, that ye use this proverb concerning the land of Israel, saying,* The fathers have eaten sour grapes, and the children's teeth are set on edge? *As I live, saith the Lord God, ye shall not have occasion to use this proverb any more in Israel. Behold, all souls are mine; as the soul of the father, so also the soul of the son is mine: the soul that sinneth, it shall die. But if a man be just, and do that which is lawful and right,...he is just, he shall surely live saith the Lord God.* See the remainder of the chapter, and Jeremiah 31. 29. That is a general repudiation of inherited guilt, the doctrine of the Decalogue; an assertion of individual responsibility, the Buddhist doctrine. For the doctrine of Aeschylus see Introduction p. 31.

761. **ἐν κακοῖς.** There are two forms of the proverb. Solon fr. 7 has τίκτει γὰρ κόρος ὕβριν, ὅταν πολὺς ὄλβος ἕπηται ἀνθρώποισιν ὅσοις μὴ νόος ἄρτιος ᾖι, but in Theogn. 153 the lines are altered to τίκτει τοι κόρος ὕβριν, ὅταν κακῶι ὄλβος ἕπηται ἀνθρώπωι, καὶ ὅτωι μὴ νόος ἄρτιος ᾖι.

762. The correction βαθύσκοτον (see cr. n.) implies the common confusion of φ and β (cf. 436, 770) and of ο and θ. Somewhat similar is Bentley's τηλέσκοπον for τῇιδε σκοπῶν in Soph. fr. 314.

771 f. **δύναμιν οὐ σέβουσα πλούτου παράσημον αἴνωι.** The best illustration is Plat. *Legg.* 870 A—C. The coining of money often marked the first assumption of absolute power.—When Bacchylides ix. 49 says οἶδα καὶ πλούτου μεγάλαν δύνασιν ἃ καὶ τὸν ἀχρεῖον τίθησι χρηστόν—τί μακρὰν γλῶσσαν ἰθύσας ἐλαύνω ἐκτὸς ὁδοῦ; I suppose that a passage on the

power of wealth must have followed in the poem of Solon (fr. 13) part of which (v. 33 sqq.) he has been paraphrasing for his young Athenian. The examples of παντοῖοι ἔρωτες became a commonplace; see Hor. *C.* i. 1. 3 sqq. with Orelli-Hirschfelder's note on v. 18.

774 ff. In this address to Agamemnon the Chorus have two objects: first, as representatives of the people, to assure him of a favourable reception; secondly, to warn him of Clytaemnestra's insincerity and unfaithful stewardship. The latter object they attain by using phrases which appear to point at her obliquely: 784 ξυγχαίρουσιν ὁμοιοπρεπεῖς, 788 δοκοῦντ' εὔφρονος ἐκ διανοίας, 796 οὐκ ἀπ' ἄκρας φρενὸς οὐδ' ἀφίλως and 799 τὸν ἀκαίρως οἰκουροῦντα. Agamemnon, when he refers to their welcome (v. 821 ff.) replies in the same manner (v. 831), showing that he fully understands them.

777. Cf. Eur. *I. A.* 977 πῶς ἄν σ' ἐπαινέσαιμι μὴ λίαν λόγοις, μηδ' ἐνδεῶς τοῦδ' ἀπολέσαιμι τὴν χάριν;—**καιρὸν χάριτος** = 'the due measure of thy content.'

779. **τὸ δοκεῖν εἶναι**, or τὸ δοκεῖν εὔνοι as read by Weil. The latter phrase is used by Lucian iii. 274 where he is reminding Samippus, who had wished to be a king, what the drawbacks of the position would have been: ἐπιβουλαὶ μυρίαι καὶ φθόνος παρὰ τῶν συνόντων καὶ μῖσος καὶ κολακεία, φίλος δὲ οὐδεὶς ἀληθής, ἀλλὰ πρὸς τὸ δέος ἅπαντες ἢ πρὸς τὴν ἐλπίδα εὔνοι δοκοῦντες εἶναι.

782. **δῆγμα...λύπης**, *pang* of grief, resembles 742 δηξίθυμον ἔρωτος ἄνθος, 1472 καρδιόδηκτον, Soph. fr. 757 ἔρωτος δῆγμα. The metaphorical use of δάκνω, as applied to *pain*, *grief*, *annoyance* and the like, is very common: see the examples collected in *On editing Aeschylus*, p. 102. δάκνω, δῆγμα are merely equivalent to λυπῶ, λύπη, the words regularly given as their synonyms in lexicons and scholia. δῆγμα λύπης is a periphrasis for λύπη just as δῆγμα ἔρωτος (quoted above) is a periphrasis for ἔρως. The same MS. error (see cr. n.) is found in Lucian i. 24 οὔτε κίνησις ὁμοία πρόσεστιν οὔτε ψυχῆς δεῖγμά τι, ἀλλὰ τέρψις ἄλλως καὶ παιδιὰ τὸ πρᾶγμα, where Cobet (*V. L.* p. 142) shows that δῆγμα is to be read.

784 ff. Two things indicate that at least a line—probably a paroemiac—is missing, the metrical hiatus between βιαζόμενοι and ὅστις, and the sense; for ξυγχαίρουσιν, if taken as a verb 'they sympathise in gladness,' is not true; they only feign to sympathise; it is the dative, 'in the guise of sympathisers,' Lucian i. 838 προσιόντες οὖν ἐδεξιοῦντο καὶ θαυμάζουσιν ἐῴκεσαν (see for the idiom Cobet, *N. L.*, p. 341), and the verb followed in the missing line. The purport almost certainly was 'they smile a forced smile only with the lips; but their eyes bewray them': Heliod. ii. 19 πρὸς ταῦτ' ἐμειδίασεν ὀλίγον καὶ

βεβιασμένον καὶ μόνοις τοῖς χείλεσιν ἐπιτρέχον. Hom. O 101 ἡ δὲ γέλασσεν χείλεσιν, οὐ δὲ μέτωπον ἐπ' ὄφρυσι κυανέῃσιν ἰάνθη. Lucian iii. 153 προσίεται μὲν καὶ προσμειδιᾶι τοῖς χείλεσιν ἄκροις, μισεῖ δὲ καὶ λάθρα τοὺς ὀδόντας διαπρίει. Plaut. *Capt.* 484 *nemo ridet. sciui extemplo rem de confecto geri. ne canem quidem inritatam uoluit quisquam imitarier, saltem, si non adriderent, dentis ut restringerent.* Fronto, p. 243 Naber ὁ τοι γέλως, οὕτως τὸ πρὶν ἄδολος εἶναι πεφυκὼς ὡς καὶ τοὺς ὀδόντας τῶν γελώντων ἐπιδεικνύειν, εἰς τοσοῦτον ἤδη κακομηχανίας καὶ ἐνέδρας ὡς καὶ τὰ χείλη κρύπτειν τῶν ἐξ ἐπιβουλῆς προσγελώντων. Schol. Plat. *Rep.* 337 A, p. 926 μήποτε οὖν τὸ Ὁμηρικόν, ὅθεν καὶ ἡ παροιμία ἴσως ἐρρύη, 'μείδησε δὲ θυμῶι σαρδάνιον μάλα τοῖον' τὸν ἀπ' αὐτῶν τῶν χειλῶν γέλωτα καὶ μέχρι τοῦ σεσηρέναι γιγνόμενον σημαίνει.—**προβατογνώμων**: he uses ἱππογνώμων in the same connexion in fr. 243:

> νέας γυναικὸς οὔ με μὴ λάθηι φλέγων
> ὀφθαλμὸς ἥτις ἀνδρὸς ἦι γεγευμένη·
> ἔχων δὲ τούτων θυμὸν ἱππογνώμονα...

which, as I learn from Burton, is the regular metaphor in Arabic; *firâsah,* their word for physiognomy, means properly 'skill in judging the points of a mare (*faras*),' an eye for horseflesh: and the metaphor in Greek was derived, I suppose, from a common Oriental source. In that science, as I have shown in the note on v. 283, it was the *eye* that told the truth.—**ὑδαρεῖ**, 'watery,' is the opposite of ἀκράτωι, 'neat' or 'undiluted' as applied to wine and metaphorically 'absolute,' 'unmitigated.' Ar. *Pol.* ii. 4, p. 1262 b 614 ἐν δὲ τῆι πόλει τὴν φιλίαν ἀναγκαῖον ὑδαρῆ γίνεσθαι διὰ τὴν κοινωνίαν τὴν τοιαύτην (*i.e.* of women and children), καὶ ἥκιστα λέγειν τὸν ἐμὸν ἢ υἱὸν πατέρα ἢ πατέρα υἱόν. For the description of the false friend cf. Max. Tyr. vi. 7 τὸ δὲ εἴδωλον αὐτοῦ πρόχειρον καὶ παντοδαπόν, κολάκων ἑσμοὶ καὶ θίασοι, σεσηρότων καὶ σαινόντων, καὶ ἐπ' ἄκραι τῆι γλώττηι τὸ φιλεῖν ἐχόντων· οὐχ ὑπ' εὐνοίας ἀγομένων κτέ.

791. **οὐκ ἐπικεύσω**: see cr. n. γὰρ may have been inserted merely for sense: see *On editing Aeschylus*, p. 121.

794 f. **θάρσος ἑκούσιον ἀνδράσι θνῄσκουσι κομίζων**, 'in seeking to recover a consenting wanton by means of the lives of men.' κομίζειν is used of the quest for Helen by Pind. *O.* xiii. 59 τοὶ μὲν γένει φίλωι σὺν Ἀτρέος Ἑλέναν κομίζοντες, οἱ δ' ἀπὸ πάμπαν εἴργοντες, and *N.* vii. 28 ξανθῶι Μενέλαι δάμαρτα κομίσαι and in the *Tebtunis Papyri*, vol. i., p. 3 (fr. 1, 1) ὦ φανεὶς χάρμα μοι φίλον ὅτε μ' ἠγάπας ὅτε δόρατι πολεμίωι τὰν Φρυγῶν πόλιν ἐπόρθεις μόνα τἀμὰ κομίσαι θέλων λέχεα πάλιν εἰς πάτραν.—θάρσος ἑκούσιον is, as Dr Verrall takes it, a description of Helen herself, rather than 'the willing wantonness of Helen,' as

Weil explained it: θράσος is used in a personal sense in *Theb.* 172 κρατοῦσα μὲν γὰρ (γυνὴ) οὐχ ὁμιλητὸν θράσος (ἐστί), Eur. *Andr.* 261 ὦ βάρβαρον σὺ θρέμμα καὶ σκληρὸν θράσος, and many other neuter words like στύγος, μῖσος, ἔλεγχος, ὄνειδος, μίασμα, ἄλημα, παιπάλημα, παροψώνημα (v. 1448) were used to describe persons not only in addressing them but in speaking of them (*Class. Rev.* xiv. p. 117).

This view of Helen's conduct would be familiar to a Greek audience so that they would not experience the least difficulty in understanding what was meant, especially after the introduction of Helen's name in v. 791. Stesichorus (before his Recantation) had declared that Ἑλένη ἑκοῦσα ἀπῆρε (Bergk, p. 215); and her conduct was a ground of discontentment both at home and in the camp. It was bad enough that men's blood should be shed for a woman's sake at all (*sup.* 62, cf. *Supp.* 486), especially when that woman was another's wife (*sup.* 455, Achilles in Hom. A 154, I 327, 339); but for a woman who went off with her lover of her own accord (see also Eur. *Andr.* 592 ff.), this was indeed a thing intolerable. Herodotus i. 4 presents the Asiatic view of this very matter; when women were carried off, it was folly to make exertions for revenge, δῆλα γὰρ δὴ ὅτι, εἰ μὴ αὐταὶ ἐβούλοντο, οὐκ ἂν ἡρπάζοντο.

796 f. If ἀφίλως is sound, a supplement such as **ἔστιν ἐπειπεῖν** seems to be required. A short line was often written at the side and afterwards omitted. ἐπιλέγειν is to *pronounce* a judgment, censure, eulogy or epitaph: Plut. *Mor.* 704 E ταύταις μόναις τὸ 'καλῶς' ἐπιλέγεσθαι. Arist. 1323 b 11 εἰ δεῖ καὶ τούτοις ἐπιλέγειν μὴ μόνον τὸ 'καλόν' ἀλλὰ καὶ τὸ 'χρήσιμον.' Philem. 128 καλὸν τὸ θνήισκειν ἔστιν ἐπὶ τούτωι λέγειν. *Theb.* 906 πάρεστιν εἰπεῖν ἐπ' ἀθλίοισιν ὡς... *sup.* 379.—**εὔφρων** means *pleasant*, *agreeable*, *welcome*, = σαίνει, προσγελᾶι, *arridet*: as in 1577, *Supp.* 19, 383, 543, 983, Pind. *O.* ii. 40, *N.* vii. 67. For the sentiment see Cope on Ar. *Rhet.* i. 11. 8.

800. οἰκουροῦντα. If nothing else had told Agamemnon that the Chorus are alluding to Clytaemnestra, this word could not fail to tell him. οἰκουρεῖν, *to keep house*, was the duty of the faithful housewife. Eur. *Hec.* 1277 κτενεῖ νιν ἡ τοῦδ' ἄλοχος, οἰκουρὸς πικρά. *Or.* 928 εἰ τἄνδον οἰκουρήμαθ' οἱ λελειμμένοι φθείρουσιν, ἀνδρῶν εὔνιδας λωβώμενοι. Lycophr. 1107 λυπρὰν λεαίνης εἰσιδοῦσ' οἰκουρίαν. Liban. iv. 115: Agamemnon on departing for the Trojan expedition is supposed to have charged his wife in these terms:—ὁ μὲν πλοῦς, ὦ γύναι, μακρός, αἱ δὲ περὶ τοῦ ζῆν ἐλπίδες ἄδηλοι· δεῖ γάρ, ἢν δέηι, πάντα παθεῖν ὅπως σωφρονῶσιν ἡμῖν αἱ γυναῖκες. ταυτί σοι παρακατατίθεμαι τὰ παιδία. οἰκούρει, καὶ φύλαξ τῆς οἰκίας ἔσο πιστὴ καὶ μεῖνον ἀπόντι πάλιν γυνὴ καὶ τοῖς παισὶ μήτηρ, καὶ πατὴρ ἀντ' ἐμοῦ. ἴσως ἐπανήξω καὶ ἐπαινέσομαί σε τῆς οἰκουρίας.

802. **τοὺς ἐμοὶ μεταιτίους** recalls the arrogant inscriptions set up by Pausanias at Delphi and Byzantium: Thuc. i. 132, Athen. 536 a.

806. **αἱματηρὸν τεῦχος**: *an urn of blood*, like μελιτηρὸν ἄγγος—*a honey pot* (Ar. fr. 440): κεράμιον ὀξηρόν—*a vinegar jar* (*ib.* 511).

807 f. **τῶι δ' ἐναντίωι κύτει ἐλπὶς προσήιει χειρὸς οὐ πληρουμένωι.** The other urn saw Hope of the hand which was to drop a vote in it continually coming nigh, but never saw it quite arrive: for when a hope arrived, it was a hope realised: Eur. *Or.* 859 οἴμοι· προσῆλθεν ἐλπὶς ἣν φοβουμένη....*Herc. Fur.* 771 δοκημάτων ἐκτὸς ἦλθεν ἐλπίς. Hopes far from realisation were called μακραὶ ἐλπίδες, distant hopes; when realised, or nearly, they were ἐλπίδες παροῦσαι: *Cho.* 694 νῦν δ' ἥπερ ἦν δόμοισι βακχείας κακῆς ἰατρὸς ἐλπίς, ἣν παροῦσαν ἐγγράφειν.

809. **καπνῶι δ' ἁλοῦσα κτἑ.**: 'the capture of the city now remains still manifest by the smoke.' Dio Chrys. i. p. 72 R. καὶ νῦν ἔτι τοῦτο δρᾶι, Menander fr. 113 (iii. 34 K.) καὶ νῦν ἔτι ἀποίητα πάμπολλ' ἐστὶν ἡμῖν.

810. See cr. n. If Hermann's reading is taken, Troy with all her insolent wealth—the cause of her damnation—is conceived as a burnt sacrifice to Ἄτη (*inf.* 1434, *Theb.* 938 ἕστακε δ' Ἄτας τροπαῖον ἐν πύλαις). Helen, who fired Troy (Achill. Tat. i. 8 τὸ μὲν γὰρ Ἑλένης τῶν γάμων πῦρ ἀνῆψε κατὰ τῆς Τροίας ἄλλο πῦρ), has been already likened to a sacrificial minister of Ἄτη in v. 736. ζῆν, which appears in ζωπυρεῖν, is a proper word of fire in Greek as *uiuere* and *uiuus* are in Latin: Eur. *Bacch.* 8, Ar. *Lys.* 306, ἄνθρακι ζῶντι Arat. 1041. The wind fans the flame into life, which is contrasted with the dying ash: Quint. iii. 712 ff. Cf. Hom. μ 68 πυρός τ' ὀλοοῖο θύελλαι.

812. **πολύμνηστον χάριν.** Max. Tyr. xxx. 4 speaks of Pausanias and Lysander sacrificing or dedicating a tithe of their spoils.

826. Tzetzes on Lycophr. 354 pointed out that πεπαμένος should be written with a single μ. τῶι πεπαμένωι is the Aeschylean substitute where poetry would generally give τῶι κεκτημένωι, prose τῶι ἔχοντι.

829 ff. By the vague **δοκοῦντας**, 'certain ones in appearance,' he conveys to them that he is quite aware of Clytaemnestra's insincerity; and then, as though he were thinking only of the Greeks at Troy, continues with **μόνος δ' Ὀδυσσεύς**, just as they had continued with σὺ δέ μοι in v. 790.—**ὁμιλίας κάτοπτρον** here means the mirror which ὁμιλία, *consuetudo*, converse or conversation, association, companionship, familiarity, holds up, the glass in which the associate's true character is shown: κατόπτρωι μὲν ἐμφανίζεται τύπος τῆς μορφῆς τοῦ σώματος, ὁμιλίαις δὲ καὶ λόγοις τὸ τῆς ψυχῆς ἦθος χαρακτηρίζεται Stobaeus, *Flor.* iv. p. 430, Gaisford. ἐν μὲν τοῖς ἐσόπτροις ὁ τῆς ὄψεως, ἐν δὲ ταῖς ὁμιλίαις ὁ τῆς ψυχῆς χαρακτὴρ βλέπεται is the form in Antonius and Maximus. Eur.

El. 383 οὐ μὴ ἀφρονήσεθ', οἳ κενῶν δοξασμάτων | πλήρεις πλανᾶσθε, τῆι δ' ὁμιλίαι βροτοὺς | κρινεῖτε καὶ τοῖς ἤθεσιν τοὺς εὐγενεῖς; *Andr.* 683 ἡ δ' ὁμιλία | πάντων βροτοῖσι γίγνεται διδάσκαλος. Aesch. *Supp.* 1004 ἀγνῶθ' ὅμιλον ὡς ἐλέγχεσθαι χρόνωι. In Plut. *Mor.* 53 A the flatterer is compared to a mirror, which only reflects foreign images:—δίκην κατόπτρου, παθῶν ὀθνείων καὶ βίων καὶ κινημάτων εἰκόνας ἀναδεχόμενον. But that is a different comparison. It is certain that ὁμιλία does not mean *friendship* (φιλία), nor is κάτοπτρον ever used of a mere reflexion (σκιά or εἴδωλον). See fr. 393 κάτοπτρον εἴδους χαλκός ἐστ', οἶνος δὲ νοῦ, Eur. *Hipp.* 428 κακοὺς δὲ θνητῶν ἐξέφην', ὅταν τύχηι, προθεὶς κάτοπτρον ὥστε παρθένωι νέαι χρόνος.

835. τὰ δ' ἄλλα πρὸς θεούς. This use of τὰ πρός, 'with regard to,' is not of the commonest and occurs chiefly with θεούς and πόλιν: Soph. *Phil.* 1441 εὐσεβεῖν τὰ πρὸς θεούς, *O. C.* 617 τὰ πρὸς σέ, *Trach.* 879 σχετλίωι τὰ πρός γε πρᾶξιν (Hermann), Eur. *Or.* 427 τὰ πρὸς πόλιν δὲ πῶς ἔχεις; 1664 τὰ πρὸς πόλιν δὲ τῶιδ' ἐγὼ θήσω καλῶς, Xen. *Rep. Lac.* 13. 11, Dem. 3. 26, Aeschin. 3. 120. In later prose the idiom is employed freely.

841. See cr. n. and for the form of expression cf. Soph. *Phil.* 765 τὸ πῆμα τοῦτο τῆς νόσου τὸ νῦν παρόν, *Ai.* 363 τὸ πῆμα τῆς ἄτης, Apoll. Rhod. iv. 4 ἄτης πῆμα δυσίμερον.

845. νίκη δ'.... But in his contest presently with Clytaemnestra (v. 933) he quickly yields the victory to her, and before long her triumph is complete.

855 f. Ford, *The Broken Heart* v. 3

> When one news straight came huddling on another
> Of death! and death! and death!

In **κακοῦ κάκιον ἄλλο πῆμα** she means him to understand disasters happening to him, his wounds or death; she herself has in mind ἀραῖα κακά (v. 1396) inflicted by Agamemnon on his wife at home, the slaughter of her child (τὸ πῆμα τῶν ὀλωλότων v. 358) and his unfaithfulness (v. 1440).

859. τέτρηται, which H. L. Ahrens gave for the MS. τέτρωται, is the right verb; a net is not full of wounds, but of holes: δικτύου πολυτρήτου Babr. iv. 4.

860. εἰ δ' ἦν τεθνηκώς.... A shade of intonation in the Greek as in the English would make a wish of this, 'If only he had been killed!' and I fancy this is the suggestion, that he deserved to die three times over, ἄξιος τρὶς τεθνάναι in the common phrase: Eur. *Or.* 1512 ΟΡ. ἐνδίκως ἡ Τυνδάρειος ἆρα παῖς διώλετο; | ΦΡ. ἐνδικώτατ', εἴ γε λαιμοὺς εἶχε τριπτύχους θανεῖν like some three-headed monster.

The 'coverlet' of earth or stones was a familiar metaphor from

Homer downwards: Γ 57 ἦ τέ κεν ἤδη λάινον ἕσσο χιτῶνα κακῶν ἕνεχ' ὅσσα ἔοργας. See the passages collected by Blomfield.

868. ἐκ τῶνδέ τοι. The real reason of course was that she might carry on her intrigue with Aegisthus undisturbed; that was the 'price' for which she 'sold' Orestes, *Cho.* 132 πεπραμένοι γὰρ νῦν γε πως ἀλώμεθα πρὸς τῆς τεκούσης, ἄνδρα δ' ἀντηλλάξατο Αἴγισθον, *ib.* 914.

872 ff. Στροφίος is so accented by M in *Cho.* 675. [Blass (*Choeph.* p. 24) says: 'Ferner accentuire ich mit M v. 679 Στροφίος gemäss der Regel wonach diese Namen auf -ιος bei kurzer erster Silbe Paroxytona sind: Ἐχίος Στρατίος und doch Φήμιος.' See also Cobet's remarks to the same effect in *V. L.* p. 59.]

ἀμφίλεκτα πήματα. Two things might happen: Agamemnon first might fall at Troy; and then the people might revolt and frame a plot to murder the young heir, and so destroy the dynasty entirely. Lucian's *Tyrannicide* ii. 151, who has killed the tyrant's son, argues that τὸ ὑπ' ἐμοῦ γεγενημένον οὐ φυγή, οὐδὲ δευτέρας ἐπαναστάσεως ἐλπίς, ἀλλὰ παντελὴς καθαίρεσις, καὶ πανωλεθρία παντὸς τοῦ γένους, καὶ ῥιζόθεν τὸ δεινὸν ἅπαν ἐκκεκομμένον.—For βουλὴν καταρράψειεν cf. Alexis ii. 329 K. (Athen. 568 a) ῥάπτουσι δὲ | πᾶσιν ἐπιβουλάς. Ael. *N. A.* vii. 10 ἐπιβουλὰς ῥάπτοντες (v.l. ῥίπτοντες), *Eum.* 26 καταρράψας μόρον, *inf.* 1604 φόνου ῥαφεύς. Similarly ῥάπτειν is combined with κακά, φόνον, θάνατον: add the compounds δολορράφος, μηχανορράφος, δικορράφος. βουλὴν καταρρίψειεν could not mean 'hazard a plot,' because Greek said ἀναρρίπτειν, or ἀναβάλλειν, κύβον βόλον or κίνδυνον, never καταρρίπτειν. If, on the other hand, the meaning were 'overthrow the Council,' we should at least have had τὴν βουλήν, but Tragedy never uses this technical Athenian term to describe a body of councillors in the heroic age. Observe moreover that she is speaking of a danger to Orestes' life.

880 ff. I take it that Clytaemnestra here is feigning just what Imogen says honestly in *Cymbeline* iii. 4. 38

> False to his bed! What is it to be false?
> To lie in watch there, and to think on him?
> To weep 'twixt clock and clock? if sleep charge nature,
> To break it with a fearful dream of him,
> And cry myself awake?

Night after night, she means, the lamp has been burning in her chamber and she waiting to receive him there, and weeping because he, like a faithless lover, never heeded it: *Anth. Pal.* v. 190. 3

> ἆρά γε τὴν φιλάσωτον ἔτ' ἐν κοίταισιν ἀθρήσω
> ἄγρυπνον, λύχνωι πόλλ' ἀποδαομένην †
> (ἀποδυρομένην Jacobs, ἀποκλαομένην Huschke)

Ah, shall I find the unthrift still awake
And sorrowing to her lamp for my dear sake?

ib. 279, 263, 150. Plut. *Mor.* 759 F Λαῒς τις ἢ Γναθαίνιον 'ἐφέσπερον δαίουσα λαμπτήρων σέλας' ἐκδεχομένη. But in truth the lamp has been alight in expectation of Aegisthus, or in Aegisthus' company, for the lamp was always witness, Heliod. i. 12, *Anth. Pal.* v. 4, 5, 7, 8, 128, 165, 166—in Lucian i. 648 it is cited as a witness, and in amatory language plays a large part as a sentimental symbol: lovers, says Plut. *Mor.* 513 F, κἂν μὴ πρὸς ἀνθρώπους, πρὸς ἄψυχα περὶ αὐτῶν διαλέγονται, 'ὦ φιλτάτη κλίνη,' καὶ 'Βακχὶς θεόν σ' ἐνόμισεν, εὔδαιμον λύχνε,' a saying Asclepiades alludes to in *A. P.* v. 7 λύχνε, σὺ δ', εἰ θεὸς εἶ, τὴν δολίην ἀπάμυνον. And if a gnat's least whining woke her in alarm, it was alarm about Aegisthus; that is why in 881 and 884 she repeats the ἀμφὶ σοί, which for that reason I have thought should be a little stressed.

In the ears of the audience the words τοῦ ξυνεύδοντος would suggest another bed-fellow than the time she speaks of. For **βλάβας** (or βλάβην) **ἔχειν**, *to suffer injury*, see *Eum.* 802 ὡς ταῦτ' Ὀρέστην δρῶντα μὴ βλάβας ἔχειν, Soph. *Ai.* 1325 τί γάρ σ' ἔδρασεν, ὥστε καὶ βλάβην ἔχειν; schol. Eur. *Or.* 542 on μὴ 'πισήμους· φανερὰς βλάβας ἔλαβε, schol. Flor. on *Ag.* 72 βλάβην ἔχοντες ἀπὸ (l. for ἀντὶ) τοῦ γήρως.

887 ff. These are familiar examples of a single ἐλπίς, a saving hope or stay, existing or afforded, to rely upon: but critics since Blomfield have been offended by the καὶ in v. 890; and rightly, on their view of the construction: some therefore would read γαῖαν for καὶ γῆν, while others take the καὶ to begin a new series of comparisons. Yet καὶ γῆν I am sure is sound, for μονογενὲς τέκνον πατρὶ (παρ' ἐλπίδα φανὲν) καὶ γῆν φανεῖσαν ναυτίλοις παρ' ἐλπίδα is the meaning. So Pindar *O.* x. 86 speaks of his late-appearing ode as coming dearly welcomed like a long-desired child granted to a father late in life: τὰ παρ' εὐκλέϊ Δίρκαι χρόνωι μὲν φάνεν ἀλλ' ὥτε παῖς ἐξ ἀλόχου πατρὶ ποθεινὸς ἵκοντι νεότατος τὸ πάλιν ἤδη. Liban. iv. 651. 10 πόσους ἐπιδείξω σοι τῶν πολιτῶν γυναῖκας μὲν αὐτῶν ἔχοντας εἰπεῖν πατέρας δ' οὐ κεκλημένους, ἀνθρώπους εἰς ἔσχατον ἤδη γήρως ἥκοντας καὶ τὴν ἐλπίδα τοῦ πράγματος προσαφῃρημένους; ἂν οὖν ἐγὼ μέν σοι ταῦτα πείθωμαι γύναιον δὲ ἔνδον ᾖ παῖδες δὲ μηδαμῇ φαίνωνται,...Hom. *h. Dem.* 219 παῖδα δέ μοι τρέφε τόνδε, τὸν ὀψίγονον καὶ ἄελπτον ὤπασαν ἀθάνατοι.

παρ' ἐλπίδα with its double meaning (vv. 278, 1042) comes with telling irony at the end: but the effect of it is weakened by three lines which follow in the MSS., and which I have omitted, believing them to have been merely an illustration quoted in the margin (see cr. n.):

κάλλιστον ἦμαρ εἰσιδεῖν ἐκ χείματος,
ὁδοιπόρῳ διψῶντι πηγαῖον ῥέος,
τερπνὸν δὲ τἀναγκαῖον ἐκφυγεῖν ἅπαν.

Fair is the clear day viewed after the storm,
Spring-water to the parching wayfarer,
Dear the deliverance from all hard constraints.

That is the construction of them, as in Theognis 255 κάλλιστον τὸ δικαιότατον, λῷστον δ' ὑγιαίνειν, πρᾶγμα δὲ τερπνότατον τοῦ τις ἐρᾶι τὸ τυχεῖν, Soph. fr. 329 κάλλιστόν ἐστι τοὔνδικον πεφυκέναι, λῷστον δὲ τὸ ζῆν ἄνοσον, ἥδιστον δ' ὅτωι πάρεστι λῆψις ὧν ἐρᾶι καθ' ἡμέραν, *A. P.* v. 169 ἡδὺ θέρους διψῶντι χιὼν ποτόν, ἡδὺ δὲ ναύταις ἐκ χειμῶνος ἰδεῖν εἰαρινὸν στέφανον· ἥδιστον δ' ὁπόταν κρύψηι μία τοὺς φιλέοντας χλαῖνα καὶ αἰνῆται Κύπρις ὑπ' ἀμφοτέρων,—this epigram repeating the same commonplace. I need only add Eur. *Andr.* 870 ὦ ναυτίλοισι χείματος λιμὴν φανείς and *Or.* 719 ἡδεῖαν ὄψιν· πιστὸς ἐν κακοῖς ἀνὴρ κρείσσων γαλήνης ναυτίλοισιν εἰσορᾶν to show that κάλλιστον ἦμαρ εἰσιδεῖν ἐκ χείματος would be little more than tautology with γῆν φανεῖσαν ναυτίλοις. Besides, τοιοῖσδέ τοι νιν ἀξιῶ προσφθέγμασιν should follow the προσφθέγματα immediately.

904. See cr. n. An alternative reading is σὺν θεοῖσιν, ἄρμενα.

905 ff. Agamemnon answers coldly, and δωμάτων ἐμῶν φύλαξ would have made another woman wince. His first remark is a severe snub, and his next, that praise should come from others, is at least ambiguous.

914. **κάλλεσιν**: a technical term of worship. Cf. Eupol. fr. 333 (i. 346 K.) βάπτειν τὰ κάλλη τὰ περίσεμνα τῆι θεῶι.

917. This line was explained by Blass *Mélanges Henri Weil*, 1898, p. 13: to walk merely over ποδόψηστρα would be ἀνεπίφθονον; but it would have a very different sound if rumour said that he had walked upon τὰ ποικίλα, which belong to the service of the gods. Cf. Damascius ap. Suid. *s.v.* χωρὶς τὰ Μυσῶν...χωρὶς γὰρ τὰ τῶν φιλοσόφων καὶ τῶν ἱερέων ὁρίσματα, οὐδὲν ἧττον ἢ τὰ λεγόμενα Μυσῶν καὶ Φρυγῶν. So χωρίς is predicative, followed by τε καί, in Soph. *O.C.* 808, Plat. *Prot.* 336 B.

918 f. **τὸ μὴ κακῶς φρονεῖν θεοῦ μέγιστον δῶρον**: Eur. *Med.* 635 στέργοι δέ με σωφροσύνα, δώρημα κάλλιστον θεῶν. In the allusion to *felicity* (ὀλβίσαι) which follows there appears to be a side-reference to the proverbial *Theb.* 612 θεοῦ δὲ δῶρόν ἐστιν εὐτυχεῖν βροτούς, *Cho.* 57 τὸ δ' εὐτυχεῖν, τόδ' ἐν βροτοῖς θεός τε καὶ θεοῦ πλέον. Jebb on Soph. *O. T.* 1529 remarks that this is the first allusion in literature to the famous adage attributed to Solon. Cf. Dio Chrys. xxviii. 13 (ii. 535 R.) ὅστις δὲ τοῖς μεγίστοις ἀγαθοῖς συναπέρχεται τὰ ἄριστα πράξας, οὗτος εὐδαιμονέστατα τελευτᾶι.

921. See cr. n. The reading of the MSS. could only mean 'if it is the case that (supposing certain conditions) I should act' (or 'fare') 'in all things thus, I have no misgivings.' This can hardly be called a meaning; nor is ὧς so used in Tragedy. Cf. *Supp.* 403 εἶπον δὲ καὶ πρίν, οὐκ ἄνευ δήμου τάδε πράξαιμ' ἄν. *Cho.* 684 τοσαῦτ' ἀκούσας εἶπον. *Eum.* 641 τὴν δ' αὖ τοιαύτην εἶπον.

922. καὶ μὴν τόδ' εἰπὲ...ἐμοί is the preface to a question: Hdt. vii. 47, Ar. *Nub.* 500, 748, *Thesm.* 740, *Plut.* 902, Plat. *Cratyl.* 385 B, *Rep.* 351 D, Lucian i. 297. Everyday language would say καὶ μὴν τόδε μοι εἰπέ. Tragic style habitually uses ἐγώ, σύ superfluously: if emphasis were desired it would have been secured by the position of the word, καὶ μὴν ἐμοὶ τόδ' εἰπέ. Nevertheless in the use of ἐγώ, ἐμοί, ἐμέ at the end of three successive lines we hear an undertone of strife between two wills. Thus, **μὴ παρὰ γνώμην** is interposed, as in the following examples: Soph. *Ant.* 446 σὺ δ' εἰπέ μοι, μὴ μῆκος ἀλλὰ συντόμως, ᾔδησθα...; *Trach.* 1117, Eur. *Med.* 768 μὴ πρὸς ἡδονήν, *sup.* 515, 897, *Theb.* 266 μὴ φιλοστάνως. Ar. fr. 473 καὶ κρῖνον αὐτὴ μὴ μετ' ὀξυρεγμίας. Plat. Com. 86 (Ath. 110 d) κᾆιτ' ἄρτους...ἧκε πριάμενος, μὴ τῶν καθαρύλλων (where μή shows ἧκε to mean 'return'—it is often used in the imperative—not, as the editors take it, 'he came back'). εἰπεῖν παρὰ γνώμην is 'to speak contrary to one's own γνώμη, deliberate opinion, conviction, advised judgement.' Cf. Thuc. vi. 9 οὔτε ἐν τῶι προτέρωι χρόνωι...εἶπον παρὰ γνώμην οὔτε νῦν, iii. 42 οὕτω γὰρ ἥκιστα ἂν παρὰ γνώμην τι καὶ πρὸς χάριν λέγοι. Plut. *Mor.* 986 B ἐγὼ δ' ἐκστήσομαι ὑμῖν, μὴ καὶ παρὰ γνώμην ἐμοὶ δοκῆι χαριζόμενος διαλέγεσθαι 'against his conviction, to please me.' Dem. 1451. 16 τὸ χαρίζεσθαί τι παρὰ γνώμην opposed to τὰ δοκοῦντά μοι βέλτιστα παραινεῖν. Plut. *Phoc.* 9 ἐμὲ...λέγειν ἃ μὴ δεῖ παρὰ γνώμην οὐκ ἀναγκάσετε. *Tib. Gracch.* 2 ὥστε καὶ παρὰ γνώμην ἐν τῶι λέγειν ἐκφερόμενον ὑπ' ὀργῆς...βλασφημεῖν. *Philop.* 6 ὡς παρὰ γνώμην βιασθεῖεν εἰς χεῖρας ἐλθεῖν. So παρὰ δόξαν or τὰ δοκοῦντα εἰπεῖν: Plat. *Laches* 178 B οὐκ ἂν εἴποιεν ἃ νοοῦσιν, ἀλλὰ...ἄλλα λέγουσι παρὰ τὴν αὐτῶν δόξαν. *Rep.* 346 A ἐπεὶ τοσόνδε εἰπέ· οὐχὶ φαμέν...; καὶ ὦ μακάριε μὴ παρὰ δόξαν ἀποκρίνου. *Gorg.* 500 B μηδὲ παρὰ τὰ δοκοῦντα ἀποκρίνου. 495 A εἴπερ παρὰ τὰ δοκοῦντα ἐρεῖς. In Eur. *Med.* 577 ὅμως δ' ἔμοιγε, κεἰ παρὰ γνώμην ἐρῶ, δοκεῖς προδοὺς σὴν ἄλοχον οὐ δίκαια δρᾶν the meaning is 'unadvisedly,' as in Thuc. i. 70 παρὰ γνώμην κινδυνευταί, Soph. *Trach.* 389 οὐκ ἀπὸ γνώμης λέγεις. Liban. i. 291 προήκατο ῥῆμα παρὰ γνώμην, κελεύοντος τοῦ θυμοῦ, *i.e.* ὀργῆι βιασθὲν μᾶλλον ἢ γνώμηι φρενῶν Soph. *O. T.* 524, 'more upon humour than advised respect.' *Philoct.* 1191 ΧΟ. τί ῥέξοντες ἀλλοκότωι γνώμαι τῶν πάρος, ὧν προὔφαινες; ΦΙ. οὔτοι νεμεσητὸν ἀλύοντα χειμερίωι λύπαι καὶ παρὰ νοῦν θροεῖν. 'Contrary to my opinion' would be παρὰ γνώμην ἐμήν, as Eur. *I. A.* 502 ὅτι παρὰ γνώμην ἐμὴν ὑπέθηκας ὀρθῶς τοὺς λόγους, where the sense is 'expectation,' as in Aesch. *Supp.* 463 γένοιτο δ' εὖ παρὰ γνώμην ἐμήν, Eur. *H. F.* 594 μὴ παρὰ γνώμην πέσῃς.

924. ἔρξειν: see cr. n. εὔχομαι in the sense '*I vow that I will*' always takes the future. Greek never said ηὔξω ἔρδειν ἂν for 'you vowed that you would,' and ηὔξω ἔρδειν could only mean 'you vowed that you were performing.'—ἔρδειν was probably the alteration of a scribe who thought that ἂν and ἔρξειν belonged together. The editors strangely imagine that ὧδ' ἔρδειν τάδε means 'to refrain from treading on dyed robes'; having forgotten that when you made a vow to the gods you did not say οὐ θύσω, 'save me, and I will—*not* sacrifice!' Vows were made in times of fear or danger (Plat. *Legg.* 909 E, *Anth. Pal.* ix. 7); you said, *Deliver me from this danger, and I vow to sacrifice* so much. Similarly in v. 954 Clytaemnestra says πολλῶν πατησμὸν εἱμάτων ἂν ηὐξάμην, 'I would readily have vowed the sacrifice of many robes to ransom Agamemnon's life.'—Agamemnon would have obeyed Calchas as he had done in the matter of Iphigeneia.

925. 'Yes, supposing the authority on ritual (the priest, εὖ εἰδὼς μαντευόμενος Hom. β 170: cf. Z 438) had prescribed (πιφαύσκων εἶπε or ἐξηγήσατο) this holy service' (τόδε τέλος, which now has a proper sense).—ἐξεῖπον of the MSS. is the alteration of a scribe who mistook the construction of εἴπερ τις.—If εἴπερ τις had really meant 'if anyone ever did,' we should have had no γε with εἰδὼς εὖ: yet γε must be genuine, for it was never inserted by scribes except *metri gratia*: εἴπερ ...γε is *siquidem*; in answer to a question, 'yes; that is, if...' (*O.T.* 369).

933. ἦ καὶ σὺ is *tu quoque*, and could not mean anything else.

934. See cr. n. and cf. Soph. *Ai.* 1353 κρατεῖς τοι τῶν φίλων νικώμενος. In v. 932 Clyt. has forced him to accept the ominous 'felicitation' of v. 919 (see Solon in Hdt. i. 32), and now contrives to make him yield of his own accord (ἑκών).

935. ὑπαί τις...λύοι: Hom. ξ 496 ἀλλά τις εἴη εἰπεῖν Ἀτρεΐδῃ Ἀγαμέμνονι.

938. πρόσωθεν marks the connexion with θεῶν: *Eum.* 297 κλύει δὲ καὶ πρόσωθεν ὢν θεός, *ib.* 400 πρόσωθεν ἐξήκουσα, *Cho.* 690, Blomf. on *P. V.* 320.

939 f. πολλὴ γὰρ αἰδὼς δωματοφθορεῖν ποσὶν φθείροντα πλοῦτον ἀργυρωνήτους θ' ὑφάς: this is the scruple that Clytaemnestra scornfully replies to in v. 949 ff. δωματοφθορεῖν is a synonym of the usual word οἰκοφθορεῖν, to squander one's substance, ruin one's estate by spendthrift prodigality. ὠλεσίοικος and ἀπωλεσίοικος were used humorously in the same sense.

941. τοὐμὸν μὲν οὕτω: so Max. Tyr. xxii. 3 καὶ τὰ μὲν ἐμὰ ταύτῃ ἔχει· ὅτι δὲ καὶ περὶ ὑμᾶς κτέ. Lucian ii. 729 ἀλλὰ ταῦτα μὲν ἱκανῶς· τὰ Πυθαγόρου δὲ ἤδη λέγε, ii. 872. Either τούτων μὲν ἅλις or ταῦτα μὲν οὕτω would be Greek, but not τούτων μὲν οὕτω (see cr. n.).

944. She, therefore, being a delicately-nurtured princess, will feel

the condition of slavery with peculiar keenness. At the same time Agamemnon wishes to convey that she has only been assigned to him according to the common practice as the choicest flower of all the spoil, and that he has no personal interest in her beyond that. A comma is substituted for the full-stop which is commonly but wrongly placed at the end of v. 944. The formula πάντες (or οὐδείς)...αὕτη δέ is extremely common. The predicate comes first in Greek, and the stress here is on πολλῶν χρημάτων ἐξαίρετον ἄνθος.

949 ff. Clytaemnestra utters not a word about Cassandra, but replies 'You talk of squandering wealth and ruining the house; surely there is the whole sea to draw from, with as good purple-fish in it as ever came out of it; purple only costs its weight in silver, and we can afford to pay for it. Besides, thank Heaven! there is a store of purple garments in the house already; we are not quite paupers; the house is surely not going to be ruined by the sacrificing of a few dyed robes.' Thus **ἔστιν θάλασσα** not 'there is a sea,' but 'the sea is in existence': cf. Ach. Tat. vii. 9 εἰ δὲ ταῦτα γέγονεν οὕτως, ἐγὼ μὲν οὐκ οἶδα, μαθεῖν δ' ὑμῖν ἐξέσται· ἔχετε τὸν δεδεμένον· εἰσὶν αἱ θεράπαιναι· ἔστιν ὁ Σωσθένης. Alexis 15. 14 ὁ ταριχοπώλης ἐστίν· ἐλθὼν πυνθάνου (you can go and ask him whether I didn't pay him as much). Acts 19. 38 ἀγοραῖοι ἄγονται, καὶ ἀνθύπατοί εἰσιν· ἐγκαλείτωσαν ἀλλήλοις. Soph. *O. C.* 506 ἔστ' ἔποικος ὃς φράσει.—**οἶκος δ' ὑπάρχει κτέ.** 'The house affords us store of these.' Cf. Theocr. 22. 222 λιγεῶν μειλίγματα Μουσέων, οἷ' αὐταὶ παρέχουσι καὶ ὡς ἐμὸς οἶκος ὑπάρχει, Eur. *El.* 359 ξενίων κυρήσεθ', οἷ' ἐμὸς κεύθει δόμος, *ib.* 870 φέρ' οἷα δὴ ἔχω καὶ δόμοι κεύθουσί μου κόμης ἀγάλματ' ἐξενέγκωμαι. If any alteration is to be made, I think it should be οἴκοι, giving the construction ὑπάρχει (ἡμῖν) ἔχειν τῶνδε: in that case cf. *Rhes.* 170 ἀλλ' ἔστ' ἐν οἴκοις· οὐ βίου σπανίζομεν, 178 καὶ πρόσθεν εἶπον· ἔστι χρυσὸς ἐν δόμοις. Alexis 127 A. λάβ' ἐλθὼν σήσαμα. B. ἀλλ' ἔστιν ἔνδον. Ar. *Pac.* 522 πόθεν ἂν λάβοιμι...; οὐ γὰρ εἶχον οἴκοθεν.

954 ff. Perhaps the thought in her mind is 'If you sacrificed Iphigeneia to recover Helen (κομίζειν v. 795), I would have sacrificed more than a few robes to recover the life of my dear daughter!'

957 ff. These lines appropriate certain familiar Oriental images, which may be illustrated from a well-known Arabic poem[1], speaking of a friend,

> Sunshine he in wintry season;
> When the dog-star burned, a shadow.

[1] Translated by Dr H. M. Posnett, *Comparative Literature* (1886) p. 135, a book full of interesting and fruitful ideas.

But these figures are so manipulated by Clytaemnestra as to allow herself an ironical side-reference to her real intention.

'Aye and when Zeus is maturing bitter vengeance for an unripe virgin, then there is coolness in the house!' ὄμφαξ was used in that sense, πικρός often means 'bitter' in resentment, and Cassandra in v. 1229 foresees οἷα τεύξεται, the deed that Clytaemnestra's workmanship designs for execution. The γε in ὅταν δὲ τεύχηι Ζεύς γε gives a meaning intonation to the sentence. Then echoing ἀνδρὸς τελείου—'complete' or 'perfect' of a full-grown man as being married and head of a household—she appeals to Zeus himself, as God of τέλος, consummation in all senses, to complete, fulfil, perfect her prayer.—σημαίνει μολόν: see cr. n. 'Warmth...signifies its coming' is the literal rendering: see v. 305.

967 f. δεῖμα προστατήριον καρδίας ποτᾶται is a metaphor from wind, such as is often employed in poetry to describe emotions of the spirit: *Sup.* 229 φρενὸς πνέων δυσσεβῆ τροπαίαν, *Theb.* 692 ἐπεὶ δαίμων λήματος αὖ τροπαίαι χρονίαι μεταλλακτὸς ἴσως ἂν ἔλθοι θεμερωτέρωι πνεύματι· νῦν δ' ἔτι ζεῖ. προστατήριον καρδίας is 'set stubbornly before my consciousness,' like πάροιθεν δὲ πρώιρας δριμὺς ἄηται κραδίας θυμός in *Cho.* 390, where the preceding words τί γὰρ κεύθω φρέν' ὃ σεῖον ἔμπας ποτᾶται; illustrate ποτᾶται here. The allusion is to the phrases technically used of wind; στάσις, properly its setting in a certain quarter, ἱστάμενος, εὐσταθής, ἀντιοστατεῖν: so οὐριοστάταν νόμον in *Cho.* 817 is an allusion to the οὖρος ὕμνων. Cf. *Pers.* 705 ἀλλ' ἐπεὶ δέος παλαιὸν σοὶ φρενῶν ἀνθίσταται.—For the confusion of δεῖμα and δεῖγμα (see cr. n.) see *On editing Aeschylus* p. 101.

970 ff. οὐδ' ἀποπτύσας...θάρσος ἵζει. The construction is slightly varied from οὐδ' ἀποπτύσας...θαρσῶ, as in *Eum.* 100. Cf. Eur. *Alc.* 604 πρὸς δ' ἐμᾶι ψυχᾶι θάρσος ἧσται.

973 ff. χρόνος δ' ἐπεὶ κτἑ. 'Time has passed since the sandy shore chafed' (or 'grazed' from παρ-αφάω, related to παραφάσσω) 'the cables cast out together from the stern when the sea-borne host sped for the walls of Troy.' Cf. *sup.* 40 δέκατον ἔτος τόδ' ἐπεὶ τῆσδ' ἀπὸ χώρας ἦραν, 437 ἀφ' Ἕλλανος αἴας συνορμένοις, Eur. *I. A.* 1319 μή μοι ναῶν χαλκεμβολάδων πρύμνας Αὐλὶς δέξασθαι τούσδ' εἰς ὅρμους ὤφελεν ἐλάταν πομπαίαν, *El.* 1022 πρυμνοῦχον Αὖλιν, Ov. *Trist.* iii. 9. 13 *dum soluitur aggere funis*, Val. Flacc. ii. 428. Thus πρυμνησίων ξυνεμβολὰς is equivalent to πρυμνήσια ξυνεμβεβλημένα: *Eum.* 751 ἐκβολὰς ψήφων. Some may prefer ἀγά, the alternative suggestion of Ahrens; for, though ἀγή is not glossed by ἀκτή, the two words appear sometimes to be confused. Thus in Pind. *I.* ii. 42 Νείλου πρὸς ἀκτάν Schneidewin reads ἀγάς and Bury ἀγάν from the schol. πρὸς αὐγάς: see also Jacobs *Anth.* xii. p. 96.

Schneidewin also restored πρὸς ἀγάς in *Anth. Pal.* v. 82 and ἀγήν in Arat. *Phaen.* 668. Numenius ap. Ath. 305 a ὁππότε πέτραι ἀμμώδεις κλύζωνται ἐπ' ἄκρηι κύματος ἀγῆι. **ψαμμάς** is taken in preference to ψαμμίς in view of the copious collection of adjectives belonging to this type which are brought together by Lobeck, *Path. Proll.* p. 442 f.

984 ff. σπλάγχνα δ' οὔτοι ματάιζει, πρὸς ἐνδίκοις φρεσὶν τελεσφόροις δίναις κυκώμενον κέαρ: In simple terms the meaning is 'My heart too is beating violently, and I know its agitation is not idle but warranted by apprehensions that will surely come to pass,' as Hecuba says in Eur. *Hec.* 83 ἔσται τι νέον· ἥξει τι μέλος γοερὸν γοεραῖς· οὔποτ' ἐμὰ φρὴν ὧδ' ἀλίαστος φρίσσει, ταρβεῖ. The metaphor is built up out of the phrase κυκώμενον κέαρ 'a troubled heart': Archilochus 66 θυμέ, θύμ' ἀμηχάνοισι κήδεσιν κυκώμενε, Tragic fragment in Clem. Alex. p. 486 οὔτοι γὰρ οὔτοι καὶ διὰ σπλάγχνων ἔσω χωροῦσι καὶ κυκῶσιν ἀνθρώπων κέαρ. As κυκώμενος was usually said of tossing waves, the heart dashing against the midriff (κραδία δὲ φόβωι φρένα λακτίζει *P. V.* 881) can be spoken of as a boat tossed in swirling eddies on a troubled sea and dashed upon a shore. These considerations support the conjecture δίναις κυκώμενον (see cr. n.), as Apoll. Rhod. i. 1327 ἀμφὶ δέ οἱ δίνῃσι κυκώμενον ἄφρεεν ὕδωρ. Plat. *Cratyl.* 439 C ὥσπερ εἴς τινα δίνην ἐμπεσόντες κυκῶνται, [Arist.] *Mirabil.* cxxx. p. 46, 16 Westermann τότε δὴ πάλιν σὺν πολλῶι μὲν βρυχηθμῶι μεγάλαις δὲ καὶ ταχείαις δίναις τὴν θάλασσαν ἀναζεῖν καὶ μετεωρίζεσθαι κυκωμένην ἐκ βυθῶν, where there are variants κυκλωμένην, κυκλουμένην. The same error is illustrated by Tryphiod. 325 ἴαχε καὶ Ξάνθου ποταμοῦ κυκλούμενον ὕδωρ, where κυκοώμενον should be read (κυκλόμενον, κυκώμενον and κυκοώμενον are quoted as variants), and by Nonn. *Dionys.* xx. 336 ἄφνω δ' ἐκ σκοπέλοιο χύθη κυκλούμενον ὕδωρ (al. κυκοώμενον). So κυκῶντες (Reiske) should be restored for κυκλοῦντες in Polyb. xi. 29. 10. The MS. reading could not mean anything but 'circling round,' not 'eddying'; for κυκλοῦσθαι can only be applied to a river which encircles or to the surrounding stream of Ocean (Nonn. *Dionys.* i. 495 etc.).

990 ff. are corrupted, but the sense is clear; probably we should begin with μάλα τί τοι... The language recalls Solon 13. 71 ff. (=Theogn. 227 ff.) πλούτου δ' οὐδὲν τέρμα πεφασμένον ἀνθρώποισιν...τίς ἂν κορέσειεν ἅπαντας; cf. *inf.* 1330. The idea of Health as a Mean appears in Max. Tyr. xxxix. 2 οὐχ ἡ μὲν ὑγεία μέτρον τι ἐστὶ τῆς τῶν σωμάτων εὐαρμοστίας; ...ἔστιν οὖν ὅπως ποικίλον τι σοὶ ἡ ὑγεία ἔσται, καὶ παντοδαπόν, οὐχὶ δὲ ἁπλοῦν καὶ ὡμολογημένον;

994. It is generally agreed that something has been lost here. The supplement adopted and its insertion in this particular place are advocated on the ground that **ἀνδρὸς** should not be separated far from πότμος, and παίειν πρός is the usage in such cases. In Aesch. fr. 99. 23 Blass restored μὴ πάντα παίσασ' ἐκχέω πρὸς ἕρματι, a reading which is made certain by Plat. *Rep.* 553 B πταίσαντα ὥσπερ πρὸς ἕρματι τῆι πόλει καὶ ἐκχέαντα τά τε αὑτοῦ καὶ ἑαυτόν κτἑ. *Com. adesp.* fr. 391, 2 (iii. 482 K.) μὴ πολλάκις πρὸς τὸν αὐτὸν λίθον πταίειν ἔχοντα καιρὸν ὁμολογούμενον.

995 ff. **ὄκνος** (nearly the same as εὐλάβεια) is the opposite of θράσος, and **πημονᾶς** is a synonym of ἄτας, so that the whole means: 'Now let but timid caution cast beforehand some of the possession overboard from the derrick of Proportion' or 'Due Measure, the whole fabric does not founder through being loaded with surcharge of Harm'—the Too Much that causes ἄτην. For the contrast see Plat. *Defin.* Θάρσος ἀπροσδοκία κακοῦ, Εὐλάβεια φυλακὴ κακοῦ, Xen. *Ages.* ii. 2 θαρρῶν πλείονα ἔθυεν ἢ ὀκνῶν ηὔχετο, Thuc. ii. 40 διαφερόντως γὰρ δὴ καὶ τόδε ἔχομεν, ὥστε τολμᾶν τε οἱ αὐτοὶ μάλιστα, καὶ περὶ ὧν ἐπιχειρήσομεν ἐκλογίζεσθαι· ὃ τοῖς ἄλλοις ἀμαθία μὲν θράσος, λογισμὸς δὲ ὄκνον φέρει: which is illustrated by Xerxes' speech in Hdt. vii. 49—50 with θρασύς and ὀκνέουσι opposed. ἡ δ' εὐλάβεια καὶ τὸ μηδὲν ἄγαν ἄριστον, as Plut. *Camill.* 6 says of believing or disbelieving miracles. Horace (*C.* ii. 10. 13 ff.) after the famous passage on the Golden Mean continues thus: *sperat infestis, metuit secundis alteram sortem bene praeparatum pectus.* The grammatical construction of the MS. reading is far from clear: **πρὸ μέν τι** (see cr. n.) is probably right. μέν marks the antithesis with v. 1004 τὸ δ' ἐπὶ γᾶν πεσόν, as in *Supp.* 452 καὶ χρήμασιν μὲν...458 ὅπως δ' ὅμαιμον αἷμα.—σφενδόνη, as is proved by an inscription discovered by the French at Delphi (see Wyse in *Class. Rev.* xiv. p. 5), was the technical term for the derrick used in discharging cargo.

1002. **τε** couples ἀμφιλαφής to πολλά, and καὶ must be taken with what follows ('even from the annual ploughing of the fields').

1007 ff. **οὐδὲ** is equivalent to οὐ καὶ 'not *even* the one who knew...': so 1524 οὐδὲ γὰρ οὗτος = οὐ καὶ οὗτος γάρ, Soph. *O. T.* 325 ὡς οὖν μηδ' ἐγὼ ταὐτὸν πάθω = καὶ ἐγὼ μή.—In reference to the death of Asclepius the Chorus say in Eur. *Alc.* 124 μόνος δ' ἂν εἰ φῶς τόδ' ἦν | ὄμμασιν δεδορκὼς | Φοίβου παῖς, προλιποῦσ' | ἦλθεν ἕδρας, σκοτίας | Ἅιδα τε πύλας· τοὺς | δμαθέντας γὰρ ἀνίστη | πρὶν αὐτὸν εἷλε Διόβολον | πλῆκτρον πυρὸς κεραυνίου. So Pindar (*P.* iii. 1 ff.) says 'I would that Cheiron, who brought up Asclepius, best of physicians, were still alive'—εἰ χρεὼν τοῦθ' ἁμετέρας ἀπὸ γλώσσας κοινὸν εὔξασθαι ἔπος. But Asclepius was stopped by Zeus, when he was tempted to restore the dead to life (*ib.* 55 ff.), as Aeschylus says here, ἐπ' ἀβλαβείαι to prevent his arrangements being thwarted—or ἐπ' εὐλαβείαι (Plat. *Rep.* 539 C) as a precautionary measure to that end; either would do. (For a possible instance of confusion between ἀβλαβέως and εὐλαβέως see *H. Herm.* 83.) Apollodorus iii. 122

says Ζεὺς δὲ φοβηθεὶς μὴ λαβόντες ἄνθρωποι θεραπείαν παρ' αὐτοῦ βοηθῶσιν ἀλλήλοις, ἐκεραύνωσεν αὐτόν. Ov. *Fast.* vi. 759 *Iuppiter exemplum ueritus direxit in illum fulmina.* Then, according to the ancient story which he himself narrates at the beginning of the *Alcestis*, Apollo, in anger at the killing of his son, destroyed the Cyclopes who had forged the thunderbolt. Zeus thereupon condemned him to a year's penal servitude in the house of Admetus son of Pheres; and while there, Apollo saved Admetus from death by tricking the Fates (Μοίρας δολώσας *Alc.* 12) whom he had made drunk with wine. In Aesch. *Eum.* 726 the Eumenides refer to this:

ΕΥΜ. τοιαῦτ' ἔδρασας καὶ Φέρητος ἐν δόμοις·
Μοίρας ἔπεισας ἀφθίτους θεῖναι βροτούς.
ΑΠ. οὔκουν δίκαιον τὸν σέβοντ' εὐεργετεῖν
ἄλλως τε πάντως χὤτε δεόμενος τύχοι;
ΕΥΜ. σύ τοι παλαιὰς διανομὰς καταφθίσας
οἴνωι παρηπάτησας ἀρχαίας θεάς.

These are the same terms in which they had reprehended the dealings of Apollo with Orestes, v. 172 f. παρὰ νόμον θεῶν βρότεα μὲν τίων παλαιγενεῖς δὲ μοίρας φθίσας. The Μοῖραι are personifications of these μοῖραι or διανομαί 'apportionments' or 'dispensations,' provinces allotted to the various divinities and severally administered by them. In the same play, the Eumenides complain that Athena, by her decision in the case of Orestes, is robbing them of their τιμαὶ δαναιαί (848), rights assigned to them in perpetuity by Μοῖρα (335 f.). Hades has his μοῖρα: mortal men have theirs; not to live for ever, but to fall one day within the power of Death. Hippolytus therefore was restored to life *Dite indignante* Ov. *Met.* xv. 535, *dis indignantibus* ii. 645: *at Clymenus* (Hades) *Clothoque dolent, haec fila reneri, hic fieri regni iura minora sui* by being baffled of their prey, *Fast.* vi. 757. And so, as Spenser says, *Faerie Queene* Bk. I. v. 40:

Such wondrous science in man's wit to reign
When Jove avised, that could the dead revive
And *fates expired* could renew again,

he put an end to it. The exact force of ἐπ' ἀβλαβείαι therefore would be 'to prevent the appointed μοῖραι being hindered by the interference of Asclepius.' From this we conclude that there exist in the system over which Zeus presides certain 'vested interests' or 'spheres of influence' assigned by Dispensation (Μοῖρα). With a polytheistic system it is evident that they will often be in opposition; just as human destinies may be: see Conington's note on Verg. *Aen.* vii. 293 *fatis contraria nostris fata Phrygum.* For, to take a particular instance, there is no reconciling the interests of Ceres and of Famine, *neque enim Cereremque Famemque fata coire sinunt*, Ov. *Met.* viii. 785; or of Artemis and Aphrodite. But each must be content to abide within his own sphere and not seek to encroach upon another's, or the balance of power will be upset, which Μοῖρα regulates, whose dispensations are upheld and administered by Zeus. There is a good illustration in Ov. *Met.* ix. 427, where the Gods murmur and complain that they should not be allowed to confer the gift of youth as Hebe does:

> *cui studeat deus omnis habet; crescitque fauore*
> *turbida seditio: donec sua Iuppiter ora*
> *soluit, et 'O nostri si qua est reuerentia,' dixit;*
> *'quo ruitis? tantumne aliquis sibi posse uidetur*
> *Fata quoque ut superet? Fatis Iolaus in annos*
> *quos egit rediit; Fatis iuuenescere debent*
> *Callirhoe geniti, non ambitione nec armis.*
> *uos etiam, quoque hoc animo meliore feratis,*
> *me quoque Fata regunt: quae si mutare ualerem,*
> *nec nostrum seri curuarent Aeacon anni,'* etc.

And in Eur. *Hippol.* 1327 Artemis explains why she has not interfered to save her votary from the wrath of Aphrodite:

> Κύπρις γὰρ ἤθελ' ὥστε γίγνεσθαι τόδε,
> πληροῦσα θυμόν· θεοῖσι δ' ὧδ' ἔχει νόμος·
> οὐδεὶς ἀπαντᾶν βούλεται προθυμίαι
> τῆι τοῦ θέλοντος, ἀλλ' ἀφιστάμεσθ' ἀεί.
> ἐπεί, σάφ' ἴσθι, Ζῆνα μὴ φοβουμένη
> οὐκ ἄν ποτ' ἦλθον ἐς τόδ' αἰσχύνης ἐγὼ
> ὥστ' ἄνδρα πάντων φίλτατον βροτῶν ἐμοὶ
> θανεῖν ἐᾶσαι.

'Aphrodite's heart was set upon it; and in such a case we none of us offer opposition to the desire of any of our fellows: otherwise, but for fear of Zeus (who upholds this system of spheres of influence with its rule of give and take), I would never have suffered him to perish.'—For πλέον φέρειν cf. Soph. *O. T.* 1190 τίς ἀνὴρ πλέον τᾶς εὐδαιμονίας φέρει ἢ τοσοῦτον ὅσον κτέ.

1022. **κτησίου βωμοῦ**, in the open court-yard in front of the palace. Athen. 189 e Ὅμηρος δὲ τὴν αὐλὴν ἀεὶ τάττει ἐπὶ τῶν ὑπαίθρων τόπων, ἔνθα ἦν ὁ τοῦ ἑρκείου Ζηνὸς βωμός.

1023. **ἀπήνης**: this was four-wheeled (τετράκυκλος Hom. Ω 324) and usually drawn by mules. In Eur. *El.* 998 it may be that the Trojan slaves of Clytaemnestra are in the car with her. In *Tro.* 573 Andromache is placed among the spoil, which is being removed in the ἀπήνη (when τετραβάμονος ἀπήνης is used of the Wooden Horse, it is compared to a four-wheeled carriage). It was commonly used as a travelling-carriage: Eur. *I. A.* 147, 618, Soph. *O. T.* 753, 803. So Tryphiod. 241, where the old men accompanying Priam come down from the πόλις in ἀπῆναι. It may be that Agamemnon came back in a car suited to an oriental monarch: thus the car of the King of Babylon is said to be ἅπαν ἐλέφαντος εἰργασμένον, ἐγγύτατα ἀπήνης Ἑλληνικῆς (Walz, *Rhet. Gr.* i. p. 531).

1024 f. This was the Greek commonplace of consolation, that even heroes half-divine (ἡμίθεοι) had not been free from human sorrows, and had submitted to the like themselves. One of the earliest examples is in the *Heraclea* of Panyasis (fr. 16 Kinkel):

> τλῆ μὲν Δημήτηρ, τλῆ δὲ κλυτὸς Ἀμφιγυήεις,
> τλῆ δὲ Ποσειδάων, τλῆ δ' ἀργυρότοξος Ἀπόλλων
> ἀνδρὶ παρὰ θνητῶι θητευέμεν εἰς ἐνιαυτόν,
> τλῆ δὲ καὶ ὀβριμόθυμος Ἄρης ὑπὸ πατρὸς ἀνάγκηι,

where no doubt he was speaking of the servitude of Heracles to Omphale in Lydia.

1034 f. Hesych. χελιδόνος δίκην: τοὺς βαρβάρους χελιδόσιν ἀπεικάζουσι διὰ τὴν ἀσύνθετον λαλίαν (read ἀσύνετον). Just below we have χελιδόνων μουσεῖον: ὡς βάρβαρα καὶ ἀσύνετα ποιούντων τῶν τραγικῶν, with reference to Ar. *Ran.* 93. Thus βάρβαρος is practically the equivalent of ἀσύνετος, and here merely strengthens ἀγνῶτα φωνήν: Hesych. βάρβαρα: ἀσύνετα, ἄτακτα. One of the tests for admission to the Eleusinian mysteries was that the candidate should not be φωνῆς ἀξύνετος; in other words, he must be Ἕλληνα τὴν φωνήν (see Cobet, *Misc. Crit.* p. 165).

1041. **πάρος**: see cr. n. πρὸς σφαγὰς πυρός could only mean that fire was to cut the victims' throats or that the victims were to cut the throat of fire; and there would be no construction for the genitive ἑστίας. Musgrave's correction removes both these blemishes and gives precisely what we want: Eur. *H. F.* 922 ἱερὰ μὲν ἦν πάροιθεν ἐσχάρας Διὸς | καθάρσι' οἴκων. *Ion* 376 προβωμίοις σφαγαῖσι μήλων. *Alc.* 162 πρόσθεν ἑστίας κατηύξατο. *Andr.* 1112 ὡς πάρος χρηστηρίων εὔξαιτο.—πάρος usually follows its case immediately, or with a word intervening as in *Trach.* 724, and may surely have as much intervening as other prepositions; see Fritsche on Theocr. 16. 109: so *sup.* 133 πάντα δὲ πύργων κτήνη πρόσθε τὰ δημιοπληθῆ. There is the same corruption in Eur. *Hel.* 870 κροῦσον δὲ πεύκην, ἵνα διεξέλθω, πάρος (Reiske for πυρός), and as I believe in *Eum.* 1050 τιμᾶτε καὶ τὸ φέγγος ὁρμάσθω πάρος (codd. πυρός).

1045. **σὺ δὲ** 'marks an antithesis, not of persons, but of clauses, and serves merely to emphasise the second clause': Jebb on Soph. *El.* 448, who quotes several parallels. Cf. Lucian ii. p. 656 οὐχ ἅπαντες, ὦ Ζεῦ, τὴν Ἑλλήνων φωνὴν ξυνιᾶσιν· ἄμεινον οὖν, οἶμαι, τῆι χειρὶ σημαίνειν καὶ παρακελεύεσθαι σιωπᾶν. [But this passage, so far from supporting the ordinary interpretation, rather favours Wecklein's view that σὺ is addressed to the Chorus. Since, however, καρβάνωι cannot be separated from χερί, Prof. Mackail suggests (*C. R.* xix. 197) that κάρβανος χείρ alludes to the forcible removal of Cassandra from the car.]

1053. **ἐποικτίρω** from the Chorus strikes the note which is meant to be in our thoughts throughout this scene. It is repeated in v. 1320, and again in 1329—their last word as it is their first. Agamemnon partly brings his own doom on himself, and we are not to feel that he is altogether to be pitied; so by heightening our pity for Cassandra Aeschylus has weakened it for Agamemnon.

1055. **ζυγόν**: cf. Eur. *Or.* 1330 ἀνάγκης δ' ἐς ζυγὸν καθέσταμεν, *sup.* 228.

1063. **προσήκοντ'**: cf. Soph. fr. 592 μὴ σπεῖρε πολλοῖς τὸν παρόντα δαίμονα· σιγώμενος γάρ ἐστι θρηνεῖσθαι πρέπων.

1077. **καὶ πεδορραντήριον.** Dr Verrall would read παιδιορραντήριον 'a place for sprinkling (with the blood of) babes.' παιδίον is not elsewhere used in Tragedy, but the sense suits admirably if it can be got out of the word.

1095. **λουτροῖσι φαιδρύνασα**: Apoll. Rhod. iii. 300 αὐτοί τε λιαροῖσιν ἐφαιδρύναντο λοετροῖς.

1103. **ἦ...γε** is used in a question, as in *Cho.* 417 τί δ' ἂν φάντες τύχοιμεν; ἢ τάπερ πάθομεν ἄχεα πρός γε τῶν τεκομένων; γε serves as a link with the previous question: *Cho.* 992 τί σοι δοκεῖ; μύραινά γ' εἴτ' ἔχιδν' ἔφυ...; *Theb.* 836 τί φῶ; τί δ' ἄλλο γ' ἢ πόνοι πόνων δόμων ἐφέστιοι; [Eur. *Cycl.* 207], Dio Chrys. ix. 20 p. 294 R. τί δέ; εἰ χωλοὶ πάντες ἦσαν οἱ τρέχοντες, ἐχρῆν γε μέγα φρονεῖν, ὅτι χωλοὺς χωλὸς ἔφθης; Max. Tyr. xvi. 3 ἆρα γε μάθησιν (*sc.* ὀνομάζοιμεν ἄν), ἢ Πλάτωνι ὁμοφώνως ἀνάμνησιν;

1107. **θύματος λευσίμου**: 'abominable sacrifice'—*i.e.* 'stonable,' 'deserving stoning' (that is 'lynching'), as καταλεύσιμος (Suid. Phot. *s.v.*), ἀράσιμος, μαστιγώσιμος, ἀκούσιμος Soph. fr. 823, ἐπόψιμος *O. T.* 1312. See *inf.* 1409, 1413.

1109. Cf. Eur. *Ion* 685 οὐ γάρ με σαίνει θέσφατα μή τιν' ἔχηι δόλον.

1110. **κροκοβαφής.** The hue of pallor—white in Northerners, and ashy in the Negro—is in Greeks and Indians green or yellow. Hence χλωρὸν δέος was the regular expression, describing the effect of fear upon the countenance. Both in Greek and Latin paleness is spoken of as 'greener than the grass' (Sappho fr. 2. 14, Longus i. 17), or 'yellow as the saffron crocus,' or 'as boxwood,' or 'as gold.'

Strictly the blood runs to the heart leaving the complexion sallow, which Aeschylus understood as well as Aristotle p. 1520 διὰ τί οἱ μὲν αἰσχυνόμενοι ἐρυθριῶσιν, οἱ δὲ φοβούμενοι ὠχριῶσιν, παραπλησίων τῶν παθῶν ὄντων; ὅτι τῶν μὲν αἰσχυνομένων διαχεῖται τὸ αἷμα ἐκ τῆς καρδίας εἰς ἅπαντα τὰ μέρη τοῦ σώματος, ὥστε ἐπιπολάζειν· τοῖς δὲ φοβηθεῖσι συντρέχει εἰς τὴν καρδίαν, ὥστ' ἐκλείπειν ἐκ τῶν ἄλλων μερῶν. ('A true account,' says Gellius xix. 6, who quotes this, 'but why is it that fear has that effect?' a question to which fanciful answers are suggested by Macrob. vii. 11.) Cf. *The Emperor of the East* iv. 5. What an earthquake I feel in me! | And on a sudden my whole fabric totters; | My blood within me turns, and through my veins, | Parting with natural redness, I discern it | Changed to a fatal yellow. Others prefer to explain κροκοβαφὴς σταγών as 'the drop of *red* blood,' like πορφυρᾶι βαφῆι in *Pers.* 320, on the ground that the dye called saffron was made from a *purple* crocus and is termed *ruber*, *rubens*, *puniceus* by the Romans. [Yet another view, that κροκοβαφὴς σταγών is the gall, is taken by Tucker on *Cho.* 183.]

1111 ff. **ἅτε καὶ δορὶ πτωσίμοις ξυνανύτει** (whose arrival synchronises, coincides with) **βίου δύντος αὐγαῖς**, the very pallor that is seen in wounded men when life is ending in a yellow sunset. Thus δορὶ πτώσιμος = δοριπετής.

1116. [The common punctuation, corrected by H., places a colon after ταῦρον instead of after βοός.]

1124. **ἀπὸ δὲ θεσφάτων.** From Soph. *Trach.* 1131, τέρας τοι διὰ κακῶν ἐθέσπισας, this would appear to be an allusion to some proverbial phrase.

1131 ff. **τὸ γὰρ ἐμὸν θροῶ πάθος ἐπεγχύδαν.** The parenthesis is an explanation of ταλαίνας. Hitherto she has seen Agamemnon's fate; now she sees that her own death is to be added to his. Cf. Eur. *Hec.* 736 EK. δύστην'—ἐμαυτὴν γὰρ λέγω λέγουσα σέ—Ἑκάβη, τί δράσω; Not unlike are *Tro.* 869, Soph. *O. T.* 1071, Oppian *Hal.* iv. 345: see also on 1225. It is evident, therefore, that θροῶ is right, and that Hermann's θροεῖς ἐπεγχέας will not stand. ἐπεγχέαι, another suggestion, is not Greek. The MS. reading ἐπεγχέασα is metrically impossible; but if it would only scan, we feel that it gives just the sense required. ἐπεγχύδαν—following the analogy of χύδην, καταχύδην, ἀμφιχύδην—seems to me the most probable correction, because such adverbs are commonly explained by participles, *e.g.* *Cho.* 65 οὐ διαρρύδαν] ἀντὶ τοῦ οὐ διαρρέων, *Eum.* 556 περαιβάδαν] παραβεβηκότα, Hesych. σπερχυλλάδην κέκραγας: ἀγανακτήσας ὑλακτεῖς ἄγαν, schol. Lycophr. 1425 χανδόν: χαίνοντες.

1140 f. **Ἴτυν...βίον.** The grammatical relation of the accusatives is not certain. A possible alternative rendering would be: 'With (cry of) '*Ityn*,' '*Ityn*,' plaining for a life luxuriant in misery.'

1142 f. The exclamatory accusative in Greek is almost unknown to the grammarians. It became much more common in Roman times, but was always introduced by some such word as αἰαῖ or ἰώ.

1144. περέβαλόν γέ οἱ. This correction (partly anticipated by Enger) explains the origin of περεβάλοντο, while the meaningless γάρ is an interpolation. When Sophocles uses οἱ, he also follows the practice of the lyric poets, *Trach.* 650 ἁ δέ οἱ, *El.* 196 ὅτε οἱ (Hermann for σοι), and so does Cratinus in a burlesque lyric verse, fr. 241, Ἥραν τε οἱ. In our passage γε is equivalent to μέν, in opposition to ἐμοὶ δέ.

1146. γλυκύν τ' αἰῶνα κλαυμάτων ἄτερ. 'A sweet life except for lamentation,' otherwise the conditions are all pleasant. I have never been able to see that κλαυμάτων ἄτερ can have any other meaning here than that which Schneidewin also had suggested: the nightingale in Greek poetry from the earliest to the latest was the type of unconsolable lamentation. ἄτερ, like ἄνευ, and many other words meaning 'without,' 'apart from,' is used elsewhere in the sense 'except.' For the general sense cf. Aphthonius *Progym.* 11 (Walz *Rhet. Gr.* i. p. 103) Niobe is speaking ἀλλὰ τί ταῦτα ὀδύρομαι, παρὸν αἰτῆσαι θεοὺς ἑτέραν ἀλλάξασθαι φύσιν, μίαν τῶν ἀτυχημάτων τεθέαμαι λύσιν, μεταστῆναι πρὸς τὰ μηδὲν αἰσθανόμενα· ἀλλὰ μᾶλλον δέδοικα μὴ καὶ τοῦτο φανεῖσα μείνω δακρύουσα. For the nightingale see Dio Chrys. ix. 19 p. 293 R. οὐκοῦν, ἔφη ὁ Διογένης, εἴπερ τὸ ταχύτατον εἶναι κράτιστόν ἐστι, πολὺ βέλτιον κόρυδον εἶναι σχεδὸν ἢ ἄνθρωπον· ὥστε τὰς ἀηδόνας οὐδέν τι δεῖ οἰκτίρειν οὐδὲ τοὺς ἔποπας, ὅτι ὄρνιθες ἐγένοντο ἐξ ἀνθρώπων, ὡς ὑπὸ τοῦ μύθου λέλεκται.

1159. There is considerable similarity to Eur. *Tro.* 460 f., where Cassandra says, addressing her country, her dead father and brothers: οὐ μακρὰν δέξεσθέ μ'· ἥξω δ' ἐς νεκροὺς νικηφόρος | καὶ δόμους πέρσασ' Ἀτρειδῶν, ὧν ἀπωλόμεσθ' ὕπο.

1167. πρόπυργοι might also mean 'before his walls.' Cf. Max. Tyr. xi. 2 καὶ τῶι μὲν Πριάμωι εὐχομένωι ὑπὲρ τῆς οἰκείας γῆς, βοῦς καὶ ὄις ὁσήμεραι τῶι Διὶ καταθύοντι, ἀτελῆ τὴν εὐχὴν τίθησι (*sc.* ὁ Ζεύς).

1170 f. See cr. nn. and cf. *P. V.* 950 οὐδὲν γὰρ αὐτῶι ταῦτ' ἐπαρκέσει τὸ μὴ οὐ πεσεῖν ἀτίμως. The text was first corrupted to τὸ μὴ πόλιν μὲν ὥσπερ οὖν ἔχει ἔχειν, παθεῖν being merely an insertion to patch the metre. Constantly, finding μὴ οὐ, scribes omitted the οὐ as περισσόν (see *Journ. Phil.* xxiii. p. 296), and it should always be written in texts, at any rate where there is any trace of it.—**ἐμπελῶ βόλωι** describes exactly what she does in v. 1290 ff. For the metaphor, see the oracle in Hdt. i. 62 ἔρριπται δ' ὁ βόλος, τὸ δὲ δίκτυον ἐκπεπέτασται, θύννοι δ' οἰμήσουσι σεληναίης διὰ νυκτός, Opp. *Hal.* iii. 465, *Cyn.* iv. 141, Eur. *Bacch.* 847 ἀνὴρ ἐς βόλον καθίσταται, *Rhes.* 730, Herod. vii. 75.—For θερμόνους cf. *A. P.* vi. 173 (of a votary of Cybele) θερμὸν ἐπεὶ λύσσης ὧδ' ἀνέπαυσε πόδα.

1179. **λαμπρός.** The metaphor shifts by means of this word, which covers the meaning 'fresh' applied to wind. As πνεῖν and πνεῦμα, *spiritus*, meant not only *wind* but *inspiration*, the spirit of prophecy is spoken of in terms belonging to a rushing mighty wind, which will wash the unseen horror to the light, as though it were a wave rolled up against the Orient rays. The wind is ἀργεστὴς Ζέφυρος)(ἀπηλιώτης.

1180. **ἐσάιξειν**: see cr. n. ἀίξαι is often used of wind: Hom. Β 146 τὰ (κύματα) μέν τ' Εὖρός τε καὶ Νότος τε ὤρορ' ἐπαίξας, Soph. *Ai.* 358 ἄιξας ὀξὺς νότος ὣς λήγει.

1181. If πῆμα is the subject (cf. Hom. Ψ 61 ὅθι κύματ' ἐπ' ἠιόνος κλύζεσκον), perhaps κλύσειν may be right.—For the image Catull. lxiv. 269 is quoted: *hic qualis fluctu placidum mare matutino | horrificans Zephyrus procliuis incitat undas | Aurora exoriente uagi sub limina solis, | quae tarde primum clementi flamine pulsae | procedunt leuiterque sonant plangore cachinni, | post uento crescente magis magis increbrescunt.*

1187 ff. The κῶμος, drunken well with human blood, refusing to be sent away, sit fast against the chamber singing; and their song is deadly Primal Sin (πρώταρχον ἄτην), the first act of Kin-murder when Atreus slew the children of Thyestes: *Cho.* 1066 παιδοβόροι μὲν πρῶτον ὑπῆρξαν μόχθοι τάλανες τε Θυέστου. For δώμασιν προσήμεναι cf. Verg. *A.* vii. 342 *Allecto Laurentis tecta tyranni | celsa petit, tacitumque obsedit limen Amatae*, iv. 471 *Orestes | armatam facibus matrem et serpentibus atris | cum fugit, ultricesque sedent in limine Dirae.* So they sit guarding the vestibule of Hell: vi. 563 (with Conington's note), 279, 555, 574, Ov. *Met.* iv. 453.

1191 f. **ἐν μέρει δ' ἀπέπτυσαν κτέ.** is part of the Image of the κῶμος explained above: Jeremiah 25. 27, Lucian i. 750.—The words admit of various constructions. δυσμενεῖς may be either nominative or accusative (belonging to εὐνάς); or we might take ἀπέπτυσαν absolutely and understand the rest to mean δυσμενεῖς τῶι εὐνὰς ἀδελφοῦ πατοῦντι.—For ἐν μέρει 'each in turn' cf. *Cho.* 331 κλῦθί νυν, ὦ πάτερ, ἐν μέρει πολυδάκρυτα πένθη.

1193. **ἢ θηρῶ τι τοξότης τις ὥς;** 'Or have I brought my quarry down?' Greek often adds to metaphors such phrases as ὥστε τοξότης (Soph. *Ant.* 1084), ναυτίλων δίκην (*Cho.* 201), which we should not express. So Eur. *Hipp.* 872 πρός γάρ τινος οἰωνὸν ὥστε μάντις εἰσορῶ κακόν.

1196. **λόγωι παλαιάς**, 'storied,' 'historic': Soph. *O. T.* 1394 ὦ Πόλυβε καὶ Κόρινθε καὶ τὰ πάτρια | λόγωι παλαιὰ δώματα (where, however, the editors of Sophocles, neglecting this parallel, connect λόγωι with πάτρια against the natural order). Hermann and Dobree, followed by Paley and others, substituted τὸ μὴ εἰδέναι in 1195, to be joined with λόγωι in the sense 'that I know not merely by hearsay.'

Apart from other objections, this is contrary to the order of the words: since the point in that case would consist in λόγωι, which must have preceded εἰδέναι, *i.e.* τὸ μὴ λόγωι εἰδέναι. See Eur. *Heracl.* 5 οἶδα δ' οὐ λόγωι μαθών. Antiphon 5. 75 ἀπολογεῖσθαι ὧν πολλῶι νεώτερός εἰμι καὶ λόγωι οἶδα. λόγωι often implies 'in word *only*': Eur. fr. 57 καὶ τὸ δοῦλον οὐ λόγωι (not only in word) ἔχοντες, ἀλλὰ τῆι τύχηι. *Theb.* 832 ἦλθε δ' αἰακτὰ πήματ' οὐ λόγωι. Soph. *Trach.* 1046, *El.* 1453, *Ai.* 813. [For ἐκμαρτυρεῖν, which has nothing to do with the technical ἐκμαρτυρία but signifies 'to testify openly,' see Wyse on Isae. iii. 77.]

1197. **ὅρκου πῆγμα**, an oath's plight: Eur. *I. A.* 395 τοὺς κακῶς παγέντας ὅρκους καὶ κατηναγκασμένους.

1205. **ἀλλ' ἦν παλαιστὴς κάρτ' ἐμοὶ πνέων χάριν**: *i.e.* 'he contended for me strenuously' (ἐπάλαιεν as ὑβριστής). Similarly Eur. *Supp.* 704 λόχος δ' ὀδόντων ὄφεος ἐξηνδρωμένος δεινὸς παλαιστὴς ἦν. Cf. generally the speech of Lady Faulconbridge in *King John* i. 1. 253:

> King Richard Cœur-de-lion was thy father:
> By long and vehement suit I was seduced
> To make room for him in my husband's bed:
> Heaven lay not my transgression to my charge!
> Thou art the issue of my dear offence,
> Which was so strongly urged past my defence.

So in Ovid *Heroid.* 5. 139 Oenone says of Apollo:

> *Me fide conspicuus Troiae munitor amauit:*
> *ille meae spolium uirginitatis habet.*
> *id quoque luctando. rupi tamen ungue capillos*
> *oraque sunt digitis aspera facta meis.*

Oenone too, according to Ovid, received her gift of medicine from Apollo (*ib.* 145).

1206. **νόμωι**, they say, to make it easy for her to confess what was so natural: cf. Hom. ψ 296 ἀσπάσιοι λέκτροιο παλαιοῦ θεσμὸν ἵκοντο.—For **ἠλθέτην** see Cobet, *Misc. Crit.* p. 279.

1210. **ἄνατος**: see cr. n. There is a similar confusion in Lycophr. 1172.

1215. See cr. n. An adjective has been lost.

1216. **τοὺς δόμοις ἐφημένους**, 'seated against the house'—like the Furies, who personify their vengeance (see n. on 1187 f.),—rather than 'seated on the roof.' She sees the figures, vague and shadowy at first; as they grow plainer, gradually she discerns the details one by one; at last they show distinct, **πρέπουσι** (v. 1221).

1223. **λέοντ'**: he was a Pelopid like the rest, but ἄναλκις: see on 147.

1224. **οἶμαι**, *credo*, 'no doubt': see on 800.

1225. **φέρειν γὰρ κτέ.**, explaining δεσπότηι ἐμῶι: Eur. *Hel.* 1193 (Helen to Theoclymenus) ὦ δέσποτ'—ἤδη γὰρ τόδ' ὀνομάζω σ' ἔπος—ὄλωλα, Ar. *Vesp.* 1297 (with Starkie's note), Ach. Tat. v. 17 (in the address of a letter) Λευκίππη Κλειτοφῶντι τῶι δεσπότηι μου—τοῦτο γάρ σε δεῖ καλεῖν. Aristaenetus ii. 5 σὺ τοίνυν Ἁρπεδόνη (πρὸς σὲ γὰρ ἐξεπίτηδες ὡς ἔχω πάθους ἀπήγγειλα τὴν ὑπόπικρον τῶν βελῶν ἡδονήν).

1227 ff. **οὐκ οἶδεν οἷα...τεύξεται.** The text, which is correct except that we must read λέξασα κἀκτείνασα (Plat. *Prot.* 329 A ὥσπερ τὰ χαλκία πληγέντα μακρὸν ἠχεῖ καὶ ἀποτείνει), has suffered grievous treatment at the hand of many critics. **οἷα** is understood with λέξασα as well as with τεύξεται as though it were οἷα λέξασα οἷα τεύξεται. The general meaning is:—'He little dreams what accursed act all her protracted words of smiling blandishment are but the treacherous cloak and prelude to.' In the speech which opens at v. 846 we have had a sample of her treacherous speech, and Agamemnon feels the hollowness enough to make the significant answer (v. 905) ἀπουσίαι μὲν εἶπας εἰκότως ἐμῆι μάκραν γὰρ ἐξέτεινας. In the *Eumenides* Apollo describes her (634 ff.):—ἀπὸ στρατείας γάρ νιν, ἠμποληκότα | τὰ πλεῖστ' ἄμεινον, εὔφροσιν δεδεγμένη | <τὰ πρῶτα μύθοις, ἡ κατάπτυστος, γυνὴ | παρίστατ' αὐτῶι θέρμ' ἐν ἀργυρηλάτωι> | δροίτηι περῶντι λουτρά, κἀπὶ τέρματι | φᾶρος περεσκήνωσεν, ἐν δ' ἀτέρμονι | κόπτει πεδήσασ' ἄνδρα δαιδάλωι πέπλωι. 'After receiving him with kindly words of welcome, she stood by while he was performing his ablutions in the bath, and at the conclusion trammelled him in a cunning robe and hewed him down.' **γλῶσσα** is of course the false-speaking tongue, as in the proverbial warning against 'the smyler with the knyf under the cloke' attributed to Solon (fr. 42):

> πεφυλαγμένος ἄνδρα ἕκαστον ὅρα
> μὴ κρυπτὸν ἔχων ἔγχος κραδίαι
> φαιδρῶι σε προσεννέπηι προσώπωι
> γλῶσσα δέ οἱ διχόμυθος ἐκ μελαίνας φρενὸς γεγωνῆι.

And **φαιδρόνους** means 'with smiling cheerfulness' in her greeting (v. 525 φαιδροῖσι τοισίδ' ὄμμασιν δέξασθε, *Cho.* 563 φαιδρᾶι φρενὶ δέξαιτ' ἄν); here, like φιλόφρων in *Pers.* 98 (a passage to be quoted presently), merely describing the *appearance* worn by simulated cheerfulness.

To flatter with such sinister intention was to behave like a κύων λαίθαργος, which treacherously fawns and bites at the same time; a proverbial verse said σαίνουσα δάκνεις καὶ κύων λαίθαργος εἶ (Soph. fr. 800 Nauck). This must be part of the suggestion in **κυνός** here, though the epithet **μισητῆς** introduces another quality.

And like the treachery of a κύων λαίθαργος is the deceitfulness of Ἄτη: with smiling blandishment she lures men into her nets: *Pers.* 94

> δολόμητιν δ' ἀπάταν θεοῦ
> τίς ἀνὴρ θνατὸς ἀλύξει;
> τίς ὁ κραιπνῶι ποδὶ πηδή-
> ματος εὐπετέος ἀνάσσων;
> φιλόφρων γὰρ σαίνου-
> σα τὸ πρῶτον παράγει
> βροτὸν εἰς ἄρκυας ἄτας[1].

And Soph. fr. 519 illustrates the same connexion of thought: ἡ δ' ἄρ' ἐν σκότωι λήθουσά με | ἔσαιν' Ἐρινὺς ἡδοναῖς ἐψευσμένον. In Pind. *P.* ii. 83 σαίνων ἄταν διαπλέκει the metaphor is applied to a treacherous person. And Helen too, as we have seen in the n. on 724 ff., is a minister of Ἄτη, just as the Lion-cub that typifies her is called ἱερεύς τις Ἄτας. In the corresponding line of the previous strophe he had been described as φαιδρωπός, ποτὶ χεῖρα σαίνων τε or φαιδρωπὸν ποτὶ χεῖρα σαίνοντα: that implies *fawning with the fatal blandishment of Ate*, δίκην Ἄτης λαθραίου.

1233. **οἰκοῦσαν ἐν πέτραισι** corresponds to Homer's Σκύλλην πετραίην (μ 231).

1234. **θύουσαν Ἅιδου μητέρα** is not '*Mother of Hell*' or '*Dam of Death*,' but '*raging*, infernal, hellish *mother*,' exactly as Eur. *Cycl.* 396 τῶι θεοστυγεῖ Ἅιδου μαγείρωι, Aristias Trag. fr. 3 μαζαγρέτας Ἅιδου τραπεζεύς, '*damned*,' '*devilish*.' The genitive is equivalent to an adjective such as these, or '*deadly*,' '*fatal*': Eur. *Or.* 1399 ξίφεσιν σιδαρέοισιν Ἅιδα, *Andr.* 1046 σταλάσσων Ἅιδα φόνον. Ἐρινύων, Ἐρινύος are used just in the same way: Ach. Tat. v. 5 ἐδείπνησεν ὁ Τηρεὺς δεῖπνον Ἐρινύων '*of retribution*,' '*avenging*.' Both genitives serve as *limiting epithets* to a metaphor: δίκτυόν τι Ἅιδου *Ag.* 1103 = 1580 = 1611, Soph. *Trach.* 1051, explained by *Ai.* 1034: *Theb.* 853, *Ag.* 650, 980, Eur. *Supp.* 773 = *Cho.* 151, Eur. *Alc.* 424: βάκχαις Ἅιδου Eur. *Hec.* 1077, *H. F.* 1119, *Hipp.* 550 (Musgrave): *I. T.* 286 Ἅιδου δράκαιναν, *Hec.* 483 Ἅιδα θαλάμους Εὐρώπας θεραπνᾶν. See also Lobeck on Soph. *Ai.* 802, Blaydes on Ar. *Thesm.* 1041.

1251. **παρεκόπης**, in answer to the question 'by what *man's* hand.' Quite failing to see that τοῖς δ' in v. 1249 may refer to a woman, the chorus assume that a man is meant (as in Soph. *Ant.* 248 Creon, never dreaming that the culprit is Antigone, asks: τί φής; τίς ἀνδρῶν ἦν ὁ τολμήσας τάδε;). Cassandra's reply refers to the confession ἐκ δρόμου πεσὼν τρέχω in v. 1244, which corresponds to her request at v. 1183 καὶ μαρτυρεῖτε συνδρόμως ἴχνος κακῶν ῥινηλατούσηι. ἀποκοπῆναι τῶν ἰχνῶν

[1] εἰς ἀρκύστατα MSS.

was used in the same way of hounds being thrown off the trail: Bekk. *Anecd.* 428. 25 ἀποκοπῆναι τῶν ἰχνῶν τὴν κύνα λέγουσιν ὅταν μηκέτι εὑρίσκηι τὰ ἴχνη. Hesych. ἀποκοπῆναι: ἐπὶ τῶν ἰχνευόντων λέγεται ὅταν μὴ εὕρωσιν. The true reading is doubtful, but it is possible that the scribes have tampered with the order of the words, putting ἄρα too soon, and that we should restore ἦ κάρτα χρησμῶν ἄρα παρεκόπης ἐμῶν. Similarly in Soph. *O. C.* 534 σαί τ' εἴσ' ἄρ' ἀπόγονοί τε καὶ (Jebb) has become σαί τ' ἄρ' εἰσὶν or σαί τ' ἄρ' εἴσ' ἀπόγονοί τε καὶ.

1254. **τὰ πυθόκραντα**: *scil.* Ἕλλην' ἐπίσταται φάτιν. Cf. Eur. *I. A.* 640 f. ΙΦ. ὦ πάτερ, ἐσεῖδόν σ' ἀσμένη πολλῶι χρόνωι. ΑΓ. καὶ γὰρ πατὴρ σέ. For the confusion of δυσπαθῆ and δυσμαθῆ see Cobet, *Misc. Crit.* p. 432.

1256. **Λύκει'**, in his character of Destroyer, as 'Wolf-slayer.'

1259 ff. **ὡς δὲ κτἑ.** The construction of this sentence is uncertain. ἐπεύχεται ἀντιτείσασθαι would be 'prays to...,' ἐπεύχεται ἀντιτείσεσθαι 'vows that she will....' **κότωι** should not be changed although it is figured as ποτόν. [The translation suggests the acceptance of the Triclinian ἐνθήσειν, with ἀντιτείσασθαι explaining μισθόν. But no final solution was approved.]

1266. See cr. n. If the reading is τῶιδ' ἀμείψομαι or πεσόντα θ' ὧδ' ἀμείψομαι, the meaning is 'thus I'll requite you.'

1269 ff. **ἐποπτεύσας...μάτην**, 'having regarded me even in this raiment laughed to scorn by foes and friends alike without distinction.' The form of phrase, which from its unfamiliarity has occasioned a good deal of doubt and alteration, may be illustrated by the proverbial sayings ἐρρέτω φίλος σὺν ἐχθρῶι (Plut. *Mor.* 50 F, Macar. iv. 12), σφάλλειν σὺν ἐχθροῖς καὶ φίλους κέρδος φέρει and ἀπόλοιτο καὶ φίλος σὺν ἐχθροῖς (Macar. vii. 95). Bergk's reading in Pind. *P.* viii. 74 πολλοῖς σοφοῖς (for σοφὸς) δοκεῖ πεδ' ἀφρόνων βίον κορυσσέμεν ὀρθοβούλοισι μαχαναῖς would be just such another phrase, 'is thought not only by fools but by many wise men also.' If the original had been καταγελωμένην μάτην φίλων ὕπ' ἐχθρῶν οὐ διχορρόπως μέτα, to take this for ὑπ' ἐχθρῶν would have been a natural error, and to transpose μέτα and μάτην a ready expedient for making a construction; but the MS., which throws the stress on ἐχθρῶν, has a very obvious meaning, 'laughed at now in Argos as before at Troy.' That would have been as well expressed by φίλων μέτ', ἐχθρῶν οὐ διχορρόπως ὕπο.

1272. Cf. Dio Chrys. xiii. p. 422 R., οἱ δὲ ἐντυγχάνοντες ἄνθρωποι ὁρῶντες οἱ μὲν ἀλήτην οἱ δὲ πτωχὸν ἐκάλουν, οἱ δέ τινες καὶ φιλόσοφον. Phrynichus fr. 33 (i. 379 K.) ὦ κάπραινα καὶ περίπολις καὶ δρομάς. Menander fr. 546 (iii. 166 K.) τὸ δ' ἐπιδιώκειν εἴς τε τὴν ὁδὸν τρέχειν ἔτι λοιδορουμένην κυνός ἐστ' ἔργον, Ῥόδη.

1274. **ἐκπράξας** = **ἀνύσας** (704): *postquam reddidit me uatem.*

1276. **βωμοῦ πατρώιου**, the altar of Ζεὺς Ἕρκειος at which Priam was slain.—**ἀντ'**: so long as a preposition can follow its case, there is no objection to its elision or even to a pause after it. Examples in iambic verse are Eur. *Bacch.* 732 θηρώμεθ' ἀνδρῶν τῶνδ' ὕπ'· ἀλλ' ἕπεσθέ μοι, *Tro.* 1021 καὶ προσκυνεῖσθαι βαρβάρων ὕπ' ἤθελες, Ar. *Lys.* 1146 (tragic style) χώραν ἧς ὕπ' εὖ πεπόνθατε, Eur. *I. A.* 967 ὧν μέτ' ἐστρατευόμην, Aesch. *Supp.* 260 αἶαν ἧς δί' ἁγνὸς ἔρχεται (rightly corrected for αἴδνης διάλγος). Here ἀντί follows its case as in Lycophr. 94 ὀστρίμων μὲν ἀντί, 365 ἑνὸς δὲ λώβης ἀντί, but does not suffer anastrophe.

1277. See cr. n. The construction cannot be κοπείσης (or κοπεῖσαν or κοπείσηι) θερμῶι φοινίωι προσφάγματι 'butchered with a hot bloody stroke,' for two reasons; even if it were possible to speak of a *hot stroke*, πρόσφαγμα does not mean (as some have wished it to mean), a *blow* or *stroke*; and μένει με κοπεῖσαν or κοπείσηι could not mean 'awaits me, *about to be* beheaded,' κοφθησομένην; it could only mean 'awaits me *after I have been* beheaded.'

The construction, therefore, must in part be προσφάγματι κοπείσης 'the sacrifice' or 'slaughtered body of me butchered.' The dative, then, if θερμῶι κοπείσης φοινίωι is sound, depends on μένει, 'a block is in store for the slaughter of me butchered'; more probably, as is generally thought, it depends either on θερμόν (Schuetz' conjecture), 'a block is in store for me hot with the bloody slaughter of me butchered'; or on φοίνιον (Haupt), 'a block is in store for me, bloody with the hot slaughter of me butchered.'

The difficulty is in κοπείσης. Cassandra, as a prophetess, might of course visualise a block streaming with the slaughter of herself, foreseeing the future as though it had already happened, as she does in 1080–1119. But μένει is not the language of visualisation; it is the language merely of prediction; and my feeling is that in conjunction with μένει we ought to have, not κοπείσης, but κοφθησομένης. Consider now two passages: Plut. *Mor.* 597 F τὸν Λεοντίδην ἐπέσφαξε θερμῶι τῶι Κηφισοδότωι 'slew Leontides while the body of Cephisodotus was yet warm.' Philostratus Κασάνδρα, *Imag.* 10, describing a picture of these very murders; after slaying Agamemnon, ἡ Κλυταιμνήστρα τὴν τοῦ Πριάμου κόρην ἀποκτείνει θερμῶι τῶι πελέκει 'with her axe yet warm.' And then consider whether you would not like to read κοπέντος: either θερμὸν κοπέντος φοινίωι προσφάγματι '*there waits for me a block, hot with the bloody sacrifice of a butchered man*,' or θερμῶι κοπέντος φοίνιον προσφάγματι '*bloody with the still warm slaughter of a butchered man.*' See now how well the plurals follow, τεθνήξομεν and ἡμῶν.

I have little doubt about the answer, —if only it could be shown how κοπέντος came to be altered to κοπείσης. Well, it was a deliberate alteration made by a half-intelligent corrector, who took the participle as referring to Cassandra, and therefore made it feminine. In this same play there are at least two other passages which have been subjected to precisely the same treatment: in v. 275, κλύοιμ' ἂν εὔφρων· οὐδὲ σιγώσηι φθόνος, f and h give σιγῶντι; and again in 283, εὖ γὰρ φρονοῦντος ὄμμα σου κατηγορεῖ, they give φρονούσης.

1286 ff. ἐπεὶ τὸ πρῶτον κτέ. Now that the capture (εἷλον: cr. n.) of Troy is avenged, I go gladly to meet death. Cassandra's speech in Eur. *Tro.* 353—405 is in effect an expansion of this passage, if read in connexion with *ib.* 455—461.

In Sen. *Agam.* 1005–1011 Cassandra speaks to Clytaemnestra: 'You need not drag me to my death; I willingly—nay, gladly follow.'

> *Perferre prima nuntium Phrygibus meis*
> *propero; repletum ratibus euersis mare;*
> *captas Mycenas; mille ductorem ducum,*
> *ut paria fata Troicis lueret malis,*
> *perisse dono feminae, stupro, dolo.*
> *nihil moramur: rapite. quin grates ago:*
> *iam, iam iuuat uixisse post Troiam, iuuat.*

But πράξω in v. 1289 is doubtful.

1290. προσεννέπω: see n. on 365.

1303. εὐκλεῶς. Honour is a medicine even against death: Pind. *P.* iv. 187 ἀλλ' ἐπὶ καὶ θανάτωι φάρμακον κάλλιστον ἑᾶς ἀρετᾶς ἅλιξιν εὑρέσθαι σὺν ἄλλοις. *Theb.* 670 εἴπερ κακὸν φέροι τις, αἰσχύνης ἄτερ ἔστω· μόνον γὰρ κέρδος ἐν τεθνηκόσιν. See *Class. Rev.* xvii. 290.

1304. ἰὼ πάτερ σοῦ σῶν τε γενναίων τέκνων is a fine answer to their empty consolations. There is a stroke remarkably like this in Marlowe's *Tragedy of Dido*, ii. 2, where the queen is endeavouring to cheer Aeneas, son of Priam and Hecuba:

> *Dido.* Be merry, man:
> Here's to thy better fortune and good stars [*Drinks.*
> *Aen.* In all humility, I thank your grace.
> *Dido.* Remember who thou art; speak like thyself:
> Humility belongs to common grooms.
> *Aen.* And who so miserable as Aeneas is?
> *Dido.* Lies it in Dido's hands to make thee blest?
> Then be assur'd thou art not miserable.
> *Aen.* O Priamus, O Troy, O Hecuba!

When Antigone is doomed to death, the Chorus attempt to console her with somewhat similar praise (Soph. *Ant.* 817 ff.); but she rejects the mockery of their words, and appeals to Thebes and Dirce (*ib.* 839 ff.).

1311. οὐ Σύριον must be taken closely together, κατ' εἰρωνείαν.

Cf. Ar. *Ran.* 1150 πίνεις οἶνον οὐκ ἀνθοσμίαν, *Plut.* 703 οὐ λιβανωτὸν γὰρ βδέω, Soph. fr. 140 κατάγνυται τὸ τεῦχος οὐ μύρου πνέον. Similarly Soph. *El.* 1500 ἀλλ' οὐ πατρῴαν τὴν τέχνην ἐκόμπασας, Eur. *Alc.* 814 ὅδ' οὐ θυραίων πημάτων ἄρχει λόγος, Plat. *Phaedr.* 242 B οὐ πόλεμόν γε ἀγγέλλεις.

1323 f. See cr. n. 'I pray...that to my champions my enemies may pay for the slaying of a murdered slave.' This is on the whole the best remedy, although φόνευσιν is a strange word for tragedy to use. [See Housman in *Journ. Phil.* xvi. p. 210.] An alternative would be τοῖ' ἐμοῖς τιμαόροις ἐχθροὺς φανεῖσιν τοὺς ἐμοὺς κτέ. Cf. Plut. *Dio et Brut. comp.* 5 καὶ Δίωνος μὲν τιμωρὸς οὐδεὶς ἐφάνη πεσόντος.

1325. For the loosely-added genitive, cf. Eur. *El.* 1195 τίς ξένος... ἐμὸν κάρα προσόψεται μητέρα κτανόντος; *Cycl.* 244 πλήσουσι νηδὺν τὴν ἐμὴν ἀπ' ἄνθρακος θερμὴν ἔδοντος δαῖτα τῶι κρεανόμωι.

1326 ff. These lines contain an Aeschylean figure developed out of the phrase σκιὰ τὰ θνητῶν (Nauck *F. T. G.*, p. 783, Eur. *Med.* 1224, Soph. *Ai.* 125, Ar. *Au.* 683 etc.), '*All is Vanity*,' empty and unsubstantial, and not real or solid: 'every man at his best state is altogether vanity,' *Psalms* 39. 5, Soph. *O.T.* 1186 ff. ἰὼ γενεαὶ βροτῶν, ὡς ὑμᾶς ἴσα καὶ τὸ μηδὲν ζώσας ἐναριθμῶ. Aeschylus makes his 'shadow' that of σκιαγραφία, as Iamblichus, *Protrept.* 8 εἰ θεωρήσειεν ὑπ' αὐγὰς τὸν ἀνθρώπινον βίον· εὑρήσει γὰρ τὰ δοκοῦντα εἶναι μεγάλα τοῖς ἀνθρώποις πάντα ὄντα σκιαγραφίαν κτέ. πρέψειεν implies that life, *when seeming most vivid*, is only a pencilled sketch: cf. v. 253 πρέπουσα θ' ὡς ἐν γραφαῖς. I formerly preferred τέρψειεν, which was proposed by an anonymous critic: pleasure of this life (τὸ τερπνόν) is short-lived and faint like a deceptive imitation: Xen. *Symp.* 4. 22 ἡ μὲν αὐτοῦ ὄψις εὐφραίνειν δύναται, ἡ δὲ τοῦ εἰδώλου τέρψιν μὲν οὐ παρέχει πόθον δὲ ἐμποιεῖ. Cf. Ar. *Poet.* 6. 1450 b 1 παραπλήσιον γάρ ἐστιν καὶ ἐπὶ τῆς γραφικῆς· εἰ γάρ τις ἐναλείψειε τοῖς καλλίστοις φαρμάκοις χύδην, οὐκ ἂν ὁμοίως εὐφράνειεν καὶ λευκογραφήσας εἰκόνα. Stob. *Flor.* 14. 24 (Socrates) ἔοικεν ἡ κολακεία γραπτῆι πανοπλίαι. διὸ τέρψιν μὲν ἔχει, χρείαν δὲ οὐδέμιαν παρέχεται. This train of thought led Greeks to the conclusion μὴ φῦναι ἄριστον, and the chorus in Soph. *O. C.* 1211 ff. is only a versification of an ancient and familiar commonplace. Thus we have τὰ τέρποντα δ' οὐκ ἂν ἴδοις ὅπου, and in Pind. *P.* viii. 88 ἐπάμεροι· τί δέ τις, τί δ' οὔ τις; σκιᾶς ὄναρ ἄνθρωπος (an hyperbole like εἴδωλον σκιᾶς, καπνοῦ σκιά) is led up to by the reflection ἐν δ' ὀλίγωι τὸ τερπνὸν αὔξεται, οὕτω δὲ καὶ πίτνει χαμαί. Pleasure is like the grass that withereth and the flower that fadeth; τοῖς ἴκελοι πήχυιον ἐπὶ χρόνον ἄνθεσιν ἥβης τερπόμεθα, Mimnermus (fr. 2) says.

εὐτυχοῦντα μέν applies to Agamemnon's fortunes, εἰ δὲ δυστυχοῖ to Cassandra's: κυριώτερα δ' ἐν οἴκτωι τὰ τῆς Κασάνδρας, says Philostratus,

Imag. Κασάνδρα, and that is what Aeschylus takes care to stress. But it is hardly for Cassandra to pronounce that her own case is far more pitiable than Agamemnon's; and I think with Weil that this final comment is as usual by the Chorus: 'vaticinatur Cassandra, non philosophatur.' For the opposition of the μέν- and δέ-clauses, expressing the contrast of the bad to the worse, cf. *Theb.* 172 κρατοῦσα μὲν γὰρ οὐχ ὁμιλητὸν θράσος, δείσασα δ' οἴκωι καὶ πόλει πλέον κακόν. Achill. Tat. i. 7 πονηρὸν μὲν γὰρ γυνή, κἂν εὔμορφος ἧι· ἐὰν δὲ καὶ ἀμορφίαν δυστυχῆι, διπλοῦν τὸ κακόν. Lucian iii. 232 ποθεινὴ μὲν οὖν καὶ νέοις πατρίς· τοῖς δὲ ἤδη γεγηρακόσι πλείων ἐγγίνεται ὁ πόθος. *Cho.* 740 ὥς μοι τὰ μὲν παλαιὰ...ἤλγυνεν ἐν στέρνοις φρένα, ἀλλ' οὔτι πω τοιόνδε πῆμ' ἀνεσχόμην. For the pity which is due to Cassandra cf. Antiphanes ap. Stob. *Flor.* 97. 1 καλῶς πένεσθαι μᾶλλον ἢ πλουτεῖν κακῶς· τὸ μὲν γὰρ ἔλεον τὸ δ' ἐπιτίμησιν φέρει.

1330. **ἀκόρεστον.** So it is said of Wealth in Ar. *Plut.* 188 ὥστ' οὐδὲ μεστὸς σοῦ γέγον' οὐδεὶς πώποτε. τῶν μὲν γὰρ ἄλλων ἐστὶ πάντων πλησμονή κτέ.

1331. **δακτυλοδείκτων,** that is, 'admired and gorgeous palaces,' show places.

1333. **μηκέτ' ἐσέλθηις.** The *entrance* of Wealth into men's houses is described in Ar. *Plut.* 234—244.

1339. **ἐπικρανεῖ**: so the MSS., and the future is the natural tense here, but it is hardly credible that it could be scanned ἐπικρᾱνεῖ, and a paroemiac at this point is unusual. Perhaps ἐπικράνειεν 'should he complete....'

1340. τίς ἂν <οὐκ> εὔξαιτο Canter, but the sense required is 'who can boast that his lot is free from harm?' (cf. Menand. 355 οὐδ' ἔστιν εἰπεῖν ζῶντα 'ταῦτ' οὐ πείσομαι'). τίς ἂν <οὖν> Porson, but οὖν cannot stand so *in apodosi.* τίς τἂν Weil, τίς <ποτ'> ἂν E. A. Ahrens, τίς <τίν'> ἂν Verrall, *alii alia*, all but Schneidewin retaining εὔξαιτο. This cannot be. τίς ἂν εὔξαιτο; has only one meaning in Greek, 'who would *wish*?' (*e.g.* Antiphon 6. 1 εὐχόμενος ἄν τις ταῦτα εὔξαιτο, Dem. in Hermog. Rhet. p. 179 εἶτα ἃ Φίλιππος εὔξαιτ' ἂν τοῖς θεοῖς, ταῦτα ὑμῶν ἐνθάδε ποιοῦσιν). In ordinary language it is very common, *e.g.* Isocr. 3. 16 καίτοι τίς οὐκ ἂν εὔξαιτο τῶν εὖ φρονούντων τοιαύτης πολιτείας μετέχειν...; (where G has δέξαιτο which is equally common, but means '*be content to*'), Ar. *Ran.* 283 ἐγὼ δέ γ' εὐξαίμην ἄν... and occurs also in Soph. fr. 327 οὔτε γὰρ γάμον, ὦ φίλαι, οὔτ' ἂν ὄλβον ἔκμετρον ἔνδον εὐξαίμαν ἔχειν· φθονεραὶ γὰρ ὁδοί. I thought once of τίς ἂν αὐχήσειε, but though Hesych. gives αὐχέω: εὔχομαι, that is the only place I have ever found it so explained, and probably the true reading is Schneidewin's rejected ἐξευξαιτο.

1346. εὖ πως: see cr. n. Cf. Eur. *Phoen.* 1466 εὖ δέ πως προμηθίαι καθῆστο Κάδμου λαὸς ἀσπίδων ἔπι. The converse error occurred in v. 557.

1355. **Μελλοῦς.** The word should be written so, not μελλοῦς, to indicate that it is a personification or idealisation of a quality. These were formed in Greek as easily by a termination in ῶ as in English by a capital letter. Tryphon (*Mus. Crit.* i. 49), quoting this word as an example of ὀνοματοποιΐα κατὰ παρονομασίαν, gives ...τῆς Μελλοῦς χάριν no doubt by defect of memory. The phrase τῆς Μελλοῦς κλέος gives me the impression that it refers to some proverbial commendation of *Deliberation*, and in this I am supported by an epigram of Antiphilus *A. P.* xvi. 136 ''Αρκεῖ δ' ἁ μέλλησις' (*Intention*) ἔφα σοφός. This may have been the very proverb, from an early gnomic poet. They, the speaker ironically remarks, are paying singularly little respect to '*that same lauded name*' *Delay*. Cf. Eur. *I. T.* 905 ὅπως τὸ κλεινὸν ὄνομα τῆς σωτηρίας λαβόντες κτἑ., Ov. *Trist.* i. 8. 15 *illud amicitiae sanctum et uenerabile nomen | re tibi pro uili est sub pedibusque iacet.*

1373 f. **φίλοις δοκοῦσιν εἶναι,** 'passing as beloved,' and therefore to be treated with dissimulation.—See cr. nn. The corrections assume that the scribe took ἀρκυσταταν to be an adjective and altered πημονῆς accordingly.

1379. I formerly punctuated after τάδε (*C. R.* xii. 247), joining it with ἔπραξα: but there is no need for the pronoun to be emphatic

1382. **πλοῦτον εἵματος κακόν** is taken to be merely a fine phrase for abundance of material; surely it implies that the silver-purchased raiment which he trampled in his pride of wealth has now itself, as it were, become the instrument of his undoing, changed into the net of Ate. See vv. 383, 940, 951, 1580.

1385 f. **τρίτην ἐπενδίδωμι κτἑ.** The third libation was offered to Ζεὺς Σωτήρ: Aesch. fr. 55 τρίτον Διὸς Σωτῆρος εὐκταίαν λίβα. See also note on v. 257 τριτόσπονδον παιᾶνα and cf. 650 παιᾶνα τόνδ' Ἐρινύων. 'My third blow was added as a prayer-offering to the *subterranean* Zeus'—as Hades may be called, for in the Underworld his position corresponds to that of Zeus among the Olympian powers above; and so in *Supp.* 160 ff. the Danaids from Egypt say, 'If Zeus Petitionary will not hear our prayer, our swarthy company will perish by the noose and make their supplication to the dark Zeus of the Earth, that Zeus most Hospitable—to all that seek rest from their labours with him, who grants entertainment freely to the dead,' τὸν γάϊον, τὸν πολυξενώτατον Ζῆνα τῶν κεκμηκότων, where the schol. has τὸν καταχθόνιον ῞Αιδην.

There is something of the same irony in the words σωιζέσθω κάτω in Soph. *El.* 438 and σωιζόντων κάτω *Ai.* 660: and there is a precisely similar implication in the mention of a third libation in *Cho.* 576

φόνου δ' Ἐρινὺς οὐχ ὑπεσπανισμένη ἄκρατον αἷμα πίεται τρίτην πόσιν, *i.e.* 'as her third and crowning draught.'

1390 f. recall Hom. Ψ 597 τοῖο δὲ θυμὸς | ἰάνθη, ὡς εἴ τε περὶ σταχύεσσιν ἐέρσῃ | ληΐου ἀλδήσκοντος, ὅτε φρίσσουσιν ἄρουραι, 'His heart was gladdened as the heart of growing corn is gladdened with the dew upon the ears when the fields are bristling' (Leaf).

1394 ff. πρεπόντων was formerly taken as a partitive genitive with ἦν (as though = ἐν τῶν π.) 'had it been among things fitting,' and Wecklein still takes it so. But Wellauer and Blomfield truly observed that in such phrases the article is used; we must have had τῶν π. Dr Verrall accordingly takes it as a genitive absolute 'under fit circumstances, with good cause,' interpreting 'Could there be a fit case for a libation over the dead, justly and more than justly this would be that case.' The natural construction, as van Heusde saw, is πρεπόντων ἐπισπένδειν, 'to pour a libation of what is fit,' σπένδειν being often used with a genitive, *e.g.* Longus ii. 31 ἐπισπείσαντες οἴνου, 22, iii. 12. Philostr. *Apoll.* v. 15, *Epist.* 39 οὐκ οἴνου σπένδοντες αὐτῶι ἀλλὰ δακρύων. Heliod. vii. 15 ἀποσπένδω τῶν ἐμαυτῆς δακρύων, iv. 16. Plut. *Mor.* 655 E Herodian v. 5. 12. In the sense 'it is possible to,' ἔστιν ὥστε is common enough: *sup.* 389 ἔστω δ' ἀπήμαντον ὥστ' ἀπαρκεῖν εὖ πραπίδων λαχόντα, Soph. *Phil.* 656, Eur. *Hipp.* 701 ἀλλ' ἔστι κἀκ τῶνδ' ὥστε σωθῆναι. ἐπισπένδειν is properly used of pouring a libation upon a sacrifice: Hdt. ii. 39 ἔπειτα δὲ ἐπ' αὐτοῦ (the altar) οἶνον κατὰ τοῦ ἱρηίου ἐπισπ., as iv. 62 ἐπεὰν γὰρ οἶνον ἐπισπείσωσι κατὰ τῶν κεφαλέων, iv. 60, vii. 167. Nicand. Thyat. (Ath. 486 a), Plut. *Rom.* 4, Xen. *Ephes.* i. 5. Here the whole point lies in πρεπόντων, for of course, to pour libations on a corpse was to give him the due rite of burial: *Anth. Append.* Cougny ii. 485, Nicet. Eugen. ix. 4 τὸ σῶμα συγκαίουσιν, Ἑλλήνων νόμωι, χοὰς ἐπισπείσαντες. By τάδε, which is explained by τοσῶνδε...ἀραίων in the following lines, Clytaemnestra means that the *proper* libations for Agamemnon would be taken from the ἀραῖα κακά (that is, βλαβερά) that he has himself inflicted on his own house. Such metaphors from libations are common in later Greek and Latin; *e.g.* in Achilles Tatius, iii. 16, a lover about to cut his throat upon his mistress' grave says λαβὲ οὖν, Λευκίππη, τὰς πρεπούσας σοι χοὰς παρ' ἐμοῦ.

1400. πειρᾶσθε κτέ. may be a reminiscence of Hector's words to Ajax in Hom. H 235 μήτι μευ, ἠΰτε παιδὸς ἀφαυροῦ πειρήτιζε | ἠὲ γυναικός, ἣ οὐκ οἶδεν πολεμήϊα ἔργα· | αὐτὰρ ἐγὼ εὖ οἶδα μάχας τ' ἀνδροκτασίας τε.

1406 f. τί κακὸν...χθονοτρεφὲς ἐδανὸν ἢ ποτὸν...ῥυτᾶς ἐξ ἁλὸς ὄρμενον; 'what φάρμακον, solid or liquid?' Hom. Λ 741 ἣ τόσα φάρμακα ᾔδη ὅσα τρέφει εὐρεῖα χθών. Apoll. Rhod. ii. 530 φάρμαχ' ὅσ' ἤπειρός τε φύει καὶ νήχυτον ὕδωρ. Longus ii. 7 οὐδὲν φάρμακον, οὐ πινόμενον, οὐκ ἐσθιόμενον, οὐκ ἐν ᾠδαῖς λαλούμενον. *P. V.* 495 οὐκ ἦν ἀλέξημ' οὐδὲν οὔτε βρώσιμον, οὐ χριστὸν οὐδὲ πιστόν. Eur. *Supp.* 1110 βρωτοῖσι καὶ ποτοῖσι. Ov. *Fast.* v. 243 *omnia temptabo latis medicamina terris et freta Tartareos excutiamque sinus.*

1409. **τόδ' ἐπέθου θύος δημοθρόους τ' ἀράς;** I take this to mean τόδε λεύσιμον θῦμα (v. 1107). Other views are that θύος here means 'frenzy,' either 'this maddened rage of thine' or 'this fury of the clamouring people.'

1418. See cr. n. Perhaps we should read Θρηικίων γ' ἀημάτων: but τε may have been merely a metrical addition, after the corruption of A to Λ.

1423. **ἐκ τῶν ὁμοίων,** 'conditions equal.' So Plat. *Phaedr.* 243 D συμβουλεύω δὲ καὶ Λυσίαι ὅτι τάχιστα γράψαι ὡς χρὴ ἐραστῆι μᾶλλον ἢ μὴ ἐρῶντι ἐκ τῶν ὁμοίων χαρίζεσθαι, where the phrase is equivalent to *ceteris paribus.*

1429. **λίπος ἐπ' ὀμμάτων αἵματος εὖ πρέπειν:** the eye shows the heart (see nn. on 283, 784 ff., 1 Samuel 16. 7 *But the Lord said unto Samuel, Look not on his countenance or on the height of his stature*). Therefore bloody heart should have a bloody eye to match. The blood will come from public stoning.

1432. **καὶ τήνδ' ἀκούεις ὁρκίων ἐμῶν θέμιν** can hardly be correct, for ἀκούεις would mean 'you hear,' 'you have heard now': it is after the law has been recited that the orator says ἀκούεις τὸν νόμον, and the same is the case invariably with ἀκούεις or κλύεις. Greek would be καὶ τήνδ' ἄκουσον (Casaubon), as *Cho.* 498, or ἄκουέ γ' (Herwerden), or as I suggest ἀκούσηι γ', *Eum.* 306, Soph. *Ai.* 1141.

1435. **οὔ μοι Φόβου μέλαθρον Ἐλπὶς ἐμπατεῖ,** 'my confident spirit sets no foot within the house of Fear.' For the metaphor cf. Ecclesiastes 7. 4 'The heart of the wise is in the house of mourning; but the heart of fools is in the house of mirth.' [Quint. xiv. 168 ἀλλὰ τὰ μέν που πάντα μέλας δόμος ἐντὸς ἐέργει λήθης.] μέλαθρον is used in the singular of the cave of Philoctetes (Soph. *Phil.* 1453), and of the temple of Artemis (Eur. *I. T.* 1216). For the combination of φόβος and ἐλπίς see Thuc. vii. 61 οἱ τοῖς πρώτοις ἀγῶσι σφαλέντες ἔπειτα διὰ παντὸς τὴν ἐλπίδα τοῦ φόβου ὁμοίαν ταῖς ξυμφοραῖς ἔχουσιν.

1437. **εὖ φρονῶν ἐμοί:** 'sympathetic' is the nearest equivalent, as in other places, *e.g.* *sup.* 283, *Cho.* 770.

1439 ff. This is the scene that Cassandra foretells in Lycophron, 1108:

> ἐγὼ δὲ δροίτης ἄγχι κείσομαι πέδωι
> Χαλυβδικῶι κνώδοντι συντεθραυσμένη·

ἐπεί με, πεύκης πρέμνον ἢ στύπος δρυὸς
ὅπως τις ὑλοκουρὸς ἐργάτης ὀρεύς,
ῥήξει πλατὺν τένοντα καὶ μετάφρενον
καὶ πᾶν λακίζουσ' ἐν φοναῖς ψυχρὸν δέμας
δράκαινα διψάς, κἀπιβᾶσ' ἐπ' αὐχένος,
πλήσει γέμοντα θυμὸν ἀγρίας χολῆς,
ὡς κλεψίνυμφον κοὐ δορίκτητον γέρας
δύσζηλος ἀστέμβακτα τιμωρουμένη.

κεῖται in this sense often begins a sentence: Hom. E 467, Π 541, 558, Σ 20 κεῖται Πάτροκλος. *Theb.* 779 πέπτωκεν ἀνδρῶν ὀβρίμων κομπάσματα. *A. P.* xii. 48 κεῖμαι· λὰξ ἐπίβαινε κατ' αὐχένος.

1445 ff.
ἣ δέ τοι...
κεῖται, φιλήτωρ τοῦδ'· ἐμοὶ δ' ἐπήγαγεν,
εὐνῆς παροψώνημα τῆς ἐμῆς, χλιδήν.

The antithetical sentence (shaped in the figure called *Chiasmus*) puts in a brief and telling way the relations of Cassandra to Agamemnon and to Clytaemnestra, and the results of them in each case: 'she was the lover of *him*,—and is laid low by his side; she dared to trespass on the rights of marriage that were *mine*,—and all that she has thereby brought to *me* is the delight of triumph.'

By the words φιλήτωρ τοῦδε she implies at least two things: that Cassandra had chosen to side with Agamemnon against herself; and that she now lies, as a lover should, beside him. Hereafter she herself and Aegisthus are to fall, as Cassandra had foretold, woman for woman, man for man (v. 1317); and in *Cho.* 893 Orestes says to her φιλεῖς τὸν ἄνδρα; τοιγὰρ ἐν ταὐτῶι τάφωι κείσηι. Perhaps by the active word she wishes to imply that the woman was the seducer; in Sen. *Agam.* 1001 she says:

at ista poenas capite persoluet suo,
captiua coniunx, regii paelex tori.
trahite, ut sequatur coniugem ereptum mihi,

'that she may follow the husband she has stolen from me.' The associations of the word are likely to have lent a special sting to it; the Cretans, says Strabo 484, τὸν μὲν ἐρώμενον καλοῦσι κλεινόν, τὸν δ' ἐραστὴν φιλήτορα. Hesych. gives φιλήτωρ: ἐραστής, and Nonnus uses it as an adjective, 'loving': *Dion.* xxi. 27 φιλήτορι κόλπωι, *Ioan.* xviii. 55 Ἰησοῦς δ' ἀνέκοψε φιλήτορι Πέτρον ἰωῆι.—παροψίς or παροψώνημα mean a *trivial extra morsel*, Pollux x. 87 τὰς δὲ παροψίδας...ἐπὶ μάζης ἢ ζωμοῦ τινος ἢ ἐδέσματος εὐτελοῦς ὅ ἐστι παροψήσασθαι, vi. 56 παροψίδα· ἔστι δὲ καὶ τοῦτο ζωμοῦ τι εἶδος, ἢ ὥς τινές, μάζης, ἢ παρενθήκη τις ὄψου, ὃ οἱ νῦν ἂν εἴποιεν παροψημάτιον. And when used metaphorically they were a synonym for a πάρεργον, as opposed to an ἔργον or σπούδασμα (Galen i. 227 ἔργον δ' αὐτοῖς ἐστὶ καὶ σπούδασμα.... Plat. *Euthydem.* 273 D 'Οὔτοι ἔτι ταῦτα σπουδάζομεν, ἀλλὰ παρέργοις αὐτοῖς χρώμεθα...' 'Καλὸν ἄν τι τό γ' ἔργον ὑμῶν εἴη, εἰ τηλικαῦτα πράγματα πάρεργα ὑμῖν τυγχάνει ὄντα'): Sotades (Ath. 368 a) παροψὶς εἶναι φαίνομαι τῶι Κρωβύλωι· τοῦτον μασᾶται, παρακατεσθίει δ' ἐμέ. Magnes (*ib.* 367 f) καὶ ταῦτα μέν μοι τῶν κακῶν παροψίδες. Philostr. *Heroic.* 284 = 662 φυτεύω δὲ αὐτὰ (these other fruits) οἷον παροψήματα τῶν ἀμπέλων. Clem. Alex. 695 καὶ τῆς Ἑλληνικῆς ἐφάπτεται φιλοσοφίας οἷα τρωγάλιόν τι ἐπὶ τῶι δείπνωι παροψώμενος. Himerius *Or.* xiv. 24 τοὺς δὲ Πύρρωνος τρόπους καὶ τὴν ἐκεῖθεν ἔριν οὐχ ὡς μέγα σπούδασμα οἷον δέ τι παρόψημα τῆς ἄλλης φιλοσοφίας.

Metaphorically, therefore, these words mean *a mere slight toy* or *by-play* beside the serious business or main action; and thus παροψίς is applied in Aristophanes Δαιδ. fr. 236 to a married woman's lover: πάσαις γυναιξὶν ἐξ ἑνός γέ του τρόπου ὥσπερ παροψὶς μοιχὸς ἐσκευασμένος. It is in precisely the same way that εὐνῆς παροψώνημα τῆς ἐμῆς is applied by Clytaemnestra to her husband's paramour.

The metaphorical meaning of these words has not been grasped; παροψώνημα here has hitherto been taken as though it were ἥδυσμα, a seasoning to enhance the appetite, εὐνῆς παροψώνημα something that gives a zest and gusto to the pleasures of the bed; and the usual interpretation has represented Clytaemnestra as proclaiming to the public, 'Cassandra by her death has added a relish to the enjoyment of my commerce with Aegisthus.' How that would be possible is not easy to imagine; still less easy to imagine any woman making such a profession. ἐπάγειν is used by Pindar thus, like ἐπιδοῦναι: *P.* viii. 64 to Apollo, τὸ μὲν μέγιστον τόθι χαρμάτων ὤπασας, οἴκοι δὲ πρόσθεν ἁρπαλέαν δόσιν...ἐπάγαγες: cf. *O.* ii. 10, 41, Soph. *Ai.* 1189. The phrase εὐνῆς παροψώνημα τῆς ἐμῆς is not the accusative and object to ἐπήγαγεν, but the nominative and subject of it—or better, perhaps, it is in apposition to the previous nominative ἥ δέ τοι. It follows that the object must be χλιδήν: see cr. n. The schol. has τὴν ἐκ περιουσίας τρυφήν, which Blomfield took to be an explanation of παροψώνημα merely. It must have included χλιδῆς, for of that word τρυφή is the grammarians' regular equivalent (see Ruhnken *Tim.* 276 = 230, Moeris 408 = 370): thus (to quote passages some of which will at the same time illustrate the sense of *luxuriating triumph*) Aesch. *Supp.* 925 Ἕλλησιν ἐγχλίεις, 242 χλίοντα, schol. τρυφῶντα, *Cho.* 137 ἐν...πόνοισι χλίουσιν, schol. τρυφῶσιν. Hesych. ἐγχλίει: ἐντρυφᾶι. χλίει: θρύπτει, *P. V.* 1003 χλιδᾶν ἔοικας τοῖς παροῦσι πράγμασι, schol. τρυφᾶν, ἀνίεσθαι. Soph. *Trach.* 281 ὑπερχλίοντες, schol. ὑπερεντρυφήσαντες.

1451. φέρουσ' ὁμιλεῖν (see cr. n.) is exactly like Soph. *Ai.* 1201 νεῖμεν ἐμοὶ τέρψιν ὁμιλεῖν: cf. Pind. *N.* x. 72 χαλεπὰ δ' ἔρις ἀνθρώποις ὁμιλεῖν κρεσσόνων, *I.* ii. 37 αἰδοῖος μὲν ἦν ἀστοῖς ὁμιλεῖν.

1456. **παράνους**. Cf. Eur. *Or.* 79 (Helen speaks) ἔπλευσα θεομανεῖ πότμωι, *Theb.* 640 ὦ θεομανές...Οἰδίπου γένος, *ib.* 741 παράνοια συνᾶγε νυμφίους φρενώλεις.

1461. **εἴ τις ἦν ποτ'**: see cr. n. This use of εἴ τις is not so well recognised as it should be; it means '*any that there may be*,' '*some or other*,' and is declinable, as in the other well-known use πλούτωι σθένοντος εἴ τινος. I believe it should be read with Elmsley in Soph. *Ai.* 179 ἤ χαλκοθώραξ εἴ τιν' Ἐνυάλιος μομφὰν ἔχων '*some complaint or other*,' '*possibly*,' '*perchance*,' for ἤ τιν', and in Aesch. *Cho.* 752 with Buttmann (*Griech. Sprachl.* i. 142) εἰ λιμὸς ἢ δίψ' εἴ τις ἢ λιψουρία ἔχει 'or thirst, may be' (like ἢν τύχηι, εἰ τύχοι, τυχόν, *si forte* Munro on Lucr. v. 720) for δίψη τις. Exactly similar is the use of εἴ ποθι in *Ai.* 885 εἴ ποθι πλαζόμενον λεύσσων, and of εἴ ποθεν in *Philoct.* 1204 ξίφος εἴ ποθεν ἢ γένυν ἢ βελέων τι προπέμψατε. It should be considered whether *Tro.* 705 ἵν' εἴ ποτε ἐκ σοῦ γενόμενοι παῖδες Ἴλιον πόλιν κατοικίσειαν may not be explained in the same way.

1463 ff. **ἐπεύχου...ἐκτρέψηις**: for the change from present to aorist in prohibitions cf. *sup.* 909 ff. For the distinction in meaning see *C. R.* xix. p. 30.

1465. **ἐκτρέψηις**: for illustrations of this word see *On editing Aeschylus*, p. 100.

1468. **ἀξύστατον ἄλγος**, *uulnus incompositum*, 'a hurt unhealable'; referring to their description of Helen as ἐν δόμοις ἔρις ἐρίδματος.

1471 f. **κράτος τ' ἰσόψυχον ἐκ γυναικῶν κρατύνεις**: Helen and Clytaemnestra are both instruments to execute the purpose of the haunting Spirit. Schol. Κλυταιμνήστραν καὶ Ἑλένην λέγει, αἳ κατὰ φαυλότητα ἴσας τὰς ψυχὰς ἔχουσι. The infatuation of the daughters of Tyndareus was an old tradition: see Hom. λ 436—9, Eur. *El.* 1062 τὸ μὲν γὰρ εἶδος αἶνον ἄξιον φέρει | Ἑλένης τε καὶ σοῦ, δύο δ' ἔφυτε συγγόνω, | ἄμφω ματαίω Κάστορός τ' οὐκ ἀξίω. | ἣ μὲν γὰρ ἁρπασθεῖσ' ἑκοῦσ' ἀπώιχετο, | σὺ δ' ἄνδρ' ἄριστον Ἑλλάδος διώλεσας. Similarly in *Orest.* 249 ἐπίσημον ἔτεκε Τυνδάρεως εἰς τὸν ψόγον | γένος θυγατέρων δυσκλεές τ' ἀν' Ἑλλάδα, where we learn from the scholiast that Hesiod (fr. 117) had said that both she and Helen (and Timandra, a third sister,) had received from Aphrodite the gift of beauty but the curse of ill-fame with it; all deserted their husbands: τῆισιν δὲ φιλομμειδὴς Ἀφροδίτη | ἠγάσθη προσιδοῦσα, κακὴν δέ σφιν ἔμβαλε φήμην, | Τιμάνδρη μὲν ἔπειτ' Ἔχεμον προλιποῦσ' ἐβεβήκει, | ἵκετο δ' ἐς Φυλῆα, φίλον μακάρεσσι θεοῖσιν· | ὣς δὲ Κλυταιμνήστρη προλιποῦσ' Ἀγαμέμνονα δῖον | Αἰγίσθωι παρέλεκτο καὶ εἵλετο χείρον' ἀκοίτην· | ὣς δ' Ἑλένη ἤισχυνε λέχος ξανθοῦ Μενελάου. This was followed by Stesichorus (fr. 26) who assigned a reason for the curse:

οὕνεκα Τυνδάρεως ῥέζων ποτὲ πᾶσι θεοῖς
μούνας λάθετ' ἠπιοδώρω
Κύπριδος· κείνα δὲ Τυνδάρεω κόραις
χολωσαμένα διγάμους τε καὶ τριγάμους τίθησιν
καὶ λιπεσάνορας.

Nicolaus in Walz, *Rhet.* i. 385 makes Agamemnon, when struck down, exclaim: ὡς ἐπὶ δυστυχίαι τῶν Ἀτρειδῶν κατέστη πατὴρ ὁ Τύνδαρος ἑκατέραις γοναῖς ταῖς Ἀτρέως ἐπὶ συμφοραῖς. καὶ πλεῖ μὲν δι' Ἑλένην Μενέλαος, ἐγὼ δὲ διὰ Κλυταιμνήστραν ἀνῄρημαι· Μενέλαος μὲν Ἑλένην τῆς Ἑλλάδος ἀλλοτριοῖ, Κλυταιμνήστρα δὲ τοῦ βιῶναι (τῶν βίων MS.) ἐμέ· καὶ κακοπραγοῦμεν δι' ἑκατέρας ἀμφότεροι.

1474 f. The ending of these two lines is doubtful: see cr. n. But, if the two words required are ἐκνόμοις and νόμοις (like νόμον ἄνομον 1137), it is plain how easily νόμοις might be omitted; and the omission would lead naturally to writing ἐκνόμως.

1476. νῦν in the sense of 'now at last,' and not νῦν δ' (see cr. n.), is required. Cf. Ar. *Eccl.* 204 νῦν καλῶς ἐπῄνεσας, Plat. *Gorg.* 452 E νῦν μοι δοκεῖς δηλῶσαι κτέ. Similarly in Theocr. i. 132 νῦν ἴα μὲν φορέοιτε βάτοι several copies have νῦν δ'.

1480. νειριτροφεῖται. The MSS. reading may be, I think, a corruption of a compound νειριτροφεῖται, like σκιατροφεῖσθαι: cf. νυκτηγορεῖσθαι *Theb.* 29. To write it as we find it would be the natural tendency of a copyist; thus we get in MSS. ἄγει κνήμων schol. Pind. p. 312 (fr. 82) for ἀγχίκρημνον, ὀνήσει πόλιν Simonides in Plat. *Prot.* 346 C for ὀνησίπολιν, κάμψει δίαυλον Telestes in Ath. 637 a for καμψιδίαυλον; while for the strengthened form of the verb they tend to write the simple form; thus (to take a case in which this often happens) in Eur. fr. 1063. 5 for ἀναστρωφωμένη (Gesner) the MSS. of Stobaeus and Choricius vary between ἀναστροφωμένη and ἀναστρεφομένη.

The form might also be νειριτραφεῖται, as σκιατραφεῖται. This word too supplies an example of the tendency to break up compounds: in Stob. *Flor.* 97. 17 (Eur. fr. 546. 8) there is a *v.l.* σκιᾷ τροφούμενος.

1481. νέος ἴχαρ 'fresh in appetite' (τὴν ἐπιθυμίαν). ἴχαρ is to ἰχανάω as μῆχαρ to μηχανάω, λῶφαρ to λωφάω, μῶμαρ to μωμάομαι, λῦμαρ to λυμαίνομαι. There is no such word as ἶχαρ (Dind. *Lex. Aesch.*); *Supp.* 863 is corrupt. The intestine murders in the House that follow in such swift succession are conceived as wounds made by a devouring monster, whose thirst for blood revives again before the last wound has had time to heal. ἰχώρ of the MSS. is taken to mean 'gore, bloodshed'—a sense incredible. Its proper sense is a *humour*, *lymph*, *serum*; never *blood*, that it should be extended (like αἷμα) to mean a *deed of blood*. And the phrase should naturally be a further account of ἔρως.

1482. **τοῖσδε** is probably a gloss: cf. 1657. Perhaps we should read ἢ μέγαν <ἢ μέγαν> οἴκοις with Weil: see on 1506.

1488. **ἄνευ Διὸς**: Soph. *Trach.* 1278 κοὐδὲν τούτων ὅ τι μὴ Ζεύς.

1506. The addition of σὺ after εἶ for metrical reasons was first suggested by Schuetz. Perhaps ἦσθα or αὐτὰ should take the place of εἶ: see on 1482.

1508. **πῶ πῶ;** is Doric. Cf. πώμαλα, not at all. [See Shilleto cr. n. to Dem. *F. L.* § 56.] πόθεν and ποῦ are used with the same force—'go to!'

1510 ff. **βιάζεται δ'...** The blood of the slain children of Thyestes lies congealed upon the earth (μελαμπαγὲς αἷμα φοίνιον *Theb.* 724), demanding vengeance (τίτας φόνος πέπηγεν οὐ διαρρύδαν *Cho.* 65), and is not to be washed away until sufficient blood of kindred has been shed by murder to atone for it: φόνωι φόνον λύειν is the principle. Soph. *El.* 1384 ἴδεθ' ὅπου προνέμεται | τὸ δυσέριστον αἷμα φυσῶν Ἄρης. Eur. *Or.* 811 πάλαι παλαιᾶς ἀπὸ συμφορᾶς δόμων | ὁπότε χρυσέας | ἔρις ἀρνὸς ἤλυθε Ταντα λίδαις, | οἰκτρότατα θοινάματα καὶ | σφάγια γενναίων τεκέων· | ὅθεν φόνωι φόνος ἐξαμείβων | δι' αἵματος οὐ προλείπει | δισσοῖσιν Ἀτρείδαις. Ἄρης πάχναι κουροβόρωι (φόνου) δίκας παρέχων, feud-murder serving as the price for bloodshed, is just like ἀρὴ ἀτολμήτων ἐκτίνουσα in v. 385, havoc and destruction paying the penalty for sin.

1524. She takes up their words δολίωι μόρωι with the retort οὐδὲ γὰρ οὗτος δολίαν ἄτην οἴκοισιν ἔθηκ'; An ellipse such as is implied here by γάρ was often explained by scholiasts, see *e.g.* scholia on *P. V.* 1015, *Pers.* 237, Eur. *Or.* 794, Ar. *Nub.* 1366: and the explanation was liable to be incorporated in the text, as οὐκέτι in *Rhesus* 17. Cobet, *Misc. Crit.* p. 323, condemns Hom. κ 190 on similar grounds. So here the lines which precede οὐδὲ γάρ were a scholiast's explanation, οὔτ' ἀνελεύθερον οἶμαι θάνατον τῶιδε γενέσθαι.

1527. Porson on *Med.* 822 (826) restored πολυκλαύτην on the ground that the less common form of the feminine is liable to corruption, and that τ' was a subsequent addition. Meineke rejected τὴν, which he thought to have been inserted with the object of avoiding a paroemiac. Errors due to the last-named cause will also be found in 87, 783 (προσεφικνεῖται h), and 791.

1528. **ἄξια δράσας ἄξια πάσχων** corresponds to ἄξι' ἀξίων; *digna dignis*, a common use. [Eur. *Supp.* 813 σφαγέντας οὐκ ἄξι' οὐκ ὑπ' ἀξίων, *Ion* 735 ἄξι' ἀξίων γεννητόρων ἤθη φυλάσσεις.]

1531. **ἔρξεν**, 'what he *wrought*' (see cr. n.), is equally possible. Hom. Γ 351 Ζεῦ ἄνα, δὸς τείσασθαι ὅ με πρότερος κάκ' ἔοργεν.

1532 ff. The construction is εὐπάλαμον φροντίδος μέριμναν στερηθεὶς, ἀμηχανῶ ὅπαι τράπωμαι. So Soph. *O. T.* 170 οὐδ' ἔνι φροντίδος ἔγχος ὧι τις ἀλέξεται, Opp. *Hal.* iii. 571 οὐδέ οἱ ὅπλον ἐνὶ φρεσὶν οἷον ἄρηρεν ἐκ γενύων. 'I find in thought no ready weapon to my hand and know not where to turn.'

1536. **ψεκὰς δὲ λήγει**: 'it is no longer early drizzle.' The phrase is based upon the word ἀσταγές or ἀστακτί 'in torrents': ἀψεκαστί might have been used in the same sense.

1537 f. 'Yet there are other whetstones whereon destined hurt is being whetted for the hand of Justice to another end.' In *Cho.* 643 Δίκας δ' ἐρείδεται πυθμήν, προχαλκεύει δ' Αἶσα φασγανουργός Destiny is the armourer who forges the weapon for Justice to employ, and here, with language very similar, we expect to find the same image. It seems probable, therefore, that Triclinius was correct in writing δίκαι, which will mean 'for the hand of Justice.' In face of Αἶσα it would be rash to alter μοῖρα: otherwise, modifying a suggestion by Prof. Robinson Ellis, we might perhaps read θήγεται...θηγάναισιν αἶρα:— supposing that could mean a chopping instrument requiring to be sharpened. It is usually explained by σφῦρα, and in a fragment of Callimachus, the only place where it occurs in literature, αἰράων ἔργα stands for 'blacksmith's work.' Hesychius, however, and Bekk. *Anecd.* 359. 19 give αἶρα· σφῦρα. ἀξίνη: and might not μαχ-αιρα mean originally a *battle-axe*? But one of the sign-posts to the sentence is the genitive βλάβης, which according to my ear should be dependent neither on πρᾶγμα nor on θηγάναις but on the final substantive, θήγεται βλάβης μοῖρα, as you have θανάτου μοῖρα (*Pers.* 919, *sup.* 1463). The only other possibility I see is that βλάβης is an error for an accusative, θηγάνει βλάβας or βλάβην. The θηγάναι are the incentives urging Orestes to revenge.

1546. **ἀδίκως**, dishonestly, like δίκην παράβαντες in v. 780. Cf. Schol. on Soph. *El.* 270 σπένδοντα λοιβάς· τὸ τῆς ἀσεβείας Αἰγίσθου κατηγόρημα, εἰ σπένδει θεοῖς, ὅπου ἄδικος φόνος εἴργασται.

1547. **τίς δ' ἐπιτύμβιος κτέ.**: *i.e.* and if you do, what praise of *yours* could be genuine? ἰάπτων is intransitive, as in *Supp.* 556 ἰάπτει δ' Ἀσίδος δι' αἴας.—**ἀνδρὶ θείωι**: Cratinus, fr. 1 (i. p. 11 K.), of Cimon, σὺν ἀνδρὶ θείωι καὶ φιλοξενωτάτωι καὶ πάντ' ἀρίστωι τῶν Πανελλήνων.

1557. **πόρθμευμ' ἀχέων.** Schuetz was the first to quote in illustration of this phrase Stob. *Ecl.* i. 49. 50 (p. 418 Wachs.), containing an extract from Apollodorus περὶ τῶν θεῶν (*F. H. G.* i. p. 429) ἐκ γὰρ τοιούτων ὁρμώμενοι πιθανῶς καὶ τοὺς ἐν Ἅιδου νομιζομένους ποταμοὺς κατωνομάκασιν. Ἀχέροντα μὲν διὰ τὰ ἄχη, ὡς καὶ Μελανιππίδης ἐν Περσεφόνηι (fr. 3)

> καλεῖται δ' <εἵνεκ'> ἐν κόλποισι γαίας
> ἄχε' εἶσιν προχέων, Ἀχέρων,

ἐπεὶ καὶ Λικύμνιός φησι (fr. 1)·

μυρίαις παγαῖς δακρύων ἀχέων τε βρύει

καὶ πάλιν (fr. 2)·

Ἀχέρων ἄχεα πορθμεύει βροτοῖσιν.

1568. **Πλεισθενιδῶν.** It is difficult to find a place for Pleisthenes in the genealogy Zeus, Tantalus, Pelops, Atreus, Agamemnon. Later writers, to meet the difficulty, assert that Pleisthenes was son of Atreus and father of Agamemnon, but died young, so that Agamemnon was commonly called the son of Atreus (Schol. Eur. *Or.* 4). There is no warrant for this in Homer, but some faint indication that Aeschylus had heard of it: see vv. 775, 1602.

1574. **πανεπαρκὲς ἔμοιγ'** is assumed to have been the original text which with ἀπόχρη superscript ultimately produced the MSS. reading. The first step was πᾶν ἀπόχρη 'μοιγ': but since πᾶν ἀπόχρη cannot be construed together, πᾶν was taken to be a predicate; and that necessitated a connecting particle in the following clause: and so we get κτεάνων τε μέρος βαιὸν ἐχούσῃι πᾶν, ἀπόχρη μοι δ'.... The rhythm alone is enough to show that this cannot be genuine; but to confirm my view that such was supposed to be the construction, cod. f has actually that punctuation, a comma after πᾶν. I had long looked with suspicion upon ἀπόχρη, for it is a prose word, not a poetical, and neither in Epic, Lyric, nor Tragedy is ever used at all. Thus it would be a natural synonym for explanatory purposes: Moeris p. 262 οὐκ ἀπήρκει ἀντὶ τοῦ οὐκ ἀπέχρη, Ἀριστοφάνης Πολυΐδωι. But poetry uses ἀρκῶ and compounds, verbs and adjectives, as v. 390 ἀπήμαντον ὥστ' ἀπαρκεῖν, *Pers.* 240 πλοῦτος ἐξαρκής, *A. P.* x. 76 πλοῦτον ἔχειν ἐθέλω τὸν ἐπάρκιον, Anon. ap. Suid. Παλαμήδης: εἴη μοι βίοτος πανεπάρκιος. See also *Cho.* 68 παναρκέτας νόσου βρύειν. Aeschylus has also παναρκεῖς *Theb.* 152. The copyist, after the habit of such with unexpected compounds, made two words of it. In Iambl. *Vit. Pyth.* § 147 Cobet (*Coll. Crit.* p. 378) for τὸ λεγόμενον πᾶν ἀληθές restored παναληθές, and the tendency is seen in *Theb.* 709 where πανάληθεῖ was the first attempt at ΠΑΝΑΛΗΘΗ. ἔμοιγε is quite suitable: Plat. *Prot.* 346 C ἐγώ, ὦ Πιττακέ, οὐ διὰ ταῦτά σε ψέγω ὅτι εἰμὶ φιλόψογος, ἐπεὶ ἔμοιγε ἐξαρκεῖ ὃς... Pherecrat. 145. 17 ἀλλ' οὖν ἔμοιγε χοὖτος ἦν ἀποχρῶν ἀνήρ.—For the general sense cf. the words of Menelaus in Hom. δ 97 ὧν ὄφελον τριτάτην περ ἔχων ἐν δώμασι μοῖραν ναίειν, οἱ δ' ἄνδρες σόοι ἔμμεναι.

1579. **ἄγη**: 'This shows you are above, | You justicers, that these our nether crimes | So speedily can venge,' *King Lear* iv. 2. 79. Cf. Diogen. vi. 88 νῦν θεοὶ μάκαρες: ἐπὶ τῶν ἀξίως τιμωρουμένων ἐφ' οἷς ἔπραξαν.

1591. προθύμως μᾶλλον ἢ φίλως: he plays bitterly on two words commonly applied to welcome, προθύμως δέχεσθαι, *eager*, *zealous*, *hearty*, and φιλοφρόνως or φίλως, *kind*. Effusive rather than sincere this welcome was.

1594 f. This passage is mutilated and corrupt, but there can be little doubt what happened (see Prof. Platt's article in *Class. Rev.* xi. p. 96), because the story is told elsewhere not only of Thyestes but of Tereus and of Clymenus and in Hdt. i. 119 of Harpagus, and when the details are described they are the same. The toes and fingers (and the head), which would have been recognised as human, were concealed apart (Senec. *Thyest.* 764, Hdt. *l.c.*, Achill. Tat. v. 3 and 5) and afterwards displayed in proof (Zenob. ii. 234, Senec. 1038, Hygin. *fab.* 88, Hdt., Ach. Tat., Ov. *Met.* vi. 658); the rest, including the ἔντερα and σπλάγχνα (*sup.* 1220), was broken small (Senec. *Thyest.* 1059) and served as meat. The separate table made it easy for the fated guest alone to have the special mess (Hdt., cf. Ov. *Met.* vi. 648—50). The general shape of the sentence therefore would appear to have been something like this:

τὰ μὲν ποδήρη καὶ χερῶν ἄκρους κτένας
ἔκρυπτ' ἄνευθεν, τἄλλα δ'...
ἔνθρυπτ' ἄνωθεν ἀνδρακὰς καθήμενος.

Cf. Ov. *Met.* vi. 656 *ipse sedens solio Tereus sublimis auito.* The kicking over of the table is also told of Tereus by Ovid in 661.

1597. ἄσωτον, spendthrift, prodigal; usually meaning one who wastes his substance in riotous living, and applied with bitter irony to the banquet of Thyestes.

1601 f. ξυνδίκως is either simply '*jointly*, *together with*,' for which sense Pind. *P.* 1. 1 χρυσέα φόρμιγξ, Ἀπόλλωνος καὶ ἰοπλοκάμων σύνδικον Μοισᾶν κτέανον is quoted; or else '*in support of*'—so that the act is symbolic. In the latter sense it has been suggested to read σύνδικον (Karsten), as in Pind. *O.* ix. 98 σύνδικος δ' αὐτῶι Ἰολάου τύμβος ἐιναλία τ' Ἐλευσὶς ἀγλαΐαισιν.—οὕτως is part of the curse: 'go perish... !'

1605. τρίτον γὰρ ὄντα μ' ἐπὶ δέκ' of the MSS. is ridiculous. ἐπὶ δύ' 'in addition to two others' would make sense and may be right; but I suspect the original was τρίτην γὰρ ὄντα μ' ἐλπίδ' 'I who was my father's third last hope.' Cf. *Cho.* 235, 695, 772, Aeschines ii. 179, *A. P.* viii. 389, *Epigr.* Kaibel 116, Thuc. iii. 57, Pers. ii. 35.

1610. See on 544. Aristid. i. 709 Λακεδαιμόνιοι δ' ἥδιστ' ἂν τεθναῖεν ἅπαντες, εἰ λήψονται δίκην παρὰ Θηβαίων· οὕτω δι' ὀργῆς αὐτοὺς ἔχουσι.

1613. Cf. Eur. *Tro.* 427 σὺ τὴν ἐμὴν φὴς μητέρ' εἰς Ὀδυσσέως ἥξειν μέλαθρα;

1618. **ἐπὶ ζυγῶι**, 'When on the main thwart sits authority.' [ζυγόν denotes here a bench at the stern: see Torr, *Ancient Ships*, p. 57, n. 131, and cf. Eur. *Ion* 595, *Phoen.* 74.]

1619 f. Cf. *sup.* 1425 γνώσηι διδαχθεὶς ὀψὲ γοῦν τὸ σωφρονεῖν.

1625 ff. **γύναι, σὺ...ἀνδρὶ στρατηγῶι** is addressed to Aegisthus. There is the same contrast in *Cho.* 624 γυναικοβούλους τε μήτιδας φρενῶν ἐπ' ἀνδρὶ τευχεσφόρωι, which is so framed that it might include Aegisthus. See also *Eum.* 628—40. For **οἰκουρὸς** cf. Eur. *Heracl.* 700 αἰσχρὸν γὰρ οἰκούρημα γίγνεται τόδε, τοὺς μὲν μάχεσθαι τοὺς δὲ δειλίαι μένειν. Enger points out that Cassandra had already so described Aegisthus: *sup.* 1224.

1630 ff. Orpheus tamed (ἥμερου) the savage breast with persuasive charm (πειθοῖ): you shall find your own savagery tamed by compulsion (βίαι): Ἔρωτος θεσμόν, ὧι πεισθεὶς ἐγώ, οὔπω κρατηθείς Aristarchus fr. 2 (*F. T. G.* p. 728). Cf. Dio Chrys. xxxii. 61 f. p. 683 to the Alexandrians, speaking of their degenerate popular musicians: τούτων μὲν γάρ ἐστιν οὐδεὶς Ἀμφίων οὐδὲ Ὀρφεύς· ὁ μὲν γὰρ υἱὸς ἦν Μούσης, οἱ δὲ ἐκ τῆς Ἀμουσίας αὐτῆς γεγόνασι...τοιγαροῦν οὐκ ἀπὸ κύκνων οὐδὲ ἀηδόνων ὁ ζῆλος αὐτῶν ὠνόμασται παρ' ὑμῖν αὐτοῖς, ἀλλ' ὡς ἔοικε, κνυζηθμοῖς καὶ ὑλαγμοῖς εἰκάζετε....καὶ μὴν ὅ γε Ὀρφεὺς τὰ θηρία ἡμέρου καὶ μουσικὰ ἐποίει διὰ τῆς ὠιδῆς· οὗτοι δὲ ὑμᾶς, ἀνθρώπους ὄντας, ἀγρίους πεποιήκασι καὶ ἀπαιδεύτους.

1638. **ἐκ τῶν δὲ τοῦδε χρημάτων...** He leaves that awkward topic hastily and cuts the matter short: *Theb.* 1052 ἀλλὰ φοβοῦμαι κἀποτρέπομαι δεῖμα πολιτῶν (the Chorus with reference to the burial of Polynices).—For the sense cf. Eur. *El.* 939, where Electra is addressing the corpse of Aegisthus: ηὔχεις τις εἶναι τοῖσι χρήμασι σθένων.

1640. **οὔτι μὴ σειραφόρον κριθῶντα πῶλον.** The *tracer* (σειραφόρος or δεξιόσειρος) had light work, as compared with the horses running under the yoke. **κριθῶντα** expresses the effect of his generous diet. He was called upon to make a special effort at the corners of the race-course, when he was thrown wide to the off (Soph. *El.* 721), and had to pull the chariot round on the pivot of the near wheel. Hence the metaphorical use of **σειραφόρος** and **δεξιόσειρος** of one who gives assistance in the time of need (*sup.* 833, Soph. *Ant.* 140).

1641 f. Cf. Eur. *Supp.* 1104 οὐχ ὡς τάχιστα δῆτά μ' ἄξετ' ἐς δόμους, σκότωι δὲ δώσετ', ἔνθ' ἀσιτίαις ἐμὸν δέμας γεραιὸν συντακεὶς ἀποφθερῶ;

1645. **μίασμα.** Cf. *Cho.* 1026 (of Clytaemnestra) πατροκτόνον μίασμα καὶ θεῶν στύγος.

1650. **λοχῖται.** Aegisthus is attended by λοχῖται or δορυφόροι (*Cho.* 764 f., Eur. *El.* 616), the characteristic retinue of a τύραννος.

1652. **ἀλλὰ κἀγὼ μήν.** Porson substituted ἀλλὰ μὴν κἀγὼ and has been generally followed, but the change is unnecessary; for (1) a similar rhythm is found elsewhere: Eur. *I. A.* 908 ἀλλ' ἐκλήθης γοῦν ταλαίνης, *Ion* 557 τῶι θεῶι γοῦν οὐκ ἀπιστεῖν, and (2) the order of the words, *i.e.* the occurrence of μήν after the pronoun, is not uncommon: κἀγὼ μὰν κνίζω Theocr. v. 22, καὶ ἐν ἐμοὶ μήν Plat. *Legg.* 644 D, ἀλλ' οὐδ' ἐγὼ μήν Eur. *Hec.* 401, *Or.* 1117, *Andr.* 256, ἀλλ' οὐδ' ἐγὼ μέντοι πεσών γε κείσομαι Ar. *Nub.* 126, μὰ Δί' οὐδ' ἐγὼ γάρ *Lys.* 130.

1656. **μηδὲν ἡιματωμένοις.** See cr. n.: most editors read μηδὲν αἱματώμεθα, 'let us not spill any of our blood.'

1657 f. See cr. nn. The true reading of these obscure lines I believe to be that printed in the text, or something closely resembling it. τούσδε, given by the MSS. at the end of v. 1657, was a marginal note, just as on Eur. *Hipp.* 1152 πρὸς δόμους ὁρμώμενον there is a schol. τούσδε, and on *Andr.* 141 ἔμολες οἴκους, though δεσποτῶν ἐμῶν follows, a schol. εἰς τοὺς ἐμοὺς οἴκους δηλονότι. καιρόν was a gloss on ὧραι or ὥραν, as was first pointed out by Prof. Housman in *Journ. Phil.* xvi. p. 289. If ὥραν is right, it is used as καιρόν Soph. *Ai.* 34, 1316, ἀωρίαν Ar. *Ach.* 23.—For **πρὶν παθεῖν** cf. Hom. P 30 ἀλλά σ' ἔγωγ' ἀναχωρήσαντα κελεύω ἐς πληθὺν ἰέναι,...πρίν τι κακὸν παθέειν, Υ 196, Apollonius ap. Stob. *Flor.* 58. 12 καλὸν πρὶν παθεῖν διδαχθῆναι πηλίκον ἐστὶν ἡσυχία, Eur. *Med.* 289 ταῦτ' οὖν πρὶν παθεῖν φυλάξομαι, Xen. *Anab.* ii. 5. 5 οἱ φοβηθέντες ἀλλήλους, φθάσαι βουλόμενοι πρὶν παθεῖν κτέ.—It is Clytaemnestra's plea that she was the executor of Doom, 1434, 1471 ff., 1498 ff., *Cho.* 909 ἡ Μοῖρα τούτων, ὦ τέκνον, παραιτία. The MSS. reading, πρὸς δόμους πεπρωμένους 'to your predestined houses,' is absurd. Thus **χρῆν τάδ' ὡς ἐπράξαμεν** is 'it was fated we should act herein as we have acted.' Cf. Ter. *Eun.* 95 *ne crucia te, obsecro, anime mi, mi Phaedria.* | *non pol quo quemquam plus amem aut plus diligam* | *eo feci: sed ita erat res; faciundum fuit.* Eur. *H. F.* 311 ὃ χρὴ γὰρ οὐδεὶς μὴ χρεὼν θήσει ποτέ. Ar. *Ach.* 540 ἐρεῖ τις, οὐ χρῆν· ἀλλὰ τί ἐχρῆν εἴπατε. Quint. ix. 493 (Agamemnon says to Philoctetes) μηδ' ἡμῖν χόλον αἰνὸν ἐνὶ φρεσὶ σῇσι βαλέσθαι, οὐ γὰρ ἄνευ μακάρων τάδ' ἐρέξαμεν.

1660. **δαίμονος**: cf. 1568 f. The metaphor has nothing to do with the spur (πλῆκτρον) of a fighting-cock: the phrase βαρὺς δαίμων (βαρυδαιμονία) or βαρεῖα τύχη was developed into the conception of a bird of prey that souses down, or swoops down, heavily: *e.g. sup.* 1174, 1469, *Pers.* 518, Soph. *Ant.* 1272, 1346, *O.T.* 263, 1300, 1311. The same figure is made out of βαρὺς κότος Ζηνός in *Supp.* 654.

1662. **ἀλλὰ...ἀπανθίσαι** is like the exclamatory use of the inf. with δέ in Dem. 21. 209 (quoted on v. 348). Cobet, *Misc. Crit.* p. 147.

1663. **δαίμονος πειρωμένους** here and in *Cho.* 511 means more than 'trying one's luck'; it means 'putting one's *predestined* fortune to the touch.' ἐξιστορῆσαι μοῖραν τύχης in *Theb.* 493 is the same thing.

1664. **σώφρονος γνώμης θ' ἁμαρτεῖν τὸν κρατοῦντ' ἀρνουμένους**, *dominum recusantes* (Ov. *Met.* viii. 848): γνώμης ἁμαρτεῖν is 'to be ill-advised,' 'mistaken' (Hdt. i. 207, γνώμης χρηστῆς ix. 79, τῆς ἀρίστης iii. 81); τεύξεται φρενῶν in 185 is the opposite, 'shall be well-advised.' 'To be well-advised or ill-advised in doing so and so' is expressed by a participle, as 183 κλάζων τεύξεται φρενῶν, 793 οὐδ' εὖ πραπίδων οἴακα νέμων...κομίζων, Eur. *Bacch.* 329 τιμῶν τε Βρόμιον σωφρονεῖς, Hdt. vii. 15 οὐκ ἐφρόνεον εἴπας, i. 116 οὐκ εὖ βουλεύεσθαί μιν ἔφη ἐπιθυμέοντα.... To be metrical here, the participle must be deponent, and I know no other which will give the sense required except ἀρνουμένους: for which see Heliod. iii. 3 ἡ ἵππος τὸν χαλινόν, ὅσα μὲν δεσπότην, ἠρνεῖτο. To deny their master is exactly what the Elders have been doing, 1633 etc., and that was proverbially impolitic: Walz, *Rhet. Gr.* i. 281, Soph. *El.* 394—7, 340, 1014, 1465; Eur. fr. 337, 93, 604; *Hec.* 404. This leads to their retort, which is the same as in Soph. *El.* 397 σὺ ταῦτα θῶπευ'· οὐκ ἐμοὺς τρόπους λέγεις, *P.V.* 969 σέβου, προσεύχου, θῶπτε τὸν κρατοῦντ' ἀεί.

1669. Cf. Soph. *El.* 794 ὕβριζε, νῦν γὰρ εὐτυχοῦσα τυγχάνεις, *Cho.* 57 φοβεῖται δέ τις· τὸ δ' εὐτυχεῖν, τόδ' ἐν βροτοῖσι θεός τε καὶ θεοῦ πλέον, *i.e.* 'they (Aegisthus and Clytaemnestra) may hold their reign of terror while their luck endures!'

1670. **χρόνωι**: see cr. n. The usual idiom is διδόναι ἄποινα followed by the genitive without the addition of χάριν. For the corruption cf. 316.

INDEXES.

I. GREEK.

II. ENGLISH.

CAMBRIDGE: PRINTED BY JOHN CLAY, M.A. AT THE UNIVERSITY PRESS.